CW01018521

MASS IMMIGRATION
Problems & Opportunities

For Lisa and Alexander
with high regard and
much affection.

Vassula

Eastern Ivy 2016

Sir Basil Markesinis QC, FBA

MASS IMMIGRATION
Problems & Opportunities

I. SIDERIS
PUBLICATIONS

MASS IMMIGRATION
Problems & Opportunities

ISBN: 978-153-05-7463-6

First edition: March 2016

Copyright © Sir Basil Markesinis

Copyright © I. SIDERIS Publications
            116 Solonos Street, 106 81 Athens, Greece
            T: 210 3833434, F: 210 3832294
            E: contact@isideris.gr, S: www.isideris.gr

To Ieta, Eugenie, and Julietta,
the three women in my life
in gratitude and with huge affection

ACKNOWLEDGEMENTS

Authors thinking about their books, like women reflecting about their beauty, are among the most delusional inhabitants of our world since they both overestimate reality which is not as attractive as they both in their own ways believe. My intention to address some problems which I regard as serious under the occasional veneer of humour may have thus misfired. Still, the serious themes of the book, indicated in its subtitle and discussed in the second half of the book are among those which worry me deeply as I note how unpleasant, confused, and even dangerous the world we live in appears to be in all the many places in which I have spent many a happy hour working and getting to know their admirable people.

I am grateful to the publishers of earlier books of mine – *Good and Evil in Art and Law* (Springer Verlag, Vienna and New York); *The Duality of Genius* (Shramek Verlag, Vienna); *Windows to an Authors Soul* (Sapienza, Rome) and *Ancient Greek Poetry – Epic, Lyric and Tragic – as seen through the eyes of artists and psychiatrists* (I. Sideris Publications, Greece) for allowing me to re –use ideas and texts from the above books though in most cases they have been either, rephrased, enlarged, or otherwise modified.

GUIDING THOUGHTS

Praise exceptional ability whenever you come across it irrespective of its politics; admire true beauty and do not taint it by morality; respect humans, whatever their religion, ethnic origins, or sexual orientation; revere the guiding value of the unidentified cosmic force which some call religion; judge rarely knowing that whatever you have decided will, at best, only be partially right; enjoy life for the short time that true happiness lasts; help others who need your help without expecting anything in return and then you will never be disappointed by their ingratitude; never complain, never explain, never apologise for being different or thinking differently since the solution to insoluble problems invariably comes from lateral thinking; and never hesitate in saying or doing something on the grounds that it may be wrong; for those who have been scared of failure never acieved anything truly original.

TABLE OF CONTENTS

Chapter Four

Chapter Five

Chapter Six

Chapter Nine

Chapter Ten

PREFACE

I started writing this book a few days after the Left formed in Greece its second government in seven months and the Right lapsed into its own proverbial squabbles among the self-appointed *Dauphins*. Combined the two events have happily put an end to my own long-rumoured involvement in Greek politics. Many had believed that I was bound, in the end, to be drawn into this messy scene because of my family's connection with Greek and, earlier, Venetian politics. Some, yet not many I suspect, even hoped I would become active in the country's political life on the plausible ground that I had been untainted by its recent shenanigans. Nowadays, however, the bulk of the population simply do not care about individuals, rightly being more preoccupied with the financial straits they find themselves in than in rumours about a possible increase in the numbers of those who wished to rule them. For my part, therefore, suffice it to repeat what I have *always* maintained namely, that I remain determined to claim nothing more than the right to speak my mind freely but keep much blue water between my private life and party politics, the media, and the banking interests which have ruled – many might argue with great persuasiveness and I am among them 'misruled' - Greek life at least since the collapse of the Junta in 1974.

The reason for my diverging views is simple even though people who are both intelligent, gullible, and in love with conspiracy theories - as most Greeks are - cannot see it. The fact was and remains that my country of birth never really held out for me any appeal to pursue within its borders any professional career. The fact is that those who speculated about my intentions, be they simple citizens or the self-interested media, had, quite simply, failed to 'understand' the personal circumstances of the individual, his professional career abroad, and his views as they matured in a 'foreign' environment.

My Greek compatriots thus simply underestimated the fact that I have spent forty eight of the seventy one years of my life in England after regaining my mother's old citizenship, married and acquired a family of my own in the country in which she had always wished me to settle permanently. This originally un-planned development (by all except my mother) altered the pattern of what, to many, appeared as the pre-determined life pattern of all children of Greek politicians. Greeks often fail to realise that nurture can often trump nature as human life finally develops; and that happens that much easier if the individual in question is predisposed in favour of such a change. Further down, I shall say more about the importance of education in character-forming and attitudes towards life and not just enhancing one's store of often useless information.

The time of writing this book also coincides with autumn. In Greek mythology this was the time when Persephone, grabbed by her husband to be, Pluto, from the world of the living, disappeared into the world of the dead, creating the kind of family dispute (between three brothers and a sister – Zeus, Poseidon, Pluto and Demeter) which one finds only too often in the Mediterranean world. Persephone's kidnapping, however, plunged the visible world and not just her squabbling family into chaos. The dispute ended with a compromise, happily not drafted by lawyers in their drab offices in their usual dry if invariably accurate written style, but by artists with a talent to generate eternal images. So, according to the agreement reached Persephone would spend six months in Hades with her husband king of the Underworld and during this time the world above would be dressed in the brown and orange colours of the autumn and the leafless trees of dark winters. Come mid-March Persephone would rejoin her mother on earth which would instantly turn green, its trees would blossom and produce their crops, the light and blue skies of Greece (and Italy), which so captivated the 18th and 19th century European artists, would return to mark the arrival of the easy days. Depressing some might call the story; romantic others might describe it. The essence, however, is that family as well state disputes are best resolved through compromises and not fighting and this was no exception.

It seems that like the ancients I, too, had a predilection for reconciliation and disliked useless divisions. To be honest, I am not sure whether this was always within me or was gradually instilled in my character when I was hardly able to understand the subtle messages which only mothers can transmit to their children. Whatever the truth, the planted seed grew and flourished mainly in England where good fortune gave me the chance to work with some of the best judges these countries ever had. Nurture changed nature to a large extent; and that has explained my life and views ever since. It did not, however, deprive me of the ability to understand the world I left behind me nor my love for its literature, its art, its scenery and the generous characters of its simple people by which I mean those who were lucky enough to escape contacts with the privileged but corrupt elites.

Am I already displaying signs of subjectivity inappropriate for a work with scholarly pretentions? Professor Peter Gay, a famous Yale historian and psychologist, once wrote "that our status, our nationality, our character, our religion, our very language mould the manner in which we see the world".[1] The statement is made to warn about the difficulty of wresting objectivity from one's overpowering subjectivity which is the result of all the above-mentioned factors.

Yet I have laboured hard to present in this book the very sensitive issues discussed within its cover and if I have partly at least escaped the dangers mentioned by Gay's words it is because my peripatetic life furnished me with ample opportunities to see with my eyes, understand, and appreciate how different worlds felt, thought, reacted, misbehaved, but also succeeded in numerous ways. This is a gift which fate bestows on cosmopolites; and in my case it came without depriving me of my affection for the countries of my paternal ancestors – Italy - the country where I was born - Greece - and the maternal country – England - which I rediscovered. Nationality, character, religion, and language were in my case thus all mixed from the very beginning and thus the ability to see (and try to understand) humans and historical events from different angles came naturally.

Since all crises I discuss in this book have been occurring in a low key way for decades but have now suddenly acquired the dimension of a true crisis because of the huge increase of mass immigration I decided it might be worth putting on paper some of my views and conclusions about the messy and disorganized world we live in, especially the one I know fairly well namely that of the Eastern Mediterranean employing the observation angle I have used so often in my professional career.

One point, however, which I will stress in this book, surprised even me. For, when comparing cultures and individuals inhabiting this uncertain, disorganized and even dangerous world I was also pleasantly

---

1. *Art and Act. On Causes in History – Manet, Gropius, Mondrian* , Icon Editions, Harper & Row, Publishers, New York and London (1974), at p. ix.

surprised to note that their growing coexistence and communication through the contemporary social media and enhanced travel of all kinds – touristic, education, business etc. - had also resulted in my life time in convergences of habits, ideas, and ways of working and behaving, though not eliminating divergences on matters where nations were, for political or economic reasons, at loggerheads. Maybe in this convergence phenomenon, which is encountered in what I describe for lack of a better term the sociological or anthropological field might represent a promising seed of optimism which we should help grow further.

There is an explicit contrast in the above images and an implicit indication of different personal attitudes towards the phenomena one wishes to study. My personal preference for similarities instead of differences may have become in early stage at home and then formally structured during a long career as a law student and then a law teacher and legal advisor to judges, politicians, and corporations from different countries. Discovering these similarities between the various legal systems helped me assist different nationalities of students or clients to work closer together; but it also made it necessary to explain to them and relegate into the background the undoubtedly existing differences.

In art, contrasts in colours and light and shade invariably add beauty to the created image. In a written text, especially in a legal text, textual dissimilarities cry out for an explanation since these dissimilarities can entail different consequences. Explaining these differences require prior understanding of religious influences, human characters, history, language difficulties, and social habits, as well as many other factors which account for the differences on the face of a text.

The more I pursued this legal work the more it seemed to fit in my growing wider interest in how people cohabited – or could cohabit better – in a world so messy, disorganised, and made, through political rivalries, appear to be even more divided than it was. To achieve this *rapprochement* in my legal work as well as in my mind I had to understand what purposes the words, terms, notions or concepts were meant to achieve and then compare these aims and see if they existed in other countries and cultures as well, albeit hidden behind different names.

As stated by background but also by conviction I always disliked any philosophy of stark confrontation and believed, instead, in *sensible reconciliation* not strife; in compromises not win all or lose all situations; in admiring and learning from what is different in others and not degrading it and discarding an alien solution or custom on the simplistic reasoning that because it was different it was also bad.

A brief excursus is here over due. If all the above may strike some as containing the kernel of an autobiography nothing could be further from the truth. For autobiographies represent a difficult genre of book and attract readers only when they come from the pen of the likes of Jean Jacques Rousseau, Bertrand Russell, or Stephan Zweig to mention but a few whose work I enjoyed reading and re-reading. The commercial success of the autobiographies of retired politicians do not disprove my thesis; for their aim is self-justification and their written style often betrays the hand of anonymous assistants who have done the spade work and, who knows, maybe even have a wider culture than that possessed by the purported author.

In writing this book my aim was twofold and more modest. First to try describe the changing habits of different people in whose lands I had spent considerable time on matters such as habits, modes of expression, styles, demeanor, attire (and how this concealed more than their naked bodies) and attitudes towards women. My purpose to describe these features was to show the kind of changes that were taking place even within my life time and slowly creating a greater degree of convergence, tolerance to others, and understanding. To the extent that I figure indirectly in it this account it is because – inevitably - my mixed origins and peripatetic life furnished me with much of the raw material that helped me 'understand' and, I hope, explain but not criticise existing differences among people with different backgrounds.

'Understanding' is thus the word which connects the set of themes touched upon (rather than examined in depth) in the nine chapters that follow. As I explain in the first chapter, for me 'understanding' is a particularly important word since it provides the first step towards civilized cohabitation within states but also in the development of ever-closer relations among states, nations and religions which are, or appear to be, far apart. That is the reason why I am interested in digesting what lies behind these differences though international literature has shown us other uses to which such curiosity can be put.

As already indicated, for me the search for 'understanding' began from my mixed background and my restless travelling, reading, and thoroughly enjoying meeting different people. Understanding and learning to tolerate the divergence of views and tastes all began at home from my early infancy. I have hinted at this but perhaps now is the best place to stress the diverging characters and attitudes of the two dearly devoted to each other parents; for, if my father taught me

Sophocles, endlessly reciting beautiful lines about characters doomed by fate or their own arrogance, my mother read to me Sainte Beuve, Marcel Proust, Jane Austen or Charles Dickens – her emphasis being on conciseness of expression, understatement and the need for a social conscience. If father loved vanilla ice cream covered in chocolate sauce - known on the Continent as *Dame Blanche* - mother never forgot throughout her long life the trifle pudding of her youth in England. If the *pater familias* was religiously inclined, his religious *interest was born from the analyses of philosophical texts* – Saint Paul was one of his favourites – whereas my mother's *faith* – and note how I use different words to describe the religiousness of both my parents - *came from the compassion that was instilled in her heart during her years at her at school – a marvelous Convent called Notre Dame de Scion* which I believe still exists.

Absolute statements thus had no room in my up-bringing. With the passage of time I came to realise that the only figure as a dark shadow in the background of my life was politics; and it was from the destructive, self-interested clutches of this profession - which in the good days was seen as the supreme form of public service -which my mother was determined to *save* me, even if this meant putting an end to a long family tradition which had begun centuries earlier in Venice (from where the paternal side of my family hailed). Everything thus had to be sorted out through calm argument and…compromise. On this both parents agreed. For instance, from a very early age I was taught that it was wrong to ask "who was the *greatest* musician: Bach or Mozart?" All I could say, after having (made to listen over and over again) to some sample works of both, was that "I *preferred* the latter".

In this world of no absolutes one thing was left for me to explore and that, in later times, was to question whether the differences in thinking and reasoning were real or only present on the surface of texts or words. My own next step, appropriate to law, was thus to search for the functional purpose performed by the different concepts or notions used by law. That way of looking at things often revealed that the interests promoted by societies of similar socio-economic development were analogous if not identical. The law of contract, in simple terms, consisted in a set of rules intended to help you become richer; the law of torts – accidents - was meant to ensure that you did not end up being poorer and unable to take care of yourself as a result of the multiplication of accident which came with 19th century industrialisation.

The difference of approach was important because it took one straight to the values or interests which societies wished to protect or promote and spared the student and the practitioner the danger of getting confused in translating often untranslatable concepts. The differences between the systems were thus often – not always – transformed into *apparent differences not real ones.*

On matters of substance, the similarity of the systems was thus remarkable; and even more remarkable is the fact how this convergence has grown through international treaties, European Directives, and the use of foreign ideas by the many supreme courts. My close contact with judges - a true gift from the Heavens to which I have already alluded - taught me that often, when they sensed themselves that the synchronisation of solutions was demanded by modern conditions but had no time or expertise to search themselves for empirical evidence supporting this 'gut feeling', they did me the honour to ask me to do some spade work for them to prove or disprove the hunches they had and I shared. This was a unique experience for me even if it often involved much and unpaid work. Maybe it was useful to them as well if I am to judge from the fact that research work I did for them often ended up in their judicial opinions. Either way, I count myself as extremely fortunate that among those who felt I had something little to offer in this respect one must include Lords Bingham, Goff, Phillips, Woolf, Mustill, and Steyn in England; Presidents Walter Odersky (of the Bundesgerichtshof) and Juta Limbach (of the Bundesverfassungsgericht) in Germany; First President of the Cour de cassation in France M. Guy Canivet and Madame Justice Fernanda Contri of the Italian Constitutional Court. An exchange of letters caused by a book on which we collaborated, with President Aaron Barak of the Israeli Supreme Court reconfirmed my long term view of the manifold advantages of talking with jurists of that great race.

The other crucial factor behind this effort was that my peripatetic life and nurture enabled me to overcome many – I hope – of the prejudices which stem from one's natural surroundings which make humans see differences, miss similarities, *and rejoice in an invariably exaggerated image of their national/ ethnic uniqueness.* I encountered this *exaggerated* sense of 'uniqueness' in *all* the countries in which I spent considerable time *though, in the last phase of my active life, I have with pleasure also sensed that the old arrogance in which it was clothed is beginning to wear thin.*

It is this slowly achieved, carefully pre-planned assimilation that is now put in serious danger by the latest phenomenon of massive displacement of people from the Middle East, Central Asia and even Africa in the direction of Europe that is threatening what has been achieved and possibly even destroy the troubled and very divided European Union.

In the first six chapters of the book I thus look at all these sociological or anthropological points in an *apparently* light-hearted manner. I adopted this approach not only because such a way of looking at the world around me fits in well with my deep-rooted feeling that people of the world are converging in the tastes, attitudes, and characteristics, sexism and race attitudes, but that they respond better to these challenges when they take place in a light and not strident manner. Serious issues are sometimes best explored if approached from a light-hearted angle.

A second reason for this 'division' of my material was my belief that I see in this sociological or anthropological kind of approach a good forerunner for the second and main part of the book which is to be found in chapters 7, 8, 9, as well as the Epilogue and which, in terms of pages, represents the bulk of this work. This deals with the modern Tsunami of immigration and is thus, appropriately, written in the more serious if not dark tones associated with the tragedies of enforced human displacements.

I stress this ordering of my materials as well as the difference in written styles adopted for the two parts because I want to highlight once again the fact that the hitherto slow convergence which has taken place in all the topics described in these first chapters had moved most Europeans closer to the idea of peaceful cohabitation with people of different races and religions, *a change which I much welcomed* but which I think is now threatened by the attitudes adopted even by the most liberal of politicians.

On the other hand, modern Islamic fundamentalism, world terrorism – again whether we like it or not both tend to be linked with Islam *even though Islam as a religion cannot be identified with violence*[2]- America's African and Middle Eastern and Central Asian Wars, along with the monumental incompetence shown by the EU and the Greek government in handling the sudden colossal increase of human displacements have combined to make the problem even more insoluble.

This means that the convergence achieved gradually, peacefully, and in a planned way among the citizens of Europe by adapting their

2. In his *East-West Poetry* (Suny Press, 2009) Martin Bidney, an eminent Goethean scholar has brought the Christina Gospel, the Muslim Qur'an together with the Torah to shape to illuminate the love and understanding that all three religions are capable of showing. But maybe it takes a poet – not a politician - to show some of the common good points of all three monotheistic religions.

attitudes and daily likes and dislikes runs the risk of being arrested if not destroyed by the abrupt increase of massive and unplanned immigration with all the multiple dangers this entails.

I regret and condemn all words containing negative connotations and included in the two previous paragraph but would like to play my part in stopping this backward move in its tracks and the only way to do this is to remain bluntly pragmatic about the dangers of the policies which I see are now being adopted by the European Union and Greece and Italy as front line states. Being objective in my account is one desideratum; remaining blunt in the expression of my criticisms of what (little) has thus far been done is quite another. Thus Europe's reaction has been slow, disunited, politically motivated, and as always failed to address the real causes of the problems instead of focusing on how to cope with its consequences. Greece, on the other hand, has clothed its reaction to the unprecedented influx of over 800,000 immigrants during the last eleven months by wrapping it in the mist which traditionally surrounds all extreme (retain and outmoded) Leftist ideology and language.

Some – maybe many of my readers - may take issue with my stating so starkly my starting position; but just as I will not be shocked if they disagree with my basic opening stance on these matters, so must they be prepared for my determination to continue to express my honestly held views freely. Which of us proves right at the end only time will tell.[3]

---

3. It is because of this 'understanding' of cultures that I also chose to ignore my original Greco-Germanic training and *tried* to omit (most but not all) footnote references in the belief that what needs backing from notes will be of little interest to the general reader and, conversely, what is already known to the expert needs no repeating in notes solely to make the author appear learned! On the whole, therefore, it is thus only where the source of my information was not easily available to most of my readers that an exception was made and a reference was inserted in the notes.

Chapter One

THE IMPORTANCE OF 'UNDERSTANDING'

Some illustrations of how better understanding can help explain what followed hurtful events

Understanding is the first cognisable act in a series of decisions or reactions to a perceived problem or events and, as such, it can be of considerable importance for it can determine what fill follow. For instance, the proper understanding of the symptoms of a sick person will determine the doctor's diagnosis of his ailment and the requisite treatment. In school exams, a correct understanding of the question asked of an examinee should lead him, if moderately prepared, to the answer sought in his test. The correct understanding of a human's mind will enable the correct assessment of a particular human conduct which may follow. Understanding correctly troop movements in a war-torn part of the world should enable military planners to decide if they form part of routine manoeuvres or represent the first moves towards military escalation and react accordingly. Understanding tremors and earth rumblings may give useful warnings of imminent earthquakes or volcanic explosions; metaphorically, too, the may give – as they should have done for we had early warnings of them coming – of massive displacements of humans because of the conditions prevailing in their own lands. At the end of this chapter, we shall examine briefly some of the possible reactions to accurate understanding of acts or events that occur around us. Before that stage, however, it might be useful to give in slightly more detail some famous examples of our current topic taken from literature as well the world politics.

A psychologically hurt person is likely to react in ways that will set in motion a series of often inexplicable or unforeseen consequences. What exactly hurt an individual more often than not may not be discernible or, alternatively, may be subject to different interpretations. The Dutch painter Piet Mondrian (1872-1944) explains his own move from being an accomplished (but not outstanding) post-impressionist painter, later influenced by the bright colours of the Fauvist school, and then turning towards cubism and, eventually abstraction. His own style consisted of constructing lines and color combinations on a flat surface representing two dimensional depictions of squares painted in black or the three basic colours[1] becoming a highly original abstract artist. His artistic conversion is described by him in numerous letters and works in abstract and not always clear philosophical terms. Mondrian's explanation of his stylistic evolution "Can never resist elevating psychological traits into metaphysical questions"

Professor Peter Gay, an historian of repute as well as a trained psychiatrist, on the other hand has, in a detailed essay,[2] explored more complex reasons submerged in the artist's sub-conscious but hidden by his aforementioned manner of explaining the causes of his artistic development. Gay's work thus suggests – reveals one might be tempted to say - not only that the person examined may (unknowingly) be giving wrong reasons for his actions and thought processes; but that the understanding the true psychological causes of his externalised conduct provide a further if not more accurate dimension of the difficulties of correctly understanding radical shifts in human conduct. The wider conclusion of this is that understanding human conduct may involve the difficult task of understanding the causative significance of the actor's subconscious. Correct 'understanding' thus becomes not only an essential word in explaining human conduct and its consequences as stated at the outset of this chapter; it becomes devilishly difficult if it involves understanding his subconscious – a task often impossible because of lack of reliable evidence. Numerous examples, more or less well substantiated by complimentary evidence, show that this challenge applies across all forms of art and this, if properly carried out, can offer researchers new rewards in exchange for more detailed *but interdisciplinary* analyses of their subjects.

Euripides' *Electra* for instance offers us an example of a young girl whose father is brutally killed by her mother while the latter's lover

---

1. His works progressively had a considerable influence on other artists, including musicians – Pierre Boulez for instance – or even Yves Saint Laurent whose one year's entire collection reflected Mondrian's designs on the cloth used.
2. *Art and Act. On Causes in History – Manet, Gropius, Mondrian,* Harper and Row Publishers (1974) pp. 175 ff, especially, pp. 207 ff.

and eventual new husband marginalises the Royal Princess by forcing her to marry a decent but impoverished minor aristocrat, to prevent her from giving birth to a son who might one day legitimately claim the throne of his grand-father. The humiliated princess is thus forced out of Court and obliged to live in a hut where day in day out she is obliged to carry out herself all the necessary menial acts while her beloved brother has been smuggled out of Mycenae by loyal servants in order to help him survive and, who knows, one day succeed in taking revenge on his father's death and reclaim his throne.

Philologists and psychologists have come to the same 'understanding; namely that it was Electra's *special closeness to her father* that lies at the basis of the subsequent revenge which she and her ultimately reunited brother carry out on Clytemnestra and Aegisthus. That is the prevailing 'understanding' of the plot of the tragedy, though the path followed by the philologists (textual) and the psychiatrists (the psychological defined by the later famous psychologist Karl Jung as the "Electra's syndrome") have not been the same. Yet a third explanation (or understanding) is, however, possible; and though the end result is the same – killing the mother – the motive of the killing is altered with the result that the character of the avenging daughter can now been interpreted in a different way, perhaps less charitably than it was before the new understanding was put forward. In literary/philological term the difference may be of interest; it may also consist of a very human reaction without having resort to Jung's theory which, almost instantly, was 'rubbished' by his teacher, none other than the famous Sigmund Freud.

We owe this different understanding – more sociological than psychiatric in nature to, among others, an eminent psychiatrist who also is very learned in the ancient texts – Professor Bennett Simon, currently of the University of Harvard. The Professor thus maintains that Clytemnestra was killed not because she assassinated Agamemnon but for denying her daughter the chance of a royal marriage and her issue the right to ascend to his grandfather's throne. Electra's ambition and not the 'pathological' love of her father, as Karl Jung had maintained, thus becomes the key point of the play. The new understanding does not alter the final result; but it does change our understanding of the protagonist's motives and character.

The different 'understanding' of the motive is significant not only because of the standing of the author who has suggested it but also because, interestingly enough, Euripides – arguably though, again this is not the prevailing explanation - also has resort to it in another famous play of his: *Medea*. For there, too, the prevailing explanation of Medea's ferocious revenge is her betrayal by her husband Jason. This, too, however has been doubted on the grounds that what Medea resented most was the diminution of her own social status as a result of Jason leaving her in the state of a *donna abandonata*.

The full implication of this is only grasped when one recalls that Medea's marriage to her husband was carried out in accordance with 'barbarian' – i.e. not Athenian - law with the consequence that once abandoned by Jason she lost all her status, her children became illegitimate, and in fact, because of her own conduct in helping Jason steel the Golden Fleece, she would have nowhere to seek refuge after their separation and, in effect, become what we now call a "stateless person". For she could not remain in Corinth, the residence of Jason's new family; nor could she return to Iolcus or, indeed, her fatherland Colchis, because of the way she had treated her family in helping Jason steel from them the Golden Fleece. Refuge in Athens, in the event, proved her salvation; but this was due to the crafty way she used to convince the Athenian King Aegeus to give her sanctuary in his city; and this, too, turned on exploiting his own psychological needs which she instantly understood when she met him by chance on his return from the Oracle of Delphi where he had sought advice as to his failure to have a son.

Many other examples can be given of alternative understandings of the event which triggers off differing consequences to or interpretations of theatrical representations of historical or mythical events. One last example will suffice.

The Trojan Women is one of the latest plays of Euripides where the playwright describes the devastating state which prevails in Troy after the sacking of Ilion. The account is so vivid that it is tempting to read the play as one standing on its own and, in one sense this is of course, perfectly correct. Yet preceding this play two different plays written by Euripides – *Andromache* and *Hecuba* – talk of the fate of two of the most famous members of the Trojan Royal family – the Queen (Hecuba) and Hector's wife (Andromache), not to mention the female slaves who went into exile with their mistresses. If read together – *and though the poet nowhere tells us that they should so be read though, equally, nowhere has he told us we must not*– the three plays can suddenly acquire a much wider and, one might add, eternal theme. For all three focus on the disasters of wars and particular the uncertainty and misery that hits the abandoned and the widowed Trojan women. Our understanding – and thus our further analysis of thus 'unofficial trilogy'[3] leads us to explore new and wider issues.

But to return to the Trojan cycle, directing the reader to a different 'understanding' of the Trojan women pushes him to reconsider the very contemporary issues of refugees and economic immigrants; how one deals with them; and, most importantly, whether those who are really responsible for their plight are those who are responsible for starting the war[s]. I shall return to these issues in chapters eight and nine and discuss them in their contemporary setting; for, once again, though the causes of wars may differ, their consequences rarely do. Indeed, the entire world is, at the time of writing this book, pressed to address them. It is only recently and manly in America that we thus came to understand that ancient works – such the *Iliad*, the *Odyssey*, *Filoktites or Hercules Furiens* and other 5th century tragedies – contain many valid clues about the troubled state of mind of disturbed people which we are now finding replicated in the men or women who spent much time in oversees wars (such as that of Viet Nam, Iraq or Afghanistan) and find themselves in need of urgent medical attention.

From the literary world but from a very different era and literary genre one more example may be considered to show how this time the motives of the author may be more complex than one might imagine when reading his work for the first time and, perhaps, have scant knowledge about his personal beliefs and circumstances. The work in question is England's most famous epic poem: *Paradise Lost*.

The poem, exceeding twelve thousands lines of verse in length, follows (fairly) closely the *Genesis* and is in many respects modelled on the *Iliad* and *Aeneid*; but even on religious issues, especially if read in conjunction with other works of Milton's, it contains interesting variations from established Protestant dogma. Hints of all these, which warn us that Milton was not only a very learned man, a deeply devout Protestant, a political pamphleteer, and an ardent but in the end also disillusioned supporter of Cromwell's - not to mention the fact that by the time he wrote this poem he was totally blind – all become very important to the proper understanding of both his motives and the correct reading of his masterpiece. Thus, all these desperate elements figure – to varying degrees – in this greatest example of English Epic poetry. More importantly, if constantly born in mind while reading his poem, they can give us a different 'understanding' of what led him to

---

3. By this I mean that the only surviving official trilogy of ancient drama is Aeschylus' *Oresteia* consisting of the three separate plays of *Agamemnon, the Libation Bearers and Eumenides*.

the 'unusual' characterisation of his two protagonists: God and Satan.

Indeed, if there is one thing which is known and accepted by most readers is Milton's magnificent portrayal of Satan – though one must hasten to remind ourselves that he is gradually degraded until he ends up as serpent 'crawling on his belly eating dust' – and a rather dull depiction of God, with only Christ (the Son and "Vice Regnant" but not yet Jesus Christ since he has not yet also become a man) receiving in a mere one page a more human image.

In my view an important explanation can be found in the section which describes why Satan decided to abandon the comfortable life he enjoyed in Paradise while still considered - in Baudelaire's wonderful sentence – "the most beautiful of angels". The Divine Court is there described as rigid, hierarchical, calling for constant genuflecting and boring and repetitive duties such as guarding Eden (which in the event the angels did not do that well) which provided no incentive for any exceptional, gifted, ambitious 'servant' – Satan for instance – to continue in the Master's service.

Aspiring for a better position in life, even if this means moving to another 'job', is the only option open to Satan and he takes it. In our times, one would hazard the guess with a fair degree of certainty that that which is seen in Milton's poem as the sin of all sins in our contemporary world would represent the reaction of most driven young men and women, indeed the one which the prevailing capitalist system would encourage not just tolerate. Was Milton foreseeing, understanding, implicitly accepting, this reaction as being one only to be expected? Or have times changed so radically that even he could not foresee such a radical change in the way ambitious youngsters think?

Now the hierarchical, ceremonial, rigid Royal (Devine) Court is very much in accordance of the image Milton had of the Catholic Church of his time; and, as a political animal, it is against this that he is really rebelling. To be sure, at the time he was living, it would have been inconceivable to come up with a different *ending* to his plot and book. Yet what he could change in the original story he did and there is thus no doubt that there are passages where Milton clearly shows his admiration for Satan (and many of his chief lieutenants) – an admiration which at times leads him to present Satan not only as a genius commander, master builder of Pandemonium– the Capital City of the Devils – within a very short period of time and courageous traveller in unexplored and unknown space, but also as very movingly human. This is precisely what occurs when he is presented weeping before his troops before he pulls himself together and makes a rousing speech to his devils, thanking them for their support and proposing to them his plan to penetrate surreptitiously Eden and destroy God's finest creations.

Crass though this summary of the poem and its poet's life may be, I hope it shows how a different, new in the sense of more adapted to our times and thus arguably more convincing understanding of what the poet was really trying to achieve can lead to a different – equally stimulating if different – interpretation from the traditional one ascribed to the poem. And let us not fear to consider such different interpretations for classic is a work which is capable of adapting to the conditions of different eras – ethical as well as aesthetic – and retain its educational value.

Let us now move to real individuals and contemporary geopolitical events and note how here, as well, the correct understanding of some fundamentals can lead us to further questions, perhaps, even novel answers, as to what individuals or governments were really trying to achieve when, though their actions, they set in motion a series of further reactions.

Those, who like the present author, have shown a deep interest in the somewhat novel branch of history known as psychobiography may have noticed how most if not all of the great musical composers were afflicted by varying psychological or other problems raising two questions – which clearly cannot to be answered in this book. The first is whether these shadows or peculiarities are discernible in their musical work; the second being whether these shadows or blemishes helped – not hindered – the extraordinary productivity of these composers. To the first question the answer must surely be affirmative; to the second ambiguous if not downright impossible to answer in any manner other than the expression of a gut feeling. A further and purely psychological question is to what extent can these pressures promote creativity and at which stage do they actually cease being inspirational and, actually, can succeed in killing all intellectual creativity.

Ludwig van Beethoven was, literally, a genius not least because his creativity like that of Mozart's was so effortless. He was also a kind man; a lonely man; and a mystery. 'Understanding', however, some of his actions remains impossible; for why would a man at the peak of his popularity and creativity allow his name to be misspelt into *von* Beethoven which – unlike the Dutch *van* – implies a title of nobility? And why would he even allow the rumour to be spread that he was the illegitimate son of Frederick the Great of Prussia? Did he feel he needed this kind of shallow recognition at a time when he had composed the Fifth Symphony?

Insecurity is a word that springs to mind; but can a man recognised and admired to the extent that he was in his Vienna days also be that insecure? How does such a feeling affect people? Where does it arise from? These are the kind of questions which lend meaning to Piet Mondrian's six mystery word: "to know, to understand is happiness." Certainly they are the answers historians and biographers would dearly wish to have.

I, for one, can offer no happiness on this score; for, as a layman, I cannot begin even to answer the questions I raised. One thing is clear, however, and that is that Beethoven's mysterious 'complex' did not affect either the quantity or the quality of his productivity. Obviously, however, these repressed feelings formed part of his subsequent loneliness which must have deepened further with the onset of deafness and nearly, as he himself admitted in his letters, often led him to toy with the idea of suicide. They may also explain the composition of his beautiful but so mysterious last quartets.

In other cases understanding the past can help explain contemporary behaviour both by individuals, even entire nations. The Greeks are a proud nation; vaguely conscious of how great their distant past was and gay – in the old sense of this beautiful word – by disposition, though happiness and melancholia often alternate in the members of this race in a manner that reminds one of the symptoms found in those who are by-polar. Faults also abound. Bouts of extremism often come with a strong and most unpleasant desire to show off. Political immaturity is rife in a nation that talks incessantly about politics, is quick to imagine things which are not there, and can be quick to give and suffer offence. The fault, however, which falls under the category that here interests me is the obsequiousness and servility which is so contrary to the sense of pride of a nation which is at heart confident, generous, and sentimental. The reason was the long – four centuries – Turkish yoke which followed the fall of Constantinople in 1453 AD.

The Turkish occupation was a mixed phenomenon. The Greek Orthodox Church was, originally, the only one to be recognised; and the Patriarchate was, to start with, well-respected as was the freedom of religion. However, the Sultan's that followed Mohamed the Conqueror did not share his shrewd political mind which led him to opt for a moderate degree of control over the Orthodox Church. His successors hardened their rule as their grip extended over the entire Balkans and, of course into the Arab lands. Young Christian children were taken away from their families at tender age and transformed into the Janissaries, a fanatical, fighting force in the service of the Sultan. Greek schools came under growing restrictions; and the so called 'hidden' – i.e. functioning in the darkness of the night – schools came to be an important source of keeping the national consciousness alive.[4] They and the Church – though a fair number of its highest ranking members opted for the easier life of collaboration with the occupier – were the two factors which kept Hellenism alive. The Islamisation of the Byzantine provinces - meticulous described with admirable objectivity by Professor Spyros Vryonis in the USA – was practised at least since the 9th century AD; but with the passage of time it increased in intensity, especially as the Empire began its long but constant down slide from about the middle of the 18th century.

In such an environment survival was hard. Though the poor peasant living in unpopulated areas off the land and their stock felt little of the Imperial administration, those in larger urban centres had to become servile, cunning, dishonest, and volatile in their friendships if they were to survive. Only those who flourished as merchants outside Greece – in Vienna, Leghorn, Trieste, Odessa and parts of current day Romania – flourished, remained educated, and admirably loyal to their roots. But the servile, sycophantic, characteristics described above became ingrained in the Greeks who never had the chance to escape abroad; and since this state of affairs lasted for over nearly four centuries, many of these features have become part of a second nature. Even the non-specialist reader, un-interested in the current tribulations of the Greek society and economy will have heard of political favouritism, tax fiddling on a huge scale, a large – many would argue with some justification – hydrocephalus public sector, and that unique Greek phenomenon of the state cheating when it can its citizen and they, in turn, returning the same favour.

This is not a pleasant state of affairs to encounter and even sadder to have to admit it in such blunt terms; yet it has to be admitted for until it is remedied Greece will continue to suffer politically and economically. How long a proper reform would take is anyone's guess. But the reasons of this favouritism, volatility, and corruption has an old history behind it; and only if one understands this one can begin trying to rectify it. Joining Europe, however, has achieved nothing – absolutely nothing – to improve this unwelcome remnant of past

---

4. Γιώργος Κεκαυμένος, *Το Κρυφό Σχολειό. Χρονικό μιας ιστορίας*, Εναλλακτικές Εκδόσεις.(2012).

subjugation. Understanding modern Greece is near impossible; but anyone who wishes or needs to, has to try by beginning to understand its past.

Understanding modern geopolitics requires a deep knowledge of past history. It also calls for a talent to see under the surface of things. This exist naturally or not at all; but its existence is helped develop if he who has it has met in his life politicians and noted, if not studied, how they think, behave, react, especially in moments of crisis.

Along with understanding human nature especially that of the protagonists of politics, it helps to know as much as possible about the countries which figure in one's writings. This is one reason for devoting an entire chapter to the countries in which I have spent much of my professional time so that it can serve as a sui-generis introduction to the points made later.

The Balkans is another region of importance in my account. They have the unwelcome privilege of being regarded as one of the traditional areas of division, instability, crime, poverty and drug-dealing. Much of all this they owe to the presence of many rivalling races, religions, and cultures which retained a certain degree of autonomy even under the Ottoman Empire. The relations with each other could thus easily flare into local disputes, even wars. They are all still there; and they remain dangerous both for the locals and for Europe as a whole. Unity and peace of sorts came to the Balkans only when exceptionally strong leaders – be they Byzantine, Serb, or in most recent times Yugoslavian in the form of Marshall Tito – were present on the scene. The importance of leadership and its notable absence – in my view – in our times will thus also be considered as this book progresses.

Religious antagonisms, even among one and the same Church - the Christian Church - played their part in the instability of the region from at least the 8th century as Byzantium and Rome quarrelled as to who had the right to appoint the Bishops in these regions. This religious confrontation between the Orthodox Church in the central and eastern Balkans, the Catholic Church, in Slovenia and Croatia, and the Muslim presence mainly in Bosnia and to a large extent in Albania, all remain semi-quiescent but not pacified, let alone obliterated even after the war in Yugoslavia came to an end many years ago. Indeed, in one sense these religious divergences remain alive and are becoming more acute as the number of Muslims in the Balkans is growing faster than those who belong to the Christian Churches and revealing their domineering tendencies with not a little help from Turkey. At the same time one must note the revival of the Russian willingness to act as the protector of Orthodoxy, something which progressively went out of fashion after the Crimean War and, the Russian political slogan for 'intervention' in the region was replaced first by pan-Slavism and later by communism. Once again, centuries of ethnic and religious antagonism cannot be erased within decades; and while the past still leaves its shadows it makes the present unstable and the guessing of the future opaque.

My last geopolitical example will be mentioned briefly for I will return to it at greater length when I discuss the modern problems of massive movements of refugees and economic immigrants. In my view, thus far Europe and the West have been caught unprepared and, inevitably, both immigrant and native populations are suffering and will suffer even more in the immediate future since the tide of immigration has not yet peaked. Collective solutions have not yet been found; and the understandable divisions within Europe, will continue to make a civilised and widely acceptable solution an unachievable illusion.

This is the situation which should make all serious Europe-watchers ask themselves what is the purpose of having a Commissioner for Immigration – a shrewd Greek in fact – when he is so obviously two steps behind and not three steps ahead of the game. The one point I wish to raise here, however, is linked to my point about understanding the causes of a problem and acting before it becomes insoluble. In fact, it is two points I am making and they are closely inter-linked. They will be looked at in greater detail in chapters 7 and 8 so here I will only sketch them out.

The first is the EU had more than ample indications that the migration crisis was about to explode and yet remained (criminally) inactive. I am not the only one who has been saying this though now leading newspapers make this unprepared for European decline the subject of articles which are splashed across the entire front page.[5] From the early 2004 ministers of the then conservative Greek government were trying to sensitise Europeans to immigrants crossing the Greek borders and being stopped from heading for Germany by an EU treaty known as 'Dublin II'. The current President of the Republic – at the time Minister of Interior – discussed this issue with his French counterpart. Sympathy was given; reaction, however, was so minimal it might as well be described as absent. The problem was seen as a Greek problem; and Greek politicians were ignored when they were

---

5. For instance *The International New York Times* of 19-20 December 2015, esp. page 2.

increasingly arguing that it was fast becoming a European problem. From 2011 onwards I kept warning in my writings that immigration would soon dwarf the economic crisis as Europe's – not just Greece's main - problem but then scholars are used to be treated as the preeminent example of a *vox clamantis in deserto*.

Then the illegal migrations from the Libyan coast to Lampedousa and, from there to Sicily, began. It is noteworthy in the interests of the discussion that will follow towards the end of this book to note that this phenomenon gained momentum after the USA, France and England bombed Libya and it rotten regime out of power with great relish, forgetting that it was they who had rehabilitated Khadafy into the world community because their oil companies needed the Libyan oil. The turn came for the Italians to complain; but even the gradual increase of drowning of fleeing immigrants was unable to move – emotionally or politically – the euphemistically called European *Union*.

Then the Turks, faced with growing internal problems with their own minorities, decided to cause some mischief of their own. Greece was the easy target; Europe, which had the money, was the ultimate aim. The Turks rarely make a diplomatic or other move unless they see somewhere in the distance a hidden pot of gold. With their help, the migration route changed; and the poor creatures escaping the mayhem affecting their countries were packed into unsuitable inflatable dinghies (manufactured in Turkey) and were expected to cross shorter distances of water and land on the Greek islands of the North-Eastern Aegean. Within weeks these island were literally swamped by refugees who were then shipped off like cattle to Athens and then either left to camp in parts of the over-run Capital or began a long walk – yes, unbelievable but true, a walk - to the northern states of Europe which were always their intended destinations. The human drama was transformed into a human catastrophe but the EU continued to talk and remained divided as it usually is.

The second point is even more rarely discussed. This is out of fear of stoking up anti-American, anti-British or anti-French feelings and it is the fact - and a fact it is not an opinion and thus must be respected - that the current waves of immigration have received a great boost by the misguided foreign policies and failed wars led – manly by the USA – in north Africa, Libya, Iraq and Afghanistan as well as a confused policy towards Syria, the Palestinian issue, the democratisation of the Gulf states, and conflicting policies towards Iran. *America's responsibility for this human disaster is equalled if not surpassed only by that of the Gulf Arab States who have done absolutely NOTHING to help their*

fellow Muslims but, on the contrary, have, for a variety of reasons, financed
fellow Sunni militants operating in Syria thus making the spectre of Mus-
lim militancy both more frightening and totally unacceptable. The truth,
however, is as Oscar Wilde's put it "rarely plain and never simple".
So what I just mentioned must be qualified by mentioning one important factor which fuels the current feelings of instability. For these
states live increasingly under the terror of the growing Iranian power
in their region and the very real danger of their destabilisation if Shia
refugees were ever to settle in their lands.

To these wounds we must add three more.

First is the weakening of the traditionally good links between Israel
and the USA. Second, is the growing instability in Turkey and the
ambivalent feelings the more recent and extreme Turkish administrations have caused in Western capitals, even among those who have
traditionally and for understandable reasons of self-interest have been
well-disposed towards Ankara. Finally, a major source of concern is
the growth of Islamic fundamentalism which, too, has profited from
the foreign policy errors of the leading Western powers. The universal
effort on this problem has been – *quite rightly* – to stress that not all
Muslims were terrorist. But there is another fact – not opinion – which
no one dared to mention for fear of being described as a racist namely,
that European terrorist activities or even just unrest has never been associated with other religions such as Buddhism or Hinduism or Tao-
ism. If true, should not this factor be *carefully* weighed?

When later we talk about possible solutions to the growing problems of immigration, bearing the above in mind will be essential. From
what the West did in north Africa and the Middle East is an important
reason for the present chaotic state on the topic of immigration; but it
will also be up to them to find ways to stem the problem by finding
ways to address the problems *before* it touches European shores. For
the current role of the Gulf States in the problem has been less than
satisfactory since they have thus far refused to take any of these fellow
Muslim immigrants into their lands and – worse still – many of them
are reputed to have been bank-rolling the emerging Islamic (Sunni)
militant movements, allegedly out of fear of the Shia sect mainly situated in Iran and the southern part of Iraq.

What can better understanding achieve

The answer to this question has, in one sense, already been given in the material provided thus far. This illustrated how the correct understanding of an event, human conduct, work of art, or its creator's true aims and frame of mind can produce the first solid foundation on which to base one's reactions to all of the above. These reactions will, in turn, be determined by such new ideas, motives, or explanations discovered in the kind of happenings or conduct referred to above. As stated, the understanding of a play or work of art can thus be altered or enriched by the discovery of new aspects calling for a re-assessment of the situation. Alternatively, they can reveal undiscovered or unnoticed information about the initiator of the conduct analysed or the work produced which may, in turn explain, or even justify a conduct which otherwise may have attracted reprobation. This understanding of the human conditions lying behind the investigated conduct or human behaviour may thus lead to greater understanding of the actor and this enhanced tolerance towards him and his ideas and beliefs. In a world increasingly antagonistic, polarised, and fractious this tolerance can be no mean achievement.

Learning to gauge the kind of risks that a certain form of conduct may entail can also be beneficial in so far as it can make humans more conscious of the need to contemplate in advance the possible adverse consequences of their action or inaction and thereby act with greater circumspection or foresight. This inability of the West, especially the Americans, to foresee major world-changing events – and let us remind our readers that they did not foresee (a) Saddam's invasion of Kuwait; (b) the collapse of the Wall in Berlin; (c) the 11th September bombing of the Twin Towers in New York' nor, finally, (d) the Arab Spring and its rapid expansion – omissions which deserve to be described as mind boggling. In the case of the current mass immigration a similar understanding of the consequences of this invasion of Europe will represent for its people should have led to the timely erection bulwarks – economic and, yes, maybe even physical, against the risks of a human inundation of their territories. Judging from the patchy ideas emerging as answers to this huge problem one is tempted to suggest that its full consequences have still not be rightly gauged.

Our inability to foresee the consequences of our decisions is not a new phenomenon though its extent probably is. Since the technological means at our disposal are greater than ever, this can only mean that the human factor is less alert, less efficient, or less imaginative in interpreting the signs. Alternative, though talents exists in various areas which could help address this problem – intelligence information, politics, anthropology, military action and the like – they remain imperfectly exploited because of lack of co-ordination both at national and international levels. That is where the huge responsibility of the EU comes in and I predict will attract even more criticism in the years to come than that it has already done.

An illustration of a seriously inadequate appreciation of the consequences of collective action can be found in the severe economic reparations imposed upon the defeated Germany at the end of the First World War. At first blush they represented an understandable reaction by those who had suffered most by it namely, the French who, among the victorious allies, were those who took the strongest line on this issue having suffered the largest number of casualties next to the German. Imposing unrealistic reparations and temporally transferring to French control Germany's units of production led to a rapid increase of inflation in that country, progressive social dislocation, and thereby laid the foundations of another and even more ferocious confrontation less than twenty years later. One of the few far-sighted economists who mentioned these dangers in a famous book of his was John Meynard Keynes; and in keeping with the spirit of the times his *Economic Consequences of the Peace* were slammed by the book reviewer of *The Times* who must have had the audacity to believe that his criticisms was so notably correct that they could take – and did take - the form of a leading article and not just a book review. Life – the Gods the ancients would claim – mercilessly strikes arrogance down. In my recent example, the name of Keynes is still very widely known; that of his reviewer is as if the man never even existed.

Such lessons are not always learnt; and this is the result of a variety of possible causes including the relentless pursuit of state interests in a world more closely linked and interdependent than ever before. This author for one is thus among those who is not convinced that the violent toppling of the former Libyan leader Muammar Qaddafi – a tyrant if there ever was one yet one who had been 'tamed' somewhat in the last phase of his rule by Tony Blair – was an act which encouraged more instability in the region. The American involvement in Syria, in concert with a continuous vacillation as to what form it should take, revealed the USA as indecisive as ever during the winter of 2013. In my view, in fact, it also revealed how weak the country was left after its exhausting and failed wars in Iraq and Afghanistan. The state of the internally troubled Turkey has also worsened partly because of the authoritarianism of its current President but also because its foreign policy has lost much of the novelty if not shine that it had gained during the early years of the Davutoğlu years.

To this list of enhanced troubled spots I would add the continuing crisis in the Eastern Europe, one which, in the beginning, was due to a serious miscalculation by EU officials – not top political leaders – anxious to offer to the Ukraine a union of sorts with the EU. The earlier lesson of the failed meeting at Bucharest, which had clearly revealed the difficulties of such an initiative, were ignored, possibly by American policy makers always anxious to take a jab at Russia and expand their influence into Russia's back yard.

This ran counter to what President George Bush (father) had promised to the Russians when they offered their consent to allow the former Eastern Bloc to join NATO.[6] My own belief is that President Obama's willingness to transfer so much power to a bunch of hard line conservative ladies who, arguably, share part of the blame for creating this contemporary crisis with Russia, the insolubility of the Ukraine problem in particular. Why on earth a Democratic and obviously pro peace candidate would ever delegate such power to conservative hard liners has not, to my knowledge, ever been clarified. I can only speculate that it may in part be the result of a belief – or hope - that this might have helped pacify restless 'tea party' Republicans and other Neo-Conservatives and leave the President free to work on his favourite social themes. If this was, indeed, even part of his planning – and, of course, by its nature this can only be guessed but not confirmed except by documents – it proved disastrous both for the President but also for his legacy in foreign affairs during the dying years of his term of office.

One may, of course, argue for long as to who are the 'goodies' and who are the 'baddies' in this instance. To this author, however, this humanly-fabricated crisis, not only was born out of a lack of deep understanding of the ethnic divergences in the Ukraine but also a blurring of the spheres of influence tacitly agreed by opposing camps after the end of the Cold War at Yalta. More importantly, it triggered off uncontrolled imaginations (such as that of the present author) to try and think ahead. He has thus been wondering for some time whether the moment may be fast approaching for *a new kind* if Yalta.

The name of course instantly invokes the image of a world long

---

6. I am not aware why such an important undertaking was never embodied in any kind of written document; but that it was given no one has ever doubted.

past when super powers could impose unilaterally their respective spheres of influence on smaller countries. Such a way of proceeding would be much more difficult to achieve these days when too many conflicting interests would be competing with one another to impose their own views. More difficult and, arguably, not desirable. Yet, subject to overcoming this kind of 'technical' problem I am increasingly inclined to believe that such an idea might just about help restore a more lasting state of peace in the centre of Europe by re-setting the red lines the opposing world camps should clearly observe.

Yet a Yalta of sorts will, in my view, have to be agreed and major powers get the message that they cannot interfere in the back yards of their powerful opponents. This would require the West to understand that Russia has historically required - and *needed* - a series of buffer states to protect the periphery of its central core. *English tanks or American missiles a few hundred miles away from Saint Petersburg have never been and will never be welcome by Russia until and unless a deeper and more obviously mutually beneficial understanding could be reached between the Russian Federation and Poland (and, of course, the Baltic States).*

I conclude this illustration by repeating that the type of solution I am envisaging and would personally wish to see occur will prove unimaginably difficult to negotiate. Yet I also feel that the current status quo with growing parts of Europe, North Africa, and the Middle East multiplying daily the geographical areas of festering wounds cannot continue for long. The rethinking, however, can only begin by understanding where we now find ourselves to be and balancing the competing expansionist moves of many countries without classing them 'as good or bad' but simply evaluating the need to respect commonly agreed red lines which can bring back the stability which existed during the Cold War period *MINUS the unacceptable human rights' violations.*

In my humble view if Russia and Europe were ever able and free to evaluate the advantages of greater financial, energy, trade, and educational benefits which would flow from a state of co-operation rather than state of confrontation, all that I dream of could be turned into reality. To be sure, America's thinking and self-interest would never, as things stand at present, allow or tolerate such moves. A more 'mature' Europe however – might, just might - emerge out of its current dislocation and ineffectiveness. If it did, I feel confident that it would see the benefits of such a closer co-operation with the Russian Federation and thus remove its lands from the list of traditional troubled spots which have, in the end, always exploded in its face. Even those countries – England for instance – who centre their thinking around the idea of free trade could see the advantage of being left free to sign direct trading agreements with huge power houses such as China and India instead of being restricted by European rules.

How can one dare make such predictions? Well, for one, the current apocalyptic prospects of massive immigration acts as a stimulus for more serious thinking. Second, because all of us can see, and see not for the first time, that the European Union is neither united nor prepared to cope collectively with crises. Why is that, I will attempt to sketch in the concluding chapters; and my thoughts are bound to raise eye brows if nothing else even more hostile. But one of my theses, which I anticipate here, is that we have failed to understand and address the main weaknesses of our times and done so because our political discourse has been conducted within the restraining straight jacket of political correctness as well as the straight jacket of servility towards the USA. For if convergence is occurring in many aspects of human life and cuts across existing national and ethnic borders, in other matters - ethnic and religious issues – they remain swept under the carpet by politicians who should be statesmen and have the courage to call openly a spade a spade and then try to discover solutions which are equitable, respect human dignity, as well as state interests, and are 'doable' and 'durable'. We do not want semi-theological disputations or unrealistic dreaming. The sooner the real issues are openly addressed the better it will be for all.

As stated this book will thus look at this need for 'understanding' from different angles and will argue that despite the recent multiplication of conflict points in our world, we must not ignore the fact that peoples' tastes, views, ambitions, easy communication among themselves, even increased (but controlled) cohabitation of different races in large cities have shown a corresponding increase towards convergence. This convergence may not be present in the geopolitical field yet. Indeed, it is also weak in the way modern economic crisis are being addressed. Yet for the reasons indicated already all these unresolved problems might force *a new generation of European leaders* to feel freer to negotiate their own future with their closer big partner in the east with whom they also share more cultural resemblances than many people either do not evaluate properly or simply ignore and who are the only ones who could ensure –if a genuinely beneficial agreement could ever be reached – a guaranteed peace in our Continent. If we cannot bring ourselves even to start thinking of such a compromise, we shall go on limping together in a future which will be miserable to all. These are important points; and maybe my line of reasoning has something to commend it, so I shall return to these ideas at the very end of the last chapter of this book.

The contents of chapter one, though only indirectly related to the contents of this book represent, nevertheless, an important if *sui generis* kind of essay on the one word which is crucial for the understanding of my work. Its main message is that only with full and correct understanding of my expressed and implied views on this complex subject -matter will the full profit – such as it is – of this book be gleaned from the chapters that follow. This will thus depend on how well my readers understand the problem; its true causes; the extent of our lack of preparedness to deal with it; the fluidity of the wider environment which gave birth to this monster and which will make it grow still further; the dangers of addressing it in a sentimental not pragmatic manner; the strength of character which those who will be called to deal with all the above points will have to show if they are to have a chance to produce viable compromises (for I see no permanent solutions in the years ahead) and the danger that the contemporary crisis may destroy such progress as has already been achieved in bring humans closer together by means of measured and planned decisions.

To assist this kind of reading – both moderate and daring - I provided some general guideline thoughts at the very beginning of this work which I found useful in my seventy one years of a highly peripatetic life which brought me in contact with people in three Continents whom many would regard as different but I found to be as interesting, as weak, and as deserving of our respect, as many of our own compatriots; for in the current climate of financial greed and rampant consumerism they, too, have also often been cast overboard and allowed to drown.

Chapter Two

LIVING IN DIFFERENT CITIES
Athens, Austin, Cambridge, Cornell, Ghent, Leiden, Munich, Oxford, Paris, Rome and Siena

Changing views

You understand people better when you see them in their natural habitat; for when outside it they may be reserved, react atypically, show off (even this is not part of the temperament) or, more likely the reverse, feel lost. Moreover, if the encounter is taking place outside the home ground they may, understandably, be more anxious to learn about the place they are visiting rather than to talk about their own. Yet it is the real person whom you must understand if you are to understand how his environment has shaped his character, the way he thinks and obeys the rules his environment has laid down for him. It helps to be a foreigner in Germany and Italy or elsewhere for then you notice more than the locals do what differences exist in the things that interest them and interest you and how varied, if at all, are their reactions to external stimuli compared to yours. This knowledge is invaluable in political and business negotiations if you wish to understand what the foreigner really thinks.

This was increasingly the conclusion I reached as I taught foreign law for forty seven years in some twenty eight universities in three Continents. The most perceptive of my legal colleagues adopted a similar broad approach even if their concern was purely legal. The late Tony Weir for instance, as his obituarist in the *Times* put it, believed that " the distinctions that emerged from the comparison of laws of countries reflected differences in their languages, *their social structure, their intellectual and cultural preoccupations, their pastimes,* their systems of law and government, even *their religious beliefs.*" The importance of the italicized words is obvious for they suggest how broad the learning of the true comparatist must be. No less important in his understanding of foreign legal system is the way the legal professions are organized; the peer influence in thinking and comportment; the historical choices made by these systems when, in their distant past, they faced problems which could have been solved in two or more different ways. Combine these elements and one sees immediately the breadth of topics one must begin to digest before one moves from law to different countries and people, and their likely behaviour in international relations.

So, back to this idea of learning more about the different settings in which people work and create.

Living in different cities, much more than merely visiting them for a few days, allows one to see their inhabitants as they really are. This is a good start for the understanding process. But this also puts one in different moods: willing to understand them, more or less able and willing to like them, or just indifferent. Depending on which of the above categories one's mind falls under one's understanding of 'the foreigner' will be greater or remain unchanged. What, however, might surprise one is the change which may occur in one's own disposition towards a wide range of issues. One can thus begin to realise more how mistaken one's own ideas or approach towards these matters has been or, conversely, make one even prouder of the attitudes and solutions prevailing in one's own world.

Living in important cities produces all of the above effects.

Paris, for instance, provokes envy not just admiration for its beauty and urban planning. In it is not difficult, for me at least, from there to lapse into a state of aesthetic hedonism which my dour environment would not normally encourage. This attraction to aesthetic aspects may also lead one to pay even more attention on how one express one's thoughts. Comparing English and French – to marvellously rich languages, can immediately reveal differences in speaking and writing, each exercising a different pull on one's imagination. But the huge emphasis on aesthetics in French can, at times, produce odd results. In French law, for instances we can find instances – article 1384 of their Code Civil where a whole phrase[1] – has been added at its very beginning for no other reason than to achieve a mere *"elegance de style"*.

Could any German lawyer think in such a way? Someone who does

---

1. «On est responsable non seulement du dommage que l'on cause par son fait, mais encore de celui qui est causé par le fait des personnes dont on doit répondre, ou des choses que l'on a sous sa garde. »

not understand the French may thus attempt to give a legal meaning to the ten added words at the end of article 1384 CC cited in note 1, above, which the legislator had, initially at least, added them as a connecting link between the preceding articles 1382 and 1383 and the following article 1385 and 1386 CC and where thus *not* meant to express an independent legal rule of their own. But, as hinted, such an innovation, followed much later – 1895 and 1896 – when the French Supreme Court, taking it queue from the Belgian Supreme Court, gave an independent legal content to those ten words and thus, at a stroke, extended widely the scope of strict liability in the French Civil Code. Surprising maybe, yet true as the above observation comes not from me but from one of France's most notable, modest and learned lawyers – the late Professor André Tunc.

From Paris to New York – from elegance to power; and power in the USA is money. The skyscraper symbolises this feeling that the sky is the limit, even if so many Americans – lawyers and bankers spring to my mind – often 'burn themselves out' in trying to reach it. Just as striking and attractive, however, is the willingness of the inhabitants of this vibrant city to experiment - like Weimarian Berliners did in the 1920's – with new ideas. This may, in turn, tempt you the observer to become willing to experiment as well. Indeed, in the USA the mentality of most people is to experiment with ideas as often as in practice they are willing to change homes or even … their wives.

London by contrast turns your mind to tradition and makes the best of it by slowly but shrewdly adapting it. Not all may regard this as being 'better' but it is different; and the English preference for evolution over revolution permeates their history, the evolution of their law, as well as their current thinking. My way of thinking pushes me towards praising tradition and well-understood continuity and criticizing the world that respects it less than it used to do and, in my view, should do. Greece is currently going through this phase of doubting its values, failing to see the beauty of its past, losing its faith in the religion that kept alive during the dark centuries of Turkish occupation. This is as deeply a damaging state of mind as are the economics of the crumbling country.

Such un-excitable rationality does not abound in the Venetian canals where romanticism overtakes all other moods and makes me push into the background cynical thoughts, even my ingrained pragmatism. Munich, by contrast, demonstrates German 'solidity' but also proves that this need not be of the Prussian kind and can thus be combined with a noisy kind of *joie de vivre*. Is it, for instance, pure chance that it is only in Bavaria and the Rhineland that they 'celebrate' carnival? Small things like the above tell you much about people but, above all, teach you not to over-exaggerate the differences you tend to be told from your early days that exist between different countries and their citizens. Differences exist but, in my view, they are also being toned down in these days where social media reign supreme. This is a theme central to this book.

Greece, since these days its capital is so polluted, riotous, and overrun by beggars, pushes you to the calmer beauty of those islands which are unaffected by massive immigration and where the light blue sky and the dark blue sea instantly turn most observers into imaginary painters. With me, however, such thoughts also work differently for they make me feel sad – very sad – since I still recall vividly the smaller, more structured, safer, simpler but attractively cosmopolitan capital city of my youth.

The more I think of it the more my mind goes even further back to a world which I only know through books. That is the heyday of the Greek civilization when leisure – not laziness – was valued as the way of giving birth to new ideas through reflection and the birth of beautiful ideas. In the midst of the current economic crisis and suffering of modern Greece, it is difficult to think of beauty and great thoughts. Only those who can lie on a beach soaking in the sun can feel relaxed; but, for better or for worse, not all of us can manage such a state of nirvana.

In short, writing about foreign lands and cities can teach humans – especially the born observers – much about people. How one then recounts all this to others can also tell the latter much about the storyteller; for every portrait of a city can, also be seen as containing in part a concealed self-portrait of the *raconteur*. Seeing a city, writing or talking about it, commenting about its inhabitants and their way of life are all sources of endless ideas of very different kinds. It is for the receiver of these ideas to do with them what he can and thereby, if possible, spread them even further for the benefit and enjoyment of others.

So it was only after I left Greece early in 1968 and began enjoying the 'gentler' English sun lying on the 'backs' of the river Cam that I felt able to let me mind wonder aimlessly over my past and the countries and people that I had visited and met. Most importantly, however, with all these thoughts swirling in my mind I was also beginning to plan –not just dream - about the future, discovering what I wanted to do and not what family tradition demanded. In the event, the intellectual revolution that was gradually been hatched on the edges of the Cam happened only in part; but something is better than nothing.

The beauty and peace of the location encourages reflection by weakening the natural tendency to worry about day-to-day concerns and allowing the mind to dart backwards and forwards, in the beginning aimlessly, but soon in the direction which I suppose it always wanted to go but daily chores never allowed it the freedom to do so. It was then that I began to realize how close to a split personality does the duality of the Greek character can reach. Certainly, this was the case with me. Indeed, how true and also how important it is to understand this Greek duality, especially the doubt that plagued the country's inhabitants ever since their Independence Wars in the early 19th century: should the new country remain part of the East or should it turn its sights on Europe and the West? This, by the way, was not a dilemma limited to Greece as a small country. The question plagued the Russians more and more as the 19th century approached its end and their *nouveau regime* was beginning to appear as a distant shadow, hopeful to some, frightening for others. This wide-ranging ambivalence was reflected in much of the written work of the time but, best of all, in Vreubel's many copies of his most famous painting: 'the Flying Damon' and the 'Pensive Damon'. Rarely have two canvases caught so well the sense of confusion of an entire nation faced with unanswerable choices.

The Greeks' daily aphorism of praising the merits of rapid action (το γοργόν και χάρην έχει) but also warning one against rushed action (όποιος βιάζεται σκοντάφτει) is another way to alert one to this Greek duality. Together, they exemplify the contradictory elements of the Greek (middle eastern as well?) character – to which we shall return in future chapters. But one thing is clear: one never escapes paying for excesses. A Nemesis of sorts thus always follows Hubris. This could be seen as an indirect way of nudging the Greeks back to the theme of the golden mean: do not hurry yet do not hesitate either. The Greeks are good and reconciling conflicting theorems in well- turned out phrases; unable, however to achieve this balance in practice.

Yet as I lay on Saint John's manicured lawn in modern Arcadia reflecting on so many disjointed ideas which I thought then - and now, decades later, I commit to paper - they did not sound quite right to me. One thought leads to another and often to a reconsideration of notions, misunderstood because they were approached through translation and not seen in the wider (historical and geographical) context to which they belong. This unplanned sequence of thoughts on the

Cam may warrant a digression because they brought me out of my slumber and sent me straight into to nearby College library to check, to verify - something not possible if studying in a University situated in a large city- to rethink the accuracy of what I thought and have now just written. This recounting of events more than forty five years after they happened shows how productive it can be to allow one's mind to wonder in a relaxed and beautiful environment. For that is the main - the best - effect that Oxbridge can have, especially on those who come to it from an urban and neurotic environment – which is what modern Athens was and has become even more so in recent times.

Hubris and Nemesis

The sequence of word "hubris" and "nemesis" used above will suggest to most English readers the idea of retribution or punishment or – better still in colloquial terms *your* "comeuppance" – which tends to follow *your* arrogance. Those who have read Herodotus will attribute the idea as well as the terms to him; yet this is only a small aspect of the underlying theory which, as is so often the case with Ancient Greek sayings, may conceal deeper reflections on life and nature if you learn how to go below their surface. Indeed, it runs through all the Greek literature, from Homer onwards and is thus not a new invention by Herodotus.

The danger of misunderstanding these texts stems partly from the ancient Greek practice to anthropomorphize or rather anthropococeptualize notions such as νέμεσις, (revenge) τιμωρία,(punishment), φθόνος (envy) whereas in fact these refer to strong forces of nature which redress inequalities or anomalies and re-establish balance (or harmony as Plato would put it) in the cosmos. It may also be due to the fact that those who have not studied the ancient world are unable to see the *continuity* of some of its basic ideas in the works of its greatest authors. We thus find repeated traces of this idea in the works of Homer, Herodotus, and Thucydides which pushes these authors to talk about what they call the "Godly or Divine law" (Θεϊκός Νόμος).

This basically postulated that "balance" is the state of affairs favoured by nature and this balance is really not varied by good or bad human behaviour but by *nature's* demand for equilibrium. This concept which characterizes the philosophy of *Iliad* is that **Moira is impersonal**. Homer this depicts Zeus as the dispenser of "moira", which does not mean "fate" – as might be translated by those who know modern Greek - but "portion" in the sense of what is your allocated portion of life, glory, power, wealth.[2] The image of scales, often associated with Zeus, depicts the notion that Zeus must maintain the order of the universe ($\kappa\alpha\tau\alpha$ $\kappa\acuteo\sigma\mu ov$) and do this impersonally, without pity ($\acute\epsilon\lambda\epsilon o\varsigma$); for he is capable of pity; but he must not exercise it.[3]

Herodotus takes up and in many parts of his work develops this very same idea and most of derive it from him. He thus attributes to this aim the fact "timid and preyed upon" creatures are prolific in nature whereas the more powerful predators are less numerous. Likewise, just as in the human body there must be a balance between the alkaline and the acid, so in life the bad must be followed by the good (and vice versa), sorrow must follow happiness, bad luck must come after good luck, injustice follow justice, bravery and obedience, work and leisure. We are, in short, going well beyond the contemporary understanding which the English have of Hubris and Nemesis (and to which I alluded already), touching the deeper belief that human society must reflect the balance of the highly regulated cosmos.

Herodotus in fact gives us a moving example of this wider sense equilibrium in life, separated by any sense of goodness, by recounting the plight of the good and just Faroe Mycerinus[4]. For when he was foretold by the Oracle that his would be a short life he "sent an angry message to the shrine and reproached the God with injustice for allowing a man as pious as himself to die so soon.... In answer to this there was another message from the Oracle, which declared that his life was being shortened precisely because he had not done what he ought to have done: for it was fated that Egypt should suffer for 150 years ...[5] and it had not during his pious reign.

So to return to Mycerinus, why one may ask should such a pious man die young? The answer seems to be provided by the aforemen-

---

2. See, for instance, Iliad, 15. 209 where Poseidon claims to be «ισόμορος» to Zeus i.e. have the same amount of "apportioned power" to Zeus.
3. Thus, when he tempted to do so to save the life of his own son, Sarpedon, his wife Hera was outraged, interfered and reminded him that he should not even have expressed loudly such a thought: "ποιον μύθον έειπες?" Iliad II. 16, 431-440.
4. Mycerinus was the fifth King of the Fourth Dynasty (2620-2180 BC), the sun of Khafra and the grand-son of Khufu (in Greek literature know as Cheops) who built the third, smallest, but arguably most luxurious of the three pyramids of Giza. Mycerinus is not the only moral and pious man to perish in the name of preserving this wider need for "regularity" and redistribution of balance in a disturbed world; Hector is another and so is Nicias, whom Thucydides, praises to the heavens. See 7.86.5
5. Herodotus 3, 133.

tioned idea of "balance". For the death of Mycerinus was a necessity so as to maintain Egypt's bad state. Why? Because necessity dictated that Egypt had to go through its allotted cycle of misfortune or good fortune (like Egypt is today?). No man could go against the divine plan and Mycerinus's deep-rooted fairness and essential goodness could not prevent the operation of such a law of nature. *For morality, as humans understand it, is not found in nature but was created by the very being which usually violates it.*

This is a deeply tragic story and Matthew Arnold's poem "Mycerinus" beautifully evokes the King's lament in the first three verses, capturing poetically the point just made. Since the verses are not likely to be widely known these days as much as they were (and admired) during the last century, here are his first three.

"Not by the justice that my father spurn'd
Not for the thousands whom my father slew,
Alters unfed and temples overturn'd
Cold hearts and thankless tongues, where thanks are due;
Fell this dread voice from lips that cannot lie,
Stern sentence of the Powers of Destiny.

"I will unfold my sentence and my crime.
My crime – that, rapt in reverential awe.
I sate obedient, in the fiery prime
Of youth, self-governed, at the feet of Law;
Ennobling this dull pomp, the life of Kings,
By contemplation of diviner things.

"My father loved injustice, and lived long;
Crowned with grey hairs he died, and full of sway.
I loved the good and he scorn'd, and hated wrong –
The Gods declare my recompense to-day.
I look'd for life more lasting, rule more high;
And when six years are measured, lo, I die."

So, in the end, balance or equilibrium reign supreme in our universe. This is a fascinating idea that calls not for a paragraph nor even a chapter but a book, preferably written in collaboration with scientists, philosophers, historians.

The Greek duality

It is to another aspect of the Greek "duality", however, to which I now wish to turn since it is so apposite to the subject matter of this chapter. I am, of course, thinking of the deeply ambivalent attitude which Greeks feel towards foreigners. Those not interested in ancient Greek history can test the accuracy of my statement by looking at Greece contemporary love-hatred relationship with Europe.

Though "foreigners" can, in a shrinking world, include the inhabitants of the entire planet, the most widely used expression is framed in terms of the West (the "westerners"), *in this instance* the Greeks seeing themselves as "easterners". This, at least was the optic angle adopted when the idea was first developed during the period of the Fourth Crusade. The Greek expression was and remains when used «κουτόφγραγκοι» - dumb westerners; and the reference to westerners – to be precise originally the word referred to the Francs – shows that this contempt really began when the Venetians suddenly turned their attention from Jerusalem to Constantinople and conquered it in 1204 AD sealing a sad fate that was to be completed nearly two hundred and forty years later.

Dandolo, their Doge, may have been blind; but his sense of political direction was superb. For occupying Constantinople and, subsequently, the better part of mainland Greece for approximately one hundred and fifty years, offered far greater pickings for western commercial interests; and his was an island Republic that was built for profit and money and this was its universally acknowledged yardstick for success. This was the least Christian of the Italian principalities since like the modern inhabitants of Wall Street (though endowed with infinitely better sense of aesthetic taste) they really believed in one God only – quick profit.

Politically, the move confirmed the decline in the fortunes of the Byzantine Empire which began in earnest during the middle of the 10th because of internal dissentions. It was at that time that it finally became clear that the East – and henceforth when we use the term we no longer refer to the Byzantine East but the Turkmen tribes that came in waves from the steps on the east of the Caspian Sea.

In the beginning their arrival passed un-noticed as they gravitated more towards modern Iran and Iraq and the eastern regions of the Caucuses. But Byzantine maladministration, especially from about 1025 AD onwards, finally gave these nomadic tribes the chance to push further westwards and triumph not only because of their youthful energy but also because they were able to spread slowly but surely the idea that they represented new social ideas. The new, invariable, wins over the old because, almost by definition it succeeds in convincing people that 'new' means 'better' which it does not often do.

Yet another idea was well seeded more or less at the same time namely, that those who were penetrating Byzantium from the West were dumb, uneducated, barbarians. In reality, the Normans were anything but that; for though numerically a lesser threat to the emerging Seljuk nomadic tribes of the East, the Normans were focused in their desire not to deprive the Empire of its eastern provinces but of its capital itself. Moreover, wherever they spread their power – which included England, Southern Italy and Sicily - they proved themselves to be admirable warriors, able administrators, and great builders.

Yet, notwithstanding its slow decline, the intellectual and artistic superiority of Byzantium continued to dazzle Western European for another two hundred fifty years or so. Thus, as all contemporary accounts of the Conference of Ferrara-Florence of 1437-9 recount - in their written or pictorial form – how the Byzantines dazzled the westerners by their clothes, their manners, their learning. Benozzo Gozzoli's (c. 1421 – 1497) "The Adoration of the Magi" - a famous mural in the diminutive Chapel of the Medici-Riccardi family in Florence, (painted much after the Conference itself) - projects the central role assigned to Byzantium even during the reign of the last Emperor Constantine Paleologus. And yet the sad end of the fall of Empire was a less than fifteen years away from the visit which the emerging Florence had so sought to host.

Such myths of native superiority are not allowed to die so I, too, was brought up with them firmly anchored in my subconscious. And yet, if Greeks were so far superior to their European neighbours why did they so wish – and still do - to emulate them more and more in their manners, tastes, attire, and so many other matters in which western prominence is taken to represent the icon to be imitated?

So here is another contradiction though not one which could be easily tolerated after the Greeks obtained their independence from the Ottoman Empire during the first quarter of the 19th century. For the liberated Greeks were living by now in a country which had heard of Byron and worshiped him as a local hero; had adopted many of Bentham's ideas in building up its early political institutions; the re-merged country was sustained by Greek merchants flourishing in most of Europe's major commercial centres; and was progressively aspiring to a European kind of functioning civil service and a superior education system to replace the chaos which had reigned during the period of Turkish domination.

The first Bavarian dynasty which reigned over liberated Greece satisfied much of the above and also brought with it Roman law, which was, as the Greeks of the time proclaimed, "the law of our Byzantium forefathers" as was the neo-classical architecture with which the freed inhabitants of the new country could aesthetically relate.

Not all Greek historians have welcomed this official shift towards the West. Some still argue that Greece would have fared better if it had retained its eastern-Balkan centre of gravity. Yet the reasons for the westernization where multiple, understandable politically, and, in my view, convincing. Among them once must include the above mentioned influence of the rich Greek merchants of the Diaspora who played a big role in the Independence War and had flourished, as already stated, among communities as far stretched as Odessa, Walachia, Moldova, Vienna, Leghorn, Marseille and Trieste. To these we must add the intellectuals of the period, also working in European cities, who also gave a big shove westward through the first journals published in the Greek language. Third and chronologically the last, the appointment of a Bavarian Prince as first King of Greece arrived in his new kingdom accompanied by a bevy of Bavarian architects, lawyers, civil servants who were not only culturally Hellenophiles but also good organizers thus laying the foundations of not only the modern Greek state but also of a long and mutually productive relationship with Germany, at least its southern – i.e. the non Prussian – half!

Yet for our purposes what is important is to describe and explain how this duality of the Greek mind enhanced its hold on the Greek psyche as contacts with new states multiplied and Greeks found reason both the admire them and to try to side-line them, to love them, and yet also to downgrade them. The rational mean was, once again, lost to the tendency towards hurried and immoderate reactions gripping their minds, something which only made it more difficult for those, like me, who were determined to understand both sides of the argument and avoid irrational xenophobia. As I write, Greece is again going through such a phase, the target now being Germany. This is precisely the kind of dispute that emanates from narrowly perceived self-interests and ends up hurting all who are caught up in such whirlwinds of passion but not reason.

Thus the initial enthusiasm with Bavaria waned quickly; the King and Queen soon (but not always justly) became unpopular; later the Germans were accused for being too rigid in their Prussianess (forgetting that it was the Kaiser Wilhelm who helped Greece extend its territory by acquiring the province of Kavala in Eastern Macedonia); the late Queen Frederica, was blamed for being part of the Hitler movement in the 1930's, forgetting the inspired role she played in the very difficult years of the Civil War; Mrs. Merkel, now seen as a new Valkyrie in her hegemonic tendencies over modern Europe, without pausing to ask whether her citizens and voters also have the right to ask to what extent their own hard labours could legitimately be mobilized to keep saving the Greeks against their own unrestrained profligacy and incompetent tax-evading mechanisms. This indicative list – and examples could be multiplied - attempts to show how wildly the Greek pendulum swings. It also gives an indication of the Greek tendency to stretch an argument to its braking point, something which does no credit to the intelligence of its inhabitants who thus lose sight of all proportion. At moments like these, you can be amused, still love them – as I do – but also despair with the lack of political realism and calm assessment of the issue that lies in front of them awaiting resolution.

England has likewise been covered in abuse for traditionally having been pro-Turkish. Such feelings persist in Greece. Yet the way to moderate them is not through abuse or confrontation with my second country but through demonstrating that Greece could also be a worthwhile economic partner to Britain's ambitions and, more importantly, offer many economic possibilities for closer co-operation in the Mediterranean world. Armaments contracts are the bread and butter of contemporary diplomacy; but the Greeks should have learnt from their modern history, that they had to keep a constant balance between their suitors if only to avoid making them adversaries. And, in any event, could we not find ways to learn from the successes and the errors made by the British in making the City a world financial centre, especially since many Greeks have pursued successful careers there? The conservatively-inspired - a few years ago - tax system drove out of London many who were useful to the English economy. They, too, could also prove valuable allies in the effort to build new and more links between the two countries – a task incumbent upon small nations like my country of origin to undertake.

The ability of my country of origin to be insulting to neighbours such as Italy has also been an error in my eyes. Italians can be accused of faults that can also be found among the Greeks. But, it is of little use systematically describing the culture of ancient Rome is inferior to that of ancient Greece instead of complimentary, or playing on their supposed cowardice, incessantly mocking a former Prime Minister for his sexual peccadilloes when we know that we too have had our analogous shameful moments as, indeed, have the Americans.

My main point is simple and remains unchanged: why see and stress weaknesses instead of imitating the amazing economic wonder that has occurred in northern Italy; admire if not envy the Italian sense of good taste, which has allowed Milan to challenge Paris as the centre of modern fashion; or try to imitate the ability of countries such as Italy to punch above their weight in the international diplomatic arena? Add to the above, indicatively mentioned success stories, the indescribably beauty of the country as well as the warmth and *joie de vivre* of their "natives" and I feel there is plenty there to admire and even envy in Italy and I do both. Years of teaching In Genova, Sienna and Rome have also enabled me to see all of the above with my own eyes and I feel obliged to maintain a balanced presentation of my ideas even sometimes the annoy the citizens of one country and on others some other group.

To me the average Greek should thus feel not contempt for modern Italy but a fair degree of envy as, indeed, it should for another country which the Greeks have traditionally underestimated but which I have come to admire deeply for its consensual approach to politics, for its hard industry, its ability to continue a diplomatically successful past in times when modern conditions could have well led to decline. I am now talking of a very different country in the north yet one equally well-endowed with multiple talents (and a sense of humour): the Netherlands. Again I believe I know what I am talking about for I lived there for over fifteen years of my life (two nights and three days per week each week) teaching as *Ordinarius* Professor at the University of Leiden. Many, coming from all strata of society, became friends and have remained friends. Their knowledge, advice, common sense, and their constant pursuit of commonly agreed policies are a feature that struck me deeply during my Leiden years and I still value greatly. Indeed, I am honoured since so many of my former students there, some from the very highest echelons of Dutch society, have honoured me with their continuous friendship.

To sum up, this ambivalence towards the foreigner, seen as stupid, dull, slow in the uptake and even boring lies somewhere in the minds of most Greeks though modern travel has mitigated the strength with which these pejorative feelings were once held by the citizens of my country of origin. To the extent that I once shared such views but managed to shake them off as I enjoyed living and working in all the cities mentioned above, I regard myself as being lucky – extremely lucky. Lucky to have been given the chance to meet and work with fellow Europeans; lucky to recognise their many different strengths concealed by ignorance or prejudice. 'Understanding' is, again, the word that says it all; the lack of it, the reason for my once distorted optics.

The changing USA

America is in a category of its own and for that reason deserves perhaps, the longest account. For it is not a country but, essentially a continent and presents variations - in number and degree - that one finds in a continent but not the usual State.

The Greeks - at least all who were not inclined too much to the Left - not long ago liked them. Their simplicity of manners and lack of pretentions was attractive; so was their generosity, noticed by their larger than usual tips (which were designed in America to make up for the lack of a minimum wage and were not necessarily a sign of greater instinctive generosity). Wide spread among Americans is the virtue – or so I describe it – of always being willing ready to learn from others and they will rarely give the impressions which Mediterraneans often project of being "know all'". To be sure, their cloths might appear less attractive to the stuffier (or more chic, depending on one's own dress code) of my compatriots, their music is loud – though Jazz represents a significant contribution to the history of music, and their food fast and cheap in more ways than one. Over time, these perceived defects became advantages as the American way of life gained more and more adherents among the young those who for business or other reasons did not enjoy making a ceremonial of a meal (as the Belgians do who, in the view of *connaisseurs* of food are ahead of even the French). Why then do I single out the USA among all of the above countries in whose cities I felt at home and could still now happily work there as an example of a country which I could never make my home? To be frank, I think the answers fall under two broad and to an extent overlapping headings: their politics and their way of life. For in all honesty though I respect both, I like neither.

What dominated American thinking at the time I began my regular visits in 1980 was the spectacular appearance of Ronald Reagan on the American political scene. What better example to illustrate Carlyle's theory "On Heroes and Hero Worship" than to reflect on Reagan's impact on America of the early eighties. Reagan began as a myth and has ended up as hero.

Few that I know would regard the former President as either particularly intelligent or cultured – writes I, with an unacceptable degree of arrogance but loyal to my determination to speak my mind freely in this book. Yet, first and foremost his appearance on the political scene marked the return of self-confidence of a nation battered twice - by Watergate and Iran - or, three times if we include Vietnam, in the space of about twelve years. For though intelligent and with a social conscience which can only attract admiration, President Carter was buried by "Reaganism" which had used as its foundations all sorts of religious, extreme capitalistic, and militaristic ideas and slogans which, when examined in depth, may not strike everyone as being particularly profound. The recipe, however, was based on the ideas of decency and patriotism and worked well, not least because the rhetoric was clever and its lines delivered with perfection which the President's former profession – film acting – must have assisted. Moreover, it worked for quite a while before it was taken to its extremes in later years and then began to disturb the tastes of many. The declining health of the President might have played its part in the mishandling of the Iran Contra scandal which was managed by loyal- but dare one suggest – second rate associates.

Reaganism also provided us with an illustration of the admirable ability of the Americans to fall (as they did in the Nixon years despite the undoubted talents of the disgraced President) and then pick themselves up, dust themselves off, and rise to grandeur again. President Ford managed something roughly approximate during his decent but unspectacular interregnum. Overall the Reagan presidency, however, despite some fumbling and errors during the last years in office, proved a hard act to follow. In my view he clinched this legacy by writing – it is said personally and without the assistance of associates – his moving farewell letter to the Nation announcing that he was suffering from Alzheimer disease and would thus never again communicate with his "Fellow Americans". Sentimentalism in written texts does not work easily; in this letter it surfaced as so genuine that it was, as stated, truly moving.

President Reagan brought with him not only a new confidence for a humiliated America but also a renewed belief in the markets as supreme regulators of the economy. This was coupled with a heightened distrust towards the state as his aphorism "the state is never the solution; it is always the problem" well shows. His and the almost contemporaneous rule of Britain by Mrs. Thatcher represented the peak of the new capitalism of "rapid profit", facilitated by "decreased regulation" and the almost official espousal of the idea that financial greed was something to be welcomed. Many made much money out of this experiment, even more eventually lost as we know from the credit crisis which hit all countries from 2007 onwards and left intact only some of those who caused it. To the surprise of many and the delight of some, unrestrained and unregulated capitalism showed its first cracks and they may not be the last unless it finds a way to rejuvenate itself. Though much ground has been regained since 2007 modern capitalist societies are still striving to fine tune if not re-invent a model which combines leaving most economic decisions to the market but also acquiring a suitable social face; for neglecting the poor and weak is no longer possible in politics and only the 'unreconstructed' right-wingers still believe that it can be done in our times.

Highs are followed by lows; and it people who usually cause them both. Excessive lending in the mid 1990's onwards, encouraged by the legendry Alan Greenspan, Director of the FED, lay the foundations of the eventual collapse; decreased regulation facilitated its happening now being replaced – in England for instance, by something approaching the opposite. Yet the calls are growing for a re-invention – not abandonment – of capitalism, an "inclusive capitalism", a "capitalism with a human face", a "democratic capitalism" which would strip the existing Wall Street version "of its self-aggrandizing excesses and made to serve the interests of society rather than the other way round."[6] To me such terms have an element of self-contradiction; though the call for moderation to avoid social unrest seems to be common to all and this at least strikes me as deserving our attention.

Reagan's presence was also felt in the domain of law, not a topic suitable for discussion in a book such as this addressed to the general reader. Yet one must note the huge influx of conservative judges at all levels of the American (federal) court system with enduring consequences on American society. The transformation of American case law from its progressive status of the sixties – especially in matters concerning family relations and civil rights - to the highly conservative phase inaugurated by the Rehnquist Court and further advanced by the (current) Roberts Court – the American practice is to call the court after the name of its President - may be liked or just tolerated within the USA. But it has deprived it the products of the US Supreme Court of the iconic status they presented for other courts for many

---

6. Words and views expressed by successful Americans to "The Nation", http://www. thenation.com , Editors note 8 June 2011.

years before their switch back to the conservatism exemplified by the highly intelligent but blunt speaking Italian American Justice Antonio Scalia. The appearance of other constitutional courts, willing to adopt more modern and or liberal positions, e.g., in Strasbourg, South Africa, Canada, Germany etc., has thus meant that in the area of human rights and federalism in general America law no longer provides the *sole* model for other, especially new, jurisdictions to follow. Competition in the market is good – we are told; and in intellectual terms it provides for thinkers and writers of all kinds of new solutions for contemplation and even adoption.

In the domain of law the Reagan initiatives received new impetus during the years of the 43rd. President, Bush Jr.. In my view these innovations, in part because of the disastrous bombings of September 11th, were innovations associated with "decline" and crisis and lack of inspired leadership. For how else can an independent-minded lawyer describe rather extreme shifts towards conservative positions in matters such as abortion, electoral donations, telephone surveillance, and confidentiality of communications, prolonged periods of pre-trial human detentions, rendition, and torture and, of course, the handling of detainees for suspected terrorist acts in Guantanamo. There is little doubt that on September 11th 1971 a terrible act was perpetrated in New York by Muslim fundamentalists; but in the legal reactions mentioned above we find everything but inspired progress.

Thus, despite President Obama's electoral promise to close Guantanamo, the infamous concentration camp remains open and Executive pardon has absolved all government agents who were involved in proven acts of torture such as water-boarding. Since I admired and still do so this President, especially when I compare him with the range of possible political opponents on the Republican side, I would like to believe that he, too, must feel unhappy at having felt being obliged to adopt this stance.

I already stated that beyond recording such changes and, in specialized journals expressing – along with others including some of Britain's most senior judges – serious doubts about their reasoning, ultimately it is not for a non- American observer to tell Americans how to govern themselves or shape their law. He can advise or suggest but not pressurize, even assuming that the pressure could ever have any effect.

But the reverse is happening increasingly, with the USA trying to impose its values and interests on other nations, and nothing in my view justifies us non-American citizens to go down that same slippery path. But one is allowed to turn the tables and say "we do not like either being pressurized by you." Indeed, one is encouraged to note that much of the criticisms here voiced are shared by anything like fifty or more percent of American themselves. So wrong one may well be in noting the above shifts in American laws and, possibly, values; but "anti-American" one cannot be described by virtue only of objecting to their content and philosophy and thus describing them as retrograde steps.

These legal changes, however, also express a more dangerous development. Self-confidence lies at their root; and self-confidence becomes a sin when it turns into arrogance. That is what happened to America during the dark years of the Bush governance; and much of this smog has not been dispelled, at least in the way in which foreign policy is formulated and then *imposed* on friends.

In the America of the last decade of the 20th century and the first of the present one, profit mutated into greed both in the Wall Street neighbourhood but also in the shaping of the overseas military expeditions of the USA. All were facilitated by a remarkable electronic evolution in military technology which, however, proved unable – or so I believe - to defeat bare-footed and raggedly dressed yet determined freedom fighters. The grounding of an American spy drone over Iran December 2011narrowly missed becoming 21st century equivalent of the "Garry Powers" U-2, spying incident over Russia in 1960 and others have been brought down since. Next time events such as these occur – and there will be a next time and another after that since the perceived danger from Iran is too great and the modern technology too tempting not to have repeat incidents – the consequences could be much more severe. This danger is, indeed, arguably increasing as Russia and even more recently China have expressed an interest to become even more involves in the battle to defeat ISIS in Syria or, if the reader wishes to see it differently, in the struggle to keep the Assad regime afloat.

Contrary to assertions made, the final consequences of the 2003 Iraq War are thus not yet clear. An American President, standing on one of his "lethal toys" once rushed to proclaim that he had won it; let not a wiser President hasten to proclaim as his last troops leave Iraq that his country solved the long term problem posed by an ethnically divided country in the middle of a permanent danger zone! We must bare this warning in mind now we effectively hand over Afghanistan to its people with the Taliban likely to get their final reward on the ground. America, of course has had its own Nobel Peace prize award given to a President who though I believe would far rather remain focused on his Health Care reforms is daily dragged by his foreign policy advisors to increased provocations of the Russians from the Baltics to the Caucuses.

I stress all of the above for I note that Afghanistan and Pakistan are not described by the emerging organized propaganda of the modern state as defeats though Generals of many nationalities who have fought there and come from different countries would see them in such terms. If I may be permitted a brief but unpleasant moment to gloat, I predicted the unfortunate ending of the Afghanistan War in an article in a major Greek newspaper as far back as 2010 referring to it as the USA's second Viet Nam.

Of course, modern political systems feed off media communications so they can brush aside a series of set-backs and present the growing belligerency as a healthy reaction against Mr Putin's aggressiveness. Who can win this sui generis war of attrition fought on a growing number of fronts remains unclear to all but those who pay the propagandists to do their job. Some facts however, cannot pass unnoticed. Among them I include: (a) American worsening standing in the entire North Africa; (b) the increased presence there of various militant fundamentalist groups operating against their interests; (c) Syria now hosting an ever growing Russian presence; (d) ISIS arguably in retreat but not because of American or English bombing; (e) Iran still on its feet with the nuclear issue not resolved; (f) relations between the USA and Israel tense to say the least; (g) President Sissi's Egypt working closer with Russia than ever; (g) Turkey, as ambivalent as ever, must be daily proving a totally unpredictable if not unreliable ally to Washington; (h) and Greece hovering over no man's land with a leadership inexperienced in handling foreign affairs unable or unwilling or both to take any bold steps, explore its sea-bed gas reserves and break away from the impasse its financial crisis has created for its foreign relations as well.

In my view, a major institutional reason for American proving so ineffectual in its foreign policy is its polyphone. For many in the Middle East and, dare I say elsewhere, are wondering who decides foreign policy in that great country? The President? The Secretary of State? The Security Council? The CIA? The military industry? All of them? Or different entities at different times? All this must be read against the background that the USA nowadays has Europe as its main if lukewarm supporter; has fractured relations with Germany while on the other side Russia and China are increasingly singing from the same hymn sheet. If that assessment is even remotely accurate, in which direction would a leader of a smaller country look at? To the many reasons I gave which make it risky to think of the USA I would add the ease with which it jettisoned Egypt during its internal troubles and the way this behaviour riled the Saudi Arabians and other nations in the region.

Brave is thus the analyst who will brush away my concerns without revealing much more evidence than that which we already have to persuade me and others of the future stability in the Arabian Peninsula. Only "paid agents" – and one cannot get lower than that on the spectrum of "friends and supporters of a particular country" – can advance theories without a minimum of circumspection and deeper thought. And yet we know from the Iraqui war, if nothing else, how America has relied on the advice of such people and fared badly. I seriously wonder if its list of individual supporters, informers and advisors in other countries is really of a significantly higher quality.

The unrest in the better part of the Middle East is thus more unsettling and NOT getting better as we are being told. To these "triumphs or disasters" – the right terms depends upon the knowledge and objectivity of the assessor - one must add the unresolved crises over Korea and the simmering difficulties in Mexico which are not only causing growing immigration concerns but also serious worries about the smuggling of arms and drugs into the USA as well as the worsening economic situation within Mexico itself following a rather unfortunate management of the country's oil wealth. The conclusion must be that the USA has "slipped" on almost all fronts of international endeavour during the last ten years though by how much observers may differ.

Despite some eloquent speeches from President Obama, the bulk of America also remains deeply sceptical of other cultures and religions. However expertly these are handled or approached, in American eyes the "Orient" - as a generic term - remains an area to be flattered and administered by "friendly regimes" with the ultimate aim of a modern form of economic colonization but not to be trusted.

What Americans seem to be constantly looking for is subservient or suspect friends not politicians whose friendship is based on conviction or personal interest. If they seek and get the former, the service they will receive is unlikely to be good. Excessive reliance on unreliable politicians has always produced undesirable information and unwanted consequences. The service of what one might call lackeys is also likely to lead eventually to the spreading political instability. For instability on the streets is one of the facts of our times. Modern technology, which makes effective easy communication and mobilization of crowds, will see to this.

Contrast the American way of colonizing foreign lands which are of use to it contrast with the Chinese, and to a lesser extent Russian, ways of achieving the same aims through careful use of investments policies. The transformation of the scene in Africa offers a good illustration of economic neo colonialism, though this time not by the West which, instead, is straining its finances by bombing the Libyan Desert in one of its self-flagellating moods of humanitarianism.

America's growing isolation from the rest of the world is enhanced by its doctrine of exceptionalism which prevents it from joining in internationally negotiated treaties even on issues which do not have a direct political or defensive meaning. This approach towards international and foreign law, which at times has been expressed in intemperate language both by high-ranking officials (Ambassador John Bolton for instance) or Justices (Antonin Scalia or Robert Borke), represents current neoconservative thinking. To most outsiders this language is offensive and to that extent at the very least intellectually and politically unwise. Moreover, it becomes distinctly more unattractive whenever it is accompanied by the evangelical undertones of religion which is furthered so aggressively by the same group of people. These, again, touch upon a wide variety of issues such as education (and the teaching of creationism), sexual identification (attitudes towards homosexuality), abortion, the death sentence and others.

My personal political concerns for such developments have been voiced in many of my recent books, legal as well as political. Though they have annoyed some, usually those non Americans who make a "living *off* America" – and I have deliberately used this lax expression so as to allow me readers to complete it at will – they are, I repeat, shared most strongly by a substantial percentage, perhaps, even more than half, of the American population. So, though my readers can reject them or accept them, in part or entirely, they should use them to reflect upon the changes which I and they have lived through during my thirty four years of working in the USA and described at the beginning of this subsection.

Continuing on the complexity of the American scene let us now switch focus to other societal developments in the USA which I find disturbing. The purpose here is a double one.

First to correct the image of America which most foreigners have based on such classic fifties or sixties films or TV series like "Happy

Days", "The Waltons", "Hallo Lucy" or the Doris Day/ Rock Hudson sagas, depicting a law abiding, family oriented, moral to the point of being prudish, America.

Second, I wish to challenge the resulting conclusion that the American way of life remains an icon which is both worth adopting by and suitable to other countries and cultures.

I have attempted this difficult task only because I believe that my prolonged experience in that country may have given me some good insights of its *present* state even though I admit that these personal impressions must be supplemented by the more complex (*and contradictory*) analyses which sociologists and political theorists have done on the large number of topics which I merely touch upon in the paragraphs that follow.

Yet, true to my wish to make people think, I offer these thoughts for further reflection and then urge those who find something interesting in them to investigate them more deeply and see for themselves how impossible it is to reach unanimity in these areas of daily life. Yet the American Right and Left have, more or less, reached unanimity on one fact. That is that American society is currently going through a crisis.

Thus, on the one hand America is a country enviably rich even though its wealth is distributed in a shockingly unfair manner. We thus see on one end of the spectrum a stunning degree of wealth whereas, at its other end, we encounter something in the region of 12.5% of the population living below the so-called level of poverty.[7] We can appreciate this problem better by using some figures and looking at them from different angles. All approaches however lead to an inescapable conclusion: the difference between rich and poor is literally indescribable. I would add also socially dangerous, at least for all those who believe, as I do, that great and provocative differences of wealth can lead to social unrest.

So, in 2007 the top 1% of the American population took in 23,5% of all of the country's income (whereas in 1979 they had taken 8.9%.) "In 2007, the latest year for which figures are available from the Federal Reserve Board, the richest 1% of U.S. households owned 33.8% of the

---

7. Source: Statistical Information of the USA, 2006, p. 472. The poverty level for four persons living in the same household is fixed at $18.810 (*ibid., at* 473), this in a country of an annual per capita income of $32.907 δολ. (*ibid, at p.* 448). Worse still, the number of person with no medical insurance (before the Obama reforms) was estimated as being 44.961.000 million or15,6% of the total American population. (*Ibid, at p.* 109).

nation's private wealth. That's more than the *combined* wealth of the bottom 90%." [8]

During that same year the capital (and not just the income) of this very same 1% of the population equalled that of the remaining 99% of Americans. According to *Forbes* magazine, the top 400 richest Americans had assets totalling $1,5 trillion! The total assets of the bottom 50% of the population – that is about 160 million Americans – amounted to just slightly more namely, $1,6 trillion.

These are not just interesting but, in my view, profoundly shocking figures. But they still do not reveal how the richer Americans are annually getting richer whereas the poor are getting poorer. To put it differently, the progression of inequality is continuing apace. Thus, between 1979 and 2008, 5% of the richest Americans saw their income rise (in real terms) by 73% whereas the bottom 20% of the population experienced a decrease in income of the order of 4%. The remainder of the population remained at the levels they were some thirty years ago! [9]

These economic differences can be reconciled with great difficulty with any notion of justice *even if we assume* – a dubious assumption to make and prove – that these fortunes were all earned legally. For legal tax avoidance schemes, enacted with the help of interested pressure groups, contribute greatly in the USA to rich people not paying their due to society. For the intricate fiscal legislation does nothing to ensure a fairer distribution of wealth. It is possibly safe to assume that this is only the tip of fiscal illegality.

The list of immensely wealth corporations that do not pay tax and even have tax money returned to them is also growing. In 2008 and 2009 we thus found among them the Bank of America, Boeing Corp., the Citigroup, Exxon-Mobil and General Electric. *None of these paid a penny in federal taxes.*[10]

---

8. Taken from the "Working Group on Extreme Inequality."
9. Many studies and reports offer figures. See, inter alia, «This is what Class War Looks Like: A National Campaign, State by State", http://www.dailykos.com/story/2011/03/17/957589/-This-Is-What-Class-War-Looks-Like:-A-National-Campaign,-State-by-State?Source=patrick.net#masthead-user-text.
10. See: http://www.youtube.com/watch?v=Sknt-UBRhxo. As well as *The International Herald Tribune* of 6th April 2011, page 8: "Who could blame G.E. for paying zero U.S. taxes". The author there supports the highly complex legislation which justifies the tax exemptions which lead to the results mentioned in the text above. A look at Greece's de facto inability to collect taxes must this be compared with the controversial American practice that offers multinational companies numerous opportunities not to pay taxes, all at a time of great economic stringency and growing public debt.

Notwithstanding the above, the said corporations distributed to the top executive bonuses which varied between 6 and 29 million dollars per person. The legislation which allows this to happen and counterbalance, for instance, losses made abroad with gains made within the USA, is so technical that it would take hours to begin to explain to all non-experts (among which I include myself even though I have advised on (different) legal matters and appeared before courts in the USA).

The eccentricities of this country exist in all walks of life and could justify a book on their own. America, for instance, is a country whose constitution contains a clause – the First Amendment – which prohibits Congress to pass any law that would recognize an official religion. The ambiguity of the phrase, combined with legal ingenuity and the country's litigation mania, gave rise to an immense jurisprudence which considers the breadth of the division between state and religion.

America is also a country of philanthropy and philanthropists. Very often, these phenomena are the result of a genuine feelings of concern for the poor and the needy, especially since the state does very little to mitigate the inequalities between them. But philanthropy and charitable giving has also been institutionalized and commercialized in the USA by its tax regime. In a country which, basically, does not recognize as England does an extended system of state honours, the tax benefits given to important donors are thus accompanied by anything from class rooms, atriums, amphitheatres, swimming pools, foot-ball stadia, and museum buildings being named after the donors and often, in the interests of sex (gender as they wrongly prefer to call it) equality, their wives as well.

But by far the most shocking and also impregnable of American vices is the transformation of the legitimate and praise-worthy notion of profit into contemporary corporate greed. American financial institutions will risk – fairly regularly one is tempted to suggest - anything to make huge profits, even criminal behaviour for which they are often caught and end up paying huge fines. But however colossal the fines may appear to ordinary mortals, they are peanuts compared to the profits made by these banks acting in an overtly illegal manner so the vicious circle continues. This greed and its results thus become the yardstick of success; and the lack of any moral stigma being attached to anyone who is caught and punished means that the temptation to go on dong the same remains very much alive.

Even when fraudulent or grossly reckless behaviour contribute to the kind of mega-crisis which the American and world system experienced after Lehman Bros collapse little is said about those who conduct the so-called bank stress tests. In the case of Lehman, the bank was given a triple A rating a few months before its collapse while their CEO was allowed to retain the excessive bonus which he had awarded himself just before the "unforeseeable" collapse! This must surely tell much not only for those who are vetted but also for those who do the vetting!

The world system is still in turmoil because of these events; millions of people were dispossessed of their homes; many others have been out of work; the country had to resort to a bail-out system which has landed it with a $15 trillion public debt which its legislators cannot agree how to trim. Yet these culprit financial institutions are now back to where they were before the 2007 crises; only a fraction of the aid received from the tax payer has been used reviving the economy through lending; and the bulk of Americans who suffered from these fraudulent or, at least, reckless lending practices are still living in misery. Quantative easing, as printing money is nowadays euphemistically referred to, also continues to feed money into the banks not so that they can stimulate the markets and assist commercial borrowing but to shield them from future losses which they are expected to incur from the international bond market. International bankers have thus become a highly privileged class and no wonder many assure me that after Lehman they now know that the state will *always* bail them out. This can only mean that another credit crunch crisis of the 2007 is more than possible; some would say probable though the ways this could be provoked are not necessarily to be sought and found within the USA.

Wonderous Bavaria

The way I feel when in Germany is the exact opposite of how cut off I feel from my home turf when in the USA. Having enjoyed prolonged stays in Cologne and Munich, as a student of their language and their law, I can only state simply and unreservedly that had my family shown the slightest interest - which they did not even though my wife's paternal ancestors were Bavarian - I would have settled in Munich a long time ago! Whether this is due to an atavistic pull back to the Bavarian days of early Greece or the physical attraction of the city and its culture I cannot say for sure. I suspect this partiality is the result of both, for one tends to love a city not only because of its natural beauty but also because of the associations it generates in one's mind. Since space is at a premium, I thus intend to concentrate on Munich because I spent three whole summers there teaching at the Law Faculty as a Humboldt Senior Scholar, writing the second edition of my two-volume book on German, English and American Law of Obligations, and also happily getting lost in the town's numerous antiquarian bookshops.

Munich, proper, is a medium to large sized city (but with its suburbs it exceeds 5.5 million inhabitants) that has many ways to stimulate memories, all of a pleasant kind; that, at any rate is how it is with me. When one sits for a coffee *al fresco* a few yards south of the *Theatinerkirche* and looks north one sees what led General de Gaulle to exclaim when once driven down the grand avenue of Ludwigstrasse that "ceci est une vraie capitale!" (This is a true Capital City). For one sees, at least I saw, grandeur, architectural beauty and colour all blending into one unforgettable picture.

Munich not only exudes the air of an important city; it is also cosmopolitan in the truest sense of the word. For in addition to an abundance of Germanic and Germanic-speaking central Europeans the city has large numbers of Greeks and Italians – one gets the impression controlling a sizeable portion of the restaurant sector – but also Turkish and central Asian refugees – not as numerous as they are in cities such as Cologne, Stuttgart or Berlin - but all peacefully going about their ways under the conservative and watchful eye of one of Germany's most conservative regions. Whether this equilibrium might be disturbed is too early to assert. The fear, however, that what has been achieved peaceably, slowly over time, and methodically been built is a real one if one is to judge by what some of my local friends tactfully externalise.

Returning to the Urban beauty if the centre - Ludwigstrasse - the avenue which runs from the *Theatinerkirche* north to the University and slightly beyond, is wide and straight and impressive, surrounded here and there by the heavy version (but still imposing) Florentine-style architectural buildings, including the central city library. The University Church stands at least three quarters up the avenue on its right hand side with its pointed white belfry piercing that very 'Bavarian' light blue sky which so resembles the blue one finds in Greece but is absent from northern European cities. Barely in sight, at the southern-most part of this avenue, lies the *Residenz* – the town Palace of the former Princely and later Royal family of the *Wittelsbachs* - which ends in a beautiful little square that branches off to the left into the luxurious *Maximilianstrasse* with its expensive shops and its superb *Vierjhareszeitung* hotel which must be, if not the best certainly the most *chic*, of Munich's many *Grands Hotels*.

At the east side of the square one also stands the Cuvilliés theatre - the work of the very same architect who gave the final Rococo facade and its yellow Mediterranean colour to the *Theatinerkirche*, modelled on Sant' Andrea della Valle in Rome by Agostino Barelli and enriched by its two towers during the second half of the 17th century (It was completed in 1690 AD). François de Cuvilliés was the man who also designed the City's opera house, notable for among other things its unique carved wood work and home of the most wonderful musical and operatic performances I have experienced in all my life.

Here, again, I have always felt the overlapping of pleasurable stimuli, the architectural beauty, the divine musical memories, that unique privilege of enjoying in the company of a few eminent Bavarian colleagues a magical performance of the *Marriage of Figaro* after having received from the City's famous University an honorary doctorate. And all this sitting next to my wife and touching her hand during than most moving of aria's – the *Perdono* (forgivenss) aria - which is sung by the Contessa who, up to this point of the opera is a decent but neglected (middle class not aristocratic) wife of the local *Seigneur* who is a 'cad'. The song shames him for his arrogant and unforgiving character even though he is the moral culprit having spent the entire opera trying to exercise the defunct *ius prima noctis* and be the first to sleep with Suzanna on the night of her marriage to Figaro. Mozart is unique in overpowering us by his truly sublime music in a way which can make us forget the significance of the all the other messages – often political and eternal - which he and the much maligned Lorenzo Daponte (his larger than life librettist) squeezed into the texts of all the operas they collaborated to produce.

Munich's architectural gems extend to its churches. The Metropolis, dedicated to the Virgin and called *Frau Munster*, is the tallest building in town and can be seen miles before the visitors have actually entered the city. Not far is a smaller church – the *Salvator Kirche* – which King Ludwig the First, the father of Greece's first king offered it to the Greeks in Munich and during my days there it was pleasant to see how many of them attended Sunday mass. My favourite church, however, is the *Theatinerkirche*. I refer to it as *my* church because I really feel that part of *me lies* in it. And that part is to be found in the small underground chapel where fate decreed that the first Greek King – Otto of Bavaria – would lie to rest his mortal remains since those whom he had ruled and dearly loved had banished him from Greece. Next to him lies his wife, Princess Amalia of Oldenburg (later Amalia, Queen of Greece).

Though I have always had the deepest respect and admiration for my Queen - Elizabeth II - I have never had monarchical inclinations by conviction, probably because I believed that the institution never suited the Greek temperament. Yet my feelings run deep as I stand before the catafalques of the first but unfortunate Greek King and Queen. For though Otto and Amalia were never considered as 'successful' Monarchs – and who could have done a good job of what they were entrusted to do with all the big powers (Russia, England, Austria, France) vying to undermine each other and in the process destroying Greece in its infancy - by common consent they loved Greece. Indeed, I would venture the thought that the country never had truer Philhellenes on its throne; and Otto's last wish even to be buried wearing the Greek national costume of the Evzon, is typical of the depths of his romantic devotion to the country over which he reigned for nearly thirty years.

Both he and his Queen, as stated, now lie almost entirely forgotten in the Chapel crypt which to me at least, in its utter desolation, oozes sadness and only provokes to the romantically inclined a few memories of a promising start which was never fulfilled. How can one return in a fitting way such romantic evocations but to dream that one day the Greeks might make a superb gesture of posthumous reconciliation and homage to a man by allowing his remains and those of his wife, to be buried in the soil they so loved. Indeed, where better place than in the central park of Athens – the National Garden - the only green expanse in the centre of the modern, progressively spoilt and highly polluted city – which the first Queen helped create. I mention this because my late father, who was a friend of Josef Strauss, for decades Prime Minister of Bavaria, had asked him during an official visit to Munich in 1953 whether he would object to an official request for the returns of the royal remains to Greece only to receive an enthusiastic affirmation. But higher standing authorities in Greece refused even this purely romantic homage and the move never took place. Such pettiness on the art of some Greeks sits uncomfortably with the well-known Greek generosity of spirit.

Munich's temptations extend beyond the mind and eye of the beholder for Munich is also a town that goes for exquisite coffee. So, *Café Hag*, situated just opposite the famous Cuviliés theatre I mentioned earlier on, sells the most amazing variety of coffee beans I have ever found in any coffee shop in the world I have visited while *Dallmayer*, a couple of hundred yards further south near *Marienplatz,* is Munich's Fortnums and Mason, smaller perhaps in size but if anything even more exquisite and proclaiming loudly that Bavarians are not only beer drinkers but expert coffee drinkers as well.

In short, this city produces a profusion of memories associated with sight and smell and taste as well as some brain activity of a professional kind! Where was my mother's 'friend' Marcel Proust to stand near me and tell me "now you know why I wrote a series of books which were inspired by the memory of the taste of a humble *Madeleine*". When there, naturally, I heard the voice though it was the mother citing something of Proust's she truly liked though I hate to admit I do not recall details.

My stays in Munich were made that much more pleasurable for being housed by the University in a block of flats reserved for their senior guests. Well placed in street - guess what? – called *Amalien-strasse,* a stone throws away from the University, surrounded by my antiquarian bookshops, an endless list of beer gardens and snack bars, and wonderful bake-houses since German cities go for neighbour-hood bakeries.

Naturally I entered but I must have stood there staring for far too long at the variety of bred rolls they baked so I was suddenly stirred out of my slumber by a kindly woman possessed of the largest (but not attractive) bosoms I have ever seen barely restrained in place by her folklore dress. "Do decide she snapped" – and in what I thought was my best German I asked for two *Brotchen* (tiny loaves) only to hear her snap back: "we are not Prussians here you now and neither are you. If you want rolls call them Semmeln for you are now in Bavaria". So much for German re-unification – that otherwise amazing wonder of 1991 which owed so much to American and Russian leaders smoothly working with their German counterparts.

Not far from my flat, on *Shellingstrasse,* was the famous (or infamous) *Osteria* which served wonderful Italian dishes. Its dark past acted as a magnet for many though I found it deeply disturbing and tried, instead, to focus on its very good Italian cuisine. For the *Osteria* was one of Hitler's favourite haunts; and to this day, unbelievable though it may appear to be, people who visit it can (and do) ask to sit on his own favourite chair which is then duly brought out to give illusions of grandeur to whoever is crazy enough to seek this "privilege". "Live and let live" says I; and I try not to think of this dark past. But this, most certainly, was not the favourite motto of the former Führer!

The Institute of Foreign and Comparative law, where I was given an office to work and access to its good library, was placed almost on top of the restaurant University Professors attended for coffee, lunch, and tea. This too was Italian but also did some Bavarian dishes and rejoiced in the name of Monopteros because it stand near the entrance of that beautiful, large adjoining garden which adorns the centre of Munich and is known as the English Garden.

Like all open expanses in Germany, this garden as well offers its own collection of beer places when the Bavarians assemble as the sun sets to consume the beer in decanters which are so large and heavy that you can only lift them by sliding all four fingers through the handle and embracing the other side of the heavy crystal with your thumb. It's a matter of luck as much as training if you still manage to lift this giant to your lips, even rarer not to spill its contents on your garments when touching your neighbours glass decanter and repeatedly wishing him or her – for Munich ladies are just as good at heavy drinking as their physical builds often attest - *prosit*!

But the English Garden holds one more surprise – delight some might even call it – and few foreigners are prepared for it if not suitably warned.

For when the weather is reasonably good and the sun is shining, half of the true natives – the most liberally minded of the citizenry – sunbathe in the nude and when I say nude I mean nude! While these free souls are in communion with nature – the remaining half of the city – the most conservative who usually inhabit the suburbs, stroll by shaking the heads with disapproval while the odd brave male, who can escape the watchful eye of his accompanying spouse, will also stoop over to take a closer link of what is on display thus deriving a fleeting moment of distanced pleasure? Proust again and *a la recherché du temps perdu*! I did the same and felt the same; and if Rousseau is right in his *Confessions* I, too, can say, that "I know other people by knowing my own feelings"!

It was the rigour of the intellectual life, however, which most gripped me when working in Germany, Munich in particular. For the University has always attracted some of the best minds in the land across the entire field of human knowledge – the truly important one's are given the name *Platzhirsch a slang word* which is given to the head stag who guards his territory and females with his life and stands above all others – as well as legions of aspiring heirs, all hard working, all collaborating with one another.

I envied and still do this collaborative spirit for it makes these institutes a hub of learning, something which I must stress as the person who created two such institutes –one in Oxford and one in Texas - failed to achieve given the inability and or unwillingness of the Oxbridge and American dons to work together with others in an effort to make their institute – and not just themselves – the centre of attraction of talent and learning.

Thus, though the Germanic institution of a *Festschrift*, a collection of papers in honour of a retiring senior colleague, has taken root in England, the equally Germanic idea of an Institute or Centre has failed to follow suit with Anglo-American academics accustomed to working as loners. As a lawyer interested in the movement and transferability of ideas I find this conclusion interesting though its full consequences can be explored further in another paper. Here I thus limit myself to the observation of how exciting collegiate life was within the framework of a well-run German institute. Exciting but also productive for the discipline for which the institute caters, since the collective work ensures continuity and renewal as new recruits gradually replace those who age or leave to take up chairs of their own.

Munich by no means exhausts the attractions of Bavaria. Exploring the surrounding of the city inevitably takes one to its beautiful lakes and mad King Ludwig II's Cinderella castles.

Neuschwanstein is the most extravagant of the lot though I find it too *kitsch* for my liking. But at *Herrenchiemsee* – a truly idyllic lake which at the turn of the last century became, because of its beauty, a retreat for artists of all kinds - one finds Ludwig's "miniature" copy of Versailles – habitable of course and not a toy, but still fairly large to all who have not seen the "original".

Not far, but on the same island, a smaller and less distinguished building, can claim its own history, again important to me as a lawyer; for here, in the mid to late forties, the German political world – under strict American surveillance (and occasional bullying) – eminent German politicians and lawyers drafted the Constitution of Bonn of 1949 which came into force in 1950. With characteristic terminological accuracy, my German colleagues did not call it a Constitution (*Verfassung*) but a *Grundnorm* – the Basic Law – reserving the accepted term - Constitution – for the day the final document, applying to the re -unified Germany, would come into force. For this they had to wait forty one years and even this would not have happened but for the courtesy and boldness of Mr. Gorbachev, the American Secretary of State Jim Baker, the German Chancellor Helmut Kohl and his Foreign Minister Dietrich Genscher. Neither Mrs.

Thatcher nor President Mitterrand were particularly pleased with the creation of this new economic super- power house, though the latter, widely known in France for his cunning as "le florentin" – the Florentine –did not make his displeasure too overt! The "Lady" on the other hand did not believe in half measures and protested to the end.

This is the right moment to leave Germany, on the eve of its post-War recovery and move to its old rival, a rivalry which thanks to the genius of De Gaulle and Adenauer, Kohl and Mitterrand was turned into long-standing and close partnership which lay the foundations of the currently tottering Europe.

I love Paris

As stated at the beginning of this chapter in urban and aesthetic terms Paris for me is the most beautiful city I have ever visited. My late mother and my wife, each for their own reasons, always struggled to find reasons to place London first. "Paris, for instance" does not have the wonderful London Parks" has been one of their arguments. Its museums may have worthy rivals, - the Uffizi, the Prado, the Hermitage – but it is still not ahead of any of the above. Another argument plausible but valid if you make clear what exactly one is comparing, e.g. size, variety of exhibits, manner of display, etc. etc.

Paris, however, has the most beautiful avenues in the world with the Champs Elysées coming top since it truly is the avenue that leads to the Elysean fields. Though London comes first as a commercial centre, and always had the atmosphere that it was (and remains) the place were trading takes place. For the wealth and older families it was never the town where one had one's main residence since had to be in the country side.

By contrast Paris was always the final destination of any ambitious French man or woman, be he (or she) a politician, an academic, a medical specialist or an artist. This adds to the aura of the place and I, for one, never ceased being impressed by its gravitational pull despite the cost of living there and the reputed (and often real!) arrogance of the Parisians. So, along with Munich this would also be a city which I would gladly make my own. For its urban lay out is unique and its streets, embraced by mature horse-chestnut and plain trees, are most attractive especially in the spring. Its *grand boulevards* also made for window shopping, and the quality of life one of the highest I have experienced not only in sybaritic terms but also in terms of artistic, theatrical, culinary events as well as exposure to a constantly renewable population of dignitaries of all kinds. All of the above appeal to my eyes, my sense of smell, my taste, the totality of my aesthetic preferences; and all are further enriched by the culture – not just the education – most obvious in its higher centres of learning such as the French Academies – and there are five bracketed by Napoleon under the term of *Institut de France* – and the *Collège de France*.

This culture is not just obvious but manifested or externalized via a language which is magnificently elegant when properly spoken. To be sure, as a language it is more flowery and convoluted than the English, often declaimed rather than spoken in an under-stated way, and in the delivery of learned papers at public events – and this is not to my liking – the text in question is too often read out from a manuscript rather than effortlessly spoken. The only place I know of where notes or written texts are strictly forbidden is *l' Academie française* where all communications must be made orally and never read!

The French are also prone to longish speeches, often (as already stated) read or even declaimed, not infrequently with a touch of exaggeration. Listen to the songs of Yves Montant or Gilbert Becaut and note how the ending "e's" are firmly pronounced rounding of the sentence beautifully! The way texts are delivered, whether in a political or university setting, has often made me feel that they miss the cut and thrust one finds in English parliamentary or university debates. Also rarely to be found are signs of humour and wit which figure so prominently in all kinds of oral communication in England, including memorial services, an English feature which tends to surprise most Continentals. Again, however, one must tread gently with generalizations for in France as well we find authors who have openly advocated characteristics which the best English speaker would also wish to display in his speeches and texts. Michel de Montainge, for instance, has asserted[11]

"that it is... for words to serve and to follow. If French cannot get there, let Gascon do so. I want *things* to dominate, so filling the thoughts of the hearer that he does not even remember the words. I like the kind of speech which is simple, sinewy, brief and short; not so much titivated and refined as forceful and brusque.

---

11. In his essay "On Educating Children" in *The Complete Essays*, I, 26, translated by M. A Screech, Penguin 1997, at p.193. The original, as always, sounds melodious but also firm.

A weakness of a different kind found in many countries but I feel excessively so in the French setting is nationalism. I understood its existence which must be partly the result of an obvious (and admirable) sense of national pride; but it is also I am sure a relic of times when France was not just an important country but *the* most important country in Europe. (At the time of the French Revolution it dwarfed the populations of all other major European states.) This is an attitude one cannot help but admire though, when it surfaces in shrill tones, one also sees how it leads to unrealistic assessments as to what contemporary France can and cannot do. Thus, this attitude, combined with a poor record in modern languages even among intellectual circles, a slipping position in the financial and banking sector, and the predominance – even in France - of the Anglo Saxon world in the area of transactional commercial law raises an interesting and probably unanswerable question: what political role does the future hold for France?

The above discussion inevitably leads us to the question how does French nationalism coexist with the increased presence in France of human being coming from different ethnic and religious backgrounds. It is too easy, I believe, to invoke laws and international treaties to which France is a signatory proclaiming tolerance and condemning all forms of racism. The recent reaction in this direction by a million or more Frenchmen who protested against racism of all kind following a racist attack by militant Muslims against a French satirical magazine would support this wide wish for a tolerant society at peace with itself. The reality, however, is much more nuanced and the existing balance between different races and religions remains precarious.

We find evidence of this not only in the presence of a large right wing party – the *Front Nationale* - which has, in recent years, been shrewdly re-positioned closer to the traditional Right than the extreme or Fascist Right from where it had begun. We also find this extreme Right wing rhetoric lurking in the traditional conservative party which, until recently, was run by former President Sarkozi who, during elections periods, would swing his rhetoric to the extreme Right to take voters away from the *Front Nationale*. Now no politician would do this unless he thought it was a vote winner! There is a third reason why, when talking of nationalism and suspicion towards foreigners, one must try hard to describe the French scene in a nuanced way. For France was, and still retains a strong minority of anti-Jewish voters and even larger one who are anti-Muslim and anti-gypsie.

Will this French 'exceptionalism' – compared to real or publicly declared racial tolerance in countries such as Germany and England – one must ask oneself how can?/ will? The current mass immigration movement affect the overall picture? I find it unwise to predict national reactions towards issues which have bother or, at the very least, concerned deeply foreign countries. My own fear is that the real or pretended spirit of liberalism adopted by many contemporary citizens may in the end play into the hands of extremists.

My own view, expressed in generalities and thus good only as a possible starting point for further discussion, is that in a world of emerging giants such as India, and China, France can only aspire to being an important part of a wider entity. The question, which entity, however, is not easy to answer. One possibility could, of course, be a return to the old Franco-German diarchy which would, essentially, control the future of Europe. Though this may be appealing to some it does not look likely that the past could be recreated not least because (a) England would never favour such a reassertion of power and (b) there now exists a new power structure in Europe which could, one day, enable Poland to claim a bigger role than is currently given to her. Most importantly, however, one must not forget the fact that nowadays the old Franco-German balance has been destroyed to the advantage of the second country.

One more question has yet to receive its final answer: where does (European) Russia fit in all this? My own iconoclastic view is that culturally and economically it belongs to Europe; and if decades of prejudice could ever be overcome and a mutually beneficial arrangement worked out, then the whole of Europe would be able to hold its own in the emerging multi-polar world of giant states (such as China, India and most likely the USA.)

The second alternative could be a northern, more cohesive, inflation proof and economically disciplined Europe built round Germany, Holland, Austria, Finland, and maybe one or two central European states, once more closely aligned with the Russian Federation. France could then assume a more leading role in a conglomeration of southern European states which would operate on looser fiscal rules allowing devaluation but also running the risk of operating in a more inflationary environment than that ever likely to be accepted by the North.[12]

---

12. In journalistic writing of a quality kind only Anatole Kaletsky has dared to voice such heretical at present but highly intriguing views. See, for instance, his most recent (at the time of writing) article "Expel Germany, not Greece, to save the Euro" in *The Times* 18 January 21012.

Both these ideas may contain elements of plausibility; but they represent only a slight improvement on the current dysfunctional state of gradual but apparently inevitable economic decline of Europe. For Europe, even if divided in two as suggested above *for an intermediary period to give it time be become more synchronized* internally than the current "whole" now is, would still be too small in terms of mineral resources,[13] markets, and finances to be a real competitor to the emerging powers in the East and, eventually, in South America.

Personally, I have a further difficulty with the above issues and it flows from the aforementioned understanding of the French sense of pride and historical importance. Unless and until the current economic crisis affecting Italy and Spain reach the French heartland, would/could the French ever settle for anything less than a truly dominant position even in this restrained Europe? Would they then not be tempted to resurrect their old idea of a Mediterranean Union as a way of incorporating former colonies and hoping that in this way their power within this group of countries would be further enhanced? Again, I have my doubts whether such ideas can be resurrected given the wider crises in the Mediterranean, Middle East and especially the unpredictability of nascent fundamentalism in the northern African former French colonies. What matters, however, is not what I think but what the French believe they can achieve.

Clearly, these are not the kind of problems I cannot answer and certainly not in a sub-section of one chapter. I raise them however as examples of the difficulties which French nationalism raises for the modern French. And this is no small danger for we have seen how on the much smaller scale of law reform France has acted defensively if not negatively towards the growing influence of the Anglo-Saxon mega law firms or the German attempts to control the legal unification of Europe. To put it even more provocatively, what once made France great may now, in the absence of a charismatic leader, contribute to making it even smaller. The "leading" role she tried to play in the destruction of the Khadafy regime could suggest a desire to appear to be able to punch above its weight but that would only satisfy appearances and not represent realities. For that attack cost much money and

---

13. In this context only the mineral resources in the eastern Mediterranean shared by Egypt, Greece, Cyprus and maybe Israel could redress the gap of a Southern EU and, indeed, make it extremely wealthy. But how would England, Germany and the USA react to such ideas? The answer is that they could only go ahead of the above four countries worked closely together and enjoyed the backing of Russia, a country which has historically sought access to warm waters.

produced no positive results either for France nor its allies,

To me all of the above thus suggests that if Europe wishes to be a player, a second rate player but still a player, in the emerging world of mega players it can only aspire to do this if it (a) strengthens its depth and (b) works out a *do ut des* accommodation with the Russian Federation involving energy for technology and perhaps, assistance to access to new funding. Without such bold thinking I fear the decline will continue even though the country has, surely, many years of civilized living to offer to those who settle with its frontiers. As stated, I would happily be one!

The Italian ancestry

They say love is blind. It is not; it just learns to minimize fault lines and forgive. I must state my prejudice, for prejudice it is, since Italy is the country of my paternal ancestors and thus holds an emotional appeal which, I confess, obscures faults which are visible to others. It also greatly resembles my country of birth and for that reason I discuss them in the same sub-section.

I love them both; I am partial to their natural beauty; I envy their laid back attitude to life which my austere middle class upbringing has deprived me to a large extent. And its defiance of political correctness has something which I find amusing and, at times, even welcome. Does all this sound self-contradictory"? If it is, it is explicable by reference to my Mediterranean background.

Well yes, for we are, after all, talking about two of the most unruly countries of the Mediterranean world. Not that unruliness was only a fault. For it was the basis of individuality, so powerfully proclaimed in the books by or about Renaissance artists, since this unwillingness to bow to rules made of ordinary people allowed these artists to develop their very abnormal talents. Read or read Cellini, Castiglione, Vasari and you will immediately marvel at the extent of self-confidence these men display. The inscription on Rafael's tomb in the Pantheon says it all: "While he was alive even nature herself felt jealous"

The vanity of Italian men concerning their bodies and looks is a subject of annoyance for some, amusement for others including myself. I compare them, especially later on in this book, in looks to the Greeks and that is certainly true for those who hail from southern Italy wearing an olive skin, with busy, dark eye brows and a pronounced noses, either hooked or bulbous at the end. But from Rome northwards, one also encounters a different figure, taller that the average Mediterranean, thin if not often emaciated, and very conscious of his "good" looks. The physiognomy remarkably frequently reminds one of faces on Medieval or early Renaissance frescoes and cities like Rome seem to survive by selling almost exclusively to male Roman peacocks. The difference with Milan, where fashion revolves around the *Donna* has been noticed and commented upon by my wife and me on several occasions.

The fashion is very different to that found in men's clothes' shops in England. Less masculine many would say, most certainly less sober. Velvet, suede, moccasins instead of tied up black brogues (slightly cracked so as not to look new). tightly worn chinos and colours – a profusion of colours such as are displayed in the Paris shops of Nannani used on indescribably expensive cashmere pullovers or leather or suede sporting jackets lined in expensive wool. Thart was the problem with fashion: it never came cheap. Actually, 'fashion' has another drawback: it keep changing quickly leaving with expensive gear you no longer wish to wear.

So clad, your average Italian will dart in an out the local coffee shops and sip standing his espresso, thus named so as to be distinguished from the 'café lungo' which is favoured by decrepit oldies like me who prefer to sip their coffee in a leisurely fashion sitting down and admiring the human sights around them. Again, what stands out and cannot be missed is beauty combined with a very special ability to project it for others to note and, if possible, admire.

But the difference between the two coffees mentioned above indicates more than age (or if you are more charitably minded, different nationality). More importantly, the Italian peacock sips his coffee standing for in such a position he can swirl around constantly observing anything that is attractive and moving on two legs *and, even more importantly, trying to gage the impression he is himself making on others.* This is the true sign of the peacock: he is looking for a female and in order to get her he must look at his best. Another way of describing a Roman.

This, be it noted, is not Mediterranean show off but pure nature. For nature requires that beauty and strength to be displayed in order to attract the best mating partner. In other words, at its roots, this display has nothing to do with love or romantic attraction but the preservation of the species through the survival of the fittest. But then, this being Italy, a romantic or sensual slant is easily added to the whole ritual dance. For this is a deeply sensual world *as only Catholicism of the*

Italian variety has traditionally allowed and depicted in its religious art, a topic to which I will return in a future chapter for it deserves closer attention.

In Italy, however, the cultivation of the body and its appearance in no way means the neglect of mind and culture in all its forms. My Italian colleagues have been among the most widely read and intellectually inventive I have met in forty five years of teaching and conducting research in many universities. Where they fall down sometimes is their natural disorganization and their introduction of politics in academic life in a big way solely to create "schools of thought" and 'intellectual hers', indirectly ensure the perpetuation of their name and prestige. Brilliant again; and again in keeping with the laws of nature even though often the way this is executed touches on the comic, the corrupt, or both.

Not that politics are absent from Oxbridge Colleges where cooping up in the precincts of small colleges amazing minds can lead to the kind of behaviour which Henry Kissinger once described as academics being "extraordinary petty since the stakes were so low". But Italian university politics can give glimpses of Renaissance rivalry in Florence or the Vatican of the kind which one reads in history books and biographies and entertain us nowadays but must have been chillingly unpleasant in days gone by. But again, if you witness all this from the outside it should amuse one rather than provoke one for these are the kind of variations which give life's patch-work quilt its amazing attraction.

The cultural openness of the Low Countries

In the Netherlands and Flemish Belgium religion shapes the work ethos and provides much of the tone, rhythm, and colour of life. The two countries are so similar and yet so different that one is constantly invited to make comparisons. In this sense I love to quote two signs on the road side at the border between French speaking Walloon and Flemish speaking Belgium for the say much about the values close to the hearts of the citizens of the two regions.

Thus in the first, the sign, situated in a Walloon area, announces to passing motorists - one suspects with a sense of pride - that: "Ici on parle français". Two hundred yards further north, as one enters Flanders, the sign proclaims with (a dry sense of) humour): "Ici on travail". Few words can say so much; religion can impact one's life in more ways than are imaginable at first blush! Examples such as these abound.

Let us return to this rapid tour of the lower countries.

Prolonged poverty, after a period of extraordinary wealth as a result of successful trade which began to decline between the 16th and 17th century – the dates differ from region to region – has preserved cities like Ghent in a time warp and thus allows them to display an architectural beauty which only cities like Bruges – also in Flanders – or Prague (and for the same reason) could rival until the latter began to be modernized too rapidly from the end of the last century. One finds similar cities in the South of the Netherlands – such as Breda or den Bosch - which display the same architectural attraction. From the outside as well as the inside, which the Calvinistic openness demands to make it visible to passers-by, the visitor sees houses which he knows has seen before. The point however is that he has seen then in Museums such as the Mauritzhouse in the Hague where paintings by Jan Vermeer and Peter der Hooch immortalised on small but perfectly painted canvasses.

To an outsider like me these two parts of the Low Countries should be joined while the southern, French-speaking, part of Belgium should have long ago joined France and put an end to the "Belgium Question" – almost as divisive and convoluted as the more famous "Eastern Question". But I am ignoring, once again, the dividing power of religion or, rather, denominations of one and the same religion – Christianity in this case in the form of Catholicism and Calvinsim. For Flemish Belgium is largely Catholic, while the Central and Southern parts of the Netherlands have a strong Calvinistic element. Apart from a shared preference for French type, old fashioned – i.e. exceptionally rich – food, the two neighbouring populations can be very different.

It bears repeating because it has to be seen to be believed but the Calvinistic work ethos - avoidance of differences in wealth, openness of private life - is manifested in the poor to lower middle class row of small houses which form the bulk of the city of Leiden which have their voile curtains of their front rooms wide open so that every passer-by can look in, stare, in fact - if he is rude enough to want to do that as I was – straight into the living room and, beyond, into the usually adjoining dining room, resplendent with proudly displayed and impeccably dusted home chattels so well depicted in the 17th century paintings of Dutch interiors, all primly arranged and shining! Catholicism in Belgium allows if not encourages more privacy. Should one suspect the presence of more dust? I simply do not know though I feel confident in every Belgium self-respecting living room one can find wine bottles from the drinking of the night before.

Who said the northerners do not enjoy life? What is different is how you do things, not what you do. I built much of my work as a comparative lawyer on this distinction and I think it has room to be expanded to cover many other aspects of daily life.

The first time I visited Belgium was in the early 1970's when my brother law was then posted at the Greek Embassy in Brussels. This was the twilight of the French dominance and the French part of the population still had – politically – the upper hand. The visiting Ambassadorial class did not conceal their preference for this section of the Belgian population – probably because most speak some French but no Flemish. The Flemish people were often described as dull, too serious, even, less intelligent. Forty years later the roles have been reversed and the dull and more backward people now have, economically at least, the upper hand. My many visits in that country have left me in no doubt that some of the most learned and astute colleagues I have come across in my forty five plus years in academic life were to be found in the Low countries if I may so bracket the two I am thinking of.

But the above observations once again raise my usual question: why take sides, adopt pejorative characterizations, be quick to criticize and not enjoy what is good and interesting in both? My long stays in Ghent and occasional visits to Leuven – I have never been invited to visit the French speaking part of the University – Louvain la Neuve – which stupidly not only decided to separate from the Dutch speaking and older part of that famous university confirm the above. But petty politics divides, demotes, degrades and so this once leading European University - Leuven - not only split into two (a French speaking and a Dutch speaking one) but both parts also agreed upon the separation of their books so that those written in one language were housed in one campus and those written in the other would stay where they always were! How can such eminent centres of learning of the past compete with the American Colossi if they take their internal divisions to such extremes and make themselves weaker than they already are?

Politics (and religion – yes, religion) more often destroy than build, divide rather than unite, reveal the worst not the best in men and women. If you allow such divisions to infect you, as they did the Ambassadorial classes stationed in Brussels in the 60' and 70's in the seventies, you fail to enjoy both and begin to understand the country in all its intriguing complexity. Incidentally, I have encountered such ambassadorial divisions on the pro-Israeli pro-Palestinian side in both the Foreign Office and the Quai d' Orsai. I have long ceased being amused by them and regret that the likes of me who try to bring people together rather than separate them have such minimal influence in this world of ours. Could whoever once said that blessed are the peacemakers been wrong? Blasphemous even to suggest such thought; but when you see divisions play such a widespread and destructive role in European life one is – unwillingly – tempted to sin and describe the picture as he sees it.

But Ghent and Leuven - Bruges as well - offer more than their architectural beauty or culinary talents to the appreciating visitor. The visiting academic will find there very learned people who are also adaptable to the reality that theirs is a small country so if it has to survive it has to make its educational wealth available to as many people as possible. Thus, not only are the inhabitants more multi lingual that one finds in the larger European cities but also willing to teach their courses in English thus attracting students from as far away as Australia, New Zealand, Russia, Central Asia, China and, of course the other EU countries.

The same was true of Leiden where I worked for over fifteen years as an Ordinarius Professor and admired how international this University was able to remain despite the fact that it was operating at a fraction of the budget of even middle ranking American Universities. Why could we not combine the strong points of the two, persuade them to work closer together, encourage them to develop more exchanges and common degrees, prepare the young students of tomorrow in a way that they could work in (almost) whichever country their fancy took them. For me this was the major part of my work for nearly two decades and even though this internationalization has progressed massively during this time, it still has not gone as far as our times require. But that is for another book.

Combining the best

I attempted above a crass but personal and very honest bird's eye view of different cities, different countries, different customs and mentalities. I loved them all: Cornell, Austin, all the cities mentioned above. Just thinking of the last forty five years working in all of the above cities dredges up from the unconscious wonderful memories which flash before me as 3D pictures – all of them memorable; only a few unpleasant, not worth mentioning. All bring tears to my eyes since they all now belong to the past which can only be relived in the form of memories. How strange; how very strange it is that pleasurable and less happy emotions of the past can provoke the same physical reaction: tears!

Yet are we talking about different things, different people, different languages, different ways of writing and expressing their thoughts, varying attitudes towards life or, at the end of the day, analogous behaviour and tastes? Is a glass containing 50% of its capacity with water half full or half empty? It is the mind not the eye which will determine which expression one will use. The mind as it was first shaped and the mind as life has adapted it with the passage of time - provided it has not been hermetically closed by bias and humanly imposed stupidity - can come to see things differently and switch from a criticizing to an appreciating mode. Changing views calls for strength, mental and moral; so does admitting that one was wrong on many things and many assessments of human characters. Good people can be found everywhere; and being in the final stretch of my life I have no doubt in proclaiming my belief that it is people who make people bad.

One becomes richer when one can achieve this switch. Yet, alas, in all three of my countries, I have found people too quick to look down upon "foreigners" rather than to relish their differences and try to learn from them. Cosmopolitanism, it has often been argued, gives you a little of many but deprives you the totality of one. I disagree. For I see it as an experience which allows one to strengthen one's sense of belonging by constantly comparing it with other cultures and being able to admit that sometimes there are better, sometimes worse, but in almost all cases can each become wiser through borrowing from the other.

The history of great civilization confirms this somewhat superficially expressed preference of mine. For ancient Greece, Rome, Medieval Cordoba, the British Empire at its best, were all confident enough to graft new shoots on an old trunk and thereby produce richer and more varied products.

Lord Annan once put some of these feelings in a wonderful essay about "The British Aristocracy of Letters" in Victorian times, partly republished in his last book entitled *The Dons*. This, he wrote, was a confident class of people, sure of themselves to be able to admire their German counterparts, honour them, and even borrow their ideas (as the American legal historians of the end of the 19th and the beginning of the 20th century did even more generously). But this did not stop them from being and remaining British, even to the point - which is so amusing to anyone who has observed British academia from close quarters - by remaining faithful to their understated, almost worn out, creased but clean apparel as a way of demonstrating that what interested them was not the changing, opulent "outside" but the deeper and richer inside: "the self". No peacocks here; just hawks and eagles, living in the wild, spiralling upwards and enjoying the most wonderful of all intellectual gifts: freedom!

A very personal postscript

I have been visiting (as a teacher or as a tourist or often both) the above-mentioned cities (and others not mentioned above such Geneva, Zurich, Sienna, Genova, Brussels and Vienna) *very* regularly since the late 1950's and various impressions about them have progressively been crystallising in my mind. This is not the kind of book which obliges me – or so I feel – to overload my statements with statistics confirming in part or in full my impressions – and that is why I refer to them and the postscript as *very personal,* warning the reader of the danger that I may be seriously off the mark. Yet I plucked up the courage to write what is in my mind for it reflects what this living abroad and the passage of time did to me and the cities in question. That my views and opinions have changed is beyond doubt and, I would add, entirely understandable; but what in my mind - and for the purposes of this book - is important is that these cities, too, have changed in the course of the fifty five years or so that I am talking about.

Their ethnic composition is one; and this is a crucial assertion given the contents of the last four chapters of this book. The suburbs of Brussels are thus distinctly more ethnically diverse that I recall them being in the late fifties;[14] and so is the perceived strength/ importance of the Walloon versus Fleming populations of the country. In the late fifties I thus recall the Francophones distinctly having the upper hand - or so they felt themselves - while the Flemish population was perceived

---

14. The modern immigrant is also very different from the old ones; for the latter sought to settle in their new countries and earn a decent living whereas the new ones are constantly putting pressure on their hosts to conform with their – the immigrants – beliefs and never –ending financial demands. These humble four lines deserve in my opinion an entire and thoughtful dissertation for they illustrate one reason why immigration has become in recent times such an acute and controversial issue.

as belonging to the lower and, certainly, poorer classes. Being a good faith but still outside observer I feel free to state this impression since many people in all these places could attest to my feelings of friendship and affection to them, their cities and their cultures.

The same is true of cities such as Cologne and Munich, in the latter detecting a general degree of liberalisation which was nowhere as obvious in the times when Josef Strauss reigned unchallenged. The changes I have noted also appear in the topics discussed in other chapters – for instance chapter five – where the Italian (and Greek) male pre-eminence has undoubtedly been dented, both by legislation and – more importantly – by a slow but obvious shift towards a position of greater respect towards women. More significantly this greater respect for the female abilities and not just feminine charm has been accompanied by the awareness that it should be reflected in their position in the worlds of business and politics. A most welcome change though one which has also been accompanied by some undesirable side effects.[15]

The above impressions – I repeat conscious of the fact that they may, at best be correct in only a limited way - are crucial for the validity of my argument of 'convergence' taking place within the bounds of the European Continent. What remains to be seen is whether this tendency, which I would describe as representing a move towards greater liberalisation of views, will one day be reflected in the political sphere in a way which will transform European (and I mean here European Union) structures and their ability to shape their own, independent and new policies on a large number of issues. On the whole, such a move does not frighten me so long as it can take place in a calm atmosphere and a planned manner.

---

15. I am alluding to the complex and often one-sided case law which has developed over accusations of unfair dismissals or sexual harassment.

Chapter Three

THE PURPOSE OF HIGHER EDUCATION

Teaching one how to think, how to reason, forming one's charac-
ter or all three?

At first glance this chapter may look as being out of place in a book
such as this. Yet this book is focused on humans and their problems
- some solved others rearing some very ugly heads. In life problems
are solved through recourse to – in ascending order - learning, experience, intuition or all three combined. Experience or precedent is, in
one sense, the easiest way to try and solve a problem; for if you have
a precedent and it has worked well you simply follow it. This way
of proceeding, however, is likely to be of little assistance if the issues
confronting one are either entirely novel or of a magnitude where
past experience can only provide the slightest of guidance. It is here
that having learnt how to reason comes into play; but not in the ordinary way we understand the words. For given what we said about
the unprecedented characteristics of some of our modern problems
the above may not be sufficient to produce workable solutions. Truly
experienced and able people at this stage will move to intuition.
    The challenges that confront us are thus infinitely more complex
and require to problem-solver one to move through different phases.
The first, as stated, will test his ability to think and reason by manipu-
lating complex if not contradictory material. If the situation is too
complex, one way out is to try lateral thinking or, as it is commonly
put, 'thinking out of the box.' This requires courage: the courage of
the unorthodox person. The second phase however, is even more
complex for it requires us to combine the mind's reasoning powers

with intuition – for those few who have it - and hope for the kind of *direct insights* [1]it can generate.

At first sight, intuition is a much more complex psychological phenomenon than we can imagine. Unlike 'instinct', which is an automatic reaction and found in lesser animals performed without a conscious adaptation of means to ends, intuition is found in the most advanced human beings who have developed this *instant insight* as a result of having, through an unusual, experienced, or even trying life and, of course, sheer intelligence, acquired this rare talent. Some people have such a natural talent to assess and react to external stimuli. The intuitive approach involves reflection – even if it can be instantaneous - at a much higher level at which the intellect, alone, immediately apprehends the problem and – more amazingly – even its solution. In some of the problems facing our societies these days – Middle East; Immigration; American/Russian relations – it may well be the kind of thinking currently missing. If I am right in this supposition, the answer must lie in the politician's mind which rarely works at such levels being pre-occupied with the lesser – but to him important issues - of political survival. The intellectual heights I envisage as necessary are only attained by the very rare persons we call statesmen or true leaders- the theme with which we will end this book.

So back to teaching and education.

Teachers understandably praise their profession but the truth, I fear, is that most of the things worth learning are picked up from life and not taught in classrooms. The next most important source of knowledge comes from home; and here both knowledge is imparted and characters are also formed. Finally, higher education should teach the young how to reason and argue; how to approach subjects in an interdisciplinary manner and, if suitably prepared from home, excite them enough to wish to make the move from education to culture. This last word derives from the verb to cultivate; and it is primarily associated with agriculture. That, in itself, suggests that it comes with much toil and also requires time for its results to become obvious. I was fortunate in having lived in an environment which provided all three; but I was also told that being instructed and guided was not enough: I had to go out into the real world; work and face its problems; and learn once again the lessons which life alone can teach.

Cambridge and Oxford are two of the four gems in the academic

---

1. To avoid burdening with long note I simply italicise the words which, in my view, deserve emphasis and would, normally, justify explanatory excursus.

crown of England (Imperial College and the LSE are the other two though they cover fewer subjects and in this respect cannot compete with the *breadth* of talent found in the first two institutions). They do not stand alone for Harvard, Yale, Princeton, Columbia, Stanford, Michigan, Berkeley, Cornell, Paris (I and II), Leiden, Munich, Ghent, Rome (La Sapienza) are comparable institutions in fame and quality of staff and students; and a few more could be added to this list.

In architectural and environmental terms, however, the first two offer their students an *educational environment* in which those (few) who are prepared to exploit it can really begin to mature. This is because these unique institutions do so much of their teaching in their (almost) unique college-based system of education which gives these places their very unusual flavour of being able to provide individualized education such as cannot be found anywhere else in the world. One must attempt to explain this briefly for the sake of those who do not know it and invariably find it difficult to understand but before doing so two preliminary points should be made about Oxbridge since I have combined - as happens rarely in England – the experience of being taught and to teach in both.

Distinguishing the two centres of learning is both difficult and easy and depends upon whether one wishes to limit one's observations to generalities or try to dwell on subtler details. This task has led to many beautiful phrases, each with a grain of truth in it. My view, mundanely expressed in the best of legal traditions, is that they are very similar and very different.

Administratively, the difference could be expressed by calling Oxford a Confederate institution since its Colleges have much – too much? – economic power and autonomy whereas the central University has less that it ought to if it is to perform its fund-raising duties with greater efficiency. Cambridge, by contrast, resembles more a Federal state with stronger central powers on the economic front delegated to the University as well as delegating more educational decisions to the faculty boards in which most Colleges tend to be represented and thus act in a more centralised manner that the equivalent of Oxford in my time.

A more literary (and witty) way of distinguishing the institutions can be found in Lord Annan's learned, nostalgic, and dazzling anecdotal book already referred to and entitled: "The Dons: Mentors, Eccentrics, Geniuses". There we thus find the following sentence attributed to a cultured, educated, and eccentric Cambridge done who "liked to contrast dry, austere, high-minded Cambridge with worldly

Oxford, where success was the currency and brilliance your credit."
All I can add to this is the word with which examination questions
often end: "discuss."

The next thing to note is that these uniquely English and thus apparently tranquil institutions are, in fact, products of intellectual dissent if not rebellion and trace their origins to the University of Paris,
one of the most eminent institutions of learning of Medieval Europe.
Dissent thus gave birth to both and in succession. Pain, agony and
upheaval of some kind thus always seemed to have preceded birth (or
cosmic creation); and this must have been the case here, as well. What
follows afterwards is to a very large extent a matter of luck!

The first building of the City of Oxford apparently appeared built
around a narrow part of the river Isis (a section of the Themes –
Tham*esis* – from which this stretch of water takes its name). Today it
is marked by 'Folly Bridge' which stands at its centre of the urban area
was chosen by Saxon drovers to "ford" the river, hence the name of
the city: Ox*ford*. A small priory, lying nearby, gave early signs of intellectual life and, apparently, King Alfred stopped there in 872 A.D. for
refreshments on his way up the river. The stop, apparently, gave him
the opportunity to engage in a long intellectual conversation with the
priors and the town's reputation for scholarly pursuits was born then
– or so it likes to believe. Myths are so attractive, especially when they
are not believable.

The Colleges proper however – and the battle for the oldest is
between Merton and University College, with Balliol also laying a
strong claim – go back to the late 11th /early 12th century when rebel
dons from Paris decided to leave their *alma matter*, cross the Channel,
and settle in Oxford starting there a new University. Some forty odd
years later new dissensions broke out among the dons now settled in
Oxford so a bunch of them moved off to Cambridge, a city with Roman origins, built on the river Cam where a bridge was erected to join
the two banks of the river and promote the trade which was facilitated
by the navigable waters of the river Cam. Both cities and Universities
thus own their names to their rivers which from the beginning were
busy with trade and often carrying from nearby quarries the special
stones they needed to construct the colleges.

As stated, disagreement and dissent were at the root of the foundation of these two great centres of learning and remain a part of life - especially of academic life - where intelligent (and often highly strung)
dons, *living at close quarters to one another, can fight over trivial causes and
indulge* with amazing tenacity in life-long disagreements over mat-

ters of doctrine. Thus, the idea that the academic environment breeds peace, calm, and civil behaviour is only skin deep. I talk from experience having lived and lectured in both of these institutions for over twenty five years of my life– *I may be the only Greek, indeed, even one of a small number of Englishmen to have had this double privilege*!

There is second feature of the old English Universities, indeed of English institutions, that often escapes the attention of their occasional or superficial visitors. Old, very old, of course they are. Parts of many building attest to this antiquity which some time goes back to the 13th century, though most of them – but by no means all – date back to the 15th to 18th centuries. The gowns, customs, and many rituals also have ancient origins. But much - much more than can be imagined - of old Oxford (or Old England) was reformed and reformulated in the second half (or even later) of 19th century, the century which really made Britain the world power it became. For the Romantic Movement at its beginning, the sense of tradition worshiped by Victorian England later, and the spirit of scientific discovery which dominated 19th century British life, encouraged this maintenance of antiquity and continuity, past and future, as the real reform and change was taking place underneath the exterior shell and not infrequently prompted to emulate precedents being laid down by (indisputably) eminent institutional parvenus such King's College and University College London.

The 19th century was also par excellence an era of discovery, scientific revolution, espousal of modernity, and thus both the University curriculum as well as most of its rules and regulations were re-drafted, even if the appearance of continuity was deliberately not disturbed. These were the times when Oxford really acquired its world fame and those who lived and worked there could truly refer to it in Matthew Arnold's famous words as "The City of the dreaming spires". Standing at Boars Hill and looking at this unique site one understands how one can paint with words as a famous Greek Lyric – Simonides of Keos - put it two and a half thousand years ago.

Much of the same observations apply to England's political institutions, including many of their rituals which dominate parliamentary life. This respect for the past, which the English have always shared with the ancient Romans, goes hand in hand with their attachment to established principle and precedent and their dislike for sudden, even more so violent, change. And if something has to be changed, incremental evolution and not violent revolution is the way forward. I find this one of the many attractions of English public life; and it has been very evident in my own subject: law.

Every advantage, invariably, has its reverse side which could be seen as its cost rather than as a drawback. And, staying still with law, I think England's (unlike America's) firm attachment to legal precedent can also have the disadvantage of slow adjustment to a rapidly changing world. This balance between adjusting the law to meet the needs of a changing society and using the law to lead society towards new beginnings is as delicate an issue as it is worth careful contemplation. This, however, is not the place to indulge in it and it will have to wait for another occasion. Suffice it however to say that the American legal system, though a progeny of the English, has from its earliest times treated legal precedent with less rigour and allowed their courts to modify, already from the 19th century onwards, many of the legal rules originally borrowed from England.

Only in one major branch of the law has America shown a greater - dare one call it more rigid - attachment to the past and this is in the area of constitutional interpretation where conservative judges insist that the Constitution must be interpreted according to the original 'intention' – or, better still – the original 'understanding' of the text drafted at the end of the 18th century. [2]British judges interpreting constitutions from the Caribbean (and other former British colonies) even though their wording was more often than not borrowed from the geographically nearby icon – the American Constitution - have gone a different path preferring that of measured adaptation.

But let us return to the collegiate life of the Oxbridge system. To understand it one must understand three other features of medieval life.

One is the role religion and the Church played in the world of learning, patronage, and social welfare, including the caring of the young, infirm, and poor in almost all of Western Europe. This role remained strong in England until Tudor times and in France it only died with the French Revolution.

Second, one must also bear in mind the extent to which the Western Church often found itself in conflict with lay authorities, a conflict which dominated political thinking during the latter Middle Ages. The fight was often expressed in dogmatic terms but it really turned on matters of money and power. Who could appoint Bishops and who could try a host of issues in which the Church had an interest. Once again, the Church was deprived of much of its jurisdictional and ad-

---

2. Anyone who can find out what were the common intentions of the Founding Fathers probably deserves a prize; but that can be sorted out by Americans one day.

judicatory powers during the reign of King Henry VIII whereas in France, the Catholic Church retained more powers and prestige until the Revolution imposed its wishes and, after a series of compromises, finally moved that country to adopt a system of fairly rigid separation of Church and State.

Finally, one must remove from one's mind any idea of the University system being founded suddenly and in a pre-planned and structured manner from the outset. Instead, like medieval cathedrals, it was a product of time where many minds and ideas played a role in shaping the final product which we now see. It is this last point I feel ought to be touched upon briefly for the benefit of those who do not understand this uniqueness of the Oxbridge set up.

To explain it, one might do well to turn again to the idea of federal structures or, more accurately, a confederate system of government. For the University stands in the place of the central or federal government, endowed with a limited number of important powers, mainly the power to give "degrees" – Oxford or Cambridge degrees which is what attracts candidates to them and eventually becomes a source of revenue by mans of gifts and legacies.

That is an important power for that is the reason why students flock to Oxbridge and are willing to pay high fees – to the University and the Colleges for their lodging and local tutorials received there in the afternoons after they have attended in the morning lectures given in University building and open to students from all the Colleges.. This power resembles the powers given to federal governments. For, in the political setting, the central government is usually given special powers in foreign affairs, defence and federal finances and in this type of University world it is the maintenance of the "external image" of the academic community typically embodied in the granting of a University degree.

The federal (or confederate) states on the other hand, in the Oxbridge system are the Colleges, each endowed with its own territory – the College premises and lands, often very extensive – their own finances, their own internal administration – Colleges are governed by their Master and Fellows i.e. the sum total of their senior academic members. These last two points, the products of history, call for some further explaining.

The colleges began life, as stated, as ecclesiastical foundations meant to look after the young men who came from all over the world to attend University- run lectures, initially given by famous philosophers, mathematicians and theologians. Since these young men could, and did, "go wild" in the nights and caused constant irritation to the local inhabitants – the well know phrase "town and gown" expresses this ongoing conflict – the Church built hostels – early YMCA's one could call them - where the young men were housed and fed and kept out of trouble, especially in the evenings. Women did not arrive in either institution until the second half of the 19th century or even later and for long they were in the minority.

The system worked and, in fact it evolved in an interesting way. For the College mutated from hostels to teaching places by starting to hire the University Professors to join them and to offer *their* students – not just all the University students – *repetitoria* or, as they become know, supervisions or tutorials – which would take place after an (early) dinner in the evenings. From about the 16th century onwards the teachers thus acquired a double "allegiance", in the morning teaching classes which were attended by all the students of the University and in the evenings, doing revisions and "disputations" – *disputationes* – with the young men who belonged to their college only. For the first role they ended up gaining, through election, the title of Lecturer, Reader – and Readerships were *ad hominem* not established posts and very few in numbers – and, at the top, the title of Professor; for the second job their title was 'Fellow of X College.' When I was elected Professor in Oxford in 1995 there were only five established Chairs; now the University has created many more to stop their younger and able colleagues leaving for other Universities in pursuit of the more prestigious title. Still, the new Professorships do not relieve their holders from carrying out their usual College duties as did and do the older established chairs and, for the cognoscenti, this a reason why the new professorships are regarded as less prestigious than the older, established chairs.

Yet in early days all who in various capacities taught at the University and were known as "dons" were by no means the equivalent of the German academic, especially of the 19thc century, erudite, productive in his writings, remote, respected, rarely lovable except perhaps by his most close pupils. The Oxbridge don was a man – in holy orders until approximately the late 1870's and in theory unmarried – chosen mainly for his sociable habits, his willingness to share in the burdens of the administration of his college, the qualities of his character, his devotion to the performance of his pastoral duties, and, incidentally, his ability to drill into the minds of his students what had been said during day time by the grand professors.

It was only in late Victorian or even Edwardian times that true scholarly merit began to count as a serious pre-requisite to appointment, a seriously retarded reaction to the pattern set by that most "awful" (in English eyes) of events – the French Revolution – which had paid so much attention to "merit". *Thus, to limit my observations to my own field of knowledge – law – Oxbridge did not even begin to resemble in scholarly excellence the better Universities of 19th century Germany until the turn of the 19th century* though, of course, isolated exceptions can be found in both Universities ever since English law (unlike Cannon and Roman law) began to be taught in 1756 in Oxford by the Vinerian Professor and 1804 in Cambridge by the Downing Professor.

But if proper legal training was late to come, it increasingly became superb, not least because it relied so heavily on a one to one tuition between don and students. This labour-intensive, small class, teaching method, which began to evolve by the time of Tudor times when the Colleges became richer as a result of the confiscation of ecclesiastical property, received a decisive boost by the end of the 19th century when meritocracy made a determined appearance in the curriculum. It was from about that period that most Colleges were able to build further on this system, enhance their own wonderful libraries, and strengthen their own autonomy within the wider University structure. To this day, therefore, students and teachers alike, have a double link – one with the University, recognized by the title of Lecturer, Reader, Professor ad hominem and, the highest, (*Ordinarius*) Professor (very few indeed compared to American or European institutions) - and another with their College recognized under the title of "Fellow" (of Trinity or Saint John's College), Cambridge and so on.

One last point must be mentioned for those who wish to apply to these universities for future studies. Application for the BA degree, i.e. the first degree one can get, invariably involves and application *to a College* (not the University) and if it accepted the candidate is then automatically also enrolled in the University, belongs to both, can use the facilities of both but...also pay two fees to cover the expenses of both. If, on the other hand, a student wishes to read for a graduate degree – and M. Sci. or Ph. D (D. Phil in Oxford) or follow a one year graduate course often known as an M. Jur or BCL (bachelor of Civil Law) in Oxford or LL.M in Cambridge (Masters of Laws) then the application begins at the relevant faculty and if processed by it in consultation with the Colleges in a positive way, i.e. the candidate is accepted as a worthy one, then his or her papers are forwarded to one of four Colleges mentioned in the application for acceptance.

This complicated structure incidentally makes it much more difficult for one to intervene and influence the outcome in favour of the applying son or daughter of a ...friend. Most of my Greek friends, however, never quite accepted this impediment, an impediment, however, which has spared me much embarrassment from having to admit that I cannot help even where I would love to be in a position to do so! It has, however, that unique of advantages of individual tuition. The knd of one to one – occasionally slightly more in the room at the same time) – which allows the good tutor to shape a mind, show it how to write and reason, encourage it to reflect wider that, perhaps, the individual question may call for, and last but by no means least, play a part in guiding his pupil towards the part of a profession which both teacher and student finally agree would most suit the young man or woman. This, at its best, can be such a holistic interference (for the good) of a candidate's mind that might well end up giving him the basis of what I earlier described the rudiments of his instinct which practical experience will finally shape.

Heading for Cambridge

Joining Cambridge in 1968 had, as I said earlier on, been preceded by a tourist-type visit with my parents and aunt to form a quick visual picture of the two main University towns of Oxford and Cambridge. While still in Athens my visit was also been greatly helped by the then Director of the British Council Mr. Close. A series of tests and interviews were thus arranged and since I somehow managed to pass them I was offered a British Council Scholarship to read for a Ph. D. for the princely amount which covered University and College tuition fees as well a living allowance of 65 pound per month. This was a princely amount since in those days a weekend return train ticket to London to spend with my wife to be would cost nine shillings and sixpence – today's equivalent of half a pound!

I suspect a kind word was put in my favour by the then British Ambassador to Athens Sir Michael Stewart who, along with his wife Damaris, were close friends of my parents. The decision to come to England and not take up the even more generous Kennedy Scholarship and go to Harvard - most generously offered by my former University Professor and well-known economist Giangos Pesmatzoglou was thus turned down after some real soul searching. All of the above, and Mr Close's invaluable Assistant Mrs Koskina, gave advice with the preparation of various forms addressed to College and University while the Ambassador himself had me over one day for tea and offered more advice on general topics of "does and don'ts" which someone who was only half British should observe. I still recall how useful they proved in later years; but even more deeply ingrained in my mind was this first chance to talk to a senior British civil servant and note the elegance and style with which the advice was offered.

It was, however, one further "chance encounter" which clinched my association with my mother's country and removed the final doubts as to the wisdom of turning down the rare offer to end up studying in Harvard. It was in later life, when I was sucked into the realm of Russian literature – the works of Pasternak, Syniavskii and Nabokov in particular – with which my wife was deeply involved when writing her Ph. D thesis under the marvellous guidance of a real scholar – Dr Jane Grayson – that I, too, became, fascinated by this idea of "chance encounters" which change the seemingly pre-determined route of one's life.

This chance encounter may be worth recounting (to the extent that one's memory allows its accurate reconstruction) not only to prove how crucial it turned out to be for me to meet Nancy Mitford but also to give a light-hearted – I hope rather than cynical - account of what happens when interesting people from entirely different cultures get together and "fail to click".

The meeting was arranged through the kind intervention of Nancy Mitford's friend Mark Ogilvie-Grant at his island-type small house and little court yard, not far from where the main Athens Cemetery lies! I, of course, was not meant to be anything more than an "also ran"; an insignificant part of the background tapestry. Naturally, I was also not expected to talk throughout the lunch which Mark had arranged for Nancy Mitford to meet my father and "advise" him about a planned English edition of his book *History of Modern Greece* which Mark was busy translating into English.

Mark's intentions were the best; but though bilingual and knowing full well the Greeks and their character, he entirely failed to take into account the strong but very different temperaments of the two protagonists whom he had brought together. For my father was entirely wrapped up, as always, in his world of politics; and his conversation in English was not helped by the fact that though his English vocabulary was huge, his ability to speak the language was rather poor. Nancy Mitford on the other hand, at the height then of her literary career – the meeting took place in 1966 if I recall rightly – focused, kindly but ineffectively, on trying to persuade my father to abridge his book if he was aiming to reach an Anglophone audience. Anything larger than, say, 300 printed pages maximum would, in Nancy Mittford's view, fail to attract the interest of any major English publisher since few of their readers would be interested in the minutiae of Greek politics. She was entirely right in giving this practical advice; but it was the wrong way to start the meeting and the remaining two hours passed pleasantly but only because my mother's English background enabled her to keep the conversation flowing on a social basis while my father increasingly withdrew into the background and sulked. That, however, was the moment when chance stepped in and, for those who see it and grab it while it lasts, it can have a life-changing effect.

For it turned out that I was one of the few – apart from Mark I suppose - who had read Nancy Mitford's books, starting with "Love in Cold Climate" (published I think at the end of the forties) and most notably her latest historical book "The Sun King", a book about Louis XIV of France, acclaimed by historians but also by the educated reading public.[3]

Since I was and remain awkward when it comes to small talk and, in any event, I was not meant to say a word during this meeting, I had, thus far remained part of the wall paper with no one so much as addressing a word to me. Yet, given my interest in observing people's behaviour and body language my imagination had been gripped by the fact that I could see how the two "big ego's" were totally unable to communicate with one another, and that not only because of the language problem. So, towards the end of that engagement, and during a pause in the conversation between Nancy Mitford and my mother, I plucked up the courage to 'but in' and mention to her the fact that I had read her book as well as some of her earlier novels. Authors love people who talk to them about their books so here ears pricked up at once. Almost stammering I then put to her two questions, my mother gradually changing colours for my having broken the undertaking to remain silent.

My fist, I recall, question was why did she choose to write about Louis XIV and not Louis' grand-father Henry IV of Navarre whom – what cheek to say so! - I regarded as being more important for having brought to an end France's religious wars. She gave a succinct and convincing answer stressing that Louis' reign coincided with the golden era of French power and culture. She spoke in a staccato way and

---

3. Her last historical book was on *Frederick the Great,* which *she* regarded as her best. It did not appear until 1970 (if I recall correctly) and soon after she died.

was both calm and convincing. My second question however, should not have been asked at all. It was: "what was Sir Oswald Mosley like in private life "- for he had married her equally charming and even more elegant (if this was at all possible) older sister Diana. "Being both such strong characters – that is Diana and Sir Oswald - how did they get on with each other?"

I do not recall much of the exchanges that followed for, in reality, there were no "exchanges" but a semi monologue by the beautiful and very elegantly dressed woman and a young man clearly out of his depth captivated by her immense magnetism! It was not, however, this minor intervention that mattered but its ending; for it proved the *piece de resistance*. Thus to our collective surprise, before leaving, she asked Mark to get in touch with one of his friends in Cambridge – in turned out to be Jean Barker, subsequently ennobled by the Conservatives and made Baroness Trumpington – to ask her "to look after the boy" while he was in Cambridge. Indeed, such is the networking of the English "establishment" that a few months later and, indeed, barely a week after my arrival in Cambridge that I was asked to go and have lunch with Jean at the Lees School where her husband was Head Master, something which I did almost on every Sunday thereafter!

It is thus not an exaggeration to say that with the passage of time Jean turned to be almost a second mother to me, introduced me to the many Conservative dignitaries who would lunch with her regularly on Sunday's, took a very active interest in my studies and later in my career and would never stop correcting me with much style if an when I made a false move (which I often did). I think, after so many years of friendship and indebtedness I feel, despite my upbringing, comfortable in calling her Jean; and without committing - I hope - an unforgivable indiscretion, when upon receiving my knighthood I was asked by Her Majesty how it all began for me in England I mumbled the only reply I could think of namely, "I owe everything to Baroness Trumpington", - an answer which was not only true but entirely appropriate and interesting to Her Majesty since Jean is a Baroness Lady in Waiting to the Queen.

All this began by a chance encounter arranged by the late Mark Ogilvie Grant to help promote my father's book in English. This never happened for the reasons which Nancy Mitford had rightly predicted. But blessed be her soul and Mark's for what they did for me. I will always acknowledge my debt for being put in touch with Baroness Trumpington and receiving for her a truly flattering and long-lasting support. Which all goes to show that planning will not always determine what happens in life: luck (or bad luck) not infrequently have a great say in such things.

Reaching paradise

In early summer of 1968 Cambridge finally became a reality.

The arrival at St. John's College, Cambridge, to begin my doctoral studies was a revelation: primarily an aesthetic one but also a psychological one. The place was beautiful but, for a moment, the beauty of the place was set aside by the feeling that for the first time in my life I found myself alone yet not lonely (as I often do, dare I admit it, during my current visits to the USA) absorbing new images as I walked by the river side; absorbing and loving every bit of what I saw.

This feeling of "new" prompted me to attempt - and I think judging from the result successfully - to begin a completely new life. I *had* to do something different; and it *had* to be good which it would be only if it was also new. The lessons and experiences of the past would not, of course, be abandoned. Yet they would now have to be poured into a new mould with different contours and take the shapes which the new environment required. Survival requires the ability to adapt and this was my *sui generis* version of Darwinian evolution. For my evolution would be dictated by my eclecticism and the requirements of my new environment. Mine would thus be voluntary not imposed by nature adaptation; and it had to be rapid for unlike Darwin's creatures I did not have eternity to wait for the acquisition of the tools that would make survival in a new environment possible. Much of what Sir Michael Steward and my mother had advised often came back to my mind.

This resolution was made walking down by the "backs" as I now felt able to pay more attention to aesthetics.

I have repeatedly stressed in this book how sensitive I am to beauty of all kinds but, especially, the beauty of nature. The architectural beauty of this place compliments that of its nature. Indeed, as with ancient Greek architecture, the architecture of Oxbridge blends into its environment and does not aim to dwarf it by standing out as Egyptian or Persian buildings impose upon you their huge grandeur. It is all a matter of scale; and scale like moderation in behaviour, does not come to all easily.

We in Greece know one or two things about antiquities. Our past has contributed greatly to contemporary aesthetics of what was once called the Western world. But in Greece the ancient past and the present are separated by the long gap of Byzantium, which, in the 6th century AD, in a mad moment of ecclesiastical fervour mindlessly destroyed some old treasures. Worse still, was the decay and abandonment that occurred during the period of the Turkish yoke which in Greece proper last from about 1453 to 1821 AD.

The result is that most of our architectural wonders of the past lie in ruins, un-restored or often badly restored. The Palace of Minos is one example, the Attalos Stoa in the Ancient Greek Agora another; and both can attract praise or blame depending on your own idea of how antiquities should be preserved and displayed to contemporary viewers. But for the romantic and the knowledgeable, even if little remains to be seen, it will still be enough to be completed by the viewer's mind. For, in architecture as in so many other forms of art, it is the "left over of latter day" that must marry successfully with the ideas of the receptive mind before it can produce the deep feeling of awe and sensitivity.

My own most romantic images of this kind were the temple of Apollo in Figalia in moonlight forty plus years ago. It was so deeply moving in its silent beauty that I did not even realize at the time how much more beautiful it would have been had I been watching it with what Goethe had put it wistfully: "eine shone Seele"-a beautiful soul - by my side. For this, however, I had to wait until 1970 when Eugenie, my beautiful girl friend, consented to marry me.

But from the Peloponnese let us return back to Cambridge. What I found there were not antiquities but old, often quite old, buildings. But they were not just old and beautiful; they were in use! This was the striking thing about this place. Though it did not quite recreate its early beginnings (as I said earlier on) it kept enough of its 16th century onwards looks to enable you to feel proud to have become part of such a continuous and still very much alive cultural tradition.

Architecture caused a shock; but the facilities of the University provided the aftershock. Library facilities and even lecture rooms were thus a huge improvement from what I had left behind at the miserable (but still beloved) Solonos building of the Athens Law Faculty. Maybe, if we, too, had such buildings, I say to myself as I write these lines, our students or anarchic demonstrators, would not destroy and deface them and, instead, as the British students respect their treasures we would revere ours. But let us leave this kind of rumination aside for maybe my thoughts will get darker again just at the moment that I am beginning to feel elated for having moved into a new world!

Libraries, given my past, and chapels stand out for special notice in these centres of learning. It is certain that lecture rooms and labs are more modern, more functionally designed and equipped, more impressive, once you see the American ones. But the Oxbridge College Libraries can be gems; gems themselves, full of gems of a different kind.

For inside them you find old oak bookcases, tall and darkened with the passage of time, replete with books that call for no expertise to assert that they are old, though the older ones in some cases remain chained to the walls as they once were! It was then that I also noticed that the binding of the really old books tended to be in dark, slightly discoloured brown leather. Coloured bindings in dark read morocco with gold trimmings seem to have become more fashionable in the 19th century. That was, originally, by view of what an old binding looked like.

For old not just antique books, their bindings are remarkably colourful since brown and dark morocco blend wonderfully to give this feeling of old, indeed, antique. The setting is completed by the huge Gothic windows, often on either side of old seats, letting in light and colour since many of them are stained glass. You want to live in them and often I nearly did for, after hours of reading provoking excitement and deep despair (for how much I still did not/ do not know) I would slumber on the table and sleep and dream and remain undisturbed. If this exhaustion lasted for too long, a kindly assistant librarian, clad in a simple but long black gown, would interrupt this wonderful if uncomfortable sleep and send me back home obliged to pay the price of this conscientiousness: no dinner since the refectory has closed by now!

Even the dust one finds in such old buildings and which I find more than charming – I simply love it – gives a special appeal to this ambiance which is often unchanged and in exactly in the state it was four hundred years or more ago. And when the rays of the sun of either dawn or dusk penetrate this sanctum and stir the dust molecules in a dance-frenzy in front of your eyes you are truly mesmerized, indeed, hypnotized and drift into another world. I thus found myself in a state of semi consciousness, neither asleep nor awake, watching the light energize the dust molecules and prompt me into thinking.

In the beginning the thinking was disorganized for as I said I was in semi conscience state unable to understand why fate had given me so much good luck. But then one moved from disorganized thinking to more focused thinking about one's life and then, one step higher and more focused, about one's work. This thinking was so "relaxed", removed from worldly cares, that, finally, one could afford to think freely and "release" the modern mind, which society and convention ties it up in knots, such new thoughts as you might have buried underneath fearful of convention disapproving their appearance. And if this reverie failed this time to reveal the new thought, next time it would fare better and, again, the next and then the next again. One suddenly was realizing what a huge asset for creativity is leisure; not laziness but leisure. Leisure which we do not have in the twenty first century to absorb and re-shape in new and different ways, the huge amount of factual information which new technology has given us. What an irony; what a loss to have so much information but not to be taught that leisure – not laziness I keep repeating – is also needed to absorb what reaches you daily and then see how you can put it to your own use.

One could talk for ages about the buildings of Oxford and Cambridge not just discussing their architectural aspects but also about their famous inhabitants throughout the ages. Newton, for instance, occupied the room next to the Great Gate of my old College – Trinity - and the crack in the window shutters which allowed light to seep in he used to do his various colour experiments. Apparently, it still, exists. So does Byron's tower on the top of which he, apparently, kept a pet … bear. When asked why he brought that up with him to Cambridge he is said to have replied "to keep the dons company". What, however, is much more original is the way in which subjects are taught in these two prime institutions of the English academic establishment and to this I must now turn. Indeed, here I found perfected what had existed in much smaller scale at my home but not at my school.

Thus, first, free thought was a *sine qua non* and even if the teacher found your views unconvincing or even wrong there was never any doubt that you would never be censored simply for taking a different view than his. In Greece the relationship with one's professor is one of complete subservience. One addresses then always using expressions such as "with respect" and there is hardly a Ph. D dissertation which does not begin by giving the first reference in the text to a work written by his or her doctoral father. To challenge in one's dissertation the view of one's professor is courting disaster; endless French and German former colleagues and subsequent students of mine assured me of that and were totally surprised when I invited them to disagree with me as the struggled to put shape to their early ideas.

Second, analysis was a key point in the teaching you being expected to present neatly and systematically the facts of the legal problem you had been asked to solve, then point out the (usually deliberate) omissions in the phrasing of the problem, just as you would ask in real life your client to give you supplementary information, and then you should come up with a structured answer. You were expected to use you raw material intelligently and you would get extra marks for good presentation of your argument even if your final conclusion was, I said, wrong or, at any rate not the one your teacher would have expected. In short you were dared to be original attempting your own critique of a well-established precedent knowing that it could bring more praise than blame. It was there I learnt that one must be willing to get things wrong for only those who did, sometimes managed to say something new. In short, this was in every conceivable way the opposite of what I had experienced in Greece and to a large extent in France. I was beginning to fall in love with the place not just liking it.

Along with this intellectual freedom came others; the ability to dress as you wished or to go out with friends for a drink or have a night out with girls because you enjoyed their company. None of this would attract glares by people who wondered what Markesinis father might say had he known this or that. His benevolent shadow – but shadow nonetheless – was simply not present. I was alone but, repeat, not lonely. Georges Moustaki expressed this idea well in one of his beautiful songs "je ne suis jamais seule avec mon solitude." He was not and neither was I.

For a long time in Cambridge I was thus totally unknown and un-observed and only began to be noticed as the years went by and eventually moved into the professorial role. Then, it became my duty to look after my students, anticipate their problems and, if they so asked, to help them resolve them The pastoral as well as academic duties are intertwined in Oxbridge and this, too, was something not found in Continental European Universities, not even the American ones. I benefited fully from it for in Cambridge I had a wonderful left-wing Czechoslovakian expert on Nietzsche – Dr Stern – as moral tutor and later, as law supervisors, Professors C. J. Hamson and D. G. T. Williams.

The importance of the Oxbridge tutor is difficult to describe since if he or she is conscientious he (or they since I was assigned two) follow you throughout your years at the University and truly act *in loco parentis*. Large American and European Universities all possess brilliant scholars. But the moral tutor/ subject supervisor is absent and in my subsequent years as teacher in the USA I tried to perform all these functions myself with the result that I made some wonderful friendships with younger colleagues. I stress these points as much as I can for, as I said at the beginning of this chapter, education is not only a matter of imparting much information on a young person. Helping him find it, training him to evaluate it, encouraging him to discuss it with you and disagree with the views of, even, Aristotle let alone you, his contemporary and very humble teacher was a true service given to those who were willing to receive it as I had been when at their age.

The most difficult of freedoms gained was to learn how to arrange my time as I wished but also in a manner which was efficient. If I wanted to play games or go punting up the river all day I could, provided I attended the agreed lectures and tutorials and produced my homework on time.

To be sure, I no longer had the purely social and utterly boring obligations I had in Athens, - cocktails, funerals, weddings, christenings, and the like which I loathed greatly and still do so. But there were other activities which lay claims on my time and one was attending the Cambridge Union and observing how the young Brits were gradually trained in the art of public speaking. For here, through observation week after week, one saw young men and experienced speakers talk for and against a proposition using humour, logic, rhetoric, sarcasm but above all a well-constructed, under-stated argument to win the final vote which always took place at the end. There is hardly an English Prime Minister who went through Oxbridge and did not participate in such debates. A better preparation for what was to come later – Prime Minister's question time in Parliament – there could not be.

The late sixties were also years of sexual and dress liberation. In both old taboos fell, new ideas became fashionable only to be replaced in time by others, usually more exaggerated. I went with the flow even when I did not like much of what I saw simply in order to empty my mind from the preconceptions of a different society and, in particular, the Athenian bourgeoisie whose strictures I loathed then as I do now.

The anti-Vietnam movement was, in those days, also producing music which my conservative ear did not find attractive. But Eugenie, still not my wife, and much younger had a collection of Simon and Garfunkel and Joanne Baez discs which I learned to like with the passage of time. Tastes as well ideas change once abroad on your own; and if your early training at home was right you knew how to separate yourself what was new but unattractive from what was interesting though totally novel.

The music of the time was the first step. But it took more time to change my views on the desirability of that American War in Viet Nam for like most conservatively brought up Greeks I saw it as a war against spreading Communism, which in one sense it was, but not as a reckless overseas venture that caused more harm than good to America's interests and standing in the world which it also did. My unquestioned faith in America was changing as, indeed, was my undiluted affection for that country itself. But all this is far too important to trace and explain as part of my maturation so I may allude to it later. The important think to note – and I understand this now more than I did then – was not to turn against anyone or anything but just to open your mind to new ideas and find room for them all in the list of endlessly new experiences which a prolonged stay abroad can only bring about.

It is easy to see all this as me becoming a pliable substance in the hands of a more youthful and liberal environment. But that would be too simplistic explanation to what was happening in me deep down. *For there, in the subconscious, what was happening was a constant re-evaluation of things known and liked after they had been exposed to a rigorous re-appraisal in the light of what I saw happening in another country which, I remind my reader, I always considered as my second country. My mother had made sure that I arrived there with this idea firmly planted in my subconscious.*

The end product was a shift towards a synthesis, a move away from extremism, an attempt to find my own niche that would give me the maximum possible satisfaction at the minimum amount of inconvenience to others. Live and let live was a better way than the Greek saying "your death is my life". Understanding on the basis of wider and different factual information could lead to changing one's views; could even give birth to a supreme gift: tolerance. Why such rancour? There is room for all of us; and for good people there is always room at the top!

This may sound as logical and even good. To a large extent it was for it gave a plan to my life. But it was also self-centred in that it led me constantly to think how I could profit to the maximum possible extent from this privilege of being in such a unique centre of learning and prove worthy of my name and country. I was enjoying myself hugely but had not sight of the fact that I was in Cambridge not just to enjoy myself but to enlarge my education and begin building a career.

This over-emphasis on "me" led me to ignore the growing gathering of clouds back home where the first easy years enjoyed by the Junta were beginning to disappear as the economic boom was replaced by harsher economic conditions at the end of the decade while the "locals" – to begin with amazingly undisturbed by and placid over the violation of the constitutional order – began to voice (carefully) their first grumbles and concerns.

Physically closer to me at the time was a young Greek who suffered as a result of the troubles experienced by his father back at home. His name was Stephanos Pesmatzoglu, Professor I believe now at the Pantios University. Though Stephanos received much understanding and succour from the College for his understandable psychological tribulations, he got no signs of interest from me, no effort to stand by him and boost his sagging moral as I should have done as a fellow Greek. To be sure, Stephanos was not a "friend" in the technical sense of the word but just a social acquaintance and much younger at that. Still, when I cast my mind back to this sad moment, I feel I could and should have stood by him, figuratively speaking held his hand, been "nice". Instead, I did nothing and just selfishly remained focused on my work.

"Though shalt not kill but need not strive officiously to keep alive." So wrote almost two hundred years ago the Victorian poet Arthur Clough. Yet inaction can, at times, be almost as bad as wrong action. Egocentricity on my part must have been partly to blame since I was so absorbed by furthering my career to have no time to spare to help a suffering younger Greek. Worse, perhaps, was the fact that my father and his had fallen out in earlier times in the context of the self-destructive political game which never ends in Greece. I suspect the real reason for this disagreement was, in part at least, that they both had big ego's. Ideologically, at any rate, I do not think there were any real grounds to justify a quarrel between them; but calm and rational disagreement is near impossible in Greece!

As stated, I now reflect back on this episode and find that though I may not have done anything wrong I did not behave "properly" either, at any rate according to the highest standards which my mother always tried to impose. Most certainly my indifference to Stephanos' plight was inexcusable for, as stated, he was a fellow Greek, young, alone, and deeply troubled as anyone in his position would have been. I felt this moral lapse even more acutely when, some twenty years later, his father, who had earlier tried to get me a scholarship to Harvard, was now one of those who actively pushed my candidacy at the Greek Academy and even made a special point of coming up to congratulate my mother who was in the congregation assembled in the big Aula.

What is the use of admitting to a mistake now? It is too late, except, perhaps, in leaving him and his absolutely charming mother Miranda feeling proud at their family's impeccable behaviour towards me. It hurts to err and even more to realize it; but admit to a mistake one must, and I do. My only consolation is that it takes courage to do so in public.

Eclecticism

Let me conclude this chapter by touching on two more themes. The first is eclecticism, and my undying desire to find and use the best in everything. I liked it and still do so for I have come to believe that the whole of one's life is a constant series of choices as we move, *par elimination*, towards our pre-destined end. The idea was to become a central theme of my work in Comparative law where by definition I was meant to compare legal systems which, in essence, required, if it was to be done well, a comparison of states and their wider cultures and values. This required an enormous amount of work' but work was not enough. It had to have a theme, preferably a new theme, in order for me to make at least some kind of contribution to my subject.

In the end the solution came by deciding to adopt an intellectually revolutionary approach. Why not stand things on the head? Why not begin and end by doing what others had been either denying or avoiding? In short why not search for the hidden similarities that existed between legal systems and not keep harping upon their differences which were over-obvious? After all were not similar societies facing similar problems and needs? This suggested similarity of results if not similarity in the reasoning process which leads to analogous solutions.

Years of effort had to go into this work; and it survived because I was lucky enough to gain the intellectual support of some great judges in my second country such as Lords Denning, Goff, Bingham, Woolf, and Steyn and of some equally great Germans, notably Walter Oderski, former President of the German Federal Supreme Court for Civil and criminal matters – the Bundesgerichtshof – the President of the German Constitutional court, Professor Juta Limbach and the First President of the French Cour de Cassation Guy Canivet. Aaron Barak from Israel also belonged to the group of like-minded judges; and in his judicial and teaching work at Yale he often talked about legal borrowings.

The gamble which began in the mid-seventies in Cambridge finally paid off. Important German scholars such Christian von Bar, my pupil in Cambridge for brief time but not too brief to fail to fill me with admiration for his idea of a European Code, Stephan Lorenz in Munich, the late – alas - Hannes Unberath in Iena and Bayreuth, Joerg Fedtke at Tulane – both outstanding and dearly loved pupils along with Angus Johnson, now a Fellow of University College Oxford, Justice Martin Kessen, a former pupil of mine in Texas and now a Judge at the Court of Appeal of Cologne (seconded to the Supreme Court), Simon Deakin, FBA, one of my most admirable students and dear friends, Guido Alpa and Vincezo Zeno Zenkovitcz, both in Rome, and many others took up this new challenge and brought it to the much more advanced stage that it was when I began teaching it myself in Cambridge in 1974/5.

In Cambridge in short the process of transformation of the chrysalis into a butterfly began. The multiple parental teachings, assisted by the new stimuli, and the realization of my own weaknesses and errors helped complete this transformation or, as Ovid would have described it more poetically, a metamorphosis. I hope it was a metamorphosis for the better; but in personal matters one is the least good judge one's own strengths and weaknesses.

Cambridge and England were thus turning points in my life. But my exposure to new ideas, habits, and ways of thinking was not going to stop there. "Restlessness", says Goethe in *Faust* "is the only way one can prove one's worth"; and I was destined by my fate to be restless both mentally but also physically.

The next move was to occur in the late seventies when, during one night in 1970 while the storm was raging Mephistopheles engineered a call from Cornell. At the other end of the phone was Dean Peter Martin enquiring if I would like to visit them and teach there for a semester.

The initiative in fact had come from the famous Yale Law Professor now Judge) Guido Calabresi with whom we share common interests and whom I had got to know quite well during his visit in Cambridge during the previous year as Goodhart Professor. Senior academics are often asked in the USA to suggest how vacant places should be filled by other Faculties and he kindly put my name forward.

The offer of Dean Martin was very flattering but it took me by surprise. I asked for time to think about it and the Dean mistook this as a bargaining posture so he immediately offered to increase the remuneration suggested. It was simply gorgeous so I accepted on the spot though postponed my visit by a year since I had accepted an offer to teach for a year at the Sorbonne. I stayed at Cornell for four years repeating every autumn my seven week visit and teaching to ever growing classes. My last class numbered 135 students including a score of 'auditors'. Indeed, such was the success that I was offered the chance to be considered for a permanent post now that there appeared to be a real need for the subject - made famous by Rudi Schlesinger - seemed to have arisen. But this time I could not say "yes". England was my home and neither I nor Eugenie was prepared to give it up. So a new phase of a peripatetic life began, all made possibly because by now I had become known in America thanks to Cornell and Judge Guido Calabresi. A short visit to Harvard followed and then two terms in Michigan in Ann Arbour.

Thirty years have elapsed since that first visit to the USA and in addition to the above-mentioned centres of learning I have taught at Berkeley (as the guest of Professor John Fleming), Tulane (as the guest of Professor Thanassis Yiannopoulos) and Texas (as the guest of Professor Charles Alan Wright and Dean Page Keeton). The last University in fact decided in 1997 to make my visits regular by offering me (for the first time ever in the history of that Faculty) a tenured chair even though they accepted that I would only be part time in Texas. So, since then, every year, once or twice depending on my other commitments, I spend seven to twelve weeks (in total) in the USA teaching three or four different classes to what I have always found was a very appreciative audience.

The new world has been stimulating and generous and kind to me, especially its youth. Yet the country has also been different and, more importantly, changed a great deal, especially during the last ten years or so of my visits there. I alluded to some of these in the previous chapter and the reader will have noticed that I did not favour this switch to an unbending conservatism. I thus moved to the side which about fifty percent of Americans – the Democrats not the Republicans - also seem to prefer. Who is right and who is wrong? Maybe we all are a little bit right and wrong. Still, living in America these days' means getting used to living in a deeply divided country with extreme tendencies and that, I feel, is sad. More than sad, for in my years abroad I had managed to shake off most of my Greek predilections towards extreme positions so I could not face up them again in my life. Because this change proved decisive in the evolution of my ideas I will revert to it indirectly below when I discuss immigration

Character formation

My second theme is education as a medium of character forming. Early Greek education mainly took this form. Memorising Homer, appreciating his terse style and impartiality, understanding his many moral and social adages about duties to one's parents, to the gods, to the country were the key things the young would be expected to digest while growing up in the company of older sages. In later years, Virgil's *Aeneid* did the same by teaching that duty towards one's country was the supreme legacy of the Roman world to posterity.

From the second half of the 5th century BC education in Athens became more structured with the appearance of the School of Sophists. The emphasis here was mainly on argument and thus likely to assist citizens in performing before judges or in the popular assembly. But the early sophists were great thinkers, paid much attention to the varying meanings of words, and formed de facto a group of high flyers citizens who exercised a huge influence on social behaviour. To be sure all this did not last long as the unending war with Sparta began to take its toll; the Athenians got dispirited, cynical, divided as Euripides and Aristophanes most than others reflected this decline in their works.

This is not a book about the ancient educational system but it does make a distinction between education which enhances human knowledge, education which teaches people how to argue – and in later years Aristotle in his *Rhetoric* and Cicero in his *Ars Oratoria* completed our instruction on the subject. But one might ask: does education make good people or good citizens? A glance at societies in moments of crisis shows us that this not the case. A simple legal example may be as good as any, not least since it comes from one of the areas of professional interest: law.

In the 1920's because of the hyper-inflation experienced by Germany society fell into a state of dislocation. From an unpromising paragraph in the Code, - 242 BGB - cleaver and educated judges interpreted contracts in accordance with "good faith" and thus felt free to adjust the mutual promises if one had become grossly imbalanced as compared with the opposite one. Paying off a mortgage with seriously devalued money was grossly unfair to the lender. The judicial innovation, however withstood the passage of time and, together with Reichsbank, they finally brought inflation under control.

The floodgates of para 242 BGB, however, had be opened and in the mid 1930' as national socialism began to take root, the same highly educated judges would use this wide escape clause – "good faith" to justify impermissible interference with citizens' rights. It was called the "flight into the General clauses of the Civil Code". Paragraph 836 was another such clause which referred not only to good faith but the unidentifiable notions of *boni mores*. The judges who used such clauses to serve the new perverse regime were intelligent and inventive; but their legal ingenuity did not make them good citizens nor good people. Education, alone, this does not – necessarily - produce good people.

This is the danger character forming wishes to avoid. Whether it is instilled through sport and teaching the players that one must never cheat and what matters is having a good game and not, necessarily winning, is the point I already made. Imparting such ideas at home and in subtle way by the state organs themselves can make a difference. In a strange sort of way, this may even be the best education one can give to the young. Make then distinguish good from bad behaviour and observe the former. This, too, is education but of a different kind.

Would I have made such a statement in my later-teens decades ago? I think not out of ignorance rather than bad intentions. Yet now I have little doubt that character forming education is, from society's point of view, *the most valuable of the two*. For character formation helps win with modesty and loose with decency. Character education, often formed through sports, helps you realise that fighting well and losing is as good if not better than winning by any means. Character education teaches you loyalty to your country, to your team, to your friends, and reminds you that you must stand by them when they need your help most. Character education teaches one how to be tolerant towards human conduct, even if one disapproves of it, by making a serious effort to understand the motives and pressures which may have led you fellow human being fall below accepted standards. Character education is learning that vengeance is self-destructive, forgiveness is a divine gift. Finally, in moments of civil crisis of the kind most European countries experience in some form of another these days, citizens must realise that, ultimately, the most difficult duty imposed upon them is to discover how best they can serve their own country; and this may need reflection and is not necessarily found in the easiest option that presents itself in the mind of the individual who is called upon to act. In short, doing one's duty requires one to understand clearly what precisely it is that he should do. Our key word – understanding – pops up again in the book as it does in real life.

Chapter Four

STYLE, MANNERS, GENEROSITY, CHARACTER, FAMILY COHESION

Style

The Shorter Oxford English Dictionary offers, among others, two definitions for the word style both of which are relevant to this chapter.

First, style is defined as a "mode of deportment or behaviour". Second, and not unrelated again to present purposes, is the definition of style as "a matter of discourse or tone of speaking adopted in addressing others or in ordinary conversation." Finally, we can bring under the term "style" all "those features of literary composition which belong to form and expression rather than the substance of the thought or matter expressed".

Because of its special significance, this last point may have to be considered separately. So here we shall deal only with the remaining parts of these definitions.

Many often associate style with class but in my view the above definitions do not support this conclusion. More linked to style is education as this is indirectly stated in the second of the above definitions but then this is more appropriate to the manner of written expression than that of "deportment and behaviour" which figure prominently in the first. My view is that if the emphasis is placed on "deportment and behaviour", and we treat the other definition as being limited to the form of written or oral communication, then "style" can be disassociated from both class and education and related just as easily to charm, comportment towards others and consideration for others. Manners, one might even say and attitude in general towards humans in general.

My interpretation of the words used by the dictionary definitions thus enables me to find style even among ordinary folk, poor and un-educated, and why not unless we begin with a preconceived idea of what style is and where only we may find it. Such a narrow approach does not conform to my experience in life.

Of course, I may well be wrong; yet both when at home in England and when working abroad I spend much time talking to ordinary people found in what might somewhat pejoratively be described as low class coffee shops or bars. If I frequent such places it most commonly is because I like their coffee, their low class edibles - such as jam doughnuts - and above all talking to the servers and, occasionally, the fellow patrons for such conversations keep my feet firmly on the ground by listening to their every-day, un-affected wisdom of the ordinary folk.

In the USA, where I spend annually between forty five to ninety days, the servers are invariable young students working long hours to make some money on the side so as to complete their education. This makes it easier to talk to them being, as I see myself, a retired teacher/ mentor – in the best tradition of an Oxbridge tutor. But it also gives me the chance to "empathize" (not just sympathize) with them since in their daily struggle to survive – always presented in an understated and dignified manner – I see many of the agonies which also affected my own children when they were at the same phase of their lives. In addition, I see in their effort to make a living, often in very posh hotels – for instance the Four Seasons in Austin – these poor youngsters constantly being alert to the risk that their very wealthy clients will attempt to 'slip' away faking that they forgot to settle their bill. The way these 'girls' – for more often than not these 'servers' are young female students - catch up with these frauds and the way they handle them must be seen to be believed. At the very least it reveals who has the style in addition to the physical ability to give a chase: the rich crook or the poor server? I thus have no doubt that style can be found and often is so found among pour people of the so-called – an awful term – lower classes which are anything but low, just disadvantaged.

It is thus an immensely humbling and salutary experience when you are forced to compare youngsters of approximately the same age and realize how privilege and parental assistance can make life so much easier for those who are lucky enough to have both. I worked hard enough to give to my own off spring the above advantages. Through oral advice and discreetly carried out but generous tipping, I have systematically over a period of thirty four years tried to help likewise my Cornell, Michigan, and Texan young servers. I have just about convinced myself that I do this not just to pacify my conscience but because forty seven years as a teacher I have come to care very deeply for those placed in my charge and felt doing what I was – and now writing about it - represents the most valuable service I have been able to offer to society in this particular context.

If I find all these people interesting to talk to it, it is not because of the high cultural content of our discussions – though often one hears pearls of wisdom from quarters which one least expects to produce them - but because of the common sense found in their views, my need to be aware of what ordinary hard- pressed folk feel about the society they inhabit and, last but not least, because – without exception – in these endless talks I have found my interlocutors stylish in the sense I re-defined the term above. For my interest in them, manifested not so much in the form of financial assistance but a genuine desire to converse with them, has always been rewarded with charm, consideration, and a remarkable will to show gratitude and generosity in return to what little I do for them. For forty six plus years I never left any of the hotels I stayed without a card signed by all – and I mean all – who looked after me and with compliments which, frankly, have moved me more than anything ever said by my professional colleagues.

I suspect that not many in England would share these views but many do both in the USA, Italy, France and Greece where I follow the same practice. In fact such behaviour towards human beings almost invariable eliminates the bad (and undoubtedly wide-spread habit) of some of them working in the restaurant business to cheat with the accounts. Thus, in the Piazza Navona, that temple for Italian restaurant cheating, after two or three visits in the same place where I had been "cheated" with the change or the pricing I ended up being "treated" by the petty fraudsters to a free glass of beer or, better still, a wonderful chocolate gelato, and few things can exceed in taste of Italian gelati! Show someone you respect him and he will return the favour. Socrates and again Socrates: Ουδείς εκών κακός.

Now nothing would be further from my mind than to try to present myself as a latter-day Gladstone out, at the end of every day's hard work, on a moral mission. If I love meeting them it is because talking to them gives me much pleasure. I raise, however, all these points for one more reason related to the overall aim of this work. And frankly it is to suggest that as our societies are all increasingly – to be sure not totally but, as stated, increasingly - populated by one class - the middle class – the risk of losing style is not lost but may even be increased given that the tone of our world is these days provided by the members of this middle group of citizens. And it is my firm belief that these people, like most human beings, will reciprocate courtesy, care, and even friendship to all you offer them and more. So, even if the upper classes may no longer dominate our world style can survive if we who value the attribute display it towards ALL that we meet. Thus, the more I have such experiences the more they make me rethink and question the traditional association of style with nobility of birth, savoir faire and even education and ask my readers to reflect what are the true components of style. Their discovery might then give us a yard stick which not only cuts across classes but also diminishes perceptions built on national characteristics. In this search I would thus recommend attention is paid to the following attributes of the individual when considered for the title of stylish.

First comes his dislike to publicize titles, nobility of birth, wealth or achievement. The more lightly an individual carries his gifts and talents with which nature endowed him the more stylish I would tend to regard him to be. My own vanity towards matters of learning and culture, alas, makes me 'slip' on this requirement; but I instantly recognise the error and regret it.

Second, much attention should be paid to one's ability to make interlocutors of whatever social background feel at ease in one's presence. This attribute will be enhanced if it is found in the treatment accorded to those who are especially weak financially or intellectually. Towards them humility, genuinely felt and sincerely displayed must be shown. It is not condescension that one is looking for; but style which subtly eliminates all signs of difference and treats the unequal as equal as he or she no doubt is as a fellow human being.

Third, admirable is the willingness to assist those in need and do so quietly, discretely, secretly, without ostentation and, above all, without any expectation of a reward. I know of at least two British academics – no longer alive - who did just that to two Central European émigrés who arrived destitute in Cambridge just before the beginning of the Second World War. No single Oxbridge colleague can identify the donors and the beneficiaries for the information reached me in the most reliable but also confidential manner. What is remarkable, however, is that the support they gave to these subsequently very eminent colleagues extended to financial assistance; and I wonder how many of my readers can relate many examples of such generosity. The help, however, they gave ended up by being fully returned by loyalty and success in their chosen professions. For a mentor, the knowledge that his backing has produced a positive result is a huge satisfaction. I often wonder at the extent of the pleasure one might experience to have been able to boast that one had done something like that oneself!

Fourth, simplicity of manners, speech and written communication are infinitely preferable to contrived behaviour or exaggerated use of language. Comparing written styles has always fascinated me, not least because I always hoped that by doing this I might pick up some good hints. In the educated English style of the first half of the 20th century I have found the style I most admire; for it is succinct, avoids unnecessarily exaggerated words or expressions, while having escaped from the earlier and at times over-sentimentalised Victorian language of the previous century. I can claim a modest amount of reading of the European literature and I honestly feel that such attributes as I mentioned above have only been encountered in the writings of Homer or, to refer to a slightly more modern and thus slightly easier Greek namely of the writers of the second half of the 5th century BC.

Finally, a well turned out but modest and un-ostentatious attire can help complete the picture of inner modesty and decency in so far as it confirms the individual's desire to be good in substance and not appear important through his choice of accoutrements, be they expensive or exaggerated for both present the same character default: more often than not, they have been chosen because they help show off the person who wears them. More about this later on but here suffice it to stress that all signs of narcissism usually conceal personal insecurity, an uncontrolled desire to be noticed and admired, and if the considerable psychiatric literature on the subject is anything to go by, maybe even a host of sexual problems.

Manners

It must be obvious from the above that the attributes I value are linked to individual not social or national characteristics and would therefore discredit generalizations that race X unlike Y oozes style race W has no manners. This, of course, is not how most people think; but it represents my views and above all fits in the general thesis of this book since once upon a time would often encounter people who would come silly phrases such as "Americans are so rude" or "Scots are all tight-fisted" and the like – all statements which stem from prejudice or animosity or plain error and doing nothing to promote easy co-habitation of nations and races in the world.

Indeed, on this issue and relying heavily on my extensive experience of people from different ethnic backgrounds I feel compelled to extend the applicability of theory to include Poles, Russians, Jews, Armenians, Arabs, Persians, Indians, Ugandan Indians, and Chinese. The existence of good manners among all the nations I just mentioned is thus not just a personal and firm conclusion but also one which suggests, once again, either a growing convergence among the attributes of different nations or, at the very least, our belated realisation that this is so and should not be denied on the basis of imposed preconceptions instilled in our minds by our own individual backgrounds.

Reference to Parisian taxi drivers, admittedly often unbearably arrogant if not rude, can help bring out my point, though it would be taking things too far if one then extended such generalizations to all Parisians or, worse still, to all French. Indeed, one should close this particular item by noting that taxis – which are very cheap in Paris compared to other major towns – are frequently driven by people who hail from former French colonies in North or Central Africa – who I mention of only to stress that they are often among the most polite and obliging one comes across.

As for the rest of France – the South which I know moderately well since I spend some two to three months every summer – I find them to be a population of exceptional warmth, perhaps because of their often mixed Spanish French or Italian French backgrounds. This compliment, of course, has nothing to do with the fact that when I am in my natural stomping grounds of Maussan les Alpilles or St. Rémy de Province I find myself kissed – three times – by anyone with whom I have even the slightest dealings!

Observance of manners in my mind contains observance of two separate set of rules of human behaviour.

First, is the observance of social etiquette which is aimed to make daily intercourse easier and more civilised. The "please", the "thank" you, the 'not butting in' the conversations of others, or not 'monopolizing exchanges at social gatherings', the not 'jumping the queue' and, if caught, pretending to have acted accidentally, the helping the aged, the 'natural and not contrived courtesy towards women', the more than usual empathizing with the poor and needy, are all found in well-run societies and help round off the good image projected by its citizens.

To return to my taxi cab example, British cabbies tend to attract compliments on all of the above points, leaving far behind the majority of their French and Greek counterparts, though even the latter, if you know how to touch 'their sensitive chords', can instantly reveal an endearing warmth and care in your well-being. I have tested this on numerous occasions when I have asked French and Greek taxi drivers to bear with my relative immobility because of my two hip and two knee surgeries. All – but, truly, all – have responded with concern and warmth; indeed, many of these 'rough' taxi drivers immediately get out of their cab to help me get in and out. After all, what all these people are trying to do is to earn a decent daily wage working in an extremely harsh environment; and it may this that should take a large part of the blame for their occasional abrupt or inconsiderate behaviour. These mini-social experiments of mine only go to prove over and over again one of my deepest convictions that if you are good to people invariably they are good to you; and this does not depend in which country you are in.

The professional etiquette is, by contrast, imposed by the person's profession and not society at large. I am thinking here of lawyers, accountants, doctors and other professionals who each have their own list of does and don'ts which ensure that their profession is held in high esteem.

The British or, at any rate, the old fashioned British attitude to use in hospitals the surnames instead of first names helped – in my view – maintain the professional relationship at the right level of formality and indirectly also made it difficult from requesting favours from one's professional advisers which might border on the prohibited. On this score, I see no difference between British, Germans and French but disapprove the speed with which in England – not in France or Germany - the relationship slides from a professional one into a "chummy" level. In Greece the moment a relationship slides into this kind of gear it is only a matter of time before "favours" begin to be asked and understood on a reciprocal basis i.e. the doctor will not charge a wealthy by 'important' client but the latter, especially if he be a politician, will be expected to favour the doctor in return.

The overall evaluation of style and manner of in different countries and whether each believes it exists in the other can only be assessed in two stages. The first is to define what we mean with this word and then, secondly, to gauge to what extent the British believe this exists in other countries with which they have regular dealings.

We attempted to set some parameters to the first question but when we set it in an international setting the issue becomes merged with that of honesty and reliability (notions not immediately obvious as necessary components of "style").

To the extent that the above do cross people's minds, the answer becomes more difficult and, probably, more negative as the British involvement moves eastwards but also westwards, namely New York! For there, bribery and corruption, at a personal or institutionalized level, are encountered, adherence to agreements can become dodgy, political interference even in purely commercial transactions more frequent and thus the possibility of unpleasant experiences grows substantially. Talking of the Middle East in particular, a long colonial history has accustomed many British to cope with such "local difficulties" but even this is becoming increasingly complicated as our contemporary demands for transparency make it more difficult and more dangerous to keep the "machinery of foreign transactions" well oiled! Greece and Russia can be included in this list; I have ample personal experience for the first, hearsay evidence for the second. In practice this can mean that the potential investor must come prepared that if his proposal for an investment is to be accepted he must have made allowances for a 'bribe component'. In Greece this is apparently known and used extensively by German companies trying to penetrate the market while it is in its present doldrums. On-going but unresolved trials suggest as much. Nothing spectacular, however, has thus far been proved conclusively, not least because Germany has not been forthcoming with its needed assistance.

The consequence of all this however on the topic here considered must, surely, be that the British citizen dealing with foreigners are unlikely to regard foreigners as easy to do business with and, to that extent it is very likely that their own ideas of probity, reliability, and style will not be easily satisfied. I am sorry to maintain that such feelings usually stem from prejudice. The very opposite will, however, happen when dealing with Europeans such as the Germans or the Dutch where reliability is a byword of these nations trading histories. As for the aberrant Greeks, the main reason for such comportment must lie in the fact that the country suffers from one major defect: it belongs and is seen to belong, both to the East and the West so unreliability, bureaucracy, bribery, and delays will only temporarily be removed out of sight of the foreigner while his potential Greek "partner" will be displaying his usual charm and hospitality. That may be a good start; but after the opening gambits, my advice is "caveat Brit!" for you are on slippery ground.

The answer to the second question above cannot be fleshed out in the absence of hard statistics. But, if here by style we mean gentlemanly demeanour and mental attitude, the Britton operating above will often be pleasantly surprised if an when he happens to deal with the very highest echelons of the foreign country. This includes the usually "suspect" Middle East and Far East where both I and friends who operate in the financial business across the world have often come across individuals whom the most demanding of Englishmen would have no hesitation of describing as a "gentleman". These "specimens" however, especially as one moves eastwards, are likely to be found among the higher strata of those societies, older people and often among them their progenies who have been educated in the West, invariably, at British public schools or American Ivy League Colleges.

Without going into individual case studies I think one cannot be more specific than that.

Generosity

Giving/ helping can be institutionalized or be treated entirely as an individual matter and disposition. The first type of generosity is encountered on a huge scale in the USA and though often stemming from a deep-rooted (and, it must be admitted, admirable) desire to "give something back" to society, or more often, the institution that "trained/ educated" the donor, it has increasingly become so refined and well-tuned through the assistance of generous tax laws that it can also be seen as a means of obtaining financial benefits and or social standing rather than being truly charitable in its origins. To this motive, useful to the donee but hardly laudable in general terms, we must add the satisfaction which stems from personal vanity. Universities and Museums have thus become experts in exploiting these human weaknesses offering a range of "rewards" which invariably take the form of naming rooms, atria, lecture halls and entire buildings after the donor. Thus the bigger the donation the bigger the space designated by the name of the donor and the more obsequious [sic] the behaviour displayed towards him and his family by the higher officials of the receiving institution. Indeed, this must be experienced to be believed is the politest thing I can say about it! A more accurate description, however, is that it takes the form of pure, unadulterated grovelling to the super-rich! It is so tempting to say more, but I must resist.

Thirty four years in the USA has accustomed me to this ritual courtship between donor and donee and though the results have undoubtedly enabled American educational and cultural institutions to rise in importance, on a human level these "giving rituals" can, as stated, be quite disgusting. I express my dislike here not just because I have witnessed the above in my long years at different American institutions but also because, in a minor way, I indulged in such shameful activities myself during my fund-raising days as Professor in Leiden, London, Oxford and Austin, Texas. Alas, I know what I am talking about!

In neither of these centres of learning is the "behaviour and techniques as repulsive (or, one might say, as developed!) as they can be in the USA; nor are our achievements in this country as impressive though we are consciously moving in that direction. Personally, I found my engagement in such activities eye-opening in so far as it revealed to me the amazing vanity of successful people who, no matter how successful they may be, remain always hungry for varied public recognition. At the same time, however, this was an occupation which distracted me enormously from my prime interests: teaching and research since so much time has to be spent identifying donors and then convincing them to part with their money. On the plus side, however, I can claim to have played the major part in setting up the Oxford Institute of European and Comparative Law which was officially inaugurated by the then German Vice Chancellor and Foreign Minister Dr Klaus Kinkel.

Personal giving/generosity is another matter; and in my view it is at its best when it is not put in a societal framework but undertaken individually and with the minimum of publicity. Less attractive, to me at least are the usual charitable lunches or other gatherings run by idle ladies in the counties, each promoting her favourite though often highly laudable cause and also filling their (otherwise) intellectually empty lives. Obviously, in terms of volume of support provided these are smaller operations; but having become personally or through (Greek) friends directly involved in a few instances I can testify to the feeling of well-being that such acts of unrewarded generosity have generated to all who even indirectly became involved in them. Incidentally, I remind my readers of my earlier comment that giving discreetly without expecting anything in return, is also a sign of admirable character and style. The problem is, however, that in none of the activities I have mentioned this is the case.

We must again conclude briefly by asking how do "foreigners" – that is for an English observer - fair in this category?

Though institutional giving in Europe is far less advanced than it is in the USA or, even, Britain, acts of charitable giving are far from unknown. Companies and institutions who co-ordinate the funds of many smaller donors, are the most typical givers who take the form of Foundations. This, for instance, is the case in Germany. Beyond a modest acknowledgement, for instance being mentioned in whatever learned paper or conference is facilitated by their gift these donors rarely demand or receive big buildings being named after them.

Much more amazing and admirable is the willingness of the British general public to respond to broadcasted appeals to help either weak categories of citizens – e.g. "children in need" – or national disasters abroad such as tsunamis, earthquakes, or natural or man-induced famines. My statistics from, say, 2010 tell me that the British public contributed to such causes a total of 11 billion pounds, a figure which now stands much higher than the aforementioned figure. Though individual giving was, on average, smaller than that recorded in 2009 – more people on the whole came forward and declare their willingness to help the needy, a remarkable result for a country which is, itself, still experiencing a severe economic down turn and is in serious need for funds to help worthy causes (such as mental illness, the homeless and other such indigenous cases of real need).

The Southern-European picture of the British being tight-fisted is thus as wrong as the equally misleading impression that they have no humour. Such misconceptions, in times of enhanced travel and communication through the internet, videos, twitter and the like are remarkable and make one wonder why the modern methods of massive communication have not been used more effectively by governments to improve or alter their image abroad.

In Greece, the ship-owning fraternity, which is both admired and disliked, has traditionally been very generous towards their own island communities from which the hail; and such giving has often been accompanied by smaller gifts to needy causes or individuals. Unfortunately, as hinted, the attitude in Greece itself towards ship-owners has been mixed, coloured – or should one say shaded – by the extravagant display of wealth by a small section of this community but also marred by political propaganda from various left-inclined quarters. Jealousy and short-sightedness – often political - have thus combined to prevent Greek governments from developing this unique Greek asset – the ship-owning class - to the detriment, I think, of all. My guess is that though most of these donors will continue holidaying in Greece they will be gradually moving to major financial centres in the Far East where regulation is minimal. The Gulf States might also some of them; though the shadow of Iran will, in my view, fall heavy on them and thus decrease their apparent attractions.

Still in Greece one has to ask one final question: will private fund raising even come to the Greek educational institutions in a big way? For the time being, I think not; but despite the objections voiced above I am among those who regret having to make this prediction. Why?

My practical objection to institutionalised fund raising cannot be accomplished efficiently by academics, especially Greek academics. They do not have either the time or the know-how to carry through such operations. If Greek Universities move in that direction they should adopt the American and not the European model which is designed to attract to the University Boards more bankers and businessmen who have the know-how, the contacts, and the ability to contact and speak to donors, that use academics. This is one move that has to be made; the other is to create a tax regime which encourages charitable donations. Like so many of my views, however, I suspect this, too, will be ignored not least because the opposition reforms such as these traditionally attract from the Left.

There is a second objection to such a development but this time it is not mine but comes from the staff, usually junior staff of Universities, The fear here is that, for instance, the donor for a specialised chair might stand to gain from such a gift himself. Years of experience in the USA and England have convinced me that such a risk is not realistic and, in any evet, is controlled by carefully drafted University regulations. Connected with this assurance is one more: in my experience donors in the USA and England have never had representatives on the electoral boards and thus never have enjoyed a say in who finally gets the chair.

Were Greek academic institutions ever to overcome these 'mental blocks' – unlikely during the reign of a Left administration – their future could, almost instantly, become much brighter.

Humour and wit

If overall "grading" is allowed the Greeks and, on the whole the Mediterranean people, score worse on these topics than the English though, characteristically, they often use the words "English humour" for amusing, funny or witty statements which they simply do not understand and to which the fail to laugh! This is largely because the distinction between humour and wit is unknown to the Greek language. In Greek, for instance, the word for wit (πνεύμα) tends to be used to describe someone who is pretending to be subtle and or amusing (κάνει πνεύμα). Even the French word – esprit – does not quite convey the English meaning of wit and, in my view, this is because subtlety and concealed display of intelligence are not the ways south-erners chose to express their feelings or their views or their intellects.

Humour in the South, certainly in Greece, is thus loud – in both senses that this word can be understood - and, as the Shorter Oxford English Dictionary puts it, "it is intended to excite amusement, oddity, comicality" and, hopefully the Greeks would add, raucous laughter.

In the Mediterranean world, but not only, humour is also very of-ten, rude and, even more frequently, scatological in content. This last-mentioned feature finds an approximate parallel in the "mother-in-law" jokes which once figured prominently in the English vaudeville and pub culture but for which wider interest seems to have subsid-ed as the effects of political correctness reached these innocent pass times.

The entertainment caused by what Americans, particularly, would regard as politically incorrect statements about women, is neverthe-less still widely appreciated in various forms in Europe, more so in the South than in the North. By phrasing my thoughts in this way, how-ever, I do not wish to say that I approve of this wide-spread American "sanitizing" of daily language which virulent feminism and political correctness combined have brought into American daily talk. In my view, as in all forms of speech, the final verdict should depend on precise content, wording, and extent.

Wit, by contrast, is a much more intellectual kind of source of amusement, entertainment or a means of stressing the ludicrous in life. The Oxford Dictionary once again makes this clear by defining it as "that quality of speech or writing which consists in the apt associa-tion of thought and expression calculated to surprise and delight by its unexpectedness". Further down, the Dictionary proceeds to stress that a wit is "a person of great mental ability, a learned, clever, or in-tellectual person". The italicised parts of the definition make a point worth stressing namely, that a witty person is one "of lively fancy, who has the faculty of saying smart or brilliant things", though not necessarily only to amuse.

Words such as the above, used to define wit effortlessly bring to mind someone like Oscar Wilde and his work. This instantly also makes it clear that this is not the kind of person that is often encoun-tered in the Mediterranean world where erudition is associated with seriousness; and in Oscar Wild's very witty (but also deep) aphorism, "dullness is the coming of age of seriousness."

Wit, therefore, is something more commonly found in England even if variants of it occasionally appear – so far as I can judge – in other countries such as America and the Netherlands. The subtleness of the language and, on the face of it, its low key tone, are also features which fit in very well with the English character, its way of thought, and the tendency, at least among the most educated, for understated language. This, I find to be key feature of the English versus the Continental European, especially Southern European, way of thinking, speaking, and writing and thus, not surprisingly, it is a form of humour which is found less frequently in these countries.

The English predilection for such forms of expression, cultivated from school and public speaking at the top Universities and Professional bodies – Inns of Court, City Guilds and Parliament thus confer upon it a higher status than humour and a tendency to spend much time in preparing the apparently spontaneous explosions which embody it in its best form. Thus the display of wit is often an essential ingredient of an important public speech, indeed so essential, that we find it in frequently in parliamentary exchanges, funeral orations and, above all that most perfected of all English types of speech: the after-dinner speech.

At its best, English wit is not just unique; it is also an admirable form of externalizing amusing and even serious thoughts in a way that can leave a lasting impression (but also a lasting mental wound on its victim). The effectiveness of this message (or double entendre) is further enhanced by a feature of the English character which is the ability to externalize amusing or cynical thoughts in a straight faced-manner, wonderfully punctuated, often through the use of another rhetorical device – likewise under-used in other cultures - the pregnant pause.

Of course, all this must be achieved with the speaker hardly ever showing any signs that he is conscious of his intelligence and linguistic dexterity, a false modesty which southerners prone to pomposity are unable even to pretend. Indeed, if there is any externalized form of approval – applause of laughter for instance – the seasoned speaker will pretend surprise and brilliantly allow it to last only for a short time so that no "awkward" gap is allowed to appear in the flow of his presentation.

All that I say in fact reveals, though what one needs to do is not just indicate but stress, the enormous amount of time, effort and experience which is concealed behind such apparently effortless displays of whit and intelligence – a thought once voiced by Clement Attlee – not a gifted speaker – who accused Sir Winston Churchill of "spending the better part of his life preparing his impromptu speeches"!

On a more personal basis I also recall vividly Lord Mancroft, an old a friend of my in laws, repeating to us the contents of a reference letter he once wrote for a departing cook while making perfect use of the aforementioned rhetorical device of the pregnant pause: "Mrs X left for reasons of health…ours!"

The above illustration also demonstrates that wit is not only the product of intelligence and linguistic dexterity; it can also conceal a sting, often quite vicious not infrequently found in the kind of hyper-intelligent people who excel in the use of words, as a way of communicating feelings, enmity, annoyance, and even down- right bitchiness. Humour, is thus generally thought of as more kindly than wit. The Mancroft letter offers an excellent example of the point I just made about wit and their accompanying stings!

The late Tony Weir, a former colleague at Trinity, Cambridge and one of the most intelligent and widely read men I have ever met, excelled in such "jabs", even at the expense of some of his students, who were unable to defend themselves (though, admittedly, he used such witticisms with great relish when conversing with his immediate colleagues). Thus, on one occasion, I received from him in my capacity as Director in Studies for Law and end-of-term report which I was meant to read out to the unfortunate girl who was the butt of the following statement: "Assiduity is not Mrs X's forte; but it might become so by the time she reaches that age." Needless to say it was read out by me in the most mundane of forms such as "doing well but can do better" and thus no unnecessary offence was caused.

There is one more feature of English humour and wit which surprises, even shocks southerners, especially Greeks. It is its use in funeral eulogies, introducing a light touch which often turns around some endearing eccentricity of the deceased into a source of mirth. Comparing it with such funeral orations which I have heard or read in French, German, or Greek, the English variant may lack the grandiose style of the most pompous but undoubtedly linguistically impressive French version or the contrived – in most cases – serious to the point of dullness Greek variety.

Recourse to humour and wit in what otherwise is a serious, indeed, sad occasion may be explicable by the fact that in England such speeches tend to be made during Memorial Services, which take place sometime after the death and are meant to offer thanksgiving for the life and times of the deceased and not the funeral proper where shorter sombre speeches are combined with hope-giving religious hymns and the reading of extracts from texts of the Old or New Testament which all of us have heard a little too often to feel inclined even to reflect seriously upon them beautiful though they are. It is different, I think with beautiful hymns sung by the congregation and which, alas, are absent from the religious ceremonies of the Orthodox Church.

Character

Greeks and Mediterraneans in general tend to praise in their classical texts moderation, balance, the pursuit of the golden mean, the danger of hubris attracting nemesis, virtues in short which they are wise enough to admire but, in their daily lives, are rarely able to possess and observe. For here, under character, we find the extremes and contradictions which are inherent in the Mediterranean temperament and which can make individuals so endearing, so infuriating, and so incomprehensible to outsiders. The best way to describe them is thus through a set of "contrasts" which keen observers – dare I add lovers of the Hellenic race – must have themselves already noted.

Kindness and vindictiveness. The heights to which a Greek, Italian, Jew, or other inhabitant of the Middle East can rise in being kind, hospitable, generous and family-centred are truly remarkable. Though northerners can, of course, be found possessing such attributes as can Scandinavians and many US citizens none, it seems to me, have them developed to the same extent. This kindness really leaves the unwary foreigner breathless when it is extended to him by the poor inhabitants of villages far of the beaten track should the imaginary foreigner chose to stray in such a direction and find himself in need of help.

Sharing their meagre food supplies is thus common, and entertaining you by proudly talking of their land will often be accompanied by an amazing willingness to praise you for your knowledge of Greek even if the only word you utter is, in an obviously mispronounced manner, "good morning" or "thank you." Italians will show the same appreciation if you make the slightest effort to speak their language, in contrast with the French – at any rate the northerners – who simply cannot help themselves to hasten to correct you for getting the gender of a noun wrong or failing to give the appropriate ending to an adjective because you have made an error over the gender of the qualified noun. The way you are corrected is, in fact, ingenuously cruel since all they do is repeat your sentence, this time however without any of your errors. I adore the French, proudly claim many friends and academic benefactors; but I find this habit especially annoying given that the French are themselves so obviously contemptuous of the need to learn foreign languages. In this context, therefore, my clear favourites are the Dutch whom I regard as Europe's prime linguists.

This quite exemplary kindness of southerners is paired with a degree of vindictiveness which is exemplified perhaps, by the Corsican or Sicilian vendetta and which, in a slightly milder form, can also be found in Greece, especially in the Southern Peloponnese. In days gone by, insulting the family honour was, I think, the prime activator of such feelings; but political rivalry is nowadays a major cause for unnecessary and petty disputes that provoke a tendency to seek revenge rather than encourage the ability to forget and forgive. Revenge, in fact, was accepted in antiquity and among its advocates we find even Aristotle though he did demand proportionality. Indeed, 'revenge tragedy' figures frequently in the 5th century BC literature with Aeschylus' Oresteia leading the famous collection of plays, and closely followed – to mention only two more instances – Euripides' Medea and Hecuba. It forms a fascinating subject to trace how subsequent generations reacted to the idea of 'vengeance' but even more exhausting to note how, starting with the Stoics and culminating with Christianity, forgiveness came to be admired even more.[1]

The price paid by societies which are prone to feelings of revenge is high, not so much because they can lead to the commission of legally punishable crimes but mainly because by being so intense they tend to be so self-destructive to those who fall easily to their pray. Another price paid is the "neglect" of talented people who are not used simply because they have voted for "the other political party." To my eyes, failing to utilize talent is a sin of sorts. In a small country like Greece, where most of the talented citizens tend to go abroad and there find their recognition, to fail to use them locally represents a terrible waste talent.

Cunning and gullibility. Here is another set of contrasting mental attributes which I find more often in the South than in North of Europe and certainly in my country of birth. I am thinking of the opposite words of cunning and gullibility.

Cunning is a form of intelligence but of a kind which gives the key word shades of suspicion, desire to deceive, outwit, out-fox, usually

---

1. I attempted to trace this development in some of works on Ancient Greek literature and ideas and so, too, has Jacqueline de Romilly in her wonderful

with a self- serving motive at the back of the mind of whoever is practicing this dark craft. Intelligence and cunning can of course co-exist; and Odysseus, that archetypal Greek 'operator' epitomizes both qualities. But cunning alone pushes Greeks into being too clever by half and thus often leads them to making fools of themselves. We see this in a near-unique way – not entirely unique that is since I believe it is also found in other Middle Eastern countries – and that is in believing and promoting conspiracy theories to the point of inventing them and then elaborately and with pathos using them to explain the political world around them.

Here cunning gets confused with gullibility for in the field of politics the American talent to operate a polycentric and polyphonic foreign policy which invites disunity, false starts, and incorrect formulation of answers, leads their adversaries to a constant effort to second-guess this American phenomenon. If it stopped there, this Mediterranean hobby would not be too harmful, but it does not. In actual fact, a simple supposition will soon be developed in an unbelievable sophisticated theory which will attempt to explain one's own misfortunes or even offer to solve the world's problems in a manner which simply makes no sense.

This is the kind of thinking process which leads to the well know "reliable" theories that the late Princess Diana was murdered by the English establishment and ended only by enriching a small number of lawyers. Most Greeks are still taken in by such manifestly unattractive rubbish; and that, frankly, sits uncomfortably with their usually developed sense of intelligence and business acumen.

More importantly, the errors committed by the American intelligence regimes –the plural is intended to highlight the lack of co-ordination – combined with the rushed and apparently ill-planned overseas wars, has given a modicum of facts to those who are quick to see conspiracies hidden everywhere and continue their hobby with illustrations that can give a new lease of life to the shred of evidence which then serves as the foundation stone of building constructed out of lies and wrong suppositions.

Widely spread but legally unproved is a conspiracy theory that the Americans were planning to assassinate a former (Right wing) Prime Minister for pursing a foreign policy which was favourable towards Russia. The icing of this cake is that the Russian secret services were those who discovered the plot and warned the Greek Prime Minister to take precautions. If true, it provides an excellent example that life is stranger than fiction.

Quick to understand slow to learn. This paragraph is not based on any scientific data that I have come across it through sheer personal experience as a teacher for over forty seven years in twenty eight universities in three continents. Now this personal experience suggests that Greeks, Jews, and Armenians are among the most fast-learning students I have ever encountered. But unlike the second two, and here I must, again, add my Dutch students for whom, I have already expressed my admiration, who always had the talent to digest methodically the new information acquired Greek sloppiness failed to reach the same desired end. I suppose this suggests that the advantages of quickness of mind were thus often betrayed by superficiality, a lack of careful follow up, lack of un-hurried study, and the acquisition of gradual experience, all of which take second place to the display of superficial knowledge and a native talent of show off.

Know- all and ignorant. This set of contradictory attributes ties in with the previous mental attitude – perhaps one should call this character flaw – since it leads many Greeks to speak, indeed pontificate, often with annoying confidence, about many topics and get away with it fairly frequently until that is they come across a serious, methodical, slow-moving but sure-footed thinker such as a German or a Dutchman. Then the original confidence evaporates into thin air as their argument is smashed to pieces.

Academic examples from my career could be supplied as illustrations but the exhausting negotiations conducted by Greek politicians and civil servants with the representatives of their foreign creditors – the EU, the ECB and the IMF – which show how difficult it has been for the foreign negotiators to understand properly the Greek crises, to discover reliable figures showing its magnitude, and the time it has taken them to realize that what the Greeks appear to agree even if incorporated into national law, was either not enforced or evaded. In recent times no political party can escape this condemnation which really amounts to an accusation of deliberate lying. This state of affairs, which I do not believe I am exaggerating, has caused much harm to the image of my country of birth; I suspect huge frustration to its European partners – who are not blameless of the current economic crisis but that is another matter – and, I believe all flows from the character flaws I am trying to sketch out above. I may thus be accused of being unfaithful to Greece but I believe and will thus put it in writing that the Greeks themselves are to blame for their greatest omission of them all during the last seven or eight years of growing crisis: a true effort to make the State work as modern states should. The Greek

State simply does not for the Greek politicians have neither the imagination nor the will to make it work.

Honest and duplicitous. These contradictions of the Greek character find their source in nature, history, and environment. The first has tended towards the first attribute; the second reflected this tendency in the name of survival. Like most Greek contradictions, they usually balance out each other out and it is – important to note – for whoever is doing business with a Greek must be aware of these inherent contradictions in his character and try to bring out the best of him. This is by no means easy, especially for those who cannot understand that life, human attributes, events, are very rarely black or white but usually shades of grey. But if one takes the trouble to 'understand' the character of his Greek interlocutor he may end up building a long and mutually successful relationship and I, for one, have been aware of many such successful 'pairings' both on the family and the business front.

Anyone who has walked in the country side, somewhat along the lines of Patrick Leigh Fermor's amazing hike across pre-War Europe, visits or, better still stays, in Greek villages, will be amazed at the hospitality and sense of complete openness and honesty which goes with it. For they will be offered hospitality, share as I already stated their meagre food, allow the visit his house or roam freely on his land and in the humble abode and never for a minute think of keeping an eye on him just in case he steals one of their meagre chattels or does something improper. All such hosts will ask from their visitors and guests is to be themselves, to talk to them about themselves, make an attempt to say a few words in Greek and praise their land and its past. From the local priest to the shopkeepers, if there any, the visitor will find nothing but welcome, and unpleasant vibes will only begin to be emitted if there are signs of drugs or drunken behaviour.

Such signs of openness, based as they are on a natural sense of trust and a sense that one's visitor is a well predisposed as is his host can be found in cities as well though here, because of size, they will begin to become apparent if you encounter people more than once, e.g. you keep returning to your favourite tavern or coffee shop and take the time to talk, if only briefly, to your waiter. Incidentally, your wealth and attire will rarely make a difference as to the way you are treated unless you obviously showing off in which the Greek's egalitarianism may awaken feelings not of jealousy but of annoyance.

But Dr Jekyll instantly becomes Mr. Hyde if you give him cause to believe that you are trying to trick him. The reaction is not just because no Greek likes being outwitted; but also because your move is seen as calling for a riposte – very much in the fencing sense of the word – namely a quick response which will show you, the foreigner, who is the smarter of the two. Admit graciously or half-jokingly that you have lost, and peace will reign again upon earth; resist, and the confrontation will escalate.

This way of reaction can also be put differently. The Greek would rather give you all of what he has than feel that you cheated him out of 10% of his belongings. This is where the struggle – and it was a daily struggle in every conceivable sense – for survival during the period of the Ottoman yoke made the Greek cunning, unreliable, dishonest. For northerners accustomed from school days to notions such as that of "fair play" such debasement of attitude and comportment may seem strange. But that is because they have never really found themselves in the kind of difficult scrapes that Greeks have had throughout their history either because they had to deal with invaders or conquerors or pirates or even fellow Christians who could treat them just as badly as those who belonged to a completely different religion.

And those "outside" bounders, one had to add the "insiders", their own politicians who would behave dishonestly but unlike the British MP's, who sinned by misusing public funds for private purposes and almost instantly got punished, the Greek transgressors of the law have developed ways for making sure that the law never applies to them. Solon, Athens' great 6th century BC law giver put it beautifully when he said that "the laws resemble a spiders; web. They trap all small insects but are pierced by the larger ones who thus escape the trap." This phenomenon of applying the law – especially the criminal law – differently depending on the status of the offender infuriated Greeks from at least the days when Solon the Law-giver admitted this practice; and disgust has grown in these days as many notable individuals belong to the media, political and business classes, are suspected of wrong-doing yet constantly escape trial.

The Greek, to use a very modern expression, goes ballistic when confronted with such behaviour and, I suspect, this is partly because his up-brining – and the humbler his background is the more moral will be his general demeanour - but also, and here comes another of this Greek contradictions, if dishonesty there has to be, why should it be one sided! If the big crook can evade the law why should the smaller fry feel its full force? There is some logic in this thinking.

Take these two features together – suspicion towards the powerful and why should he be treated differently than you, the weak person –

and you begin to understand the time-honoured mistrust, animosity and the desire to cheat and trick the other side once we begin talking of the citizen and the state. Thoughts like these have often made me argue – and not I think out of excessive idealism – that (a) offer the Greek a reasonably low level of taxation; (b) keep the tax regime steady and do not alter it constantly – as all the government of recent times have been doing with alarming regularity and (c) ensure that the tax officers with whom the citizen has to deal with do not, themselves, expect bribes to approve his book-keeping and it is then more than likely that Greece would find many of its tax-collecting difficulties disappear quickly.

The conclusion of this sub-heading may strike some readers as somewhat eccentric, its judgments harsh. It is, however, consistent with two ideas which run throughout this chapter.

First, is the belief that the Greek character is full of contradictions, the product of nature but also history and environment. Second, learn how to handle the Greeks, respecting their good points, admitting that you share some of their weaker ones; do not hector them but argue calmly with them; and do yourself what you would like them to do to you. Try out this advice and, at the very least, you will encounter a race which is as good as any, maybe even more sensitive and even with a sense of loyalty that is surprising.

Where do all these contradictory attitudes stem from?

1. Some general observations

There is a certain degree of repetition in what will be said in this sub-section and what has been hinted in the previous ones or maybe repeated later on. Yet as an introduction (or summing up) it will cause no harm to put forward some suggestions that may provide a partial at least explanation for that complex topic we have discussed under the heading: the Greek character. Before we mention the three, in my view, cardinal sources which have generated these antitheses and contradictions in the Modern Greek character, we must, however, say something about the disruptive if not destructive effect which the years of Ottoman yoke – 1453 – 1821 - had on the indigenous character and traditions. This is no easy task even to contemplate let alone explore successfully not only because of its complexity but mainly because this is a book addressed to the general reader whose tolerance threshold of political and cultural history, especially if *condensed*, may be very low. Frankly, I do not blame him or her for such a reaction.

I italicized condensed for what follows involves, per force, a measure of generalization which like all generalisations is bound to contain – though I hope not too many - misleading statements or inadequately thought conclusions. In such circumstances the hope of attaining a modicum of objectivity is seriously reduced. The reason for this result as well as for my caveat lies the complexities of Byzantine history and the subsequent Ottoman occupation – the way lay and religions institutions operated; the differences between local fiefdoms; the unequally explored archaeology and art of the different regions; the fact that our knowledge is not geographically the same (for instance we know little about the Dervish movement) – all of which combine to make the picture one wishes to draw about modern Greece as it emerged from history patchy and incomplete.

To these historiographic, if I may so to describe them, difficulties, which experts in the field readily acknowledge, we must add the distortion brought about by the contemporary exploitation of history to further current state propaganda. This can be found in both opposing camps - the Greek and the Turkish not to mention the various races inhabiting the Balkans - and they only *tend to make an opaque picture even murkier*.[2] It is on the italicized words that I wish to place my main emphasis but, before I do so, I must accept the risk of making a controversial factual assertion.

Quite simply amidst the growing mêllée of refugees and economic migrants pouring into Europe it would appear that it is the Muslim entrants who demonstrate the greatest unwillingness to settle down peacefully and not create pockets of militant groups with the realm of different – now invaded - states. I stress this point for I am not aware of Indians, Chinese, Ugandans or other displaced emigrants being so unwilling to adapt to the customs and possibilities of the host country. This, I believe, probably applies to all of Europe and not just Greece.

---

2. I have drawn much of my quotations but not all the information used in these few paragraphs from Professor Speros Vryonis Jr. FAAAS masterly, detailed, and calmly phrased treatise *The Decline of Medieval Hellenism in Asia Minor and the Process of Islamization from the Eleventh through the Fifteenth Century* (1971). Since his work is extremely well documented and my intention is not to discuss facts but speculate as to the effect they had in shaping the contemporary Greek character I have resisted the temptation of adding more references or notes to my text.

The example I mentioned briefly earlier on about the new immigrants in the suburbs of Brussels illustrates my point about the change in immigrant expectations and behaviour.

Let us then begin first with some indisputable facts before we look at their subsequent political deformation through apparently scholarly and media revisionism. Though these facts refer to the earlier migrations of the Selzuk and, later, Ottoman Turks, they are characterised by the same zeal to convert the defeated local inhabitants to the religion, customs, and political aims of their conquerors.

Let us recall that the Turkish migration began from the steps east of the Caspian Sea and moved towards the furthest north-eastern frontiers of Byzantium. This did not really become noticeable[3] in Byzantium until a few decades before the fatal (for the Byzantines) battle of Manzikert in 1071 which marked the first big military retreat of the Empire. But this must not be taken to deny that patchy migrations occurred at earlier dates, at times taking a more southerly route towards Persia or modern day Iraq. This is one of the major migrations of history and like the previous one by the 'barbarians' which destroyed the Roman Empire, demonstrates aptly the destructive effects of mass migrations. We in Europe are living through the latest example and should seek in history useful lessons of what may well happen to us all.

The second and saddest feature of this rise of power of the invading Turkmen peoples and the corresponding decline of the Christian (mainly) Greeks was largely facilitated by feuding within the Byzantine Empire which peeked after the death of its last great Emperor, Basil II, known as Bulgarian Slayer, in 1025 AD. This manifested itself as a clash between the rising power of bureaucrats and intellectuals situated in the Capital – Constantinople - and the corresponding weakening of the military aristocracy based in the provinces – in western European terms we would call them the noblesse d' epé which had, until that moment, successfully discharged their role of defenders of the frontier lands, both in the East and in the Balkans.

The third, according at least to the classical historians (such as Vryonis), was the increasingly systematic weakening of the Christian Church by the Ottoman Empire before and immediately after the fall of Constantinople. In Vryonis words

---

3. I have italicised the word deliberately for, during their earlier phases – 8th, 9th century AD - these tribal invasions of Byzantine frontier lands, were small in size and, we are left to believe, without lasting effects.

"This [enforced or enticed] religious conversion and linguistic Turkification" [in Anatolia] lead to the absorption of the major portion of the Byzantine Population."

To the above, I add my own belief, widely shared in Greece, of the transformation of the Greek character in the ways described in the preceding paragraphs and chapters as a way of surviving purges, neo-martyrdoms of unbelievable ferocity, persecutions – religious and financial - of their leadership along with progressive impoverishment through systematic confiscations of private property which was then handed over to Muslim institutions or magnates. Even a number of Patriarchs did not escape death during the years of Ottoman dominance!

Four hundred years of such practices must surely make the subjugated cunning, duplicitous, sycophantic, a natural turn-coat if this was the price which he had to pay in order to survive! The Greeks so transformed became known as 'ραγιάδες'; and by common consent Greeks admit that this demeaning form of behaviour – the ραγιαδισμός - remains alive. This is the main thesis of this subsection; and it remains a plague of Modern Greek politics since many Greeks still display some of the symptoms of this character flaw in their dealing with their government and their officials. This is the very same defect which leads them to promise things to their European partners knowing full well that by instinct if not intention they will not keep their word.

It is this picture which contemporary Turkish historians have vigorously tried to amend trying to portray the Ottoman Empire as modern, non-colonial, tolerant to religions and ethnic diversity, and increasingly during the 19th century willing to introduce into its own decaying feudal structures elements of western-liberalism. The last point is correct though these imported (mainly from France) reforms did not grow well in foreign soils.

Notwithstanding the above, the way Turkish historians, with the financial support and guidance of their politicians, have proceeded to implement this revisionist policy has been both intense and admirably successful, especially since it has been combined with an enhanced role in foreign policy which was facilitated by shrewdly exploiting the end of the Cold War and thus allowed Turkey to play the role of "necessary ally" of Russia and the USA, Europe, and the rebelling Middle Eastern world. One may agree or disagree with such a policy but there is no denying of the fact that one finds in Turkey many a highly intelligent businessmen, politician, journalist and historian which makes it even more frustrating to those who like this author would like to see one day a peaceful and honest modus vivendi being invented by both sides and truly acceptable to both. For such people tend to be carried away by their power or the success of their diplomatic offensives in way which makes the idea of sensible compromises impossible in practice.

All of the above was to be expected and, beyond admiring it, nothing more need be said in a book of this kind. But in its current and continuous state of economic, political, and moral decline, contemporary Greece has generated an intelligentsia of sorts, both with Left and Right wing pre-conceptions, who have favoured this revisionist approach. This minority but well-organized group has benefited greatly by the financial assistance and political backing of a number of Non Political Non-Governmental Organizations which promote the dogma of "Atlanticism" – stay close to the USA at a time when both the approaches of Europe and the USA towards both foreign policy and economic crises are diverging – and see with a welcoming eye the growing influence of Turkey both in the Balkans and the "changing Middle Eastern world". Once again, the apathy shown by the modern Greeks, battered by a largely self-inflicted economic crisis, was also displayed during the early Turkmen migrations and, in the end, allowed the watering down of the Greekness of the flourishing merchants in what is today's western Turkish coast.

Understanding, as I have said from the very beginning of the book, is implicit in its title and it is overtly one of its main aims as explained in the first chapter. To understand the ethnic and religious divisions in Turkey, Greece, and the Balkans, the history of these countries must be put straight and the perverting influence of 'scholarly propaganda' on indigenous populations appreciated for what it achieved. More importantly I fear that many of the new immigrants, especially if Muslims, if they are settled in Thrace, they may well attempt, with the support of Turkey, to try to alter the Eastern border between Greece and Turkey.

Of course, many of these assumptions and modern reinterpretations of Ottoman attitudes towards the conquered nations may have been exaggerated in my text just as I believe are unconvincing the high political expectations which the West continues to place on contemporary Turkey, including the vain hope that it can become a genuinely democratic and multi-racial state. If, however, I have erred in my assessments I will bear the consequences and cannot be accused of hiding my doubts about the difficulties encountered in unravelling such a complex historical picture.

The above assertions, ideas, suggestions, however will only prove unconvincing to those who do not detect the twisted use of sources or ideas to build gradually the image of tolerance and justice which is currently taken place by government and historians in all Balkan and Middle Eastern states. The great bulk of citizens, Greek and non-Greek, are not, however, in a position even to detect the propaganda behind the apparently 'scholarly' historical writings. A frighteningly small number of even educated Englishmen really know next to nothing about the history of this part of the world; and one cannot blame them since it is highly complex and requires the ability to use many oriental languages as well a frequent visits to the places concerned, but not of the kind which involve lying on beautiful beaches being roasted by the hot sun.

Thus, as far as religious tolerance is concerned, the starting point is the Koran itself and its proclaimed Muslim toleration of "people with a revealed scripture". In theory this refers to Christians and Jews. In practice however this proved a deal letter if we are to judge from the many wars which Mohamet himself conducted against the Jews during his life time. For even the most elementary readers of Koranic history know how from the earliest years of the new religion – indeed while the Prophet himself was still alive – substantial persecutions took place against Jews suggesting that the "tolerance" text was more a desired aim than a principle applied in practice. Christians suffered as well during this first wave of Islamism.

More importantly, in the Greco-Turkish context, the Koranic principle of toleration was adduced from the earlier Islamic history and was never supported by the Turkish conversionary enthusiasm at the expense of Christianity. The italicised sentence is of huge historical importance and must be examined bearing this belief in mind. Such focused examination of what actually happened rather than what was in theory proclaimed by Islam – not Turkish history - is shrewdly concealed by those who, for contemporary political reasons, favour modern revisionism.

What, however, is even more surprising, at least at first blush, is that the Greek revisionists have jumped on this bandwagon of Turkish propaganda – infinitely better financed and promoted than the Greek, especially in the Universities in the USA – as part of the foreign promoted idea that neo-Ottomanism is continuing - in a modern context - the principle of tolerance which enabled it to keep for so long under its dominance so many different races and religions.

This image of the contemporary moderate Turk has been accompanied by the theory of "zero conflicts" with Turkey's neighbours brilliantly expounded with monotonous regularity by Mr. Davutoğlu even though as a doctrine it progressively crumbled. To be fair to Mr Davutoğlu his theory was shaken to its core by an unexpected event: the so-called Arab Spring. That attempt to turn an academic theory into the foreign policy of a nation was a unique experiment of its inventor and, to start with, it looked as if the doctrine fitted in well with both Turkey's revived ambitions to become a major regional power and also fitted in with contemporary USA ambitions. For it appeared at a time when the USA was beginning to grope in the dark to find allies as the Bush foreign policy dogma in the Middle East and Central Europe had begun to crumble, leaving his great country both financially and militarily in an ever-diminishing state. To put it differently, Turkey's rise, using the Davutoğlu theory was facilitated by America's downward slide while also taking advantage of Russia's pre-Putin weakness and indecision. In reality, however, this image of Turkey being a centre of stability and tolerance in the region hardly sits comfortably with the image President Erdogan has, himself, acquired in the last two years or so of his period in power.

With the above in mind, let us return once again to the idea that the above-mentioned resulting state of political and social chaos was bound to alter the character of the conquered and bemused races. This leads us to explore a number of inter-related causes for this phenomenon which are best addressed in a section of their own.

2. Specific causes explaining the plethora of contradictions in the modern Greek character

We shall look at three in ascending order of importance.

Struggle for survival. Greece is a mountainous country. A small percentage of its land offers itself to cultivation. As a country, it lacked a serious electrification program until the period after the Second World War. It was also deficient in its exploration and use of its raw materials and thus traditionally found its main source of wealth in the sea, trade, and, in later years, in tourism. Life thus remained tough for most of 19th century and a good part of the 20th. As if all this were not enough, in 1922 the small and struggling country had to face the forceful expulsion of 1.5 million Greeks living on the western coast of Asian Minor. This landed the mother country with the huge social cost of absorbing refugees amounting to almost one quarter of its own indigenous population. It struggled but it succeeded! Comparison with how California faired with its South-East Asian émigrés in the seventies, or Texas is coping now in the light of growing difficulties from its under-belly, are instructive for they suggest that what the Greeks accomplished in the 1920's with NO resources was little short of a miracle!

Such harshness in the social environment assisted the modern variant of the "acquired" or "inherited" habit to alternate between being passive or rebellious, to cow-tow and submit or stand up, to cheat and evade and yet under normal circumstances to be generous and kind.

All forms of authority – the student towards his professor, the peasant towards his priest, the citizen towards the state representative - have traditionally throughout Greek history, been treated with suspicion but also flattered or politically supported, for the sake of a favour, survival, religious salvation or, nowadays, for the sake of obtaining posts and other such financial advantages from those in power. The natural tendency of the Greek towards freedom from restraints – political, intellectual, emotional – was, once again, subordinated by the vicissitudes of life. To criticize such surrender is easy; to understand if not excuse it difficult; but the effort has to be made.

Yet the insincere and unstable nature of this kind of obedience is obvious from the rapidity with which such "allegiances" and voting patterns change when a regime, or the term of office of an individual, is seen to be approaching its end and a new strong man is appearing on the scene. But change or not, the fact remains that a relationship of "clientelism" along the lines described above reveals the very real danger of favours being (literally) bought or, to put it differently, economic corruption becoming embedded in the civil administration. Of the centre-right politicians currently in the Greek parliament few, I suspect very few indeed, can avoid this stigma of "clientelism", i.e. using their patronage power to bestow benefits, often even of dubious legality, in exchange for votes and power for himself and his family.

The above should not be taken to imply that such form of corruption is unique to Greece for everyone who has "done business" in the entire Middle East (including Turkey) and, even contemporary Russia or the part of Italy where the mafia is dominant, will attest to such practices. The problem with Greece, one is sorry to say it in public, is that such practices are so widely spread and tolerated (if not encouraged) even by senior politicians that the ability to clean up its Augean

Stables will, if at all possible, prove truly a herculean task! And all this is occurring in what we regard – or, at any rate the Greeks regard – as being part of Europe.

(ii). *Mediterranean volatility.* The previous thought leads naturally to the next. This inclination towards shady deals, found in the entire Mediterranean region, is the result of an inherently unstable environment and distinguishes its inhabitants from the more stable and less excitable inhabitants of Northern Europe. This inherent instability, largely the result not only of "absolute poverty" but also of unfair distribution of wealth, thus translates into unreliability of character and shifting loyalties which make the smooth running of a modern state difficult. For the message is soon picked up by all concerned – clients and servants – that "sweeteners" of all kinds form part of daily realities - indeed a historical relic for the reasons given above - and thus can be resorted to in order to keep the "machinery of government well oiled".

Such indisputable unfairness, which the state itself can show through some of its officials in the domain of Revenue collection, has, in fact, proved one of Greece's most incurable problems and one which has greatly contributed to the current financial crisis of the country. For inspectors have been said by many (but never adjudicated in courts of law) to be deliberately pernickety when inspecting the books of the tax payer but to relent and "close their eyes" to real or made up deficiencies when enticed through "sweeteners" to do this. This disgraceful practice in turn promotes widespread and deep distrust in the tax authorities and thus the desire of the citizen to evade as best he can and not only to avoid, i.e. minimize, as he is entitled to do so, his tax obligations. We thus end with one more cause for deep mutual distrust between different categories of the citizenry. Few would thus dissent from the rather damning conclusion often expressed by senior German politicians that the Greek tax system is not just grossly inefficient but down right corrupt. Most, I suspect, in the EU so feel; and on such limited (concrete) knowledge as we have, I am forced – very reluctantly – to agree.

In short, a modern state, which was suppressed by a brutally conqueror for four hundred years, missed the European Renaissance and the subsequent Industrial Revolution and reached modern statehood without a middle class was bound to start life in the most difficult of conditions and is now in a near--impossible position to shake off inherited bad habits.

Do the above explanations justify many of Greece's less attractive contemporary features? Most certainly they do not; but an examination of the causes, here only sketched briefly, may go a long way towards explaining how they came about and, perhaps, even put on guard foreigners working in that otherwise beautiful country! The above also suggest – to me at least – that the corrective action needed will be long and must be severe.

(iii). *Ottoman Rule.* The Islamisation and eventual Turkification of Anatolia and, eventually, the whole of Greece took well over four centuries to be accomplished but most accounts of this process bring out the violence of the process. More philosophical accounts will focus on the causes of the Byzantine defeat and they may be geopolitical in the nature or, if written by men with a religious link or penchant, will explain events by reference to the will of God. But there is also a fair amount of what Professor Vryonis describes as "belle lettristes" – e.g. the Arab historian Ibn-KJhaldun or the Greek Thedore Metochites - who focus on the cultural changes brought about by this gradual elimination of the Greek-Christian factor.

To be sure, this literature makes no direct mention of the character changes that will emerge with the passage of time as a result of this upheaval. But these texts constantly talk about how the conquered have to comply with the tastes and wishes of the conquerors, of the lives of the conquered being left in a state of inconsistency, uncertainty, oscillations, of their feelings ranging from envy, stupidity, abuse of religious life, and general apathy. All of the above represent major destabilizing emotional reactions which, over time, will generate character changes of the kind described above for no other purpose than to facilitate survival.

Was the Ottoman behaviour any different once the conquest and subjugation of the Greeks was complete? The question how tolerant the Ottoman Empire was towards the people it conquered was traditional answered by stating that such tolerance as was shown was dictated by pragmatic considerations rather than feelings of justice, understanding, and brotherhood. To put it differently, if the subjugated behaved themselves or, better still 'collaborated', they were given a certain amount of autonomy though they always remained "second class citizens".

The same is true of the alleged tolerance shown towards the Orthodox Church which, we already noted, is not reflected in the writings of the classical authors on this topic. But even the explanations which aim to suggest tolerance on the part of the conquerors seem contrived and reveal a small part of their true motives.

For instance, the pre-eminent role given for to the Patriarch of Constantinople, at a time when no privileges were granted to the Slavic churches in the Balkans most of which were in fact closed down, offers a good illustration of Ottoman cunning and diplomacy, not tolerance. For, first, the position of the new rulers was anything but stable and was thus anxious to befriend the Head of the Church which controlled spiritually the majority of the newly conquered people.

Second there was another very cynical reason behind such "generosity" and this was the fear that the Orthodox Church might turn wholeheartedly to the Catholic Church and complete, so to speak, the work never fully implemented by the Conference of Ferrara Florence (1436-1438) in which the former ceded their religious primacy to the Pope in exchange for military support in the battle against the Turks.

Gestures of this kind, however, dictated by political calculation and not a genuine feeling of reconciliation did not stop the Turks from being brutal in the collection of taxes, inhuman in the forceful kidnapping of young Christian children and their subsequent conversion into Janissaries, or the exploitation of the confiscated ecclesiastical lands, monasteries etc. leaving the indigenous populations rudderless, in a state of permanent poverty, if not outright hunger.

The brutality of the Turkish occupation is confirmed by the massive and successive revolts of all conquered nations during the 19th century the moment the sensed that the old vigour of the conquerors was in the wane. For why would so many nations, including Muslims Arabs who retained increasing hatred towards the Ottoman Empire, begin their massive "exodus" from its supposedly benign occupation from about the middle end of the 18th century onwards if the conditions of life under the old Empire were as good as Turkish historians (and the trendy Greek allies) now claim to have been? To allege that such bloody liberation wars began under the influence of intellectuals inspired by the ideas of the French Revolution is pure invented mythology aimed to disguise the depth of discontent felt by all the subjugated races towards their Turkish masters!

Yet the harm caused by the prolonged and brutal occupation harm could not be underdone. By the time salvation came, after four hundred years of foreign yoke, it was too late to straighten out the character deformations which had grown out of the harshness of the occupation. For it takes time to erase such acquired characteristics, especially in a country which had become depopulated by the invasions, had lost its middle class (since it never experienced the rejuvenating effects of the industrial revolution of the early and middle 19th century, having missed the advantages an industrial revolution) and had its cultural links with its glorious past not only severed but not even renovated intellectually by the intellectual achievements of the Renaissance which enriched western cultural life but left Greece out of this picture. The character flaws engineered by an extremely harsh environment have thus been hard to eradicate, a fact which is not easily understood nor appreciated by western audiences who have a very sanitized picture of what the dislocating effects caused by the invasion from the steps east of the Caspian Sea set in motion from about the 9th or 10th century AD.

3. Past suffering as a cause of modern character features: a postscript

This, inevitably, short account of the psychological traumas and character flaws caused by the Ottoman yoke over the Greeks deserve a study of their own. To my knowledge such a sociological 'cause and effect' study has not been undertaken with any degree of detail, perhaps because it would call for a combination of the talents of a psychologist, a sociologist, and an historian. Yet, from my experience, I can invoke another, parallel, example which is based on the same idea: past sufferings leaving their traces on contemporary character features. On this, at least, and as far as the Jewish people are concerned,[4] there is more factual information. Once again, however, and according to my limited knowledge of the relevant literature, inadequate work has been done to bring to the surface the causal links between past sufferings and current attitudes.

So here let us focus briefly on the Jewish race having always admired its many strong features – devotion to education and betterment, closeness of family ties, loyalty towards the members of the race and towards its friends – and having repeatedly been impressed by the way this race has constantly put to use in their contemporary lives the lessons of the past. It is difficult not to respect such a race, even if, for whatever reasons, one happens – as I have done – to disagree with some of their unnecessarily harsh reprisals on protesting Palestinians.

The feature I wish to stress – apart for the above-mentioned three

---

4. Another illustration can be found in the repression of free speech by violently anti-communist phases of persecutions such as the McCarthy era in the USA. In this case, however, the 'cleansing' of the Universities of suspected sympathisers of the Left pushed many into the free-lance and unregulated existence of the "public intellectual".

important attributes – is, for the purposes of this chapter, especially notable since it was born out of past confrontations. Additionally, however, it has helped shape the Jewish art and practice of negotiation, be it on purely legal or diplomatic matters.

The Jewish tendency towards a bargaining strategy which aims – or appears to aim – towards compromise and is, in tone, characterized by a constant effort to avoid confrontation must, I feel, stem from times, not entirely gone, where this race was forced to keep a low (if not subservient) profile to minimize the persecutions brought about by jealousy and bias. For their indisputable Jewish economic and cultural success was bought at a very high price and one of these must be the development of a quiet, low key, at times almost submissive way of bargaining or reacting to pressures. I have noted how exaggerated this tendency to keep a low profile to avoid provocation can be in some of my New York and New Jersey Jewish friend and academic colleagues for only when you get to know them better, as I did over the years I spent teaching in the USA, you realise a different persona hidden below the self-effacing confrontation-avoiding exterior.

At the negotiating table for instance –be it a university or political context - I have, time and again, noted how Jewish colleagues will be quick to switch the discussion to the points where there is even minimal agreement and try to rephrase the areas of disagreement in an ingenious - at times, it must be said, ingenuous way - in the belief that this might help move matters further. Compliments will thus be paid to the other side, declarations of a willingness to "give in" in exchange for "minor concessions" will all be aired in a fast and furious manner, the difficulties re-formulated in a way that make them shrink in consequence. Those gifted in this way of bargaining are a pleasure to watch in action, though equally important is not to miss sight of the fact that concealed under the velvet glove one always finds a steel hand.

This Jewish attempt to conceal adroitly their unbending determination to get their way is surely the result of past sufferings having taught them that force is best avoided where talking can do the trick. In most cases attempts are made to use diplomacy as a form of force and not use force as a way of giving content to diplomacy. This ties in perfectly with an eagerness not to cause waves and get on quietly with one's work.

Combined, however, with the angst that seems to accompany the estrangement with many American Jews feel from the basically Christian civilization which they find in England and the USA it can also lead to a special kind of craving for acceptance and recognition which, in its turn, reinforces the belief that an uncontroversial public life combined with hard work may lead to the desired outcome: social acceptance. This "craving for social acceptance" will not lead in eliminating one's Jewishness; but it can lead to its suppression in as decent a manner as possible. We shall return to these points in greater detail in chapter eight, below.

The above thoughts stem from many talks I have had with Jewish colleagues in the USA, in London and Cambridge. In the latter University I indeed recall many conversations with a hard-working Jewish comparatist who somehow (and totally erroneously) got it in his head that I had been asked to write in advance the first draft of his obituary for The Times. Naturally, I disabused him of this obsession of his since it was entirely unfounded. Yet he simply would not let go and kept telling me that he had been marginalized in the past by an even more eminent Jewish law colleague of his in Cambridge for abandoning the Jewish religion and thus did not wish his Jewishness to figure too prominently in this obituary! In particular, he was anxious for me to under play both his Jewish and his German ancestry. My reaction – and I recall now with horror at my rudeness – was to reply: "Well, my Dear X, what remains of you if we down-play the German and Jewish past?" I strongly suspect he would have liked me to say that I believed that he was...English! At the time I felt there was something amusing in his behaviour; in retrospect I realise – and repeat this - how wrong I was to say what I believed instead of letting the discussion die out. For never having experienced the feeling of not belonging I was totally unable to appreciate the loss that people denied of their roots can feel.

Yet such 'placidity' has, in my experience, been limited; and in New York the economic impoverishment suffered by many Jewish immigrants was invariably by-passed through a vast respect for education and culture as ways for social betterment. These factors, together, encouraged many of the Jewish émigrés to begin the academic careers as radical intellectuals, quick to complain through their pens against discrimination and injustice.

Yet authors like Russell Jacoby, who has divided intellectuals into two classes – those who operate among the intellectual bohemia and those who have opted for the more secure but more conventional life of the University world – have argued that "the radicalism [of the first group of Jews which included eminent sociologists such as Lionel Trilling and the half Jewish half Lutheran Richard Hofstadter] steeped in anxiety [over time] slide[d] into conservatism" while the

Irish/Texan, Puritan or Scottish identities of C. Wright Mills, Gore Vidal, or John Galbraith gave rise to a bony radicalism more resistant to economic and social blandishment."[5]

Thus Mills, for instance,[6] one of the most influential Marxist dreamers of the fifties and sixties, did not cease to lambast the "petty hierarchy" that prevailed in the university world which began to emerge after the death of the McCarthy era and "segregated completely the intellectual [of the university world] from social life". The price, always according to this school of thought, was the inability of the University world to "draw" into its embrace "men of brilliance, energy and imagination". Even up to the time I first came to work at Texas in 1985, that famous University had difficulty in accepting a very talented fund-raiser as Dean of the Law Faculty because – it was claimed – he was Jewish.

This is no place, nor indeed the kind of book, which can discuss the American conception of intelligentsia and the role the Jewish émigré played in its various forms. My point, however, is to stress the role the persecuted past of the Jewish race combined with an anguished present and discover how together they played a part in the shaping of the characters and work of these brilliant but often (socially) ill-adjusted pioneers.

Thus, where all of the above came from, how this background made them feel and, indirectly, affected not only what they said but how they wrote it is what we have to understand – hence the contents of this book and the importance I laid in chapter one on the word 'understanding'.

Nor is this difficult to do so long as we know what we are looking for. Thus the authors themselves do not conceal their anguish for having to think and write away from home. The writers, in their books, their letters, their interviews, help us in this search. We thus see it clearly in the 'troubled' writings of Theodore Adorno (Jewish); we see it also in a revealing way in the masterpiece[7] of Rich Auerbach (also Jewish), where he tells us not just of his loneliness of writing in Constantinople, away from his home and books, but also makes the inter-

5. *The Last Intellectuals. American Culture in the Age of Academe*, (Basic Books, 1987, and a new Introduction in 2000), at p.90.
6. The sociologist C. Wright Mills (1916-1962) thus wrote in his *White Collar* (NY, OUP 1956) pp. 130-1; 158-9. His collected essays under the title *Power, Politics & People*, edited by Irving Louis Horowitz 1963, paperback edition 1967).
7. *Mimesis: The Representation of Reality in Western Literature*, tras. By Willard Trask and reprinted by Princeton University Press in 1968.

esting but not entirely surprising confession that his work might not have been created at all in the comfort of his familiar surroundings![8] We see it, finally - and in order to avoid endless lists of names I mention one only - in the work of Edward Said (Palestinian),[9] and this even though his ceaseless and original views never stopped earning him academic recognition. This penned up sadness, loneliness, pain and frustration emerge most clearly in his last small book written after his cancer was diagnosed. Beautifully written it was; but I found it so depressing I never managed to finish reading it.

This leads us to the most interesting though, probably also most controversial of suggestions made in this chapter namely, that this unavoidable 'longing', these 'inherited complexes', this 'enduring angst', in the end went a long way towards assimilating the sufferings of those who in their homelands –be they Jewish or Palestinian - maintained that they were irreconcilably different in every conceivable way.

So it was through suffering – to differing degrees to be sure but suffering nonetheless – that the a miracle of sorts occurred and the displaced Jew and Palestinian came together and attained, in a city such as New York (or, in Weimarian Berlin) - i.e. a cosmopolitan environment – the sameness or uniformity which their own parochial settings denied them. To some extent I find this is also true of the Greeks of the diaspora; for though they remain there as politically divided as there are in their homeland, they are often infinitely more proud at being Greek than when they find themselves on Greek soil.

Yet the uniformity I am talking about is not of a healthy kind; for it is the uniformity of marginalization, loneliness, rootlessness which, in the case of imaginative individuals, generated an amazing intellectual productivity which otherwise might never have surfaced favouring similar liberal values. Auerbach in his work admits as much quite openly!

Moreover, this was a 'unity' which had the same beneficial effects on these displaced people as well as the rest of us. For, in prompting those who were the most resilient and most original of the 'affected' to offer us their innermost and thus original 'cries of agony' - born from their state of psychological wilderness – this 'unity" made their intellectual thoughts much richer. Perhaps, the above also made the mixed

8. Ibid, at p. 557.
9. There is this hardly a book of Said's in which this loneliness and anger of the émigré is not made obvious, even in works of (mainly) literary criticism. See, for instance, his *The World, the Text and the Critic* (Harvard University Press, 1983), passim.

societies where all of the above live (or lived) if not more tolerant, certainly more vibrant. I will keep maintaining the lite-motif of this book: understanding leads to tolerance, affection for the fellow human being, proper appreciation of his work. We must learn to appreciate the work of others; more importantly still, we must realise how important it is for us to let them know this!

Finally, this coming closer through the shared difficulties of geographical displacement strikes me as an idea worth pursuing further for its suggests that not only time but also geographical displacement, especially displacement accompanied by hardship and the frequent calls to compromise in order to survive, diminishes the hardness of dividing lines which extreme religious teaching or local fighting tends to make even harder to eradicate. I may, of course, be wildly wrong; but my readers will at least note that I am always valiantly pursuing my self-confessed policies of rapprochement which were so cardinal in my legal work throughout my life as a pre-requisite to understanding each other better and also became a key element during the years when I naively believed that by preaching reconciliation to my contemporary compatriots I would have some effect on their thinking.

Family cohesion

Go back one hundred years ago (or more) and one will find considerable similarities in family structures and habits across European borders. Paternal powers, for instance, were considerable; family unity strictly observed (often including in all family rituals - including the Sunday lunch - grown up and married children and their families) and a sense of mutual family obligations that went beyond the limits of mutual help and assistance required by the law. Progress, or perhaps one should refer to it is as change, has changed many of these original precepts, on the whole at the expense of family unity and cohesion. The family Sunday lunch has gone up like a puff of smoke as has the notion of a family holiday.

Precise details belong to another book but the variations wrought by societal changes have not been the same in all European countries and where this is true the old unity and cohesion of basic principles has given way to new ethics and habits. Thus, whereas in the South the family tendency to look after tits old members as age moves them towards various forms of disability or infirmity, in the north working conditions mean that more often than not there comes a point where the older relative will have to be packed off to an old people's home.

The Mediterranean tendency to attribute this to Northern coldness of character may often be an unacceptable simplification. Anyone reading Alan Bennett's book about his mother's mental infirmity and final commitment to an old people's home will immediately recognize how flawed generalizations can be. Those interested in the way feelings are externalized, either through behaviour but also through writing, will admire deeply this author's unique written style and his ability to capture the human condition, at is strong or weak moments, with such elegant understatement. Texts such as these to me should be used widely in teaching of writing classes, be it in any language, simply in order to illustrate the fact that loud of violent externalization of emotions does not make them more real or profound. Bennett, in my inexpert view, is a gem of contemporary English literature; and his talent for understatement is the key to his unique style. I read him with indescribable pleasure and huge envy.

The family obligation to help those who are most in need is, however, shown to be stronger when we turn our attention our attention from the old to the young. In the Mediterranean world the Middle Eastern included the help towards ones children thus continues well beyond the attainment of the age of majority by allowing the young children to remain at home during their (often over-prolonged) university years. Contemporary Greece shows that this support can go even beyond that time limit and extend to help – in terms of money or physical assistance with the children – when the general economic situation is putting families, especially of middle or lower incomes under strain. It would thus be no exaggeration to stress that in the presence economic crisis in Greece the support given by parents and even grand parents have enabled many families to keep their heads above water. I cannot give comparative statistics on these matters, indeed, I doubt that there exist any, but my strong guess is that we are faced here with a distinct difference between North and South Europe.

One social change which has affected family life and cohesion in a deep way is the tendency of women to work. This increased considerably after the end of the Second World War, partly as a result of the need to improve family finances but also because of the rapid emancipation of women in the domain of work which received a great boost by the 'War Effort'. The wider political environment of a particular country could also hasten or slow down this trend as the comparison of West and East German shows in the 1950's. Thus, the poorer East was forced to "push" more women into factories and, as a consequence, liberalize their legal status of women in matters employment but also liberalize other parts of the law – abortion for instance – which could also have some bearing on the continued presence of a woman in the household. West Germany, on the other hand, which was not subjected to similar financial constraints, was slower in achieving legal equality of man and woman even though article 3 of the (new) Constitution which came into force in 1950 required it to amend all laws which failed to give effect to this new constitutional requirement within three years of the Constitution's coming into force. A Texan colleague of mine – Professor Inga Markovitz – once described this phase of German legal history in an excellent article published – if I recall correctly the Stanford Law Review. Unearthing it will repay careful reading.

Similar changes occurred in Greece from about the late sixties onwards and received new impetus with the legal changes that were implemented during the second half of the 1970's. The beneficial effects of these changes on the status of women was immediately observable though it took rather longer to give birth to the (legitimate) concern about the effect that this "both parents" at work had on the brining up of children. In his wonderful work on "The Law of Misbehaving Children" Professor Nestor Kourakis of the University of Athens has thus described many of the adverse effects that this new type of family life had upon youngsters increasingly left to their own devices. One, which Professor Kourakis examines in some detail, is the growing tendency of parents suffering from this syndrome of not looking after their children as much as they ought to or would like, making up for this omission by showering the children with expensive presents. This substitution of gifts for personal care of attention, however, proved unable to keep strong the old-fashioned links of affection and care while also helping to instil in the younger generation this strong feeling of consumerism which has affected younger Greek and accustomed to have things just for the asking or making them think almost exclusively in terms of rights but less so in terms of corresponding duties.

The topics here discussed do not lend themselves to the inevitable summarizing attempted above. Yet, enough has been said to suggest that, once again, modernization or globalization of customs, behaviour, patterns of family life, have affected the Greek family probably more than it has changed the more western model. This change has, in turn, resulted in yet another rapprochement of cultures, a homogenization of values and patterns of behaviour. Whether this can be described as a good or bad change will, no doubt, be a matter of individual predilection. Personally, I incline towards a reaction which if not outright negative is dominated by doubts and concerns.

Chapter Five

COMPLEXITIES BEHIND A VERY NATURAL HUMAN URGE
Sexual upbringing, sexist behaviour, sexual standing, equality
of treatment, conveying a message through apparel and posture

Greek middle classes

The middle classes have, certainly since the 19th century, been considered to be the backbone of all societies; for it was they who took
the risks with their own money and created new wealth. They were
also the section of society which came to embody the moralistic – not
moral – principles of what is referred to in England as the Victorian
era. Having lived as I have done during the second half of the 20th century and the beginning of the 21st I beg to differ on a number of points
though I also hasten to clarify that the doubts I have about the validity
of the opening statement stem from my Greek experience. Since this
assertion will cause surprise if not (considerable) annoyance in my
country of birth – maybe elsewhere as well - I must try to justify it.

First of all, the middle classes in Greece – except for those above
sixty – have become, especially since the mid-sixties – politically extremely volatile. As a class they give the impression of being com-
plexed for never quite attaining the societal and wealth heights they
believe that they deserve; and their voting patterns reflect this frustration by shifting from conservatives to socialists and even the new left
in the hope that newly created links with whomsoever is in power will
help them climb one more step up the social ladder. Financial and social advancement is therefore what makes the members of this class
tick; and, in Greece at least, they will espouse any ideology which aids
their spiral move upwards.

The above suggest – to me at least – that ideologically they are
hypocritical rather than psychologically confused or merely politically

ambitious. Thus, though it is fashionable these days to be liberal and 'open minded', the Greek middle classes are both these things but only in appearance. Deep inside the bulk of the modern Greeks, especially their middle classes, we find conventional, not infrequently racist and deeply sexist individuals. Sexual fidelity is, in theory espoused, but hardly any Greek male who is given the chance to sin with a beautifully curvaceous girl – and in contemporary Greek aesthetics 'curvaceous' is an important ingredient - would refuse to give in to such a temptation. Those who though 'macho' in appearance are, in truth, of a cowardly disposition, will be content to externalise their true feelings about women through obscene language or malicious gossip. Promiscuity in Greece is thus as prevalent as it was among their Ancient Gods though, unlike them, concealed under a veneer of prudery. For years I saw all this at first hand; and, in the spirit of frankness in which this work is written, I must dwell into this matter somewhat longer.

In my time teenage years – the late fifties/ early sixties – sexual education was totally unknown. Sexual urges, however are not arrested because no one explains to a sixteen year old boy what is happening in his body at a time when it is going through a genuine physiological transformation. The slightest amorous contact with a girl in one's social milieu, however, ran the risk of an immediate threat of marriage. This was a highly pronounced attitude among the so-called upper middle classes where parents were – maybe still are - prepared even to pay huge dowries in order to 'arrange' what they regarded as good marriages. Another example here of what I have already stressed elsewhere namely, that Greece often resembles the East more than the West though the effort is made to keep this resemblance concealed.

The young men who found themselves in such a state had recourse to prostitution and this solution was, in my time, widely adopted. Better still, however, was sexual experimentation with a more emancipated visiting foreigner or when one found oneself abroad, as I frequently did at the time, in the midst of the more liberated unbelievably vibrant environment of the London of Carnaby Street or the Beatles in the early sixties.

I need not dwell more on this subject expect to say, moving away from the sombre middle classes to the true upper classes – and the species simply does not exist in Greece - for I have always had high regard for most of its members whom I met. Not that those whom I met in England, France, and Germany were without their eccentricities which often mutated - as I discovered with a gorgeous looking German Baroness - into aberrations; but none of the above made them loose their style, their manners, their air of supreme confidence, and an outlook to life which was engaging if not even enviable in the sense that they were so 'relaxed about life' and able, not just willing, to enjoy it.

Just as attractive – perhaps, even more to me at least – are those who belong to the extreme opposite social rank – the working classes. This preference for the polar social extremes of any society may need explaining yet to me it was always obvious. Though I am not a pub crawler, I love my coffee shops wherever I happen to be; and the ones I have come to visit fairly regularly were frequented by unassuming, simple, working, retired, but to man (or women) friendly working-class people. That is where my acquaintance with them began and has been maintained during my peregrinations in various countries.

In the English variants, the warmth is obvious straight away by the way the often refer to one: "love" or "Gov." are the appellations which amused me most with the latter resembling the Italian *Commnenda-tore*. In both cases, however the grand-sounding title was just a joke for as an Italian friend once explained "no one can be just referred to as *Signore* when all the rest were referred by their professional titles such as *avvocato, ingenere* and the best of all *Eccellenza* which, in moments of excessive generosity can be used even for persons who are not really Excellencies by any stretch of the imagination. This, in other words, was not pretension but teasing not the person so 'elevated' but of themselves and the Italian love for titles and, just as importantly, verbal exaggeration. The patrons of such coffee shops, be they Austrian, Greek, Italian, or English, are thus possessed of a naughty sense of humour while, invariably, overflowing with kindness. Just as admirable is their stoic patience towards the many health problems of the kind that I, too, have experienced which visit ageing people. Indeed, Greeks and Italians love talking about their health!

Sharing experiences invariably makes me remember how lucky I have been to have been attended by my loving wife and caring children during a double hip operation which was both painful and left me pretty immobilised for weeks on end not to mention grumpy. At the time, I thought I was being brave and undemanding but I am assured I was awful. Yet my fellow tea or coffee drinkers – in Bicester's 'Nash Tea Room', or Maussane's 'Le Café dé de la Fontaine', or Paris's 'Rivale' – towards the end of the rue Marboeuf -, or the Beer Garden at the entrance of the Beethoven Park at Cologne – had all gone through the same experiences but all coped without a single complaint, not infrequently alone. I could not have coped with such 'neglect'; and shudder at the thought of such loneliness during my confined immobility at home. Nonetheless, I was and remain envious of all these 'mates' for being endowed with such endurance and a character that enabled them to face the vicissitudes of life with humour and a constant smile on their face of the kind one would imagine was designed to advertise perfect dentures! At the end of the day, therefore, for me these, and not the other two social groups, are the salt of the earth. Incidentally, in Greece, this is an attitude which has rendered me very 'suspicious' in the eyes of people of 'my background' – if I may be permitted to use this awfully snobbish expression – many of whom even believed that my years in England had turned me into a "lefty". Well, they had not; but even if they had what is so wrong with that? Was not democracy invented in ancient Athens and allowed everyone freedom in his beliefs?

The Mediterranean peacock

In the animal kingdom it is widely found that the male of the species is the more handsome as well as the more powerful of the two sexes and this pre-eminence helps attract the "best" of females for the purposes of procreation and successful perpetuation of the species. With humans opinions seem more divided, the male being described as the stronger while the female being considered (not by all!) as the more attractive. In my view, nine times out of ten, it is also the most admirable – and I end this sentence with the typical examination question: discuss.

For most intents and purposes generalisations, of course, are of dubious value; yet the one with which I began this sub-section strikes me as exceptionally debatable for two reasons. First because I feel that women are in many senses, especially psychologically, tougher than men. Secondly, because the emphasis on their beauty can minimise the power of their guile, cunning, and even sheer force which they possess and, at the right moment, display.

The list of women that fall into this admirable (and frightening) category must surely be endless but, as one interested in history, the ones who instantly spring to my mind include the Empress Theodora of Byzantium, Catherine of Russia, Queen Elisabeth I, Eleanor Roosevelt, and, of course, Lady Thatcher. I could easily enlarge this list to include formidable women who were not politicians such as, for instance, artists. Elizabeth Vigée le Brun, who gained a formidable reputation as a portraitist of the aristocracy in France, Italy, Germany and Russia, all at a time when (a) women could hardly make a reputation in painting and (b) travelling conditions across huge distances, which she endured by coach were, for a single woman, difficult if not dangerous.

Whatever nature or history teaches, and however much women's lib has gained ground, the fact is that in the Mediterranean world man reigns supreme. Or, to put it in colourful terms, he is the male peacock, as quick to fan out his tail to impress as he is stupid enough to believe that others see him as he believes he is and not as he really is. Yet what he often really is, is little more than a male peacock whose feathers are damaged or have fallen, grey beneath the colour, mundane in its awkward walk, once the imperial posture has been removed.

Do I exaggerate? Go to a café in Rome or any Italian city – Florence, Siena, Rome or Venice – the ones I know best and see the males swan in, gently turning the head to see who is there and, above all, to notice if he and his attire have been suitably noticed. The visit to the Café of his choice is, allegedly, to get his daily shot of an *espresso* though, in practice such visits take place two to four times per day. In reality, however, the escape from the office is to see but above all to be seen and, one hopes, impress! *That is the real fix* that comes from the quick visit to the coffee shop mid-morning!

The best example of such human vanity comes from my days in Texas where I would co-teach with an erudite Italian Professor who was the peacock's peacock. His name escapes me - or at any rate it should - but his face will remain engraved on my mind since it is one of those Giotto saints, almost as emaciated, with a long and, at times, slightly hooked nose and with a thin beard pointed at the end. Since all have halos round their heads, they are meant to be saints. But do not let that golden semi-circles trick you to see them as anything other than proudly posing Italian peasants undoubtedly believing the role they were asked to enact as the "master catches" on the canvass precisely the features my friend possessed. My modern Giotto 'saint' gave away that he was a modern Roman by his swagger which really revealed how much in love he was with … himself.

Is it unrealistic to argue that men like that are likely to extend this vanity to their workplace or fail to reflect in their written work whether it is a novel or one which discusses legal issues? Anyone inclined to say that the social demeanour is unlikely to be manifested in the work needs more illustrations of the vainglorious and sexist attitude of the Mediterranean male. My legal colleague's presence at my American university provides more illustrations but one more will do.

Now one day he and I were invited, as is customary in American Universities, to the Dean's house for a barbeque party and a swim in his pool which, in reality, was little more than a glorified Jacuzzi in which you lounge around drinking your lethal margaritas. Our host, I should add was Jewish, my short-hand way of saying brilliant, rotund in shape if not more, and with a bathing costume of the 1930's almost designed deliberately to reveal his over-hanging belly and short and hairy legs. Aesthetically, the result may not have been pleasing, at any rate to most Europeans. But what the display underlined was that what matters is the "inner beauty" and, of course, the fact that he had risen in the world through his undoubted intelligence. In the light of the above, one might be tempted to describe him as a fox; but a peacock he most certainly was, showing that male peacocks can be found wherever the female of the species also attend.

My friend arrived at the party late and was immediately shown to the bathroom and asked to change. He did, and soon appeared in a G-string which pronounced every spare bone and "anything else" that protruded in his emaciated body. With an un-paralleled *sang froid* that drew the breath out of all participants, he approached the water and then plunged into the Jacuzzi as if it was a full sized pool. Happily he did not concuss himself so when he emerged to a round of applause from the surrounding colleagues, not so much for his feat but for the fact that he was still alive, he proceeded to join the others and sun his body or, at any rate, expose to the sun the 99.9% of it which was not covered by his G-string.

He thoroughly enjoyed the experience and so did I observing with a hawk's eye the prudish Texans, with bathing costumes reaching their knees and lower still, furtively exchanging meaningful glances about the indisputably charming, intelligent, entertaining, but very unusual guest. But the pleasant day ended with an anti-climax since our prominent guest left forgetting to take with him his bathing costume. So the following day this was dutifully returned to him inside a thin air-mail envelope addressed by the Dean: "To whoever lost this at my home yesterday afternoon". Moreover, to ensure proper publicity and mirth, this note and envelope (containing the by now famous G-string) was pinned at the entrance of the mail room so as to be seen by all who went there to collect their daily mail!

Can one condemn someone for being provocative? Yes if one is secretly jealous of that person and cannot admit it to himself. And why should one be jealous give that the indigenous peacocks were better paid and just as intellectually noteworthy as the imported one? The answer is easy: because the latter was free, felt totally unrestrained by the prudery which exists in the USA a country which, at the same time, could well be among the most promiscuous. So, this minor if not amusing illustration raises a serious question: are people from different countries truly different? Or do they appear different because it takes time to rid oneself of the prejudices and preconceptions one inherits from one's background? If the second answer is the correct one then this, like so many other differences in the comportment of people who come from different backgrounds is likely to fade in today's globalised world and easy inter-communications which makes the borrowing of ideas and behaviour both easy and tempting.

This little vignette describes beautifully the mores and attitudes of two countries, the vainglorious attitude towards the male body and contrasts brilliantly the atypically (in the minds of some) tolerance of Catholicism towards sensualist versus the prudish and austere attitude towards life favoured by the more dour Protestants, Quakers, or Jews of, inter alia, the American variety.

This sensual exhibitionism of Italian Catholicism is both a serious matter and one worth *studying through the ages* for it tells you so much about Italy and its exceptionally gifted people. In fact it goes quite far back and shows how this exceptional freedom stems in part from the self-confidence of the people and, in its turn, helped produce some artistic masterpieces for their artists dared to go where others had never gone. Of the many such works one in particular can be found painted on the ceiling of the cathedral of Orvietto (which once formed part of the Papal States in the centre of Italy), by Lucca Signorelli.

In this mural we find depicted one of the most frightening but also moving scenes of religious literature, the moment when the dead emerge from their graves at the "sounding of a trumpet" to be judged by the Lord for their earthly behaviour. Though God has already made up his mind – no justice here in the legal sense which ordains argument and detests a pre-determined judgment – those to be saved and those who will be damned are still left in ignorance. Agony thus is expressed in the expressions of most of the dead as they break the stone cover of the ground in which they have been buried and heave and claw themselves out of the earth to hear the verdict. Will they see the sun and stars again; or return to a complete darkness illuminated only by constantly burning fires tormenting the condemned sinners? How could such terrible images have been allowed to coexist with such a total devotion to the beauties of the nude human body? Freedom, again, provides the key clue; for genius can never flourish where the rules of morality and legality - devised for ordinary human beings - restrain their own creativity.

Yet what catches the eye is not just the sense of order and disorder that prevails in the two main parts of the mural which depict heaven and hell. Nor is it the deformed faces of the devils or the tortured by agony faces of those condemned which make us pause and think. It is their amazingly perfect muscular bodies and the even more pronounced…buttocks of the dead that invariably attract one's eye simply because the artist skilfully directs our vision to that part of the body which most interested *him*. The theme the artist had chosen to depict may thus have been religious; but it takes neither imagination nor psychiatric training to imagine on what his mind was focused!

The overall conception of the subject is impressive, in itself; yet even more intriguing is to imagine the Italian peasant in the Cathedral attending mass and raising his sights to the Heavens only to be confronted by perfectly rounded buttocks. What message would such a peasant get? And what do we? One word only applies and it is: amazing. What makes the entire mural so original is the contrasts it contains: the scene depicted versus the way this is done; the order of heaven versus the chaos of hell; the light in the first, the darkness of the second. Only one other man has exploited these contrasts dealing with the very same theme and achieved the same stunning result: Mozart. In the part of his *Requiem* (The Mass for the Dead) entitled *Confutatis* he makes us *feel* through the medium of music the same picture we *see* through the eye in Signorelli's painting. The fires of hell destined for the sinners are thus indicated by the opening bars with their fast tempo only to be followed by a much slower tempo, sung softly, or humbly one should say, since it contains Mozart's own hopeful plea to his God that will not forget him and place him with the blessed: "voca me cum benedictis".[1]

None of the above could have ever happened in the Escorial or any other Spanish Catholic Church or even in the stylized and austere painting of the Greek or Russian Orthodox environment which exude their own kind of severity. Only in Italy – and he Renaissance in particular which drew its life from supreme human confidence bordering

---

1. Here is the first verse in Latin and then in English; but it is the music which make Mozart's cry to his God not to forget him which makes this piece so indescribably personal.

Confutatis maledictis	When the accused are confronted,
Flammis acribus addictis	and doomed to flames of woe,
Voca me cum benedictis	*Call me among the blessed*

on arrogance - could the artist have dared to tempt the faithful down below listening to preaching of theological doctrines such as that of transubstantiation, yet thinking of naked buttocks and the gratification of the flesh. Signorelli did all this, combining them in one picture by exploiting the effects of contrast found in light and colours, his superb draftsmanship, and using his excellent knowledge of the rules of perspective. His mural makes us understand instantly why he had such a huge effect on the artistic future of Raphael and Michelangelo, the two greatest artistic geniuses of the high Renaissance.[2]

Tracing this trend to combine the religious with the profane, the sublime with the unexpectedly mundane, and do so in an artistically masterful way and doing this all through the ages to my friend's amusing behaviour would demand a book on its own; and interesting, I venture the thought, its contents would be. But what I find remarkable is that this Italian, wonderfully sinful display of combined sensuality and religiosity could have survived even during the supposed severe climate of the Counter Reformation and, indeed, displayed by Bernini in his tomb of Urban VIII in the Sanctum of Sanctums of Christianity: the Cathedral of Saint Peter's in Rome. Moreover, not only did it survive but the artists chose to do so in the very heart of religion namely its cathedrals.

For in the Basilica of Saint Peter's no less we find the tomb of that great patron of the arts who also happened to be the Pope; and on the right side of his catafalque, situated at the feet of the Pontiff, sits Christian Charity – *Caritas* - (taking precedence over Justice – *Justizia* - who sits at the left of the Pope) with her right bosom (originally) exposed in a manner which is entirely reminiscent of Bernini's likewise semi-exposed busts of his mistress - Constanza Bonarelli, sculptured in Rome but now to be seen in Florence. For its time, and given the object of the marble bust, the Bonarelli experiment was *avant garde* for its time. To do the same at the feet of a Papal tomb was, however, taking Bernini's licentious predilections too far so he was, eventually, obliged to construct a small triangular piece of marble and attach it to Charitiy's garment thus semi covering her previously exposed breast.

I am fascinated by this indiscriminate display of human sensuality but even more intrigued by the difference shown towards this wider theme by the two Christian denominations: Catholicism and Protestantism. Though the churches of the latter are notably austere and

---

2. I do not mention Leonardo da Vinci simply because he carries with him yet another gift – that of the scientific observer and inventor - which puts him in a category of his own.

devoid of all colour and depictions of the human bodies, dressed, and certainly not nude, one can still find these difference in mentality if or when one can ever put side by side these two religious communities and see how austerity versus the search for a pleasurable life are manifested even in daily life.

As it happens our cottage in South of France is not that far from two French towns that visibly display these contrasting characteristics: Tarascogne[3] and the less well-known town of Baucaire. Thus, both have approximately the same population; both are semi-walled by similar looking ramparts; both straddle the river Rhone, barely separated by 100 yards of water. Yet more different they could not be! For the first is Catholic and, in the evening it is teaming by night revellers, while its neighbour, devoutly Calvinist, is almost dead after 10 p.m. For after having eaten – not enjoyed - your daily bread, what else is there to do? I encountered the same phenomenon in Leiden, in the Netherlands - where I worked for sixteen years as a tenured but part time Law Professor - a Calvinist city saved from the dullness of Beaucaire by its large student population which gave it life.

Living and observing different towns, people, religions customs, helps understand (and appreciate) the rich fabric of humanity and even correct assumptions which may be widespread but which are nevertheless wrong! But it is also interesting to note how such different modes of comportment can be transplanted into prudish environments. If that is so, must not one wonder whether different behaviour will not, eventually, penetrate strongholds of conservative introversion and, eventually, be reflected in an adapted way of living? Leiden, mentioned above, is an example where the mixture of citizens – young and old and not just of a different ethnicity or religion – can help bring changes about which may or may not please everyone but will, nonetheless, reflect our gradual move towards social convergence. Such transformations happened; and they work provided they do not occur suddenly and in an unplanned manner.

So my conclusion, still based as much on impressions than hard evidence, is that even in such matters as sensual show off or display subtle changes are taking place. Mediterraneans may be more hot blooded than northerners but they too are learning that in the new world they inhabit old sexiest comportment may no longer help them attract the (wrongly considered) weaker of the species. For more of the

---

3. Made famous by Alphonse Daudet's novel *Tartarin de Tarascogne* and, by history, because it was the seat of the mediaeval "Good King René.

latter are climbing the social and business and political ladders, are aware of the protection – excessive some might argue at times – which the law offers them against provocative behaviour. More importantly, being placed in positions of authority they also know how best to handle such awkward situations for once they suffered themselves from old practices and attitudes. In short this, too, is an area where human conduct is becoming more uniform. Whether such uniformity and conformity is in all cases a source of contentment is, I repeat, another matter. For me, however, this is a secondary matter; and I only touch upon it because I am one of those who still believe in individuality and the right to be different.

Wives and meaningful others

The second term in this sub-title predominates in the USA though rapidly spreading in England. It is dictated by political correctness and is, frankly, "twee" and awful. But it is the form widely used in invitations to social events and, what is worse, even when these are sent out by institutions of high social and educational standing - such as National Academies, Museums, and Universities - to indicate that the female companion or partner (a slightly better term) of the principle invitee is included in the invitation. Because such invitations are issued *en masse* and there is little time to distinguish between those whom the host knows and those he does not, this stupid reference is applied to all, even to old and highly respected couples who can easily be shocked and disgusted by this modern practice.

Personally, I find it a variant of (apparent) modern egalitarianism which one encounters in places like hospitals where the un-known to you and often young nurse will address you by your first name. Alas, I have had some experience of hospitals and only rarely was I given the choice to turn down such familiarity; and only in one – the King Edward Hospital in London – was one automatically accorded what I would regard not only the old fashioned but also the far more courteous form of address suitable to professional relationships.

The twee ambiguity of this term – meaningful other - is not only annoying to relics of the world of yesterday such as me; it has also caused problems in the law. For in many commercial settings it is often customary to offer "perks" to employees and their wives. Typically, a rail or shipping or airways company might thus offer to employees an extra free ticket, especially during periods of reduced work. Such perks are often extended these days to spouses; but this term or other vague terms such as "partner" have raised the legal question whether homosexual cohabitees can also take advantage of such offers. Most courts in most systems have, in relatively recent times, accepted such wide interpretations of the company policy and in my view this is entirely right and proper. But why could not all this be clearly stated in terms of "the *permanent* companions or partners of employees (irrespective of sex) are entitled to the same privileges." If –rightly - sex discrimination is barred and if – rightly again - the determination of one's sexual identity is left to the individual concerned to determine, why not be frank about all such matters rather than coyly beat around the bush?

There is, however, one major drawback which flows from this decrease in the numbers of marriages and the formation of large families. It is demographic; and is affecting adversely most of the West, certainly Europe and Russia. It is thus a fact that the reduction of the reproductive patterns of what might describe as Western white males and females is producing more older people for the countries and an average often over fifty years. Other races, by contrast, - Turkey for instance - continue to have more children and enjoy and average age of around thirty. Few officials in the European countries seem to me to be taking seriously this growing imbalance though I suspect it will not be long before ways of reversing this trend will have to be considered. The recent decision of the Chinese authorities to abolish their own older rule prohibiting families from having more than one child is an example of the fact the governments are beginning to take this overall trend very seriously.

The meaningful other 'issue' touches upon homosexual cohabitations. Whether these should be and referred as 'marriages' is a debatable issue; but that they should be allowed is nowadays beyond dispute and this despite strong opposition from some Churches as, for example, the Greek Church. The views of the Church will weigh heavily in the minds of many individuals; legally, however, they cannot prevent the legally reached result, not least because of the binding jurisprudence of the Strasbourg court. Personally, I find it more difficult not so much to give an answer on the legal domain but express a view on the substance of the following problem namely, should homosexually cohabiting couples be able to adopt and rear children? Medical doctors and psychologists whom I have consulted for their views insist that there is no scientific consensus as to whether the cohabitation of a child in such a 'family' would not affect it in its future life. Personally, I suspect that reliable data will take time to collect and evaluate. In such circumstances my instinct suggests caution so that I, for one, would refrain from taking a biding decision. Legally, however, I believe that the Strasbourg jurisprudence might prove an obstacle to any attempt to bar such possibility by means of legislation.

I need hardly add to the above two observations. The first is that personal preferences must obey the legal regime applicable in any country where this issue arises. So, the Strasbourg case law, would not affect the Russian hostility towards homosexuality though, as stated, it could not be ignored in Greece. Second, and important for the purposes of this book, the emerging if not actually prevailing result on this very personal and moral issue seems, once again, to be underlying my overall feeling of an important convergence of views and attitudes happening among the citizens of different countries in our times.

The male predominance in the Mediterranean world

The "predominance" of the male in the Mediterranean world has been a well-established fact. Though Muslim countries have retained much of the original rigour, in the rest of the Mediterranean the phenomenon is in decline. This legal equalisation is noteworthy; but it must not lead us to believe that women did not enjoy greater power and indirect influence even in the days when the law refused to recognise to them legal rights.

So, once again, one could be misled by appearances, especially if they were derived solely from legal texts. Simply reading legislation in force, or other literature describing society in days gone by, one could lead one astray into believing that male dominance *was in all cases* real and absolute even though it was neither. Conversely, though the days of male dominance have - *in legal terms* – come to an end, in practice this male dominance has – in many instances – only been dented rather than totally extinguished. We will examine the validity of both (opposite) observations; the first in the paragraphs that follow, while the second – which deals with the new scene *–de facto* not *de iure* - will be reviewed in the next but one sub-section.

Male dominance in legal matters

In the days of the last century (and, of course, earlier on) the male dominance was manifested in various ways.

Some consequences were thus economic: the wife, for instance, could not work, at any rate without the husband's permission; her property, if she had any, often took the form of a dowry and was thus administered by her husband in a near-uncontrolled manner. Her spending power was fixed by her husband and her duties were usually limited to looking after the household and it is only within this sphere that some limited spending power was allowed. In social and wider terms now, it is also worth noting that the husband retained the power to decide all matters of importance such as were to live, where to spend one's holiday, and who would be entertained at home on formal occasions. The wife's right to work was also determined by the husband and was rarely granted short of dire economic need. The wife's tax return was also part of her husband's and she was not allowed to submit her own accounts and be taxed accordingly. The marriage of daughters largely passed through the father's hands even when the family or religion did not opt for arranged marriages. Last (for present purposes) but by no means least, there was considerable difference in the domain of sexual liberty. We shall return to this topic further down.

In terms of parental power, the real say concerning the upbringing, education and administration of such economic assets as were set aside for the exclusive benefit of the children were administered by the father. In most systems, especially those operating under legal structures different from the "trust mechanism", if the father died these powers were not transferred to the mother but were handled by the courts or, eventually, by the "family council". The woman, alone, clearly could not be trusted; and the laws did not really begin to change until the early- mid 1960's.

The French system and its derivatives was an example of the above. After the father's death the administration of the children's assets and all decisions referring to their education were entrusted to a "conseil de famille" – a clear sign that the mother/woman could not be relied upon to exercise these duties alone. It is truly remarkable, at least with hindsight, that these legal remnants of sexual inequality were not removed by most legal systems until the early sixties or even later!

Finally, sexual activity, before and during marriage, was determined in a different way, the man being allowed much more freedom in practice than the wife. This is obvious in the way in which marital infidelity was treated which some European legal systems even tolerating it in some cases by law – for example during the period of the wife's confinement. This is a topic, however, which deserves a sub-heading of its own, not least since the legislators who backed such views were even to draw support for them on the some writings of the Fathers of the Orthodox Church such as Saint Basil's essay *On Virginity*.

The reality: Female weakness was often removed or minimized through the back door

Sexual inequality was a feature of most (not all) societies from the most ancient of times. Many would argue that this state of affairs remained unchanged for a long time in both Greece and other European countries (including England), perhaps for far too long. Womankind was thus everywhere in a subservient state and real change did not begin until well after the Second World War though both Wars, by bringing women into the war effort i.e. mainly into factories, found it impossible to send them back home and demote them to their lesser status after they had come to an end.

In most European countries the changes thus really moved in forward gear after the end of the Second World War, first thanks to judicial decisions of their supreme courts which updated provision of their or older Civil Codes and then by means of constitutional amendments and international conventions on human rights. Yet even well before these changes occurred openly by means of legal instruments or judicial decisions, the Mediterranean and Oriental woman had found different ways to gain some of the lost ground through the back door. This may still be worth studying in Muslim countries (such as Saudi Arabia, Afghanistan, Pakistan etc.) where the inferior status of women is still maintained in law.

The matriarchal form of family is thus a feature of the oriental and Mediterranean worlds in so far as it implies that women had, in Greece, Italy, and further East, considerable *influence* even during the days of diminished legal *rights*. Thus, whether because of force of personality, love and affection, or pure guile, women in reality –and not if judged solely on the basis of legal appearances - were often not as powerless as the classical image suggests. To understand the extent to which they escaped the widely accepted stereotype requires a considerable amount of reading for the signs of emancipated behaviour are revealed by history, local anthropological studies and even (reliable) anecdotes. I call this the 'concealed influence of women'.

Ancient Greek (and Roman) history is full of examples of *concealed* influence. The Greek Goddesses, if no other, show us how often they outwitted their husbands and their lovers. Yet it is in relatively more modern times that we must seek to find illustrations of how what was not allowed through the front door occurred through the back window. Herodotus offers us a superb example of how this worked on one famous encounter in ancient Sparta.

He thus recounts how Aristagoras, Tyrant of Miletus, while preparing an insurrection against Persia, visited Sparta and asked the Lacedaemonians for their assistance, simultaneously offering rich gifts to their King, Cleomenes I. During that evening while King and daughter were alone in his apartments the daughter - Gorgo, later to become the wife of King Leonidas of Thermopylae fame, scuppered the deal by warning her father

"to go away from this deal [for] the stranger will corrupt you."[4]

It did not take long to convince the King and daughter's advice was accepted.

Such an approach to the study of women's *influence* in history aims at getting a 'feel' or 'understanding' of the situation being investigated but conceals pitfalls at every step and one must therefore guard against the danger of committing erroneous generalisation determining female power in this way. Yet the example I offered above, however, suggests that this feel for the Spartan mentality can only come by studying the numerous negotiations that the leaders conducted with foreign counterparts and digesting how they finally, after listening with few interruptions, reacted to them. Additionally, it shows that often supporting evidence can be found from a written source, historical in this instance, but perfectly suited to support our proposition that what matters is the *influence exercised behind the scenes*, and not necessarily what is said in a public debate or what the letter of the law dictates.

Similar illustrations come to us from later centuries and show that there is something worthy of consideration in what I am trying to

---

4. Herodotus, *The Histories*, 5, 51, Penguin, revised 2003, trans. by Aubrey de Sélincourt. Herodotus claims the daughter was only 8 or 9 at the time, but most scholars believe she was in her late teens. To this day we find communities on many islands – Crete for instance – where wives and daughters both serve and advise their husbands or fathers.

fathom correctly. Indeed, here are two further illustration of female influence coming from the Seljuk and Ottoman courts as they were gradually proceeding to erode the power of Christian Byzantium, effectively from the 9th century AD onwards. Though they are relatively unknown they are also intriguing since they show women managing to overcome not only the obstacles posed by deep *ethnic divisions* but also those associated with their sex. In these illustrations we thus find Greek wives and/ or mothers of Turkmen Sultans trying to persuade the husbands or sons to alleviate the position of the persecuted Greek citizens. Their entreaties were successful.

The first example refers to Seljuk Sultan Izz al-Din who was half Greek in origin. Since his maternal uncles were rather too overtly running the political affairs of his state, Turkmen citizens plotted his assassination so that he would be succeeded by his brother who had a Turkish mother. The female cabal prevailed though not for long.

Even more daring were the actions of the Byzantine Princess Theodora, daughter of the writer, mystique, and thinker Emperor (between 1347 and 1354 when he resigned and retied to a monastery) Johm Cantacuzene who was given to marriage to the Ottoman Sultan Orhan Orhan (1326-1362). The marriage was an arranged affair; and most women in the position of Theodora would have waned in the shadow of such an arrangement.

Theodora, however, was made of sterner stuff. She resisted conversion to Islam and, obviously, in this she succeeded because she managed to gain her husband's tacit support. Emboldened, she then went on to spend much of her own wealth in ransoming captured Greeks. Again, her luck did not run out so she thus repeatedly tried to convince Greeks who had converted to Islam to revert to their Christian religion. This was behaviour that carried with it the death penalty; but she avoided it thanks to her tact and highly developed brain power!

Old and new examples thus demonstrate that in the Mediterranean world - Greece most certainly – strong-headed women always found a way to exercise influence even where, legally and socially, they had no power. Indeed, this power of theirs was further enhanced if and when their family was socially, economically, or both, more powerful than that of her male spouse. In such instances, through their fathers or brothers, they thus ended up by applying equilibrating pressure to improve their standing or, even, subjugate the financially weaker male, thus turning him into a fully dependant and even docile husband. Such pressure, however, was rarely exercised in an open or brutal manner. But where the conditions were right, it often meant that the man's predominance was only nominal and apparent but not real in substance.

A not insignificant factor in the reversal of roles was often due not only to the power of the woman's family's fortune but also her strong personality. The Byzantine examples given – a few among many - attest to the veracity of the above statement. But this continues to this day, especially with those women who came from professional families which had had no sons (or their sons had died young) and the woman had in divers ways then come to be seen, especially by her father, as the male heir he never had (or lost). In such cases - and I have known many who fall into this category - the girl was, essentially, brought up as the boy that never was and was thus seen by her father as the real "continuer" of the family business and traditions and even the family name through child bearing with her husband. Their desire to prove to their father that they were as good if not better than the son he never had gave then a ruthless character and in their comportment enabled them to display female as well as male characteristics. It is a shame that one cannot give names to prove instantly the correctness of one's thesis; but then, at times, an author is entitled to hope that his reader will give him the benefit of the doubt, especially if he emphatically asserts that he has very specific examples in mind.

The restraining habit that sons are named after the paternal grandfather thus made it clear that the family continuity was strongly desired and maintained in one way or another. Moreover, even though the Russian practice of referring to someone always by using the patronymic was never accepted in Greece (or Italy), the paternal Christian name always crept in the son's name and signature by inserting it between the Christian name and the surname as if it was his second name. To this day Englishmen are thus confused by this practice and tend to treat the intervening name as being a Christian second name.

From my pupillage days at the English Bar one final and very personal example will demonstrate the preceding assertions. In those days as "pupil" I was allowed to sit in legal conferences chaired by my pupil master, a learned QC, and subsequently a well-known commercial judge. On one those occasions, whenever the legal issues involved a shipping case I was always quick to notice - and point out to the senior lawyers with whom I was working - the presence of the wife. Thus, though invariably silent, she always was crucial in making up her husband's final decision. Colleagues whose legal practice was largely focused on shipping law thus took extra care in keeping the present female spouse "on board" in whatever was decided and avoid at all costs the risk of addressing her husband thus giving the impression that they were ignoring the real power completely.

I conclude this unorthodox – arguably even original - sub-section with a warning. My thesis is that examples such as those I have assembled can show that female influence in the oriental including the ancient Greek world could be more extensive than the legal powers recognised to women would allow us to imagine. To extent that this assertion can be generalised and re-enforced by more specific example it represents an important dilution of the established and widely accepted principle that women in the East were always condemned to an inferior status.

The reality of the female position in this part of the world thus actually varied from time to time and region to region. This applies to ancient Greece as well, an issue I examined at some length in my most recent book *Greek Poetry – Epic Lyric, and Tragic through the eyes of Artists and Psychiatrists*[5] which should be consulted for those interested in this topic.

Sexual liberty and prowess

Less than fifty years ago prenuptial sex, especially in the Mediterranean world, was much rarer than it is today. For women in particular it could have disastrous consequences since it invariably scuppered all chances of – at the very least – a good marriage. The greatest victims of this rule were domestic servants, exploited sexually by their masters or their sons. The fate of such a *donna abandonata* was harsh: joining a Convent or suicide – the Seine in Paris even had a place favoured for such final acts of desperation!

Men on the other hand enjoyed much great pre-nuptial and post-nuptial freedom with prostitutes or even married women. Other ways for sexually relief were also in use. In ancient Greece, for instance, or 15th and 16th century Europe, France in particular, male homosexual sex was not infrequent with young pupils or male pages. In France they were often referred to as *les mignons,* and Henry of Poland, later Henry III of France, has a pronounced predicletion for such kind of amorous encounters. Though the aforementioned King is what, these days, we would describe as 'gay' as far as the Mignons were concerned they did

---

5. The current edition published by Sideris Publications (2015) is in Greek; an English edition will follow.

not, necessarily imply such a permanent predilection. In practice, they were often little more than temporary ways of solving the sexual needs of young men, preparing the heterosexual boy for the next and normal phase of his life i.e. heterosexual marriage. In fact, for those willing (and able) to make huge intellectual jumps in time these boys often remind one of the young teenage girls in Sappho's 'finishing' school were young girls were taught music and dancing and may have experienced lesbian love before entering into a formal heterosexual marriage and living the restricted life that was imposed upon married women of that time. In this last context it is noteworthy that nowhere in the surviving fragments of Sappho's poems is this love presented in a vulgar way but seen an initiation process in what, eventually, become the girl's final kind of heterosexual married life. Most scholars who have analysed the relative few fragments of her poems which have reached us have even claimed that less than 10% of them deal with erotic themes.

The change in sexual practices which has taken place in the recent four or five decades is partly the result of liberalization of public morality but also progressive improvements in contraception techniques. However, this change of behaviour has also been accompanied by the growth of teenage pregnancies, extra-marital pregnancies, and a growing number of single parent families. This increase is remarkable given that in some countries – Greece for instance - social security support for all of the above categories is minimal if non –existent. Such financial support that comes for these categories is thus predominantly emanating from family support, a source of help which covers a significantly wider range of needs which the present economic squeeze has saved many from complete destitution. The continued existence of stronger family links alluded to earlier on has thus been one of the reasons which has kept many Greeks afloat during the present difficulties.

To a large extent males also retain and cultivate a macho image through real or boasted polygamous links. For a Greek, even if belonging to one of the country's elites, sexual philandering can still be seen as a symbol of virility, youthful health, and power, though nowadays it may attract more easily than it did in days gone by a variety of family and social consequences, including divorce. However, it is the open boast about one's sexual prowess, even if that implies adultery, which may strike (many or most I cannot tell) western observers as odd if not amazing!

Such attitudes are not limited to particular classes of society; and the problem is that if such behaviour is adopted by those standing higher up on the social ladder the easier it is to find imitators among those who are less privileged.

In the late 1980's former Greek Prime Minister Andreas Papandreou became involved in such an incident when he, eventually, chose to abandon his wife of long standing in favour of an air hostess whom he ended up marrying. It is a sign of how moral attitudes had been changing after the fall of the Junta in 1974 that the event shocked some but left most citizens undisturbed, which is not to say, however, uninterested. To the extent that Mr. Papandreou was attacked it was his socialist politics since his opponents (wrongly) saw in this incident a chance to try and dent his huge popularity with the electorate.

In the same vein, Prime Minister Berlusconi's more recent reputed sexual antics for a long time did not disturb his compatriots anywhere near as much as they shocked northern Europeans. When I discussed this attitude with my mainy Italian friends, the reaction was entirely the reverse. Berlusconi was primarily seen as a *most* successful businessman, a *fairly* successful politician, and an *enviably* virile man! In later years however some of these accusations made against him ended up in court because the consenting women were, apparently, under age. It is thus something of an irony that the final downfall of Italy's self-made multi-millionaire came about not because of financial mismanagement of his personal or the country's economic affairs but because of his private life.

An example of the 'apparently prudish' New World is found in the life of former President Clinton whose indiscreet behaviour with a female intern at the White House nearly led to his political impeachment. The details of the affair were truly sordid showing serious lack of judgment on the part of the former President. Once again, however, the main motive of attacking the ex-President was American prudery and, above all, political opportunism. Giving the attack a political slant and making a big fuss of this event proved a fatal error for those who saw in the scandal a chance of getting rid of the President. For once the event became politicised, and the battle was between his popularity and that of his challenging opponents, the outcome became a foregone conclusion. Clinton was infinitely more popular than the Republicans who succeeded him. The indisputable charm of his personality thus triumphed over the dullness of his Presidential opponent drowning the latter's probity.

The above-mentioned examples of men in the lime light illustrate much more than the fact that male infidelity is a fact life tolerated by modern societies even when it appears at their highest levels. In recent time French President Hollande's amorous peccadillos actually went a step further, causing mirth and gossip but no real concern, perhaps, because his popularity rating have been so consistently low and the French simply did not care about their President's sexual antics.

Escaping from the consequences of philandering will vary on the circumstances and, as stated, the popularity of the philandering official will, in the end determine the extent of his rehabilitation. But how the 'culprit' handles his indiscretion may also shorten the period of reprobation. Thus, the example of a contrite Prime Minister Major having had an affair with one of his former female Ministers would never be encountered in Italy or Greece. In practice, of course, it remains debatable whether such contrition as he showed minimised the immorality of his behaviour; my guess is that very few these days judge these issues in moral term. It did, however, help get the indiscretion forgotten more quickly by the public.

The conclusion must thus be that such male indiscretion, even if it is still criticized by sections of society - e.g. the Church or moralizers – for the bulk of modern citizens nowadays seems to remain something of little concern. Now, suggesting that matters of male indiscretion are of little concern to most these days does not mean that the practice has ceased. It does, however, suggest yet another move towards equality between the sexes in so far as it will automatically be treated an as amusing matter even if, at first instance, it is not condoned.

A related matter is whether males inclined to such infidelity feel able/inclined to brag about such feats of theirs. My guess is that in the North this was not such a wide spread practice, whereas in the South the tendency to be more open about such adventures was far more usual and even boastful in its nature. My point is best made by a true story which I have heard recounted not once but twice by two good friends: an Italian and Greek. They are so identical and in many ways so amazingly indifferent to their betrayed spouse's sensibilities that it may be worth mentioning in some detail.

Thus in both cases and in the presence of their wives I found myself as a latter-day Gladstone trying gently to advise my friends that their openly admitted practices were unnecessarily hurtful to their spouses. (The Italian was married to an American, the Greek to a Greek who, I repeat, were present when this discussion took place.) In both instances, when my wife and I wondered – naturally *sotto voce* – whether such behaviour and boasting were unbearably hurtful to the wives we were overheard. Almost instantaneously our dear Italian friend replied with a prolonged "Noo", stressing the 'o' almost to infinity. The assertion that it was almost inconceivable for his wife not to be proud at the husband's wider 'appeal' was instantly rebutted with the disarming assertion that "x [the name of the betrayed spouse] is proud to hear that her husband is so desirable [sic] that other women cannot resist having sex with him!" If the confidence that accompanied this statement had not been so earnest, both of us would have laughed at such insensitive audacity by an otherwise charming and learned colleague.

In both cases the wives present at the time of such boasting smiled benignly, giving the impression that it was all a matter of a joke. But under the surface, it was deadly serious and both my wife and I felt that it must have been deeply hurtful for the betrayed Italian wife as well. I cannot imagine such a conversation taken place in Holland, Germany or England unless the married couple had an "open or free" marriage agreement allowing to both the freedom "to sleep" with anyone they fancied.

Paradoxically (though also mercifully) the liberalisation of sexual relations in our times seems to have made such bragging un-necessary and thus, I get the impression, it happens less frequently. After all, bragging concealed an element of bravery and courage for it invariable took place in the company of all-male groups where the participants for some reason felt the need to make clear their sexual prowess, even if this often meant vicariously enjoying the 'glory' of the philandering friend of theirs.

The conclusion of this brief survey is that sexual prowess is a feature which is more openly admired (if not envied) in the Southern hemisphere and is or, probably better to say was, tolerated more than one would have normally expected giving the teaching of the Church and the (original) overall conservative nature of the southern societies.

This difference of attitude may, indeed, be clearly reflected in one of art's greatest works – Mozart's *Don Giovanni*. For the opera, music and libretto, have given rise to endless discussions by moral philosophers and psychiatrists most hailing from northern countries whereas it is perfectly possible that for Mozart and Daponte the young Don's sexual prowess was something to be expected in the Andalusia of his time (and, maybe more so in ours). Certainly, both of them treat the Don almost as a hero and moralists who have opted for condemnation have not found much material in this 'difficult' opera to use to back their views.

*Female education, employment (and unemployment), pay in-
equality and their consequences on bringing up children*

This *de iure* but not always *de facto* subservience to the male was legally
reversed in Greece after the fall of the Junta in 1974 when a series of
constitutional and ordinary laws swung the legal pendulum strongly
away from the male-dominated model which had prevailed until then.
Thus, article 22 of the Constitution of 1975 established – along lines not
dissimilar to the (earlier) English Equal Pay and the Sex Discrimination
Act - that "all workers have the right to equal pay for work of equal
value." The 2001 version of the Constitution, amended under the influence of the earlier Amsterdam Treaty, took matters further by stating in article 116 that the State encouraged "the adoption of positive
measures for the promotion of equality between men and women".

The extent to which theory and practice, however, differs varies on
the consequences of inequality e.g. employment, unemployment, pay,
childbirth, etc. Even these distinctions, however, give at best a general
indication of how much the degree of persisting inequality can differ.
Just as confusing can be the real reasons for the unequal treatment.

Thus, the grounds for unequal pay can be confusingly varied. The
most traditional is obvious discrimination which, for various reasons,
can remain unreported. This is true not only of Greece but, as I have
been told by knowledgeable colleagues in Texas, it is also true in the
USA; for a law is as effective as its application is in practice.

But the discriminatory practices may have been brought about
subtler reasons which stem from choices made by the women themselves, unknown in many cases, that they had hidden consequences.
In Greece there is thus statistical evidence[6] to suggest that reduced
pay may be the result of educational choices made by women when
planning their future higher education and thus career. Thus the higher risk-aversion tendencies exhibited by most women often lead them
into seeking degrees in the realm of education, languages, and the
humanities, which are known to command lower wages.

These are important impeding obstacles on the road towards greater sex equality so they do not justify the conclusion that the days of
male dominance have now gone simply because the law, from the
Constitution downwards, has changed.

---

6. See, for instance, "The Gender Wage Gap as a Function of Educational Degree
   Choices in an Occupationally Segregated EU Country (Greece)" at http://mpra.
   ub.uni-muenchen.de/19166/ Paper No 19166 posted on 15 December 2009.

Genuine and complete equality between the sexes thus does not prevail in Greece. For though most traditional legal inequalities, including the obligation to give up one's maiden name, have been swept away, old habits die hard and society still, in doubt, gives preference to male interests and display greater interest in male reputation.

The disadvantaged position of women is seen not only in the lack of equality of pay for equal work but also in the lower levels of female participation in the labour market, lower of the EU average, much lower than that found in the UK. Ironically (and unfortunately) Greece moves up on the scale when it comes to levels of *unemployment* suffered by women compared to men[7] for here their numbers exceed those of men. On the unemployment front, the women most affected are those under the age of twenty five and those with University degrees.

Divorce numbers have also gone up drastically in recent years – from 3,675 in 1971 to 11.309 in 2000.[8] But the burden of such divorces also tends to fall more heavily on women, even if the level of allowances or, generally speaking, the re-allocation of matrimonial property after divorce is gradually becoming more favourable towards them than it was in the past. Also, the 'stigma' of divorce, to the extent that such term can still be used, seems to affect women more than men, at any rate in so far as the chances of remarriage are smaller in the case of divorced women than men.

But the greatest differences may still be found in the area of education and unemployment. For though women now join Polytechnics and Universities in numbers which equal and in some subjects exceed those of men, their ability to reach the highest paid and most responsible jobs varies according to professions.[9]

Thus, though women are well represented in the civil service, and moderately well in politics, their presence among the highest echelons of banking and business is much weaker than that of men and they do not achieve equal pay with men nor the same visibility and power. Thus, only very recently Greece obtained its first woman President of its Supreme Court; it was only recently that a highly educated woman made it to the Chairmanship of a large bank – the National Bank of

---

7. Useful statistical information can be found in I. Livanos, Çagri Yalkin and Imanol Nuñez "Gender employment discrimination: Greece and the United Kingdom", *International Journal of Manpower*, vo. 30 no. 8, 2009, pp. 815-834.
8. On this see Magda Kaitanidi, in daily *The News* (Τα Νέα), 22- 23.11. 2003.
9. Though note the point made earlier on about their own choice of degrees and how this predetermines the entire career development.

Greece - or become a CEO of a large corporation, though a small number have managed to be elected to Administration Boards. Though a number of strong minded women have held ministerial post since the mid 1950', Greece also acquired its first female Prime Minister June 2015 when the (female) President of the Supreme Court held that post for a limited period of time solely to preside over the government during the electoral period. By contrast, the (extreme) Communist party had for many years a feisty woman as its leader. In politics the highest political position was recently occupied by a highly intelligent and loquacious woman who was elected by a very large majority Speaker of Parliament.

Different kinds of jobs and different pay are also reflected in all statistics which show that the prime bread winner in almost all families is the male. Unemployment in women also seems to be higher suggesting that for some reason (and for reasons which could technically amount to breaches of sex discriminating laws) tend to be made unemployed or choose to take early retirement in days, such as the present ones, when economic instability is persuading many to cut their losses and leave before they are made redundant.

The most worrying statistic however, comes from the figures on unemployment. Generally speaking unemployment in Greece has followed a steady upward trend moving from 4% in 1981, 5% in 1983, to 7.65% in 1991, to 10.4 in 2001, and near 18% in 2011 (and rising).[10] Youth unemployment in 2011 has in fact reached a record level of close to 44%, the percentage being some 15% higher for young girls than young boys. As stated, though women are higher than men in all categories, the increased percentage of unemployed prime bread winners – men – has also gone up, contributing to a dramatic fall in the earning of the population during the last two years. In November (2011) for instance the Bank of Greece announced a figure that largely passed un-noticed namely, that 14% of Greek *households- that is close to half a million people -* had none of its member in employment. The figures remain unstable though the overall bleakness of employment conditions in Greece remains stable and not very likely to improve dramatically in the near future.

Such figures contribute, though they are not the sole cause of the dramatic drop in the willingness to marry and start families. Thus, while in 1971 73. 350 marriages were officiated the figure had dropped

---

10. For detailed figures (and explanation) up until 2004 see Nicholas Apergis, "An estimation of the national rate of unemployment in Greece", *Journal of Policy Modeling* 27 (2009), pp. 91-99.

to 49,000 by 2000 while during the same period the number of divorces had gone up from 3,675 to 11.309. Such figures, and the economic background briefly sketched above, has led to a halving of the child population with statistics suggesting that by the end of the last century Greece was among the sixth country in Europe with the oldest population with an estimated 25% of its population being above 65 years age. Compared with the exact reverse trend found in contemporary Turkey, these figures pose a huge ethnographic danger for the country future viability. Overall, however, the whole of Europe – including Russia – face a serious ethnographic problem.

Growing divorce rates and enhanced sexual liberation, unaccompanied however by proper sexual education have also led to an increase in single parent families (which in Greece as indeed in the rest of Europe predominantly means single mother families). [11] Who exactly qualifies to be included in this category has never been conclusively settled by researchers; and the available EUROSTAT figures can be confusing and, indeed, misleading. Two points however, seem to be incontestable.

The first is that Greece is among the countries which has among the lowest figures of single parent families, compared for instance with Denmark, the UK, Germany and the Netherlands all of whom attain substantially higher levels.

Second, there is near unanimity among those who write on this subject that this growing trend is set to continue and is, indeed, irreversible. Whether, in the end, this will lead to the re-definition of the traditional family unit and cease being seen as a social anomaly or, at any rate, a state of affairs which tends to have serious and prejudicial effects on the children living in such families, remains a subject of some discussion.

Figures such as the above only reveal the tip of the iceberg of the contemporary Greek crisis. Its political and economic reasons are not within the purview of this comparative study but the consequences

---

11. Slightly dated in its figures – since it was published in 1995 but still thorough and informative – is the treatise of Professor Dimitra Kogidou entitled *Single parent families: reality, perspectives and social policy* (in Greek). Chapter six contains an interesting if especially depressing account as to the deleterious effects this form of family unit has for the children that grow in it while chapter eleven contains much useful information about the position, status and rights of women who find themselves in such a condition. The overall conclusion on this topic of single parent families is that in Greece various forms of inequalities – economic, social policy, attitudinal, educational etc – make a situation which is by definition fraught with problems even more serious within the Greek context.

which are linked (but do not entirely depend) on the pay structures of society, the decline of the family bond because of changed working practices, the break-up of families partly the result of stressful financial conditions, and the possible results which all these factors can have on a rise in criminal behaviour must be noted even of not discussed in detail. Though extremely serious demographically for the future of the country, they also show a similarity in trends found in countries as different to Greece as the USA. To the extent that such comparisons can be meaningfully, they thus acquire an even more menacing meaning.

Apparel and appearance

All cultures practice a wide range of activities with the aim of self-definition. The enactment of constitutions does just that; so do holding of national days or anniversaries of great victories. In their private lives humans are no different. Apparel and appearance, in other words how people dress and present themselves to the world, is an important part of their need for self-definition though how this is done and what form it will take with vary between the "show off" versus the "restrained", depending on the society to which one belongs, his temperament and his class background. Otherwise, however, the urge behind it will be the same whether the self-definition determines sexual comportment or aims at social advancement. In the case of some religions – Jewish for instance and Muslim - apparel as well as head gear is determined by religious rules. Though as we shall note below there exist significant geographical variations as to what precisely must be warn, where and when. Additionally, as we shall note, there has been a civil rights legislation and litigation as to whether these religiously imposed rules must be observed or, alternatively tolerated, in European and, generally Western countries.

The preceding paragraph contains some clues of the importance of our topic; but not enough. For, in my view, this issue about 'apparel' is more important than may strike the reader at first sight and this for two reasons.

First the word itself can be used literally, as I use it in this chapter, to refer to clothes, vestments, official garments, ceremonial robes etc. The importance of these is that they help create the external impression of style, power, or authority for those who wear them and wish to generate for the sake of some personal advantage or the more efficacious discharge of their duty. A Bishop's robes, the judges' gowns or a general's uniform, are all designed to achieve precisely this effect. The psychological importance which this 'disguise' (the judicial aims, in part, to conceal the everyday face of the judge) can have on the intended onlookers in these days of (often only) pretended equality is often wrongly underestimated; but, like it or not, there is little we can do about it.

Second, apparel could also be used metaphorically to refer to the way speakers intentionally 'cloth' and project, through speech, gestures, mannerisms, their thoughts, ideas, values, and future plans. Exaggerated, unusual - tasteless some might argue - apparel is increasingly used to attract media attraction. One could argue it is also a way of attracting attention to a new policy or a new approach to politics. To me, however, attempting to present a message as new by means of ridiculously colourful apparel is more likely a sign of narcissistic behaviour or, simply, pure bad taste. The same is true of a relatively informal trend for men not to wear ties and keep the top of the shirt unbuttoned. Being different is here, once again, the underlying reason; though the public statement made is, largely, one of a literally minded if not Left-thinking individual. This trend, of course, can also be seen as the ever-evolving trend of simplification and liberalisation of daily life; a trend which has these days penetrated even the work place. Where such trends assume more extreme forms, the suspicion of lurking narcissism can also not be excluded. All of these 'liberalising trends' must thus be seen as being part of the human desire to use their apparel to make a public statement about themselves and their views. Those accused of such deeply concealed urges are likely to externalise them through the way they talk and walk, and generally use their body language to project an image of super-self-confidence (even though often what may lie beneath such behaviour is the reverse namely lack of confidence in one's selves, looks, or profession attainments. Such reading that I have managed on a topic which has attracted many authors since Freud first raised it in an essay in 1914 makes me suspect that various complexes lie hidden behind the projected image of differentness and confidence. Interestingly, however, this debasement of aesthetics is not found among the otherwise very similar in character Italians. For in that country, from houses to vehicles, apparel or general comportment, the Italians remain visibly more sophisticated in matters of taste providing a salutary warning that stressing similarities between these two countries and its inhabitants must go so far and no further.

Ambiguity accompanies such sartorial exaggeration; and, as stated, it is often introduced in the language used by such persons so that discussion as to what the meant can, in turn, cause more discussion about them than clarify the issues they are addressing. History offers us a wide variety of examples but among the most famous is General de Gaulle's famous sentence to the European Algerians who brought him to power in 1958. Thus, to an excited crowed of Algerian Frenchmen in Algiers shouting that France should not abandon them he famously replied "J'ai vous ai compri" (I have understood you.) He had; they wished to remain part of metropolitan France. But they did not understand him; for understanding them did not mean he was agreeing with them. Upon his return to Paris he thus set in motion the traumatic – for the French Algerians but necessary for France - process of independence and separation, a decision politically courageous and one which even lead to a – happily – unsuccessful attempt against the General's life.

The example, one of many, shows how those who possess the verbal talents of clothing their thoughts in ambiguous ways can succeed in presenting cynical or pragmatic decisions in an ideological or, worse, deliberately misleading garb. In technical subjects - such as law – the terminology used can help keep hidden important similarities between legal systems because they remain concealed behind the technical verbiage.

In politics, the dangers are even greater for they can mislead friend and foe leaving only the speaker happy to bask in an atmosphere where his ambiguous if not meaningless sentence is being discussed. Though this last point is understandable and explicable, for those who work in the global context of contemporary politics this can present a serious set-back to understanding what really is happening, especially if the Press is unaware of these psychological techniques of using language to confuse and mislead.

The above observations are, I believe, valid the world over. But the way we externalize our thoughts through speech and gestures differs and these differences may, to put the idea in common parlance, 'work' in one environment but not in another. In these days where both business and politics are more internationalized than ever before, realizing the importance of this obvious statement can make the difference between success and failure in presenting one's case in different countries and different audiences. Legal advocacy in international courts may be one of the rare examples I can think of where the Anglo-Saxon orality of litigation offers the advocates of these countries a universally admired advantage over their otherwise equally intelligent and able 'foreign' adversaries.

The comments made this far apply to westerners – European, American or Asiatic but not to populations who have espoused different religions. The Muslins and the Jews are two among the most notable exception and in these two cases religion is the cause of the difference; as we shall see note these differences also have – rightly or wrongly is not for us to comment upon – also retarded European integration and assimilation among different races with different religions; and this fact may even take a turn for the worse as a result of a growing number of Muslims nowadays seeking refuge in European lands.

The Muslim Burqua – differently spelt in different countries – is a full length cloak which covers a woman's body. There are fond in the Middle east, many parts of Africa, especially North Africa and Central Asia where the name, however is Chakri not Burqua. The colour varies from light blue, brown, occasionally white, though typical it is black. Differences, however do appear in a square peach of clothe which covers the face and is sown to the top part allowing it to be lifted upward and expose a fair part of the entire face, Alternatively, however, only a small part is allowed to expose the eyes of the wearer to public sight.

Religious reasons lie behind the dress code including the over-riding Muslim preference of modest attire but also the wish to avoid the giving rise to sexual temptations or even impure thoughts. Burqua are only warn by Jews who belong to the religiously more extreme citizens. Otherwise religion infleuce the male habit to wear small caps over the crown of the head known as Kippah;s or Kipa (and in Yiddish Yamaka's. The reason is to show repect to God who stand above ordinary humans and it is warn continuously by Orthodox Jews or, by those who are less religiously inclined, only when praying or at funerals.

The religious reasons behind the wearing of special apparel distinguishes those religions who opt for such rules form Westerners who pick their clothing on the basis of personal, psychological or other, considerations. In principle the difference is one which should allow each region and ethnicity to do what their religion and custom dictate; but in recent times, more than, say in the immediate past, these requirements have led to dispute, at times fairly aggressive, in and outside the courts of Justice and Legislative Bodies[12] of the European

---

12. This, for instance, from 2010 onwards laws have been passed in France, Belgium

and other Western countries and have impeded the social and daily assimilation of different races inhabiting in Europe. The reasons are mainly two; but for the same of completeness we shall a third and link what is said here with some more general points raised earlier in the book.

The first reason is linked with increased ordinary criminality and the corresponding increase of electronic surveillance in street, shops, and other public places. Obviously women (or men pretending to be women) could ensure complete privacy if covered from head to toe in a Burqua and the majority – according to statistics – of European citizens object to them being worn and used in this way.

Secondly, on a number of occasions – appearance in court, educational examinations, employment interviews – many feel their decision to judge witnesses, examinees or applicants for posts if they cannot see their eyes.

The third and final reasons is the aforementioned tendency of the most recent immigrants in Europe to adopt a more aggressive attitude in asserting their rights compared to immigrants of thirty or forty or more years ago who were content in obtaining refuge in Europe and demanded little more. This last excuse, to the extent that it is valid if not even the dominant factor in opposing – on the whole unsuccessful legislation prohibiting the wearing of Burquas in public places is the most worrying of all, not least because of Europe's current swamping of predominantly Muslim populations. To put it differently, this problem is part of the wider and more dangerous issue of what consequences with the massive influx of Muslim immigrations may cause to the internal orders of European Nations. Political correctness or not, the issue will have to faced squarely one day.

Conclusion: apparel and way of speech can be combined if the speaker is cunning enough to realise that this combination can be helpful to him but unhelpful for his superiors, his company, his party or even his country. It is certainly a habit or a practice which does not favour clarity of expression. The problem of apparel may become more acute in some cases in the years to come.

---

and the Netherlands have been passed by the parliament of these countries and this legislation has not been found to offend the European Convention of Human Rights. In the UK, though something in the order of just under 70% of the population oppose the wearing of such gear no legislation has yet been passed.

Conveying a message through apparel and posture

I touched upon this topic in the preceding section but we must return to it for it is linked to modern psychological studies of human apparel and body language intended to produce desired psychological reactions. Time and again in my lectures and books I have advocated interdisciplinary studies, especially the combination of psychology with the understanding of history, politics, and law. My success has been negligible, perhaps because each discipline has its own jargon which others do not understand and thus cannot use. Still, here we are talking about mass psychology, which is very different to individual psychology, and extremely important in political discourse. The whole topic is almost totally ignored in Greece and political debate, especially on television, is a highly unattractive display of anything between four to eight people talking simultaneously, shouting at each other, at times resorting to abuse, with very few of the moderators empowered to interrupt such hecklers –for the do not deserve the title of speakers or debaters – and even kick them out of their studios. It is in this context of wider political discourse, that apparel once again entails its own consequences.

At first blush, the differences in apparel hit the eye of the observer and can cause admiration or disapproval or even surprise. On deeper analysis however, they give, as just stated, helpful additional clues about the wearer's character, apparent indifference to trivia, even signs of inverse snobbishness. Judging the external appearance is thus, in my view, more than a simple matter of aesthetics since it says much about the person 'hidden'- not 'clothed' by the apparel!

How one dresses thus says much about one's confidence (or lack of it). You are pretty, or feel pretty, you are thus confident and in a 'show-off" mood, so you dress up accordingly. You dress to impress; you dress to kill. The dress will be in fashion, even daring; designed to attract attention; for though you feel confident or, perhaps, because you feel so sure for yourself, you wish to attract attention. A provocative decolté is often used in Greek politics to attract comment if not gossip among the usually over-sexed Greeks; but to my knowledge; it has never affected the view of voters as to the mental gifts – if any – of the so-semi-exposed female peacock. To me, and arguably, not only to me, such a display of a woman's cleavage is only a manifestation of insecurity on behalf of the person showing off part of their exposed bosoms. For if the case is strong, their argument unanswerable, the way they are presented calm and pleasing to the ear, why does the speaker feel the need to have resort to the provocative dress or the daring bikini?

Women as well as men display these characteristics. A handful of female candidates for Parliament have even resorted to being photographed in provocative bikinis. The purpose of such behaviour is obvious to those who know how to study them; but it would be ludicrous to suggest that beyond a fleeting reaction none of the above have left any real mark in politics for Greeks may like to be titivated in such crude ways but are intelligent enough to distinguish appearance from performance. Body language re-enforces one's psychology and helps project the image one wishes to project which boils down to two words: "notice me." The Italian or Greek man or women who enters the bar or restaurant with such feelings in his or her mind does not keep them concealed. He is showing them, by showing off, and the clothing –modern, expensive, chosen to bring out his or her strong bodily features – helps in this ego-projection. The effect of such behaviour, however, in substantial terms remains, as stated, debatable. Cotemporary political experience thus suggests that in practical terms a provocative feminine appearance may help a female politician in her political career only if for sexiest reasons such image attracts the personal attention of some old millionaire or senior politician who possess patronage power.

Remember, however, that we are talking of public appearances or, in the case of politics, public discourse. Aristotle in his *Rhetoric* and Cicero in his *Ars Oratoria* taught us that how you talk varies (and must vary) depending on the occasion. In short you talk differently in Parliament, in a court of law, a University auditorium, a small gathering of political supporters hurriedly organised in a barn or tavern. The same applies to apparel. A colourful shirt worn in a parliamentary debate or in a senior court of law would be totally unacceptable in most countries in which I have worked and spoken in the kind of contexts mentioned above. Greeks, however, do not seem to realise the deeper significance of what I have just mentioned. At best, they might explain the departure of widely accepted practice on the shallow argument of modernity (as they understand it). Shallow, not least because the psychological consequences of such 'innovations' have not been studied and the wider relevant literature remains ignored. Often, far too often, Greeks - and I suspect many other Mediterranean nations - feel confident that they can get away with murder on the strength of their native wits. My training at the English bar taught me that there is no substitute than hard work and even harder preparation before you stand up on your feet to speak.

For the reasons given above the English – dare I add most advanced western Europeans - do not like displays based on cheap tricks or speeches based on generalities and not backed by detail. The male suit, especially if bespoke, will be sombre, stylish, well-fitting, and serious. The impression it will make will be that of the professional who is wearing it. Gravitas and under-statement are images valued in apparel; and they often succeed to transfer this very same image to the image or idea which a speaker is trying to project. In England in par-ticular, the obvious display of a famous brand – the Gucci shoe or the Hermes tie – will not necessarily impress; probably they may even be scorned. The impression a speaker finally makes comes from the way his knowledge of the subject is projected, the confidence he shows in doing this so long as it does not border upon arrogance, and the background on which his views are based, the way of speech avoids excessive gravitas and may even be lightened by the odd flash of wit. In short, it is the inner confidence which finally does the trick; not the image-seeking ego that dictates the apparel or is projected by it. But then: attention! This is how things work in England; if an Englishman or woman thinks that the above values will also impress foreigners, he or she may be wildly off the mark.

I have noticed all of these characteristics with what I would call the dignified looking old boys who one often encountered in days gone by at the London clubs, Inns of courts, the most fashionable of the medical practices, or the most traditional – often the older – mem-bers of the civil service. The "location" influenced once upon a time the man, his comportment and apparel and he, in turn, added to its very special ambiance. But attention: all of the "environments" I men-tioned above - the club, the Inns of Court, the ministries – have grown in size and the people who populate them today are very different from those who did, say, forty years ago.

Speeches as I said vary depending to whom or where they are de-livered. They also vary upon the nation that is listening. The art of speaking, arguing, debating is not uniform. It constantly adapts, even while it is being delivered since a good speaker must be constantly aware whether he is winning or losing his audience and adapt his message or its tone accordingly.

The changes which have occurred in such matters in all these coun-tries are often due to the changes wrought on their societies by the passage of time, This "opening up" may be due to the fact that the complexity of modern government has made it necessary to hire more people or attract people with different talents or because of the need to attract money – donations, subscriptions and the like – have forced such institutions to open their doors to many who would not that long ago have been seen anywhere near them. And these "hoi polloi" do *not* appreciate the shoe that shows cracked skin, albeit, perfectly, polished; the suit which bears visibly the signs of extended use, and certainly not the suit case which is neither colourful, impeccably new, nor equipped with wheels and unfolding handles that make its use easier to move around and its appearance more noticeable.

The academic forms his own sub-category. The older specimens will still be wearing three piece suits projecting the distinct impression that they are as old as those who wear them. I never met face to face Sir Isaiah Berlin but his published photos clearly convey his preference for such suits! At the other end of the spectrum will be the young and trendy don, in the day clad in chinos or jeans and with a loose pullover on top while in the evenings, where like all good egalitarians, he will be getting plastered with Madeira or old (and thus expensive) Port, he will be sporting his black tie suit, completed by a pair of black shows with … rubber soles. The latter-day black patent shoe has thus all but disappeared, no doubt in the belief that the amount of expensive wine consumed will have clouded the vision of the socialite socialist and thus killed off such aesthetic judgment as he may have ever had!

Female apparel in England is equally sombre, often two-piece suits made of good material rather than silk, or chiffon, or displaying the characteristics of elegance and sexiness' which French or nowadays north Italian couture does. Such garments may be worn by younger ones, the "Sloanes", the ones who are married to wealthy husbands and drive four by fours simply to take their children to the local nursery, four blocks down the fashionable street they live. Depending on age all of the above will have fallen under the spell of Feragamo, Armani, and Versace, succumbed to the modern and the beautiful, and abandoned the traditional English low key dress. Many judges wives, most certainly the wives of dons, may admire such "European "fashion" but avoid it, either because they cannot afford it or, if they belong to the older generation, because the value simplicity, austerity, detest show off, put all their emphasis on the inner self, value, ability on which they trade best.

The European man or woman, especially the younger one who can also afford (or just barely afford) the most expensive items will do the exact opposite. He or she will spend choosing shirts, wonderfully colourful silk shirts if she is a woman, and with a talent which can only be described as natural to all those who inhabit in cities like Rome, Milan, Paris or the like, will know how to combine them with accessories like scarves which, with minor changes now and then, can help give the impression that the apparel warn has radically changed since your last saw it warn by its owner.

The Parisians, but even more so the Athenians and the Northern Italians, do not only wish to catch your eye; they wish to project their sexiness. In this exercise, beauty is secondary to the ability to project a sexy, lively, enticingly moving body and these tricks, if competently mastered and performed, can even make up for lack of exceptional looks or...brains. The French even have a term to indicate the physical attractiveness, even where physical beauty is absent. They talk of a "jolie-laide" the "attractive/plain" – the woman who has the irresistible "animal appeal" which, the French again, in a wonderful though nowadays somewhat dated expression would apply to a woman and say that "elle a du chien."

There is a host of such expressions in all the languages, especially those, who attach much importance on how you look and dress; and these phrases, like the apparel and make up used to create the final image, tell you a great deal about different nationalities, how they think, how they see themselves, and how they put down those who do not conform with their own aesthetic (and *underlying intellectual*) values.

Two more thoughts before concluding this essay, prompted by the two words italicized above.

First, the "matronly', sombre, unchanging apparel of the intelligent, well-read, impeccably behaved and often charming middle-aged (and more) English woman is not necessarily prompted by a desire to save money or attempts to conceal the lack of it by invoking some kind of "socialist" beliefs found so often among the intellectual upper middle classes since both they and the socialist or egalitarian husbands. For poverty, real or pretended, evaporates as a concern when indulgence in expensive wines, priceless tickets to Glyndebourne or the Covent Garden and, perhaps, even in frequent foreign travel prompted by the thirst to recharge one's intellectual batteries, takes over their life.

And as for the ladies of the shires, there the urge to differ would come by showing off the garden, maintain the upkeep of the ancestral home if they are still clinging to one, and keeping alive the hallowed way of country life including their hunting sport lives with all the expensive accoutrements which these entail.

None of all this, of course, is unworthy, let alone condemnable. But it is very different to the sensuous, aesthetic, and egocentric view of how life should be lived in countries where the climate encourages the cultivation of emotions rather than the valuing of utility, functionality, and modesty – not always genuine - above all else.

Second, one can only conclude this short essay dealing with the eternally fascinating topic of sex with one last thought.

Sex is not only the main method of procreation, one of the best ways for occasioning deep but momentary pleasure, but also provides a wonderful but little used mirror into different societies. Approached from this angle, it "says" much about the mentality and character differences which separate them. If one wishes to go beyond "saying" - i.e. "describing" - and move to "explaining" the said societal differences one sooner rather than later will find oneself lost in psychology and psychiatry and the multiple meanings of words used by them to understand the complexity of human emotions.

A long and fascinating subject this, but best left to a book of its own! Until then one final, all-inclusive, piece of advice: how one speaks and how one dresses should depend on a vast array of circumstances and conditions. Study them carefully; follow the guidelines of the environment, and then…be yourself.

Chapter Six

GREECE AND THE GREEKS AS SEEN BY THE BRITISH

General ideas

The knowledge of a foreign language helps one better understand one's own thought it also helps one understand the way one forms and externalizes one's unexpressed ideas. Later in life I was to extend this thought to law arguing that an important if not the main advantage of studying a foreign legal system was that it improved the understanding of one's own legal culture.

For years I felt happy with this formulation until I discovered that someone else had phrased the thought better and in a way which went beyond law. That someone else was the Nobel Laureate Thomas Mann who, in his epic novel "Joseph and his Brothers" published in 1935 wrote:

«*Denn nur durch Vergleichung unterscheidet man sich und erfährt was man ist, um ganz zu werden, was man sein soll*» ("For only through comparison does one distinguish one self and discovers what he is so that he can become what he should be.")

Let us not be retained here by the depressing thought of how difficult it is to be original and just accept it as a fact. Let us instead reflect on how willing we must be to think "out of the box" in order to try and take our subject of learning one step further than others have done. For Mann did just that, (unconsciously I believe) extending a shibboleth of comparative law to the entire domain of human psychology. Let me now bring his idea into my present subject.

In this chapter I would like to give a selection of extracts, mainly from English writers, who talk about my country of birth and its people. My aim is to make the Greeks see how the foreigners – the British in particular – have seen them. This may make them learn from the different or even clearer view that others have of the Greeks and thus to reconsider their strengths and (if possible, reduce) their weaknesses or, at the very least, reflect on them. I was, originally, tempted to offer the Greek translations to the original English texts reproduced in the text but then, for reasons of economy of space, I decided this was not necessary for present purposes. I kept this decision to an absolute minimum for occasionally it was instructive to illustrate translation difficulties or reveal unexpected similarities of style. This last sentence may sound odd to many – differences yes, but similarities in style between the two languages, how could this be so? Yet I did this in my legal work for over forty years and it seemed to work so I have been extending this in recent times to my work on ancient Greek poetry, epic, lyric and dramatic. I think it works if one can compare different languages but at a similar phase of their evolution (which, of course, cold be many centuries apart).

This occasional excursus into more technical linguistic points may slow down the average reader who is not proficient in two or more languages or even make him in the end skip altogether the Greek renderings. Yet most educated English have some knowledge of Greek - many very good - and it is those whom I occasionally wish to "force" – not just encourage – to reflect on the original versions in the hope that such reflections will lead them further afield in the understanding not just of a Greek text but of the Greek thought at its best. For it is in the original that one appreciates the full effect of the words chosen by the original (ancient) writer to externalize his thoughts when first encountering magical scenery; and it is in a good translation that one discovers the unexpected similarities which always intrigue me since no one expects them to be there. And the psychological perspicacity of my very distant ancestors was truly quite amazing even in subjects like psychology and psychiatry which had not, at the time, even been invented.

To my endless list of confessions – and confessions even when revealing tend to be boring to the reader who is uninterested in the writer's apologies for his shortcomings – I must thus add one more. It refers to my own preference, already made clear in the previous chapters, for the succinct and poignant sentence one finds in good English texts of a certain period – I would place it roughly during the first half of the 20th century - but which is so absent from German and Greek writings.

The verbosity found in many modern Greek texts whose authors cannot understand that less means more is thus noteworthy and makes the studying and imitating of the short sentences of English texts highly desirable. Just as important, however, it is to discover that this conciseness in expression and this restraint in expressing emotions existed in ancient Greece as it was a pronounced feature of the English educated elites during the period I set above. But, the staccato tone which the short sentences give to English texts and which Lord Denning used in his judgments to perfection, conceal the fact it takes more time to write less than to write more! The ancients knew this as well; for in the absence of computers writing on slabs covered with wax (or later papyri) and then carving on to them one's text required one to have an absolutely clear idea of what one wanted to say before one started ... scratching!

In England to a large extent these virtues were born of the English educational system, *especially that of the past*. The training with précis' at school where children were taught to shorten long sentences by omitting superfluous words provided the first step. Their encouragement to emphasize facts and, where possible, omit adjectives, leaving them to readers to add mentally, also has its reasons. For it taught future users of the language the art of deciding how much the author has to say and how much is best left to his reader to complete using his own imagination. Homer did this to perfection. He described, for instance, *la belle Helen* simply as being λευκώλενος[1] - white skinned - and left to each and every one of us to complete the missing elements – colour of eyes, height, hair, large or small bosom etc. – in a way which suited our own conception of perfect beauty.

This last thought leads to another and even more important one. The very *deliberate decision to encourage* the reader's imagination to *complete* the author's images by encouraging the former to allow his mind to play freely with the writer's *carefully chosen* vocabulary. And because the author is under a *duty* to choose his words carefully he places his reader under a *corresponding obligation* to savour them at his leisure and only then attempt to interpret them.

Why stress so strongly this symbiosis of author-reader? Why allude to the agony, at any rate of those who care about written style, to find the right words to express their thoughts? Why emphasize to the reader the importance of understanding the mental state in which the author was when writing a particular text? Why, finally, emphasize so strongly the reader's obligations towards his author's texts?

---

1. Other descriptions refer to her as καλλίκομος (with beautiful hair), καλλιπάρηος (with a beautiful face).

One answer lies obviously in the fact that the pleasure of writing corresponds exactly to the pleasure of reading. As Nabokov once put it so eloquently in an interview with Playboy Magazine (of all places) in 1954

> "…the felicity of a phrase is shared by the artist grateful to the unknown force in his mind that has suggested a combination of images and by the artistic reader whom this combination satisfies."

Such thoughts lead to others, related for many, even surprising.

Begin thus to realize that what Nabokov expressed so elegantly about words applies to all forms of human communication with the outside world. This is because the pictorial artist as much as the musician must engage the mind and not just a particular sense (sight, hearing) of the person who is looking at or listening to his work. It is this "coupling" of creator and "receiver" in digesting the former's product which allows the work to appeal to different people in different ways at different times, in other words to make the work eternal. For if a work "talks" to one person at "one time only" it is doomed to be short lived. To put it differently, longevity or endurance is, for me, the best test that something is truly classical. The Greeks achieved this not only by dealing with eternal themes but also handling them in flexible ways to allow subsequent geniuses to adapt them and then adopt them in a way that suited the aesthetic demands of their times. If the original creator and subsequent imitator dovetailed, the old work survived into a different era and the new one became a classic in its own right. I am thinking of Racine's *Phèdre* so close (but by no means as psychologically profound) as the original – *Hippolytus Stefaniforos*. This is not meant to demean in the slightest Racine since we know from his own notes how carefully he had studied Euripides and, indeed, a wide variety of Greek authors.

It is not surprising to note that once we move from the obvious – you see with your eyes – to the less obvious but more profound – you "see" with your eyes *and* your brain - that we realize that physiology and psychology enter once again into the picture, not to *confuse but to enlighten*. (I have italicised the last few words to stress my long-standing dispute with classical philologists who rigorously oppose using psychology as an additional instrument in 'undersantding; more fully the very rich ancient texts.)

Sir Ernst Gombrich in his wonderful book – one of my favourites which I would insist upon taking with me on my desert island - entitled "Art and Illusion" presents these ideas and illustrates them through numerous pictures (of all sorts and not just works of art). His book has all the virtues I said I admire; it shows how complex ideas can be presented simply if the speaker or writer really knows his subject; and it confirms the enriching beauty and depth which interdisciplinary studies can offer to the study of the topic under investigation.

In everyday life, I found this idea embodied vividly in photographs of semi-clad women not shown in full nudity. Shades of grey, especially in black and white photographs - for I believe are the ones which give greater scope in turning photography into an art - and the curvature of the posture or the ambivalent way the scant clothing is worn, can thus end up being more sexually suggestive than the presentation of complete human nudity. For the first may engender curiosity, romance, even desire, whereas the latter can, at best only, achieve the arousal of transient sexual feelings. The difference between the two sets of emotions is qualitatively enormous since the latter, though possibly intense, are fleeting by their nature whereas the former can produce a more lasting pleasure which Jaqueline de Romilly described as *bonheure contemplatif.*

British texts describing Greece and the Greeks

The texts I have selected fall into two categories and must thus be read in this way. In both of them the reader should go through them slowly, perhaps twice over or more, savour them like sipping a precious wine and not gulp them down like a man who quenches his thirst in an unexpectedly discovered oasis.

The second set of selected texts describes some of the features of the Greek *character*. Most refer to classical antiquity; though the modern Greek reader will instantly recognize in them his own strengths and weaknesses. If he does, he should reflect about himself but also admire the observing and expressive powers of the foreign writer. British writers – Runciman or Bower – or artists – like Osbert Lakaster or, before him, Edward Lear – captured the Greek scenery, Greek light, Greek churches and priests, and the Greek character – in all its beauty and, occasional, abysmal darkness– in ways which few Greeks have. A Greek can learn from the observational powers of a cultured philhellene.

Could our imaginary Greek attempt to do the same about the English, French or Germans whom he has encountered in his life? Or would he instantly fall into the trap of well-warn stereotypes? Similar-

ly, were he to be asked to talk or write about his own people would he
see their strengths and weaknesses as clearly as the "naïve" outsider
or, as the Greeks often call foreigners: the κουτόφραγκοι; (the stupid
franks, dating back to the early crusaders occupying the mainland of
Greece, then part of the Byzantine Empire?)

The first set of texts describes the Greek *scenery* and, again, one
must note the photographic talents of some of the authors who produced them for what they do is what Simonides of Keos, one of the
most famous of the Lyrics, wrote that "writing was painting with
words."

I, for one, have been an avid reader of Laurence Durrell – an intriguing if not "dark" individual in his complex private life – but one
of the English authors who has best "painted" the Mediterranean
landscape with words in the five "travel" books he wrote about Corfu,
Rhodes, Cyprus, Sicily and the South of France. Incidentally, I use the
word "painted" for this is how Durrell, himself, describes Corfu's famous "Mouse Island"

"In the dazzle of the bay stands [the island] whose romance
of line and form (white monastery, monks, cypresses) defies
paint and lens, *as well as the feebler word.*"

Durrell, like Goethe before him, was a writer with a painter's eye.
The latter's most famous poem – Kennst das land wo die Zitronen
Bluhn – bears evidence of his artistic virtues and his deep knowledge
of colours. Durrell gives us a similar illustration in another beautiful
passage from his book about the Dodecanese – "Relfections of a Marine Venus". Here is a key passage which, from beginning to end does
not allow you to forget pictorial art, he writes:

"The Aegean is still waiting for its painter – waiting with all
the unselfconscious purity of its lights and forms for someone
to go really mad over it with a loaded paint-brush. Looking on
upon it from the sentinel's tower at Castello. From the ancient
temple at Lindos, you begin to paint it for yourself in words.
Cerulean sky touched with white cirrus – such fleece as grows
between the horns of nine-day goats, or on the cocoons of silk-
worms: viridian to peacock-tail green where the sea thrashes itself out against the cliffs. Prismatic explosion of waves against
the blue sky, crushing out their shivering packets of colour, and
then hissing black intake of the water going back…But to paint
Greece one would have to do more than play with a few colours…An impossible task, when all is said and done. It is pleas-
anter not to try, but to lie dozing in the shade…"

Haven't we all who know these lands done just that? And don't most who have and then read Durrell envy the fact that he – a foreigner - tried and succeeded in conveying the beauty of our landscape in a way that most of us cannot?

Durrell's ability to paint with words is thus rare and indisputable. Reading him in England made me *feel* my land when I was far away from it. I *saw* before my eyes the blue sky even though all around me a grey England represented the reality of the north. I *heard* the cicadas singing their monotonous tune while trying to snooze in the afternoon heat, whereas around me were the sounds of a huge metropolis. I could *imagine* those sunsets, which I watch in awe every time I am in Elunda (in Crete) and note how they turn the mountains in the distance light pink, then mauve, until dark blue finally swells up from the cold sea and engulfs everything around making the sea seem alive with sea monsters. Not the time to want to go for a swim!

So, let me end this poor attempt to show the effect which our landscape has had on gifted foreigners, that very same landscape which modern Greeks, concerned with money more than aesthetics, have worked so hard to destroy! Naturally, I have again chosen a description of the sea since of all the countries of the Mediterranean - and their history – Greece has through the centuries been largely defined by it. So, in "Prospero's Cell" we find Durrell's marvellously naturalistic account describing this time the waters of Paliocastrizza in Corfu:

"...drenched in the silver of olives on the north western front. The little bay lies in a trance, drugged with its own extraordinary perfection – a *conspiracy* of light, air, blue sea, and cypresses. The rock faces splinter the light and reflect it both upward and downward" so that, staring through the broken dazzle of the Ionian sun, the quiet bather in his boat can at the same time look down into three fathoms of water with neither rock nor weed to *interrupt the play of the imagination.*"

It's the (bad) habit of the teacher which prompts me to italicize a few words in order to encourage the reader who reads fast to notice each word chosen and ask what would happen to the impressions created on his mind if he changed them with others apparently similar but more prosaic. Note for instance the word "conspiracy" instead of the more likely "combination"; and, above all, note the concluding words - the "absence of rock and weeds" - that had they been present might "interrupt the play of the imagination" provoked by the effect of light on calmly moving waters.

The word, itself, - imagination – is meant to tell the reader that, at least for the writer, these unique combination of light and clean waters provoked many, changing, adaptable, images and thus ill-defined and in this sense indescribable for the benefit of others. These were sufficiently strong to "move" him enough to attempt to put them in words such as the above. How should we react? Surely not, by continuing our reading with uninterrupted breadth!

I think I know what he is trying to tells us for my kind of mind has allowed me to share these kind of reactions. The (failed) painter is still sufficiently alive to fulfil my youthful ambition to become an artist but frustrated by the stifling attitude of the bourgeois mentality alluded to earlier in this book and thus allows me to understand and appreciate the successful one. The sentences that follow Durrell's text set in motion a new set of emotional reactions which anyone who has taken a deep dive and then swims upward noting the light become brighter as he rises from the depths until he breaks the surface of the water must have also experienced. Yet look how beautiful his text is.

"so that diving [the quiet bather] may imagine himself breaching the very floor of space itself, until his fingers touch the heavy lush sand; so that rising to the surface borne upward by air and muscle he feels that it is not only the blue sky that he breaks open with his arms, but the very ceiling of heaven. Here are the grottoes. Paleocastrizza has two of them, one reachable by boat and beautiful. The walls are twisted painfully out of volcanic muscle, blood-red, purple, green, and nacreous. A place for resolutions and the meetings of those whose love is timid and undeclared."

Texts such as the above touch all of one's senses as the water touches your body, you smell the air, instantly feel the warm sun, and only miss the saltiness of the water. They please but also shock one's sense by avoiding the use of ordinary language– recall the words and phrases "conspiracy", "twisted volcanic muscle", "waiting with all the unselfconscious purity of its lights and forms for someone to go really mad over it with a loaded paint-brush". They make you wonder why should it take a foreigner to see – and more crucially to describe - your land so much better than you can even see it? More importantly, one wonders – one should marvel – at the deep feelings our land can cause to others and yet can leave those of us who have it free all day every day so unmoved!

The Greek character

The foreign eye, enriched by the formidable training the good - by which I mean both disciplined but also sensitive - schooling can give has also presented us with some wonderful insights of the Greek character. The fact that most of the extracts that I choose to quote in this sub-section come from classists and describe ancient Greeks should, again, not be seen as being dated or invented accounts of a romantic but dead past; for in the lines that follow I, as someone born in Greece and understanding both ancient and modern Greek, can see clearly my contemporaries. Moreover, when I first read these extracts, I wondered, once again, why did I have to find such penetrating accounts of my past in the writings of foreigners?

The answer, of course, is easy and yet complex at the same time. For those who wrote and I now cite had the benefit of a demanding education that taught people how to analyse texts and think. Their disciplined training, however, did not bore them to death. On the contrary, it stimulated their imagination and made them come and to love a distant people who were extrovert - unlike themselves; who could love and hate with equal intensity; who showed feelings which they had been taught to suppress; who enjoyed the liberating freedom of an unregimented life which was denied to the English by the old family system which left all responsibility to the nanny and later the boarding school.

Contrasts attract just as complimentary colours create a special visual effect precisely because they "compliment" each other and thus please the eye. Maurice Bowra, describing the Odyssey, captures the contradictions of the Greeks which are not only so obvious in this epic poem but also, it seems to me, so irresistible to the more predictable, law-abiding, "fair play" northern temperament. He thus writes of the poem

"...what delightful and poignant accuracy does the poem describe the modern Greeks; it is a portrait of a nation which rings as clear to-day as when it was written. The loquacity, the shy cunning, the mendacity, the generosity, the cowardice and bravery, the almost comical inability of self-analysis. The unloving humour and the scolding. Nowhere is it possible to find a flaw."

This bunch of contradictory virtues and vices, often all taken to extremes (as exemplified not only by Odysseus but also that other archetypal Greek, Alcibiades) may also help us understand why the Greeks placed at the top of the Delphic list of virtues the «Μηδέν Άγαν», an idea very close to the ideal of pursuing the "Mean" or middle road.

On this that most talented "barrel-shaped, vain, red faced, voluble, always to be found at parties, celebrated Oxford wit" of the second half of the 20th century – Sir Maurice Bowra – had much to say. For like the ancient Greeks he admired the idea of the "golden mean" though he often ignored it in his pronouncements which were meant to shock. Here, then, are some further thoughts from Bowra's pen, thoughts which, as Sir Isaiah Berlin, one of England's most celebrated Latwian, German, Russian émigrés put it, were expressed in words "which came in short sharp bursts of precisely aimed, concentrated fire as image, pun, metaphor, parody, [and] seemed spontaneously to generate one another in a succession of marvellously imaginative patterns".[2]

"Poets and philosophers dwelt on the merits of the Mean, of the middle state between obscurity and excessive power, and claimed that only if a man follows this is he likely to be happy. While poets expressed the idea by saying that a man must not climb the sky, or try to marry Aphrodite or sail beyond the Pillars of Heracles, the philosophers took the conception of the Mean and built moral systems on it. But when Aristotle seeks to explain the several virtues as means between opposite extremes, he fails to convince us either in logic and experience. Such a doctrine as the mean works well enough if we are already persuaded that a quiet life is best. But it is no final deterrent to those who believe in action for its own sake and feel that the greater the risk, the greater the glory. The attention which the Greeks paid to the mean suggests not so much that they observed it as that, in the fullness of their blood, they felt they needed some curb for their more violent ambitions and more reckless undertakings. The Mean might at least have the virtue that it gave some consolation for defeat by explaining that too much had been attempted, but as a guide in the practical government of life it was as much neglected as it was observed."

We thus have here an excellent adage for prudent and happy life as well as explanation of its limited application. More importantly, we have an illustration of people who could think high but live the life of an ordinary - that is frail and often unreliable - human being consumed by his passions and ambitions and returning to humility

---

2. Michael Ignatieff, "Isaiah Berlin" (1998), p. 51. The physical description of Bowra is Ignatieff's.

only when finally defeated by his vices. It is this realization of the frailty and final and irresistible defeat by fate that motivates ancient Greek tragedy but which also led the Ancient Greeks –as Nietzsche so eloquently argued it in his "The Birth of Tragedy through the Origins of Music" - to create their goods at their own image thus proving to themselves, if no one else, that their life was worth living.

But Bowra takes us further by remarking that

> "Greek religion shows its essentially Greek character by not conforming to any plan and by its generous freedom and inclusive tolerance."

A few lines before he has thus stressed that

> "Greek religion [was/is] unusual in its very lack of system, of any organization such as we find in the dominating religions of the modern world. It begins at no fixed point and has roots which stretch indeterminately into an unchronicled past. It has no eminent prophet or law giver who expounded the nature of goods, no sacred books whose authority us final on doctrine or morals, no central organization for its hierarchy, no revealed cosmology, no conception of a dedicated religious life, no insistence on orthodoxy, no agreed eschatology, to accepted scheme for redemption."

What a formidable summary in a few lines of some of the salient features of the religion (and the character) of the ancient Greeks and, for those who wish to, a starting point for a comparative discussion of religions!

Tragedy was not the only widely taught lesson available to Greeks. To be sure, it taught them misfortunes which fate brings to most, alerted them to the volatility of their Gods, reminded them of their many foibles and how easily they could destroy them. In expecting their plays to be financed through what we would today call the "private sector" they also showed us a shared way of financing the state's duties towards education but also honouring – in today's terms rewarding – those who had assisted in this task.

What was staged, while maintaining public consciousness of the continuity of the Greeks and the superiority of their culture, also was meant to humble people before their goods, accept that fate was often cruel, and educate them in the art of government and moral obligations. Tragedy, in short, in ancient Greece was a source of education but also entertainment.

But it could be argued that many of these aims were also achieved through Greek mythology which, however, beyond its educational function went further than tragedy by becoming a fertile source of artistic inspiration throughout the centuries that followed. This double influence was achieved because their contents have appealed to the intelligence, the emotions and the imagination of humans of all times. Bowara explains this triple appeal thus, and his compact statement calls, once again, for special attention.

> "The [myths] appeal to the intelligence because some solid consideration underlies their dramatic events, some positive assertion, concretely presented, about existence, which invites conclusions to be drawn from it…They appeal to the emotions, because what happens in them evokes horror or fear or admiration or delight and forces men to compare their own desires and aims with them and to wish to rival their moments of felicity or to avoid their moments of catastrophe. They appeal to the imagination, because every man needs some image against which he can set himself and see his own limitation, only to transcend them in the light which is shed on some familiar situation or in an unforeseen expansion of his faculties. Whether they guide his fancy to the golden mansions of the gods or the unfathomable night of the Furies or the stricken fields of long ago, they take him out of himself to another order of things, where his insight is sharpened and his sensibility purified."

A people, in short, get the gods and myths they deserve and the Greeks got the best. No extra-terrestrial power therefore of the type adored in ancient Egypt; no dark and demonic Gods vying for gold and power of the sort that flourished in forests of medieval Germany and were glorified by Wagner in his interminable operas; no superhuman asceticism of the kind that Christianity spawned in some parts of the East and led some to spend their lives cross-legged on top of a column. Give me a thousand times Saint Francis earning his sainthood by talking to the animals, the sun, the moon and ministering to the ill and living in their midst at great danger to himself and you can keep the rest. He is my kind of saint; there is something very Greek about him in his Platonic love for Claire.

But to return to the Greeks, theirs was a religion and, on the whole a cosmology, which was not overtly concerned with good and evil, justice or injustice but with living and enjoying life in the midst of very human rivalries and weaknesses. An over-simplification perhaps, but one which appeals to me and which, I think, merges arguably from the works of English and French scholars who leave me with the unanswered question: did they just admire this world but also nourished a sort of secret envy for its humanity? I suspect the latter for that is how I feel.

Two concluding observations about how the British see the Greeks.

Frist, their descriptions of them, their manners, and of the treasures they have created through the ages combine the benefits of an accurate eye, the unreserved admiration for beauty in all its forms but also... humour. It all takes us back to points made in earlier chapters and the belief, which I so share, that humour enlivens even the most serious of topics: for instance, Hell. To prove this point let me quote a few lines on how Sir John Colville, Churchill's Private Secretary throughout the War, describes[3] a wonderful 14th century Fresco in the leading of the Athos Monasteries, the Grand Lavra:

"I never fail to be enthralled by the imaginative powers of mediaeval fresco-painters. The largest [one in the principal church] was a representation if the Last Judgment in which the principal figure was the Devil [early echoes here of paradise Lost?], *contentedly munching* sinners *as if there were whitebait*. Down below him was a lake of blood where hundreds of diminutive devils, armed with pitchforks, were playing hide and seek with some *tadpoles* which, on closer inspection, turned out to be more sinners. The small devils and their *elusive prey* were having such a *joly game* that it was quite *depressing to turn to the heavenly* part of the fresco where a score of priggish saints, with worn *or second-hand* haloes, were gazing down on the scene below and, I thought, *probably wishing they were allowed just half and hour's frolic in the sinner' lake.*"

No place this to analyse each of the words chosen to describe this most frightening of events in the religious calendar but I have italicised some - *contentedly munching, elusive prey, jolly game, gazing at Heaven being "depressing", priggish saints, second hand haloes* – not only because their use can be traced to English education of a naughty young boy but also impress by the understatement of serious idea, the love of sports, but also to the instilled habit to bring in humour even in the most serious of occasions or analyses even if this, incidentally, does injustice to the aims pursued by Byzantine hagiography.

Thus, this is the effect of describing the depicted saints as "priggish", since it fails to consider the aims of Byzantine art which are pursued through the deliberately ascetic and two dimensional por-

---

3. *Foot-prints in Time. Memories* (Michael Russell, 1976) at p. 57. This is as good a point to express my gratitude to this icon of the English establishment since I owe to him the regaining by British citizenship.

trayals of saints. Yet, however interesting and, indeed, correct my objection may be, the taught way of expressing oneself - in journalistic writings, books for the generally educated reader, and public lectures - in light, witty, or paradoxical terms is what gives the English language its ability to shine over and above other accurate and rational ways of expressing ideas which, however, are utterly lacking in "entertainment" value.

Writing styles (which once converged)

My second concluding point requires some space simply to sketch it out and it will elaborate my belief that the classical Greeks and the well-educated Englishmen of the Edwardian and George V years both wrote with admirable conciseness and accuracy. How best to make the point: by giving two examples.

First what is probably the most elegant passage from the most elegant speech by Pericles delivered to honour the dead at the end of the first year of the Peloponnesian War. The comparison of a mere nine words in the classical Greek text with the equivalents in English, French and, even modern Greek, demonstrates the *impossibility* of matching the *poetic* [sic] beauty found in the language of the *Funeral Oration*. The text, in its original, reads as follows:[4]

"Φιλοκαλοῦμέν τε γὰρ μετ' εὐτελείας καὶ φιλοσοφοῦμεν ἄνευ μαλακίας."

This very famous phrase is rendered in English by Martin Hammond as:

"We cultivate beauty without extravagance and intellect without loss of vigour"

Before commenting on it, in order to enlarge our sample of comparison, let us provide the French rendering by Jaqueline de Romilly[5]

" Nous cultivons le beau dans la simplicité, et les choses de l'esprit sans manquer de fermeté."

Now, indubitably, all three versions render the original meaning correctly, though in terms of words we must not forget that, as against the nine of the ancient Greek, English needs eleven and French seventeen. The comparison, however, cannot stop at the number of words

---

4. Bk II, para. 40.
5. *Thucydide. La Guerre du Péloponnèse*, with an introduction by Claude Mossé, vol. I, XL.

needed to put the text in another language; other features of the text of Thucydides also have to be noted and replicated if possible.

In terms of trying to capture the rhyme which exists between the two parts of the Greek sentences one must note that they both end with similar-sounding words: ευτελείας and μαλακίας. Only the French attempts to replicate it by choosing two words with similar endings: 'simplici*té*'/ferm*eté*. No such effort is even attempted in the English version.

Yet even the partial attempt to capture the rhyme of the original, evident in the French translation, does not go anywhere near achieving the poetry of the Greek language as Madame de Romilly has disarmingly accepted in one of her books[6] by admitting that her translation "*ne rend pas l' echo entre les deux verbes qui marquent le goût de la beauté et des choses de l' esprit*" of the text. For the words used in Greek – composites using the same verb – φιλεῖν (love) – combined, the first with the word καλόν (beau/beautiful) and the second with the word σοφία – i.e. wisdom – are in Greek parallel composites, containing the same number of syllables, and thus providing the Greek text with further, *internal* rhyming: Φιλοκαλοῦμεν = φιλοσοφοῦμεν.

If this is the attention paid by Thucydides when composing *ex post* Pericles' text, then he was a remarkably fastidious author. If, on the other hand, such poetic writing came naturally to Pericles when he spoke, then his natural talent must amaze us and the purpose of including this sub-section in this chapter should, by now, be fully justified.

My second example takes Greek conciseness to amazing depths – the reader will forgive the pun as he reads on – and, essential leads straight into the realms of psychology. This illustration appears at the very beginning of *Antigone*. For one to understand the Greek word and render it with equal conciseness into English, or come to that in any other language, is near impossible; and I submit it is literally impossible for one to complete this feat to rendering in rhyme. Its full richness becomes obvious only after careful reflection on the entire play and a longish (and I fear somewhat extended explanation of the key word).

Sophocles thus uses a participle (μετοχή) to give a one word description of the character of his heroine.[7] It derives from the verb καλχαίνω

6. *Petites leçons sur le grec ancien*, Ed. Stock (2008), at p.51.
7. Line 20 of the original. Robert Fagles, in his Penguin Classics translation – page 60 of the 198 reprint – renders it as "dark and grim". Greek translators – e.g. K.

which comes from the nown κάλχη which describes a dark version of purple. I repeat, it is an inspired choice for not only does aptly describe Antigone's character but also alludes to the source of its peculiarities and even to something that will happen at the very end of the play.

To do all this in one word is quite a feat; so, if I am to justify my hyperbole, let me begin by stating my belief that written language is capable of unlocking mental reactions in the reader; indeed, the more carefully selected are the words by the author the more varied these reactions can be. For here the eyes recognize words which the mind then, with the help of stored information in the conscious, as well as its unconscious layers, can make the text infinitely rich and rewarding.

With this in mind let me now give the dictionary definition of the key word: "καλχαίνουσα".

My *Pocket Oxford Classical Greek Dictionary*[8] needs 16 English words just to give us its meanings which, I repeat, are all substantiated as the plot of the tragedy moves towards its climax. This is the dictionary definition:

Georgousopoulos, *Αντιγόνη*, Kaktos editions (1994) at p.31 – uses the word φουρτουνιασμένη which in English means 'stormy', invariably used to describe the condition of the sea. Of the numerous versions I have looked at, Professor Giangos Andreades' comes closest to the full meaning, though in modern Greek it requires three words to render the one which was sufficient in ancient Greek. Andreades' rendering of Ismene's words (line 20 of the original) thus reads: your word "πορφύρα σκοτεινή κοχλάζει» which in English would be rendered as "your words are bubbling up with dark purple." See his *Antigone 2* (in Greek) (2008) at p. 183. Why this approximates Sophocles' idea is explained in the text above.

8. (2002) page 170. For more details see Liddel / Scott, A Greek-English Lexicon, 9th ed, (1940) at p. 871. The word attracted the interest of Sir Richard Jebb as early as 1900 when his 3rd edition of *Antigone* appeared. The word comes from κάλχη which is a murex, (a kind of shell fish which yields a purple dye) or purple limpet, (a gastropod mollusc with a tent-shaped shell adhering tightly to rocks) and also producing the purple colour. From the above we get the verb καλχαίνω which means to make purple. Metaphorically this can be taken to mean that it makes the sea dark and "troublous". This last (and old fashioned word) aptly describes the sea in a turbulent, restless, and disturbed state. The sea metaphor is particularly apt for a seafaring nation but, figuratively speaking, also captures well *Antigone's* dark and troubled mind. Jebb, ibid, and others also state that this explanation may also explain the name of the soothsayer Κάλχας, "the seer who *darkly broods* [sic] on the future". The Greek version of Liddell/ Scott (1916 ed. by Prf. Xenophon Moschos, at p. 590) also suggests that the verb indicates anyone *examining something in depth* which the English version also accepts by using the words "pondering deeply" – which is different to darkly brooding. In the light of the above and since seers, with the exception of the sui-generis Cassandra, examine signs to foresee the future in general and not search (and find) only 'dark events', the second rendering of the verb explains the name of Calchas better than the first.

"[to] be agitated in mind, ponder deeply, make purple, make dark and troubled (like a stormy sea)."

Rather than tire the reader with a long exegesis I hope I will be allowed to content myself with a bullet kind of presentation of the relevant points which this one word has for the play.

(i) We find here, at the end of the definition, the recourse to marine metaphors so liked by the ancient Greeks. This point suits well a marine nation so that sea metaphors were frequently used from the days of Homer onwards so little more need be added at this stage (though much pleasure could be derived by looking at many examples of such use and enjoying the plethora of images they have helped create.)

(ii) We note that the allusion of the sea sediments rising (bubbling up) in disturbed (but not yet stormy) waters to the surface and giving it a dark (red) – at first instance the emphasis should be given to "dark" and "red" – colours which are both accurate as an observation of nature, but also dramatically significant for this plot.

(iii) The deliberate allusion to purple – πορφύρα – as a colour often associated with blood receives its full justification at the end of the play when Haemon commits suicide at the feet of the hanged Antigone, splashing his red blood on her white innocent cheeks.[9] In colour terms, this verse is amazing; in dramatic terms: eerie; for blood marks the beginning and the end of the tragedy.

(iv) Taken as a whole the word essentially describes Antigone as 'ταραγμένη' – in turmoil. The metaphor with the disturbed water is thus once again quite apposite. As Sir Richard Jebb however noted the Greek image is subtly phrased in so far as it is describing a 'troubled' sea - mind - *before the breaking out of the full storm*. No thundering 'white horses' yet but an ominous sea swell nonetheless. No fully blown 'madness' yet for Antigone; but most assuredly the first signs that she heading in that direction.

(v) Finally, Antigone's 'disturbance', we can assume, is or will become mental, just as the sedimentary material which discolours the surface of the water originally stems from below. So, one could argue, that her behavior becomes increasingly disturbed by the turmoil in her sub-conscious which ends up affecting the conduct of the conscious.

---

9. Lines 1119- 1120 of the original.

Foreigners and how they see the modern Greeks

How many of these qualities and vices do foreigners still see in the Greeks today? By asking this question we move into more difficult areas of enquiry. For we have to set aside the beauty of the artistic description of the values of a race and civilization and move to the mundane world of semi-culture and cut-throat economic competition, greed, and politics. With the exception of shipping, in none of the above are the Greeks particularly successful or praiseworthy though when it comes to lack of inspired political leadership, from which they undoubtedly suffer, not that many countries can boast higher – or should be saying lower – rankings?. Europe in particular, which is Greece prime area of activity, is – dare I say this openly – just as affected by the lack of inspired and inspiring leaders. If, therefore, they is an area where they are distinctly performing better than the modern Greeks is in the area of their civil services and the idea of a functioning, modern state. On both, Greece's record is abysmal though its political world carries the major part of the blame for this sorry state of affairs since it is to blame for the size and quality of the employment in the public sector by filling it with their political friends rather than making a genuine effort to select the best. Current European criticism of Greece on this front is thus, in my view, entirely justified.

But let us return to our main theme: how do foreigners see Greece and the Greeks these days?

I pose the question broadly for I wish to attempt a general overview; but even that calls for some narrowing down and I will do it on the basis of somewhat dated – at times otiose – distinctions resulting from class and or profession-oriented classifications. For obvious reasons, I will also limit my observations to how the English see the Greeks for, I feel, I have better grounds on which to base my views. Overall, however, I am not sure that other northern European states have a better view of the Greeks these days.

Generally speaking Greece does not enter the mind of the average English man or woman except as a tourist destination. My bet is that the same is true of most other Europeans though I have found central Europeans more informed about the country's past. Sad, even offensive, for Greeks to admit this; but it is true of the average Englishman as it is true of the average French, German or Dutchman. Their knowledge of ancient Greek history, poetry, philosophy and literature is sketchy in the extreme; the awareness of the country's modern history entirely non-existent. Knowledge and interest increase if we move to the subject of beaches, climate, indeed they can even turn into an obsession, provided what attracts most can also claim to be "cheap". Nowadays, however, Greece is even loosing on this score to Turkey.

Mussáka, is probably the only Greek word most foreigners know even though they mispronounce it, maybe "kalimera" (good-morning) is the other. Zorba is the only Greek they recognize but are unclear as to whether he is real or a character of fiction. The image of him, however, is clear and, in fact it is that of Anthony Quinn; and the music is seen as the only kind that exists in modern Greece. Mikis Theodorakis may be known as a political activist and not the serious composer he was; and Xatzidakis songs, though a winner of one or two Golden discs, if heard will be un-identifiable, even though among them one finds some true gems. To the extent that they are known, it will be thanks to Nana Mouschouri whose talent has received wide recognition in many European countries.

Odysseus, the most intriguing (if not very flattering) model of a Greek surviving any adversity which fate might throw at him, will only be known in very vague terms among most visiting foreigners. Antony Quinn, the homonymous Zorba, is, as I stated, better known though he, of course, is not Greek and the character he portrayed on the silver screen never existed. Add to that the music of the film and you have the sum total of the information the average Englishman who decides to visit contemporary Greece. This is not entirely due to the fact that general culture has come down so much these days everywhere, including England; it is also due to the political insignificance of the country which has been enhanced by its largely self-inflicted economic crisis.

Wrong! In my list, I forgot to mention the middle aged – upwards – spinster who sees in Greece the place for one more, perhaps, her last sexual fling with an over-sexed Greek male before old age condemns her to the twilight of the wholesome but dull existence of becoming a Member of her local "Women's Institute"! Oh, how ever-lasting those memories of sex on the beach with the waves tickling one's toes will prove to be during the dark cold nights of northern England! But from Greece's point of view, this is not much to be proud about.

The educated or cultured classes will have a better knowledge. At times this can be quite impressive but then one must instantly clarify the fact that this knowledge is mainly that of the Greece of Antiquity. Indeed, in the University world which I have inhabited I have come across many such Englishmen and Englishwomen who can recite more long passages from the ancient tragedies or Homer than most of my

Greek contemporaries. Indeed, I was, myself, often stumped by Cambridge dons who, when I first met them and they realized that I was (half) Greek, they would break into long recitations of the *Iliad* or the *Odyssey* which I had to pretend I had not understood because of their "accent" and not because I had forgotten (if indeed I ever recognized) the passages I may have learnt during those afternoon tutorials with my father in the mid-fifties. In short, those who read classics at the good Universities knew Greek literature better than their Greek equivalents.

Most, if not all of these persons, were and remain Philhellenes in the historical, cultural, sense but in their views on matters of contemporary Greek politics they would be ranked as being somewhere between indifferent to mildly opposed to our "antics" as they would describe our economic profligacy, our mercurial temperament, and our tendency to exaggerate our feelings, opinions and reactions to external stimuli.

Are we in part responsible for this dreadful picture? If I am to stick to the high standard of veracity I set myself before beginning writing this book, my answer must be "yes" for the faults they pin on the modern Greeks are often – not always - real and not imaginary. Moreover, senior politicians including previous Prime Ministers as well as former Ministers have, in the course of this last decade, been quick to remind them of how dishonest and ungovernable Greek officials have been. If Greek Ministers of Finance tell Europe that their country has cheated or misled them, what can you expect the ordinary foreigner to say or believe?

Worse still, perhaps, is the impression given of the state mechanisms not working and the responsible ministers being unable to make them do so. To the question "why is this so" most Greeks, who have come to disapprove (if not detest their current political elites) would answer "because the only thing they care about is retaining their own positions as Ministers." In my view, the British elites, through the thoughtful articles which appear periodically in the more serious publications, are beginning to realize that personal ambition prevails over the sense of duty. But let us not get carried away too far in one direction; modern politicians the world over are increasingly putting their own interests above all others. This is particular true of those who smell blood because the current Prime Minister may be getting ready to with draw to a more …economically profitable life. So let me rephrase my views and accusations: the Greeks are sinners; but by no means the only ones around. What makes them more visible is the crudeness they reveal sometimes in their behaviour.

This clash of "aims" was at the core of British administration, certainly in its days of glory but, I think, is still largely resolved in the way it should be. To provide one example among many I would like to cite, again, from Sir John Colville's memoirs, not least because he uses this clash as an excuse to praise Clement Attlee even though he was no political supporter of his. He thus writes:

"Attlee was endearing in his simplicity He may well have been the only British Prime Minister in all history without a touch either of vanity or of conceit. Service was his motive as an undergraduate for social work in the East End of London; service was the basis of his gallantry at Gallipoli; service was his reason for going into politics and the mainspring of his effort as Prime Minister. Personal ambition played no part and he cared nothing for money or position."

This expression of priorities – duty over personal interest – best exalted by Virgil in his *Aeniad* once had a huge influence in the character shaped by generations of worthy teachers in the best of our public and grammar schools. Once upon a time, it was also keenly felt in Greece; and the result was that much of this sense of duty to one's country was transmitted to a fair extent to the younger generations. Not any longer, not least politicians of many shades of political opinions tend to downgrade the teaching of ancient Greece as well as their own Religion. Politicians have found it profitable to espouse such movements and have thus tolerated such moves if not actually encouraged them even when they do not believe these views. Yet if the economy remains shattered and the teaching of the Greek past is neglected what future can Greece expect other than to become one of the chief summer holiday resorts of, on the whole, the cheaper type of European tourist?

But the Greek character, in terms of perception, does not stop there. The country's diplomatic representations abroad – and here I am talking in terms that go beyond Britain – should be quick to rectify these errors of our elites and make sure that the country is better projected abroad. Yet this organization has never given signs of the degree of organization, professionalism, and planning which one encounters in the Embassies of, say, Germany, Italy, Israel or Turkey, to limit myself to some which I have been fortunate enough to get to know. Again, it is deeply painful to make these admissions; but I am recording bona fide experiences not writing a "paid page" about modern Greece to be inserted in some English or American newspaper.

This, however, is NOT to suggest that Greece lacks intelligent diplomats, for the country, truly, has a surfeit of intelligent, cunning, and successful people, especially in the business world. What I am saying, however, is that in my experience the posting in Embassies such as Paris or London, Berlin, Washington or Rome is in the large majority of cases –though not always – seen as a party-political reward for "loyalty" to whoever happens to be Prime Minister or Foreign Minister at the time. The cleverest of our Ambassadors, by which I mean the most adaptable, in fact seem to serve solely in such good posts because they have mastered the art of shifting allegiances at the critical movement when one set of people is on the way out while another is *ante portas*. Forty eight of my seventy two years of life having been lived abroad so, again, there is much truth reflected in this disillusionment which is not aired lightly!

When we move to the English business world - the City – the picture gets more complicated. Exceptionally able Greeks work there and, on the whole, though hard working and appreciation for their undoubted talents live a ghetto kind of existence once out of their office. Their ability, indeed, interest to improve their image of the country of origin among the inhabitants of the country of choice is, however, minimal since their attention is fully focused on their professional improvement. Given the kind of atmosphere which prevails in the City who can blame them? Lack of foresight or lack of interest thus deprives the country of yet another way of improving its image abroad. To this we must add the lack of interest on behalf of the central government to use this Greek talent which flourishes once it has got out of the Greek borders; and there are quite a few, both in the USA and Britain who should have been enticed back home by governments of all political hues.

Their isolated existence of many of the above alluded to is not because they are seen as "unreliable", "dishonest", "shifty", "volatile" or "arrogant" for most who work in the City and, indeed, in the Wall Street, have to some extent at least these attributes and even feel proud of them so none of them would mark the Greeks out from others of their sort for this reason. However, if they are socially "accosted" by natives it is because they are, or seem to be, rich and thus their English "suitors" expect some sort of personal gain or favour from this relationship. For here, too, we encounter a hypocrisy which goes both ways. The London based Greek – indeed the multitude of foreign races who work in the City - "survive" in London for the sake of good pay but criticize incessantly their hosts. Conversely, the latter, from the lowest to the highest, are particularly susceptible to the possibility of "freebies" from rich or powerful Greeks and, in subtle and less subtle ways, they will do all they can to gain them.

What we encounter in this City group is thus a form of behaviour (and often unbelievably vulgar speech especially found in the trading floors of the declining species of investment banks) which has originated in the macho environment of Wall Street, spread to the City of London, and affected all who work there. Even to enquire of these people if they have any kind of Philhellenic feelings would be an entirely idle exercise. For this group, as groups go, is entirely bereft of all feelings of loyalty to everyone and anyone, including their own companies! As for their own country, if they can speculate – in an economic sense - against it in moments of economic crisis they would probably do that as well. For "number one" is themselves; and the world stops there. This is the spirit of modern capitalism and very different it is of the capitalist system of, say, one hundred years ago when institutional loyalty was alive. To that extent, therefore, the Greeks in London are no worse, probably better, that they American counterparts who work in Wall Street proper and which has been the main inspirer of the ruthless kind of capitalism exemplified by a handful of New York Banks.

Cynical, some might ask? No is the frank answer: just simply true for again I have met many of these characters on both sides of the Pond and speak from personal experience. These faults were, of course, always there; but they grew in intensity and from the 1980's onwards came to be seen as "business virtues". These were the Reagan and Thatcher years when 'financial gain' became the by-word of the philosophical system known in Greece and elsewhere in Europe as Thatcherism. Like all complex social changes, these new fashions and working ethics brought distinct advantages both to individuals and the state; but they also brought a serious decline in social behaviour, morality, idealism, manners, institutional loyalty, family stability and much more besides.

Finally, in this attempt to describe the current Greek image in Britain I move to the English political elites. Here the picture is, from a Greek point of view, just as discouraging though more complex to explain. The starting point, however, is a laudable one (for the English) and one which Greeks, it seems, can never emulate since they cannot even begin to understand.

For the English political (and I include civil service) elites are highly professional so that if any "sentimentality" enters their decision-making- process it is simply and quite rightly "what is best in the interests of Britain". In this context, Greece has again totally failed to understand the English, their history, their mentality and find a way

to handle these relations in a professional and thus mutually beneficial way. Britain's handling of European issues offers a fine example of
the professionalism of the English political elites and one cannot help
but admire how a country which has kept itself outside the core of Europe (a) controls so much of what happens in Europe and (b) rigidly
observes what European obligations it accepts.

The UK as a whole may remain deeply sceptical of the European
Union, Brussels, its gravy train, and the unceasing multiplication of
highly paid posts. The antics of some of the Continental politicians
– especially Italian but also French - are also scorned by most in the
UK. Yet the UK, despite its Euroscepticism and even Europhobia, is
also the country with the best record of observing Union decisions
once taken. If there is respect and even hidden admiration for one
European country this must be Germany; and if we are talking about
an individual, we must be thinking of Vladimir Putin, though next to
no-one would ever admit this in public, especially during our times
when a concerted attempt to revive an new Cold War climate is or-
chestrated by the Americans and to some extent the British. Horror
of horrors therefore for a Greek to add that if there is another person
who might be added to this list of ruthlessly able politicians, for this
person would probably be Mr. Erdogan. If I am to be honest, I oppose
his policies; his ruthlessness, his show off mania and even, secretly,
hope that his incessant rush to rise may bring a sudden fall. But his
record of "leadership" has thus far been impressive though the signs
of hubris are also evident these days; and we all know what follows
hubris.

Thus, if the English find the Greeks "unreliable" to work with or,
simply, not "useful" to their own aims, the opposite is true as far as
their attitudes towards Turkey are concerned. History has much to do
with this, the old English imperial tradition, the appreciation (not always accurate I feel but then the Greeks have never made a concerted
effort to rectify these images) of the political significance of contemporary Turkey, win the day.

With that rationalized appreciation of Turkey comes, as well, a
wonder-lust for the Orient – which extends from Turkey to Saudi Arabia – which we find in diplomats, writers' (e.g. Lawrence of Arabia,
Freya Starck etc) and experienced travellers' longing for a different climate and a liberating environment from their own grey-covered skies.

Once again, however, Greece own political elites should realize the
measure of their contribution to this state of affairs, something which
in no way is improved by the fact that most of the politicians, military

and civil servants who periodically visit London for business purposes often do not even speak English and spend as much time as they can in...Harrods as they do seeing their British counterparts!

How my education altered the way I see people differently than before

I conclude this chapter of impressions - I hope not too misleading though no doubt most annoying to my Greek readers – by stating my own deep debt to the English educational system, especially that of Cambridge and Oxford which I spent a total of twenty five years serving in various teaching posts. I am tempted to put my conclusion in the form of ten precepts or commandments inherited from some very gifted teachers and colleagues which I had in both Universities.[10]

I feel these precepts or commandments say much about what university education really is about and I would hope that some, especially the younger of my readers, might take some time to reflect upon them and, who knows, copy them in Greece one day. Since university reform seems to be a fashionable topic in Greece these days here, then, are my major premises.

First, the object of University education is to not primarily to obtain a top mark but to elevate and strengthen one's character for life.

Second, no great University owes its name and reputation merely to one man. The debt is to *all* who studied there *and* maintain throughout their lives their allegiance to it.

Third, institutional loyalty has always come before personal friendships and help preserved and improve all great Anglo-Saxon centres of learning.

Fourth, university teachers do not teach subjects they teach human beings.

Fifth, the real service teachers render to their students comes not through teaching but by making their students have confidence in themselves. One ounce of inspiration is worth ten of transmitted information which is likely to date very soon.

Sixth, instilling in a student a sense of pride in their own high standards can make them able to tolerate a wide variety of beliefs.

---

10. I have borrowed some from Lord Annan's last book *The Dons* which is not only informative about the lives of some important Oxbridge figures but also offers an excellent example of modern English prose.

Seven, in university a young man or woman should appreciate the true purposes of life. One of the most important is to learn to distinguish in conduct as well as in concept the genuine from the sham, the appearance form the reality.

Eight, a university thrives on a diversity of talents and interests. Any centre of learning which consisted only of first class students interested only in the subjects would be a place full of unhappy and unfulfilled people. The interest of English Universities to recruit not only potential high flyers but also young men and women good at sports, music, debating, theatre and the like once used to jar me imbued as I was by the Continental way of looking at education. Now I feel that this varied way of recruitment makes these places of learning much more varied and exciting.

Nine, the best scholar should be taught to write with a sense of form, of drama, and conscious of the possibilities that language offers. The ultimate aim is not to write for a scholarly clique but for the intelligent public.

Ten, universities should teach people not to be afraid to make mistakes; for anyone who fears making a mistake will never come up with saying something new and original.

I have come passionately to believe in these ideas so it grieves me to suspect – probably correctly – that most of my Greek compatriots might not be able to appreciate the wisdom that lies behind these few lines. Maybe that is why "three year spells abroad", writing doctorates instead of reading for an undergraduate degree and learning more about the foreign country and its system, can come to represent the least profitable way of wasting one's time and one's money. I always advised students who sought my view to use their time in England to try to understand the English legal system and the country rather than write a thesis on a narrowly focused topic but not one ever took my advice. The law of statistics suggests that I may be entirely wrong in the above-proclaimed belief. Yet, like Luther, a great man (though arguably a rather unattractive individual): "Here I stand and can do no other."

Chapter Seven

THE MIXING OF CULTURES
Exiles, refugees, economic migrants,
and the psychological problems of displacement

Population movements

These are phenomena which we find occurring throughout the ages in all parts of the world. They could be massive – using the term loosely one could call them world-wide if the affect many lands – or more restricted in scope. The migrations of various ethnic groups from the steps of Russia into the lands of the Roman Empire, starting approximately towards the end of the 2nd century AD and continuing non-stop for at least three to three and a half centuries – would fall into this category. More limited, but also involving extensive numbers, was the forceful expulsion of the Greeks from the western coastline of Asia Minor in 1922 or the earlier – mid- 17th century – expulsion of the Huguenots from France.

Whether massive or, simply extensive, such movements of people can provoke serious economic consequences and social dislocation in the invaded neighbourhoods but also physical and psychological suffering to the migrants themselves. In most cases and modern jargon these are 'lose/lose' situations. On the whole, therefore benefits for the invaded countries may flow only if the immigrants are economically self-supporting or trained enough to fill posts which cannot otherwise be filled by the host countries. However, such trained or economically self- sufficient immigrants are likely to represent a small, if not very small, percentage of the displaced people.

Such migrations can conceal unexpected elements which one might even describe as ironical. For instance, the 'barbarians' who invaded the Roman Empire were not entering its provinces to destroy but simply to partake of the manifold advantages of belonging to a more advanced and structured society. They were mainly nomads and were anxious to settle in 'empty lands' – there was, for instance, much unused land in the north Balkans at the time - where they hoped to settle and become farmers. With the passage of time however, this understandable aim did not prevent the occurrence of huge material damage and human suffering to much of the Empire contributing, in the space of less than three centuries, to its final collapse. What happened has often been described as vandalism, a word, however, which more accurately describes a particular race among these immigrants – the Vandals - who, eventually, settled in lands which today (approximately) belong to western Libya, Tunisia, and a small strip of Eastern Algeria.

In other instances, concerning what we called 'lesser' migrations, the settlement of 'displaced populations' from foreign lands brought to their host lands new blood and experience in trade which – eventually - worked to their great advantage. It is thus generally agreed that France lost much by the departure of its Huguenot population after the Revocation of the Edict of Nantes which had granted religious tolerance to Catholics and Protestants alike a century earlier. This was because those expelled were middle class merchants or, otherwise, hard-working humans who settled in what was later to become the Kingdom of Prussia, giving it by common consent a huge and beneficial impetus towards attaining it subsequent prominence in the 18th and 19th century. Likewise, the fleeing Greeks from Turkey forced the hardly rich homeland state to absorb at a huge social and economic cost something approaching one quarter of its then total population. The incoming refugees, however, brought talent, trading experience, and a hard-working mentality which, in the long run, helped make Greece richer and, correspondingly, impoverished the re-founded Republic of Turkey under its charismatic (if idiosyncratic) leader Kemal Ataturk.[1]

---

1. This statement was made to my late father in Constantinople in 1972 when he met the Turkish General Fahrettin Altay Pasha who, as leader of the Turkish cavalry, crushed the Greek forces at the battle of Afyon Karahishar (some 250 km SW of Ankara) on 27. 8 1922 setting in motion the ensuing and disorganised retreat of the Greek army which ended up in Smyrna where many were slaughtered as they sought refuge by the quay sides waiting for ships to take them over to the newly acquired by Greeks island of the East Aegean. The meeting of the Turkish General, ninety two years old at the time but with a crystal clear mind, with my father was extremely cordial, both sides sincerely regretting that the war could not have ended without the exchange of populations which was finally sanctioned by the Treaty

As I write these lines the problem of massive immigrations is taking place and since it is by no means over but lies ahead as a veritable pan-European crisis of the highest order. I have been calling it a European problem for years now in my TV interviews and public speeches in Greece and predicting that, as an issue of wider concern, it will dwarf, sooner rather than later, the constantly discussed but hardly resolved economic difficulties of current Europe. The prediction was based in my belief that Europe these days is rarely prepared to face major crises and even more rarely able to co-ordinate her internal decisions as to how it should face them when they actually do occur. Events so far are proving me correct.

My sketch above suggests *the minus but also plus* consequences which such huge events *may* entail. The careful reader must, however lay great emphasis on the italicised words For the two examples summarily – indeed, superficially - mentioned in my introductory account to this subsection make it clear that the social dislocation caused by such massive movements of people can, to some extent, be both faced and their consequences even 'tamed' *provided the new arrivals consist of trained humans, able to provide assistance to the host states of the kind which they actually need.* It bears repeating therefore harsh as it may sound that this, however, is highly unlikely to occur when the incoming migrants are totally untrained and seeking refuge not just to avoid political persecution but in order to escape from local conditions of abject poverty and unemployment.

The distinction is, these days, reflected in international treaties; and the different treatment accorded to these two broad categories of displaced humans is encapsulated in the two terms used in current parlance: refugees and economic immigrants. The problem is that it takes much time and even more money to separate in practice those who belong to the one category from those who come under the other; and in many cases erroneous determinations are more than likely to be made, especially when one is talking of huge numbers.

---

of Lausanne of 1923. The General received both his surname and his exceptionally high title by Ataturk himself in 1934, the year when the Turkish Leader witnessed his name being changed by the Turkish Assembly from Gazi Mustapha Kemal Pasha to Ataturk which means "father of the Turks."

Getting off to a bad start. Displaced persons and their hosts know next to nothing about each other

The recent, especially since the sixties, colossal increase of travel through the medium of the package holiday has enabled huge numbers of people to visit foreign lands. What images they had of them before such visits were generated first by books and pictures, later by films and, the most vivid source of all, the travellers' own brains. But, how accurate were these images of the foreign land and, conversely how reliable was the image the hosts had of their visitors? And how were these both distorted by varied factors such misinformation, natural prejudice, or even ingrained enmity?

Excited or not about their visit to foreign lands the fact is that most knew little about them before going there and returned to their own homes as tourists only slightly better informed mainly about trivia. However, all this mattered very little; for the purpose of the whole visit was a brief holiday, nothing more.

Other types of visitors - then and now - ended up seeing more than the simple tourist does. How much more depended upon whether they were visiting students, legally entering the host country as 'guest workers', expatriates seeking a different or better life usually in countries with a milder climate than their own. Their impressions they received would prepare them for their stay in the host country; but this was not necessarily intended to be a permanent move so mistaken expectations would not be fatal. Return to their homelands was always possible for most of the 'visitors' who belonged to these categories.

Things were and are radically different for illegal economic émigrés or genuine refugees. They, as we keep stressing, belong to a very different category. For them the first impressions could be even more seriously deformed. Their different status, once again, will be influenced by how much they see of or know about their host country; how accurate their first impressions are; how these are or can be influenced – for better or for worse – by the general disposition shown towards them upon arrival in their potential host locations. The first indications of how well these new arrivals would do in the future and how able they would prove in adapting to their new environment could in some if not many cases, be discerned quite soon. Tens of thousands of people currently stranded in various frontal areas of what were once regions forming part of state of Yugoslavia can attest to the veracity of the points just made.

Accurate or not, in all of the above cases, what people know about each other forms only a tiny part of the reality that awaits them. Indeed, when they arrived in a new country in many cases they saw what that had been led to expect to find and not necessarily what was really there. The images which both sides – moving humans and, for lack of a better general term, let us call the receiving side their 'hosts' - are seriously incomplete. The first are motivated by hope; the second by the spirits of humanity and charity. It is crucial here to stress the opinion, depressing though it may be to some, that it is unclear how deeply these feelings of charity and humanity will last or, conversely evaporate into thin air, something more likely to occur when the hosts are faced with vast numbers of immigrants *ante portas*. Worse still, the expectations of the new arrivals are in most cases unreal. To be sure, they could be made to be more positive than negative depending on the kind of reception given upon arrival. In most cases the chances are that the euphoria of having 'reached' the imagined 'paradise' will soon give place to the realities of 'exile'. It may sound harsh to admit it but it cannot be otherwise.

The reality of the situation was – and remains – that what the new arrivals see only minimally depends on what their eyes tell them; what will really matter, however, is how their brains will interpret the local conduct they find.

Status was and is the true determinant of impressions and feelings; and it will not take long to realise that this group of 'visitors' is locally placed at the bottom of the pecking order. This feeling of despair is thus bound to set in the case of the totally untrained immigrant for he will realise very soon that "the locals will have *no use for him*". The words used were deliberately italicised to illustrate how horrible the reaction can be though one sincerely hopes that the majority of hosts will at least show care and compassion. Yet, I fear, my sentence has a strong whiff of reality; and the consequence of this is that it will generate a sense of 'nothingness' – I do not know how else to describe it – which will slowly grip the mind of such an unfortunate human being who suddenly finds himself displaced from the mountainous regions of Afghanistan into the urban surrounding of modern Munich. To me this is one more reason why we should not be too quick to give the false impression to such people – as Frau Merkel recently did by sending out the signal - that 'all will be welcome" in Germany (or Europe). They will not; and they cannot be.

If one cares about the immigrants' dignity – *and like all humans they, too, have their own which deserves appropriate treatment* – it will be fairer to them to make the kind of circumstances that await them clear from

the very outset; and doing this at sorting centres *within* the broader
geographical area in which they wish to settle is too late for it is already encouraging misleading expectations. We will discuss the problems of our current massive population movements below. Here suffice it to say that for this particular category of economic immigrants
the European idea of paying to set up 'sorting out centres' *within the
boundaries of the EU is wrong* - totally wrong. Wrong to the immigrant
for the reasons just mentioned; wrong and, indeed, an unacceptable
burden to the location in which such massive settlements will be set
up even if the EU is, or appears to be, paying for their creation. If I
were a citizen of Lesbos and was told the above I would literally be
up in arms!

Types of displaced entrants

To understand better the series of statements made above let us begin
with dictionary definitions concerning the nature and possible status
of foreigners moving to a particular country.

Exiles These are persons legally banished, or otherwise by means
of an enactment or administrative order of some kind, legally forced
to leave a country, sometimes their own (though, legally, this may not
be as easy as it sounds). The reasons for such forceful expulsion were
invariably 'political'.

Refugees were persons who, likewise, because of religious or political persecution, were forced - *directly or indirectly* - to seek refuge – i.e.
shelter or protection - in another country. The difference between the
first and the second category is the absence of a formal document
'banishing' the person who belongs to one country to reside in another. To put it different, the refugee leaves of his own accord though
in reality it is unbearable local circumstances that force this decision
upon him. Otherwise these two categories tend to present the same
problems so I will, unless otherwise stated, treat them as one.

The economic immigrant or *émigré* is a person who has left his country
of origins or residence to settle permanently or semi-permanently in
another country, usually for economic reasons. His move is, in effect
prompted by the abject poverty prevailing in his country from which
he is trying to flee in the hope of finding a better future elsewhere. He,
too, will figure in our discussion though the main difference between
this and the previous categories is that those fleeing a country solely
to find an economically more bearable life are not as easily allowed

to settle in another country; indeed, they will normally be repatriated back to their homes.

The expatriate, in a very general sense belongs to the same species, but is usually leaving his country around or after retirement for a country with a better climate or tax system or both. Unlike the previous category he is, obviously, in a much better economic position and *his move is dictated by free choice and it is not forced upon him by economic adversity.* Indeed he tends to be moving to another country because he expects to find a more favourable tax system and thus, if all goes well, he will end up being financially better off than he was in his own country.

The *metic* is the resident alien in another city, one notch above the simple expatriate in so far as he, at least, already has some of the privileges of citizenship of the country to which he has moved. In days gone by metics were found in ancient Greek cities and were those who were, for instance, Athenian only from one side of their family; nowadays, the modern citizens of the EU fill fairly adequately this definition, especially in so far as they carry many of their social security privileges or acquire – often instantly – new ones when they move to another EU country as students or guest workers. Acquisition of full political rights, including a full citizenship may, however be delayed or even denied. These people, and we are still talking those who belong to the EU, pose a special problem given that their cross-border movement cannot be prohibited. What may, however, happen to this category of citizens of the EU moving from one member state to another is that some of their social benefits conferred by the host country may not become payable to them at once. How long this delay may be has not been decided and may vary from country to country. Nonetheless, most countries, such as Britain, are deeply worried that citizens from much poorer EU countries – e.g. Rumania, Bulgaria - wish to move to Britain solely or mainly to take advantage of our country's more generous social security system. The growing wish is, indeed, to find legal ways whereby such benefits will be denied to such people, at least for initial period of two to three years. It is, however, difficult to predict if this will be the reaction of one, a few, or all the EU members.

The dual national is, finally, the person who, for divers, usually family, reasons may be a citizen of two states and can thus settle in one or the other. As a term, however, it does not tell us anything about where he resides (or most feels "at home" – in English term where he is domiciled). For persons in this category the major problem they will face is how to arrange their tax affairs between their two countries.

Otherwise, they are the most privileged of all of the above so they will not occupy us at all in this chapter.

The words used above suggest differences – sometimes subtle - between these six categories of 'moving' persons; all have occasion to see and experience life in more than one country, the question is how well they end up knowing them and how much they manage to integrate in their new environments if the move is to acquire a more or less permanent character. The answer to these broad questions depend on a variety of factors, including the displaced persons ethnicity, religion, national and individual characteristics. In the hope of avoiding the impression of any racial basis one could, in this context, point out that historically some moving populations manage to adapt and integrate better than others.

The rest of this chapter will be concerned almost exclusively with the categories (i) to (iii) above.

Refugees and economic migrants

In many instances the differences between these categories may be easier to state but not always easy to apply in practice. Separating the refugee from the economic immigrant – as stated, our major concern in this chapter - can thus depend on documents which may or not exist, international police records, or administrative determinations of individual facts *which should* – in theory - be conducted at the borders of the intended host countries *and not within them*. Invariably, such enquiries will take up time – often much time – besides being very costly if not almost technically impossible to conduct *impartially and thoroughly* where large numbers of migrants are involved.

Though this distinction is, for the reasons stated above, well established in theory it presents an additional difficulty in practice. The legal framework differentiating between who can come to your country and who cannot was designed at times when small (or at any rate manageable numbers of possible entrants) were considered. This was certainly true of so-called 'asylum laws' which were geared to deal with individuals or, at any rate, small number of annual and, if I may add, obvious applications. My own guess is that even these laws, rightly designed to protect the most vulnerable kind of displaced or fleeing persons, may have to be adjusted to the need to process many more such cases in these days of mass movements of populations. Striking a right balance between the competing interests of the person *escaping a country to save his life* and the country which wishes to help him must not be determined in a manner that prejudices the latter's own safety. At a time of spreading international terrorism this is not always going to be an easy affair.

The category a particular person belongs not only plays a key role in his ability to move to another country; it is also likely to affect the type and extent of psychological disturbances he may face for many years to come if he finally makes it to the 'host' country. These are the main issues considered in this chapter while further down I will focus on mass immigration and how one might be able to deal with it at a time when it looks set to continue growing in the immediate future. Before I deal with their problems however let me resolve a dilemma which has been bothering me while writing this chapter.

I am aware of the fact that wise commentators and politicians refrain from making political predictions for the future. An author, on the other hand, should, I think, not be bound by such a rule and on the contrary be willing to hazard guesses if for no other reason than to stimulate the thinking of his readers. My prediction thus is that the numbers of immigrants will continue to grow exponentially – I would not exclude figures described in terms of millions – and this state of affairs will thus NOT be tolerated by European nations. If I am right, we will then witness something which most observers or even simple citizens cannot even imagine at present; and herein lies the essence of my prediction; for its crux lies in the consequences of the first part of my reasoning.

The consequence is simple though dramatic. The continued validity of sacred principles which so-called civilised countries agreed - *during good times* - to observe and thus enshrined them in important documents will be seriously tested and, in practice, will be severely diluted under public pressure. For idealists of all sorts the sheer thought that such a reversal of thinking might occur is as unlikely as it is unacceptable. *But life is ruled by pragmatic not idealistic principles*; and my guess is that political pressures from the *mass of citizens* will prove irresistible.

Experience in the USA during the War with Japan and Korea and, most recently, following the September bombings in New York shows how in the USA even entrenched constitutional rules were *always* temporarily set aside to meet the fears of the general public. To be sure, such results suspending legality and alien protection, even where they were embodied in decisions of the US Supreme Court, were, in later times, revoked and condemned. But while the crisis was at its peak they remained unchallenged.

There is an irony here which must not be missed by anyone; for human rights are needed precisely when a country is stalked by fear, uncertainty, civil unrest. The possibility of suspending some of these principles at precisely the moment they are needed most may thus be unthinkable; *but in real life the unthinkable often happens*. In our current situation, the chances of such a *volte face* occurring will be all the greater until the other great issue of our times - spreading Islamic fundamentalism - is successfully reigned in. Since in my view this unlikely to occur in the near future, the chance of not watering down the good old humanistic but purely idealistic principles is real and may be fast approaching.

Returning now to the question of the kind of psychological disturbances likely to be suffered by refugees as a result of their forced displacement all we can say is that they can and will run the entire gamut of emotions. Many may thus simply feel unhappy; others may experience varying degrees of depression; yet others may fall into the trap of criminal behaviour, ranging from dealing with drugs to joining extremist groups operating in the countries in question. Just as interesting will be the fact that those with creative minds will reflect they manifold disturbances in their work be it in writing or in some other artistic form, e.g.; paintings, books or, perhaps, making a film.

A single ray of light in the midst of darkness

Creativity in the midst of physical and psychological suffering - is this really possible? Yes, is the answer since artistic inspiration stems from deep emotional moments and nowhere is it decreed that only happy ones generate masterpieces. The source of inspiration is the depth of the commitment to a person, an idea, a human feeling, it being love, life, suffering or death. One or two examples might help get readers thinking.

In the last notions – suffering and death - *Käthe Kollwitz*, one of Germany's most influential female lithographers, sculptresses, and creator of endless etchings, of the first half of the 20th century found inspiration. Her entire work deals with sorrow, hardship, and deep heartache but earned – even while she was alive - unique recognition.

Born in 1867 in the old Prussian Capital of Koningsberg (now Kalliningrad), she experienced a variety of anxieties and neuroses from early youth. She, too, was among the artists who, in more ways than one, were not entirely 'normal'. Her mood worsened as life developed and the death of siblings and later children and husband hurt her deeply yet also inspired her work depicting suffering. As a committed socialist and later communist she found among her beloved but suffering proletariat plenty of scenes of deep suffering which she would immediately proceed to record.

Official recognition was not her concern; in any event as a woman and, eventually a fully blown communist, she was unlikely to get any. Yet fate, if given a chance, occasionally – not often - ensures that recognition reaches those who deserve it with neither politics, religion or ethnicity – happily – being able to prevent it. She thus became the first woman ever to become a Fellow of the Prussian Academy Arts having a few years earlier been awarded Germany's highest Academic distinction – the Order of Merit[2]

Weimar was a crazy, unstable, and yet exciting period to experience life, especially in Berlin. Its art, even if studied through arts books, posters, and cards of the times, reflect these contrasts by being either extremely colourful or very, very dark (as Kollwicz's etchings were). This reflected perfectly an era which was born at the end of one disaster which, a mere fourteen years later, died by the hands of the man who brought the next one. Thus, it was Kollwicz's fate to see the same fanatical Corporal strip her of the two aforementioned honours during the very first year – 1933 - he came to power. As always, those who destroy are quicker to move than those who wish to build. Indeed, if it were not for Kollwicz's international reputation which, in those early years of the Reich still made her untouchable, she would have ended her life in a prison camp. As it were she died a fortnight before the end of the Second World War complaining to those around her that "Death and War had been with her ever since her birth".

Kollwicz's life is a paradox: the paradox of a huge talent bestowed upon a very miserably disadvantaged life. It may be nature's way of achieving in life the balance – Plato's αρμονία - which dominates its workings in the natural world. History thus shows us that not infrequently amidst great gloom we find rays of light which appear when the darkness begins to become unbearable. *Within limits* – alas impossible to define even by trained psychiatrists - melancholia, depression, mental suffering, have also been known to stimulate different

---

2. In Germany the French term is used to describe it - *Pour le Merit* - since it was founded by Frederick the Great who loved things French – in part because of his friendship with Voltaire. This, incidentally, was the decoration which prompted Queen Victoria and later her son King Edward VII to create our own similarly-named Order of the Merit with exactly the same aims.

forms of creativity; and we have many modern examples as well to prove this point to us beyond all doubt.

Woody Allen's amusing, at times brilliant films, ooze of their creator's anxieties and complexes. They tend to stem from his Jewishness and his own negative appreciation of his looks. Nature has endowed the Jewish race with many talents; their lives however, added more than their fair share of sufferings. To be sure, Alan's screen versions were entertaining for most of his viewers, not least because the actor/producer has learned over a long and successful career how to handle them. But to the keen observer, even his expert acting, reflects deep inner agonies and anxieties which most persons who have gone through similar pressures almost certainly would have been crushed by them not being, as the popular actor and film director was, strong enough to defeat them – partially at least - by pushing them aside and even exploiting them.

The displacement traumas related with explosions of human talent deserve deeper studies, ideally carried out by members of different disciplines such as history, art, psychology, sociology and so on. One wider point, however, remains to be addressed. That is that the study of human creativity born out of adversity need not be linked only to physical displacement of humans. I once tried to look at some of the issues this paradox raises and did so in a rather large and richly illustrated book entitled *The Duality of Genius*.[3]

My aim was never to bring down from their pedestals great people affected by a huge variety of physical or psychological ailments. Goethe - and I am one of those who deeply admire his multifaceted work - was one of them. In fact, what I set out to do was quite the reverse of what I might be accused of doing i.e. bring such people off their pedestals; far from it; for I was trying to demonstrate the link between suffering and exceptional talent. Additionally, however, I also wanted to make such geniuses more lovable by the ordinary man and women; for ordinary people cannot even begin to imagine genius, his or her imagination, creativity or mental torments; but they will instantly understand, and thus sympathise with, those who suffer from the ailments which they, too, recognise.

Our purpose here is thus to focus on the traumas associated with displacement so we must turn to this subject now.

---

3. Published by Jan Sramek Verlag, Vienna, in 2007.

Copying with the traumas of displacement

In the preceding paragraphs it became clear that different reasons may have pushed a foreigner to settle in a country other than his own. Understanding these reasons can help determine both what kind of reception such a person will get in the land in which he is seeking refuge. Just as importantly, however, it will reveal the extent of the psychological difficulties he will have to cope with once settled in it.

How such a displaced person will cope in his new country – assuming he is accepted to settle in it – will depend on a large number of factors which will be both determined by his conduct, his mood, his character and will be revealed by and through his work (especially if he is a writer or an artist). The harsher the conditions he encounters in his place of settlement, the more difficult the adaptation will be and, in turn, his psychological problems will be deeper and may take different forms. Loneliness, the first and most obvious reaction, can thus easily turn into despair; 'unhappy visitors' can become more wilful, adopt an exaggerated behaviour, become hypochondriacs, be easily led to overstatement, resentment, or even more serious instances of medically diagnosed depression.

Edward Said, an eminent displaced author put his experiences in writing in many of his widely admired works. In them we thus find first rate clues on how these people feel and react. The "exile" – but I think his idea also applies to all persons *forced* into displacement - he thus wrote [4]

"is offered a new set of affiliations and develops new loyalties.[5] But there is also a loss of critical perspective, of intellectual reserve, of moral courage."

On the other hand the uncertainty and instability which often ac-

---

4. "Reflections on Exiles", in *Reflections on Exile and Other Essays*, Harvard University Press, 2000, at p. 183. See, also his "Introduction" to that volume, pp. xi-xxxv.
5. Said talks so often about exile and of the psychological state of the mind of the exiled that - to me at least - his sentences and the description of the latter's feelings are not free from ambiguities. See, for instance, his comments on page xxx of his *Culture and Imperialism* (Vintage books, 1994). Does his reference to New York, for instance as the "exilic [what an acoustically horrible word] city *par excellence*" implies that it forces cultures to 'blend' making people feel that they 'belong to [two] worlds without being of either one or the other"? Or is it more accurate to suggest that this city leaves its ethnically diverse inhabitants 'stranded' in their respective cultures and only conscious of the existence of other separate world's ling around them in their won ghettos? My own feeling is the latter; but then my knowledge of New York is nowhere near as extended as his.

companies exiles and enforced immigrants may also make those who have lost so much become more daring in what they do or, to put this differently, become less willing to respond to the pressures of 're-straining logic'. This can make their work either unacceptable to their new environment though it can also make it very original since the exiled person's thinking process is now working in a novel environment and freed by convention.

Whichever way the exile or émigré reacts it is unlikely that it will come without deeply debilitating psychological feelings; and it would be an error to believe that these cannot occur in major cities where one is living cheek to jowl with multiple nationalities; for huge cities do not necessarily provide ideal conditions for companionship. After all Said, a Palestinian educated in Cairo University and – eventually - intellectually widely acclaimed in New York, a city of some eight million – still managed to feel alone and lonely, and even persecuted. Accumulated frustrations such as the above thus figure prominently in his collected essays so they must have been real and not prone to fade in the background with the passage of time and the advent of success. Wounds heal slowly; mental ones may never heel at all.

So in Side's life there came times when he could no longer hide the depths of loneliness if not depression with the result that his style of writing took the form of open denunciations and came close to being strident. Said, as I have stressed in everything I have written about him, was an exceptionally perspicacious writer. His very last work, however,[6] describing his early youth in the Middle East and written with the consent of the medical staff who were treating him while he was dying of cancer, reveals the extent of the bruises and complexes he carried within him almost from birth and the ways he used to overcome them if, indeed, he ever overcame them completely.

This is such a deeply distressing text that I confess I had to stop reading it half way through though I returned to it as I began writing these lines knowing that my first reaction was one of personal weakness and could not write about it or its author without having read and digested it in its entirety. This turned out to be good idea not just because it gave me one last chance to study the man's ability to write about the human suffering which those who find themselves "out of place" experience but mainly because, by re-reading it, he made me realise how - if I may say so - right I have been in including in my descriptions of Mediterranean habits etc. those of the of the Middle

---

6. *Out of Place. A Memoir by Edward W. Said*, Granta Books, London (2000).

Eastern communities. Indeed, much of what he describes would, I feel, apply to Greeks as well or, at any rate, it contained truths which applied to me as well.

There is, however, one more related question to which, I confess, I cannot give an unhesitant answer but one which, nonetheless, is crucial on the issue of 'convergence' of habits and practices which will be looked at again in the chapter nine. Said's feelings and behaviour in the early sixties on matters such as sex, courting, relations with women in general and parents in particular, paternal compared to maternal authority in the house, women at work, and so on, seem remarkably similar to those one would have encountered in Greece *at that time* (i.e. early sixties). However, does this hold true today? My doubt is due to the fact that what Said wrote about the Palestinians, Lebanese, and Egyptians may, at that time, resembled the comportment of the Greek youth but does this still hold true? I ask this question rhetorically for, I feel, the modern Greek youth and couples have moved in mind and comportment very close to that found among western European youths of today.[7] Has such a shift also taken place among Lebanese and young Lebanese? I suspect that here the religion of the young in question – i.e. whether they are Christian or Muslim – might well produce different answers. Indeed, a sizeable section of Muslim youth may have moved further towards a conservative application of their religion though we have also seen in recent times remarkable young girls fighting at the risk of the lives for a more liberated role for themselves.

Invaluable though Said's work is – largely I believe because of the frank way he speaks about matters involving him - he is not the only exile who left us written evidence of how people like him feel when 'out of place'. Other accounts – over-intellectual one could describe

---

7. The explanation in part must be sought in the liberalisation of thought (seen in the Constitution, the laws, and language, and many other elements in societal life) which brought to an end the conservatively inclined era of the Junta (1967-1974). This does not mean that these changes were welcomed by all in society; but it does provide a reason for the fact that more women joined the workforce, partly because they welcomed this emancipation from their more traditional family roles but also in order to increase family income. As a result of the above and in the fullness of time more children began to escape strict parental supervision from their early teens onwards. My explanation, though partial, also explains why this change in societal attitudes came in Greece on average ten or more years later than it did in other European states (including, for instance, England and the Netherlands) a conclusion which ties in with my earlier view that the state of family and their younger member in Greece was not that dissimilar to the one which Said described

them - tend to adopt a more intellectual approach to the cluster of problems they faced and to that extent lack the immediacy which characterises Said's writings.

Thus, the mental state of the émigré – enforced or even indirectly forced to adopt such a status, was explored and presented in detail by the eminent German Jewish philosopher, sociologist, gifted musicologist (composer and performer) as well as a keen student of psychoanalysis -Theodore Adorno (1903-1969) in his *Minima Moralia. Reflexionen aus dem beschädigten Leben*[8], - another work not at all easy to read but worth delving into it for those who are interested in understanding the spirit and general disposition this time of a *self-exile forced to leaving his country for the usual and well-known ethnically-related reasons.* One or two sentences from this important monograph can give a first flavour of his views on this topic. Thus on page 33 our author writes:

"Every intellectual in emigration is without exception, *mutilated*, and does well to acknowledge it to himself...he lives in an environment that must remain *incomprehensible* to him...*His language has been expropriated*, and this historical dimension that nourished *his knowledge, sapped."*

Adorno was not an ordinary refugee. Adorno was an intellectual and rejoiced in making this obvious both in his texts and even the deliberate opaqueness of his German style. That is the first thing we must note about him and thus be careful not to extend (or if we do extend, to do so with caution) what we discover about his character to others less intelligent, less deeply affected, less pugnacious in his attitude towards people – his audiences for instance - than he was.

Adorno, a hard-lined Marxist, was an unusually highly educated person and for that reason I italicised some of the words he used in his text quoted above for I am inclined to pay to them special attention fully convinced that as a German educated polymath[9] he used them in a

---

8. Available in English translated by E. F. N. Jepcott, Verso, New York, (2005) first published by New Left Books in 1974. The last part of the title – "Reflections from a Damaged Life" says much about the effect which his mixed background and, above all, his fifteen years of exile, had on is life. Adorno, much studied for his strident views on almost everything he wrote – from Marxism (which he favoured on the whole) to Jazz have been much discussed. But his public and private life, along with his many quarrels with colleagues and students alike have not – so far as I know – been considered from a psychological point of view. Still, even the little I say here about his deeply contradictory ethnic and religious background, combined with his exile, may have contributed to a personal disposition which veered easily towards criticism and quarrels and not just produced a restless character.
9. Adorno's German idiom is difficult to read and, I am told by many German friends,

very deliberate manner. They are thus all strong words which suggest, once again, awkward if not complex feelings, likely forced upon him by his own decision to live in another country. Even more interesting to speculate, on the basis of what is suggested in note 9, below, is the question whether the enormously rich variety of his background and interests, all experienced in the context of a highly stressed life, may have also influenced the syntactically perfect but convoluted way he expressed his thoughts.

Edward Said, who admires Adorno deeply, showed his usual courage in talking openly about his friend's difficult character describing him as a "forbidding…paradoxical, ironic, and mercilessly critical"[10]man. Yet the few sentences of Adorno cited above raise – for me at least – a number of additional questions which go beyond written style and the character which may lie hidden behind it. They touch his possible psychological complexes which, I suspect, must have also existed in 'less prominent' refugees. All I can thus do is ask some questions which might conceivably offer the beginnings of tentative answers but accept from the outset that not all refugees are likely to display the same degree the same psychological reactions to the fate they are suffering. To determine whether these answers may be relevant to different refugees, additional questions may well have to be asked of each person – a near impossible empirical survey to conduct. The conclusion of this first paragraph must thus be that we should not rush to generalise about the psychological condition of refugees but simply explore the possibility that more or less all of them may share *some broad characteristics*. At the same time we must not assume that immigration will affect more adversely the less educated and poorer of the species.

Returning to Adorno, however, on whose academic life we have enough information to begin some kind of analysis we must ask whether his mind (and language) were shaped by his status as a *semi-voluntary* exile *or* his original *character*. This, in my inexpert opinion, is the place where we must begin all searches for the answers we seek?[11]

---

that is accurate characterisation. His German thus is in keeping with the style of most of Germany's most learned philosophers and novelists of modern times such as Hegel, Heidegger, Habbemas, Horkheimer, Marcuse, even Thomas Mann who, also pose problems for their translators. In Adorno's case this often result in excessive literalness in the translation which, in my humble view, makes the English texts as well hard going!

10. *Representations of the Intellectual*, Vintage Books, New York (1996) at pp. 54-55.

11. Adorno left Germany for Oxford in 1934 and moved to California in 1941 just before the USA entered the War. As a result, he was classed as an "enemy alien" and

Second, how much of Adorno's character was affected by (a) his exceptionally mixed background which (b) his family which kept altering national characteristics. For the father was half Jewish who then became an 'assimilated' Jew by converting to Protestantism. Was this in the mind of the son when he was later to complain that the *émigré has his historical conscience sapped from his mind?* His mother's *entirely different* background *must* also have played a part in enhancing the confusion in his mind as to what he was; for she was a strong woman of Corsican origins[12] and ... a devout Catholic. So we must again ask to what extent had two cultures and three religions battled with each other inside his mind over his entire life, shaping (or sapping?) it as well as his soul of all signs of a life at ease with his background.

Adorno's is obviously an exceptionally complex case but then he was an exceptionally complicated, able, and energetic man and there is no reason not to wonder whether these complexities in his background generated feelings of *penned- up anger* which came out so clearly and so often in his criticisms in *all* the different kinds of work he wrote about politics, aesthetics, music, and psychology. Anger which often even surfaced in the lecture halls where he and his students would become involved in clashes which fell just short of even being physical!

Third, Adorno's distancing (if we may call it that) from Judaism may have started with his father conversion to Protestantism, continued by his mother *insistence* that he add her name – Adorno – to his own very Jewish 'Wiesengrund'. This is hardly an example of early feminist behaviour given that this occurred in 1903; but what was the reason for such a firm stand on her part? We will never know for sure; but forty years later he will complete this process himself when he chooses to eradicate his Jewish roots from his name upon becoming - while in California - an American citizen. Henceforth in his writings as well as his private life he will be known as Theodore Adorno – plain and simple without anything more.

Again, questions arise which call for answers and I cannot but feel that they must be addressed for the answers received might suggest that "losing one's roots" and "sense of belonging" can affect displaced persons of particular intelligence or eminence, *especially if they come from ancient races where they take their ethnic background, their religion,*

---

his freedom of movement severely restricted until he was naturalised American in 1943.

12. And we know from the well-documented history of the influence Napoleon's mother had on his life how strong this was.

and their home customs very seriously. A long cultural tradition behind one can be something to be very proud of; but few also realise how restraining it can also be.

One further observation needs to be noted. These difficulties of adaptation and assimilation are not only encountered in the lives of persecuted and often (and wrongly) perceived as "underdogs" but also by émigrés of high intellectual standing *and even wealth.* I came across a few such persons; and Adorno was one – whom I never met – but who was one of them as well since by that time he had arrived in California in 1941 he was already both an accomplished musician, a promising philosopher, and *in no state whatsoever* of financial hardship.[13] This complicates our effort to understand 'foreigner immigrants' by attributing in a simplified manner all their miseries and mental tribulations to possible financial difficulties.

So when we are talking of feelings of "loss", "lack of roots" or "feeling of not belonging anywhere" we are not necessarily talking of a phenomenon linked to the financial conditions of the geographical displacement of the person concerned but to psychological reactions associated with race, religion, or ways of life prevailing in the land which has been "left behind" and now lost – or perceived to have been lost - but also the individual's own character which predisposed him towards such state of uncertainty, hesitation, hypochondria, loneliness, insecurity and anger and reflections along the above-mentioned lines.

My own enquiries and 'gut reactions'[14] suggest that what was a fairly common feeling among most of these individuals is their feeling that they did "not belong" to the new country or, even, to any existing country except the vague idea of being part of a once famous but ceaselessly persecuted race. In short, such people tend to experience this feeling of loss more acutely even though in practice their moves had been accompanied by recognition of their worth as human beings and as professionals. This apparent incompatibility of confidence and

---

13. For this he was cruelly teased by his fellow Marxist, the Hungarian Georg (György) Lukács who castigated him for being part of the "German intelligentsia, [who] have taken up residence in the 'Grand Hotel Abyss'…a beautiful hotel, equipped with every comfort, on the edge of an abyss, of nothingness, of absurdity…". *The Theory of the Novel*, (1916), English translation by Anna Bostock, The Merlyn Press, (1971), at p. 22. This sentence appears in the lengthy introduction he wrote for the 1962 reprint of his book.

14. I call them gut reactions but I also feel sharing so many of the characteristics and experiences of these people that I feel being much closer to them that their average Oxbridge colleague.

insecurity may, in part, be traceable to this "need to belong" which, moreover, *seems* to be more developed in some races than in others.

Simone, Weill, a French Jewish philosopher who died in 1943, expressed this feeling tellingly when she wrote[15] "To be rooted is perhaps, the most important and least recognized need of the human soul." To suggest that this is a phenomenon encountered in most Jews and not only those living in France, where traditionally they received and still do at times a cold reception – to use the politest expression I can think of - is something I will attempt to do below.

But I also wish to put down a pointer which stems from my own experience: why can't this sense of belonging be satisfied by having this feeling of "roots" not just in one country but in more or, even, in one wider entity? Americans can feel Texan – and I know from experience how strong this feeling is – but they can also belong to the USA. Why could it not be the same with us in Europe? Simone Weill perceptively – I think – added in her posthumously published work (with a lauding introduction to the British public by no lesser a poet than T. S. Eliot) that "Every human being needs to have *multiple* roots." Is not cosmopolitanism the answer as well – perhaps? - the cure of uncertainties flowing from mixed backgrounds of the kind which obviously troubled Adorno?

Anathema, nationalists would argue; impossible, those with a scientific bend of mind would supplement. Yet it has not been so for me since, as I wrote above and repeated in many different works, in my case it was the most natural and satisfying of feelings to see myself as a citizen of Europe, born in Greece, originating in Venice, and English from my mother's side whose family had arrived in London from Chios (just after the famous massacre of the first quarter of the 19th century) settled in England, sweated up the financial ladder, with my maternal grandfather even managing to get appointed to the Board of the Bank of England in the mid-19th century.

Immigrants can succeed but still be burdened by silly pre-occupations

Albert Einsitein, Enest Gombritz, Karl Popper, Isaiah Berlin, F.A. Hayeck, Hans Kelsen, Walter Ullmann, Francis Mann, Otto Khan Freund, Max

---

15. *L' Enricement* (1949) translated into English as *The Need for Roots*, Rutledge & Kegan Paul *(1952)*, p 43.

Rheinstein, Albert Ehrenzweig - the list of Central European Jewish refugees who emigrated from their countries and came to our shores and settled in England or America is endless. To Hitler's madness, the Anglo-Saxon world owes an intellectual debt of gratitude; for their arrival represented the greatest infusion of new blood this world has had for centuries. For Western Europe as a whole the last time something like this occurred was the gradual fall of Byzantium.

To be sure, like Dick Wittington, those who arrived did not find the streets of England laden with gold; nor did our top academic institutions open their doors to them instantly, declaring their willingness to entrust to their care their own undergraduates. The émigrés had first to battle to learn our language,[16] simultaneously they faced the difficulties - to greater or lesser extent - of economic survival; and then, finally, they had to vanquish the psychological traumas of displacement, before – it must be said with pride – they finally got from their new countries a degree of recognition which was not only unprecedented but can be seen as a token of the openness towards talent which the English establishment, as few others in the word, was and is willing to show towards immigrants of promise.

Of these troubles, I venture to suggest, the psychological difficulties were if not the most serious certainly the most long-lasting and of the kind which could have broken lesser men. To pick up the terminology used at the beginning of this chapter, these very able displaced people also seem to have experienced difficulties in putting down roots; and the effects of these difficulties stayed with them for the rest of their lives.

In this subsection I wish to talk about a problem, not uncommon to other émigrés and exiles as well but found, in my experience, in a particularly pronounced form among those who belong to the Jewish race. The yearning is for roots, the homeland, and the sense of belonging, feelings which I suspect overlap to some extent. Though I know personally a fair number of Greek, Italian, French, and Armenian displaced persons, the only other race I have come across which feels it has lost its bearings if removed from its natural habitat are the Russian intellectuals.

To me this coincidence of reactions between two otherwise very

---

16. Walter Ullmann, one the greatest medieval political theorists of our time, arrived in Trinity just before the War and could only converse in Latin with his host, Professor Buckland. Eleven years later he was elected to his chair, and getting chairs those days was infinitely more difficult than it was in my time – the 1990's – and even more so now!

different races is inexplicable. Their nostalgia is openly displayed *even when* the states in which they sought refuse showered them with praise and honours. For instance, can anyone who followed closely the Solzhenitsyn sagas of the past ever forget his triumphant 'invasion' of the USA and his subsequent 'escape' – no other word can describe I think how he felt finally leaving the USA behind him - and return to an admittedly more welcoming Russia than the one he had left years earlier?

But let me return to the Jews with whom I have always had close professional relations.

I suspect but do not know that this yearning has probably been so strong among the members of this race because of the successive persecutions they suffered during their long and troubled history has made them depend on one another and also dream of their own fatherland, even when they did not have one. It thus seems linked to the idea that if they ever had – which they now do – a country of their own this feeling of insecurity would be reduced if not extinguished. For, like the Greeks whom I know even better and who still carry the scars of the Turkish yoke, contemporary Jews remain conscious of the discrimination they suffered in the hands of all European nations until well into the 19th century. It is an irony but true nonetheless to say that they were rejected not because they were of "no use" but because they were too clever, closely knit, and fiercely loyal to their friends.

This sense of "separateness" was, possibly, enhanced by adhering to and not forsaking their own religious observances and customs – a problem not faced by Russians, Armenians and Greeks - and my guess is that those who followed this line the absorption into their new environment proved that their full acceptance may have been more difficult for this 'dilution' of their full Jewishness must have kept eating into their souls. Again, and for the sake of completeness I add that this is what I was told by 2 or 3 colleagues to whom I was fairly close and who confided in me along these lines.

At this point, I must make clear that I have attempted to describe these complex feelings only because I found them very prominent in these close friends and thus forced myself to try to understand them because I never experienced them myself. Thus, despite my efforts and wider reading on this subject, the chances of my getting things wrong cannot be excluded; and if I have done so, I apologise in advance for any unintended offence my observations may cause to a race which I deeply admire and in which I have been fortunate enough to discover truly genuine and loyal friends.

Nor were these difficulties encountered only in England but also - so far I know through personal knowledge - in Russia, France, and even in the USA which, in many ways have not always proved to be the most tolerant of hosts. The problem is, however, that though many learned books have been written about the Jewish lawyers who sought refuge in Britain and the USA,[17] the psychological effects of adapting to a new country were never discussed in a scientific manner nor any serious attempt made to link them with the work these people did in their new homelands.

I regret this omission for four reasons.

First, because it would be fascinating to demonstrate how, if at all, these problems affected the work done in the new country compared to that done in the one from which they were fleeing.

Second, was it different in kind? Foreign lawyers for instance who suddenly found themselves in Anglo-Saxon countries typically turned first to Roman law. This was understandable since this was a subject they knew already how to teach it. But these were clever people and realised that could not keep careers going only by teaching one not immediately useful subject to the Common lawyers. So the next forward step was taken; and their switch to comparative law explains why the vast majority of comparatists – dare I say in the whole western world including South America – were central European immigrants. The best of these immigrants in fact showed the extent of their talent by showing, eventually the extent of their adaptability and intelligence; for scholars like Max Rheinstein, Albert Ehrenzweig, Otto Kahn- Freud became acknowledge experts even on the laws of their host countries. Was there and if so to what extent, any diversification in their occupation?

Third and just as important, it would give one the chance to pay tribute to these people and to this race by revealing their full grandeur, which is only understandable when one realises their loneliness and insecurities they must have experienced while being intellectual productive – sometime admirably so - in their new lands[18]

---

17. For instance, *Second Chance, Two Centuries of German-speaking Jews in the United Kingdom,* co-ordinating editor Werner E. Mosse, Tubingen, (1991). More recently and devoted to layers is *Jurists Uprooted. German-speaking Emigré Lawyers in Twentieth-Century Britain,* (OUP 2003).

18. Such a book would be successful only if it gave correct information not only about their peregrinating lives and work but also included information about: (a) the *true* reception given to these people by our old Universities and (b) to attempt to describe the feelings and loneliness and multiple insecurities these emigres felt while in our country.

Finally, one must devote more time in noting how their host countries – England in particular – were able to keep themselves so well informed of the excellence of some newly arrived refugees and go – often through Prime Ministerial initiative – and offer them the highest honours this land had at is disposal.

A book describing by a "friendly outsider" the sometimes amazing complexes and inner insecurities these people suffered from, as much as the reverse complex of contemporary German *intellectuals* (with whom I have also remained in close contact) towards the sins of the forbearers, remains to be written and I hope one day soon it will appear since I am tempted by such a difficult task to try and jot down some ideas myself. I repeat, my reason for this is plain and simple. Quite frankly it is to illustrate and explain to the ordinary reader how great men through the ages owe much of their creativity to their mental suffering. Clearly, however, if such a work is to be carried out properly and successfully it needs the combined talents of experts from different fields of knowledge to complete the ambitious task I can imagine in my mind's eye.

Since, at present, such a book lies beyond my capacities, I will only attempt to give sketches of two great men – an Englishman and American – who carried these scars with them throughout an ever-more organized, successful and richly rewarded life. Understanding them slightly better through these efforts have made it easier to deal with other worthy people of their race in my own much more modest surroundings as a student of the law. But their lives have been to all those who got to know something about them a source of inspiration and imitation.

Isaiah Berlin and Felix Frankfurter offer my two illustrations. Their host countries bestowed upon them everything they could possible offer them in terms of recognition and appreciation. They, themselves, never ceased to proclaim their gratitude for the treatment they received and proudly proclaim their Englishness and American citizenship respectively. Yet they remained in some senses unfulfilled, insecure, and uncertain, features which could even make them quite aggressive at times.[19] They felt throughout their life confused and as if they did not belong anywhere which, frankly, was never quite correct yet also never quite wrong! They even felt a kind of resentment combined with admiration towards their local peers who were citizens

---

19. This was certainly the case of Frankfurter with the result he frequently failed to carry his other colleagues on the Supreme Court with him and this despite his formidable intellect and reasoning powers.

of their host countries and had the courage to criticise them, a thing they, too would have liked to do but did not even dare to consider except when thinking while on their own! Reading their biographies carefully one is not left in any doubt that their lives, in their own eyes, were missing something.

Sir Isaiah Berlin [20]

First, one must start with the cause for the difficulty to assimilate fully in the new country: the feeling of not belonging, the yearning of home. "The loneliness of a child exiled into a foreign tongue is easy to imagine. English schoolboy lore – football teams, cartoon characters, dirty songs and jokes, snobberies and cruelties – was beyond his ken, while all the impressive things he knew seemed worthless or an embarrassment."(33-4) He shared, in short, entirely what was in my case half of my up-bringing -the Greek half – which places emphasis almost from infancy on being serious – σοβαρός – as the hallmark of a well- brought up and properly educated young boy. The wisdom of Oscar Wilde's quip that "dullness is the coming of age of seriousness" sank in my mind thanks to my mother's different ideas about the up-bringing of children; but Sir Isaiah had none of that!

Yet early years and the race culture at the background leave indelible marks; so Ignatieff continues the statement just cited by making it clear that "The marks of exile remained *faint* but visible throughout his life: abstractly, in his respect for the need to belong; politically in his Zionism; morally in his fascination with the marginal, excluded or enraged figures of nineteenth century history." (34)

Ignatieff writes beautifully; and this sentence is a staccato statement of his subject's polarised interests. But then, one also finds the word which I italicised above: faint. Is Igantieff suggesting "faint" in order to smooth the transition from émigré to Englishman and suggest the disappearance of the "complex"? I cannot say; but if that was his intention, deliberate or subconscious, it is negated by statements which follow later and refer to the more mature phase of Sir Isaiah's life. Thus, at the bottom of the same page, we find a key sentence: "… *eagerness to please* figured at the top of his list of *vices.*[sic] He always

---

20. All the citations come from Michael Ignatieff's authorised and most readable biography *Isaiah Berlin, A Life* (1998). To avoid filling the text with footnotes, I give the precise page number of the book where the quotations can be found in the form of a simple number in parenthesis after the end of the citation.

worried that a Jew should not be so emollient and accommodating. It was a central moral dilemma in his life to reconcile a *sense of dignity with the eagerness to fit in.*"

For me the two sets of italicised words simply do not fit together. "Pleasing" mostly suggests kindness; "reconciling dignity" – i.e. do not bend too much backwards to please – for the "sake of fitting in" suggests calculated moves intended to ensure survival and success, something which is clearly perceived to be more difficult for someone who is not English. The attempt/ wish to "fit in" is a dangerous desire for it may be a small step from obsequiousness.

The above does not only mean being "accommodating" for the sake of his own advancement; it also suggests as the author clearly stated that "as a Jew and outsider, Berlin felt he was not cut out for taking public stands" (53) though of course, this did not prevent him from talking abstractly about the value if freedom and liberty in his writings. Thus, later on in the book, when his years in the USA are being described, we are told that "Englishness and Jewishness came into conflict with him."(79) At times he must have even contemplated that living the life of a Jew in England must have been impossible. This had, indeed, been advocated by Arthur Koestler in an article in *The Jewish Chronicle* in 1950 but Berlin, a year later, and in the same journal, tried to distance himself from such extreme position. (183).

This psychological (or cynical) inability to "commit" to one side or the other may have been one of the many reasons which brought him so clear to Turgenev whose "middle course" he so extolled in his wonderful introduction to Turgenev's "Fathers and Children" which was based on his Romanes Lectures in Oxford in 1970. This unique sense of loneliness and yearning for "home" thus figures once again towards the end of this revealing biography where Ignatieff tells us that Berlin felt that "to be a Jew…was to have a special understanding of this loneliness. It was also to know how deeply men and women needed to be at home somewhere in the world. Belonging was more than possession of land and statehood it was the condition of being understood itself." (292). To me at least this can only mean that though the English establishment had honoured him in every way they could and he, in turn, never ceased praising the virtues of the country which had given his refuse, *he still did not feel quite at home here.* Perhaps, I may be wrong in this conclusion; but let us consider what all this internal turmoil did to his character.

The way he saw himself and behaved in his private life suggests an immense accumulation of complexes. This is not unusual among great creators though I have only encountered so many combined in one other person – Johann Wolfgang Goethe. Thus, in the longest – two volume – *Psychoanalytic Study* of Goethe I am aware of by K.R Eissler and published in 1963 we find in volume 2 (1054) the summary conclusion that "Goethe exhibited a score of phenomena belonging to the realm of psychopathology" which included: fear of heights, fear of darkness, hypochondriasis, compulsions", fear of menstruation, pre-occupation with his health etc. etc.. Eissler, a few pages further down (1097) adds for good measure that: "I believe that every genius is potentially psychotic, because the production of great art is due to the deflection of a psychosis."

Berlin' views of himself and his behaviour in private suggests a very complex and insecure character lurking behind the public persona. He apparently was quick to tell people how "intolerably ugly" he was (4) and thought of himself as (fat, oily, white-skinned and deformed and he [again] made a point of telling people so." (65). Yet he was also noticeable for his narcissistic form of "hypochondria". Thus, he "liked"[sic] being mildly and curably, ill. He love[d] doctors regimes, nursing homes" and "would take to his bed at the slightest provocation" (5). He "had a vivid sense of the difficulty of knowing what one feels and expressing these emotions without sentimentality" (56).

His first romantic encounter was seriously "repressed" he, himself, describing it as not "involving any kissing, any touching [and being] very inhibited." (57) Some attributed to him " a touch of feline malice" while most found him priggish, disapproving for example, of couples holding hands in public."(65). He also had a tendency to ascribe different meaning to words when used about Jews. Thus "Jewish energy was described as pushiness, cleverness became arrogance, and exuberance turned into vulgarity, affection was seen as sentimentality." Such terminology moves uncomfortably between irony and self-dislike.

Sir Isaiah was also a social snob. In Disraeli he detected an attempt to avoid his Jewishness by becoming associated with the aristocracy so he, too, developed a "lifelong affection for aristocrats… The quality he admired in the well-born was the indifference to convention that went with a sense of being at ease. But how was a Jew ever to be fully at ease?" (223), Finally, so as not to prolong this list too much, let us mention how his biographer finishes the book. He simply states that "a survivor's guilt always shadowed his happiness."

What can we make of such combination of personal anxieties reaching the level of neuroses, insecurities, complexes and phobias when combined with energy, talent, productivity and un-doubted fame. To what extent the former helped produce the latter; to what extent, the former were the result of his ethnic origins and the sense of guilt and anxiety and insecurity it seems to endow them along with an inexhaustible list of talents? Can the past, often the very distant past, affect an entire race, even blight it, with characteristics which sit uncomfortably with their virtues? And the key of all related questions: how is all this reflected in the lives and works of these great achievers? We found parallels in the development of the Greek character; and we suggested there as we do here that the more you know about people the more we understand them and should praise them for overcoming such "inherited character flaws".

Perhaps, if one searches deep enough, one will also find lessons for ones' self-worth learning. Thus neither Berlin, as we saw above, nor I, would find much virtue in being "too accommodating" to anyone and everyone simply for the sake of penetrating a social group to which neither of us really belongs. But here we also part in so far as I, at least, feel no need to change my image in order to penetrate any social group however high or wealthy. Either one "clicks" with people or one does not. And if one does not, each can happily take his own course without rancour, bitterness, or a disagreement. There is room in the world for all of us. If only people realised this, much strife would be minimised or even be eliminated. And, even more importantly, there is always room at the top provided you deserve it. That, at least, is the romantic meaning of a sentence I first heard uttered in the French Academy and it stuck in mind with glue: "honour is the recompense of merit"! It is a wonderful sentence, especially if you can bring yourself to believe it.

Felix Frankfurter [21]

There are some similarities and differences between our first and this example of the psychology of a Jewish émigré. For one thing, as we

21. The better ways to understand the lives and characters of American judges is to learn about them by reading books which concern not only their own lives but also those of their immediate colleagues at the US Supreme Court. Here, in the interests of the oft-proclaimed intention to keep footnotes at a minimum I only refer to Professor H. N. Hirsch's biography *The Enigma of Felix Frankfurter* (1981) and, again, the numbers in parentheses given at the end of each quotation refer to the pages of this book or the further references therein given.

shall note, the characters of these two eminent men were different, the second being – on the surface at least –more assertive and domineering. But it is the insecurities experienced by both, the ambition to rise and the psychological cost at which this rise was achieved that brings them together. Also, and perhaps most importantly, we have here, too, not only evidence of the insecurities suffered by such people as a result of finding themselves in a new environment but also of the importance of understanding their characters - warts and all – in order to understand their work and the limitations that the character flaws had on the overall impact of Frankfurter's legacy. So, let us once again, begin at the beginning.

Young Felix was born in Vienna in 1882. His father's family had been rabbis. Though the family was moderately well-established they lived in a moderately isolated Jewish community in pre-First World War Vienna which we know from the works of many, including Stefan Zweig's readable (and moving) *The World of Yesterday*, how biased it was against the Jews. Not surprisingly therefore the father moved his family to the USA and settled in a German Jewish neighbourhood of Lower East Side of Manhattan and then upgraded somewhat to the neighbourhood in the East Seventies. In such Jewish circles, education was seen as the best if not only way of advancement. But on arrival and at the age of twelve Frakfurter was, like young Berlin, totally unable to speak or read English so that he had to start the difficult way.

The father, who never made it to the rabbinate but had to end up as a petty businessman, was weak, unsuccessful, and gentle and, as Felix would later write to his future wife, "joy was his emphasis". The mother's "accent", on the other hand, was "on duty"; and she was the person who, as the saying goes, "wore the pants". In subsequent letters written by Felix, family tensions are skilfully concealed though he pays them a cunningly phrased compliment when he writes "I've said…when I was nearer in time and feeling to my youth and my relations to my family. That the greatest debt I owe my parents is that they *left me alone almost completely.*" Since young Felix developed a talent with words, one can choose for oneself how to interpret the italicized words!

Though the education progressed well the young man's physique remained small – he never grew beyond five feet five inches – and contributed to a character which was intense, nervous, arrogant, domineering and determined to acquire eloquence and intellectual power to keep the world of taller men from overlooking him" (18). Thus, when he attended his first class at the Harvard Law School in 1903 he described his feelings by writing "I had one of the most intense frights of life. I looked about me. Everybody was taller...I was a little fellow... they are a lot of big fellows...robust fellows, self-confident creatures around. (20) It is an irony that his mentor and friend, Oliver Wendell Holmes, was a tall and very handsome man not to mention self-confident to the point of arrogance. But then, maybe, one reason for choosing him to be his mentor was precisely his imposing physique.

Yet these complexes also encouraged the cultivation of wit and charm and – most deadly of all - a unique ability to flatter those he wished to impress and win over. The result is a considerable number of letters blatantly flattering his mentors – in chronological order – Attorney and Subsequent Secretary of Defence Henry L. Stimson, Louis D, Brandeis, subsequently an Associate Justice at the US Supreme Court, and Oliver Wendell Holms, who likewise was appointed to the same high judicial office and is nowadays widely considered as the greatest of all American judges.

Reading some of these letters one is amazed at how sycophantic he could be. Thus on one occasion he wrote to Holmes - whose height, looks, background, war record, whit, elegant prose and superb intellect impressed him, as already stated, so deeply that he immediately decided to model his life on that of the Justice – "You l know, of course, the great stimulus you are too many of us...but you are also a source of despair. For what can we creeping worms do, and what good is it – when you toss off ... an opinion that illuminates so much so brilliantly in a few pages." (42)

It is difficult to believe that Holmes, who was, as stated, a superb stylist and accomplished social snob, could stomach such cheap grovelling. But he did; and on one occasion, in receipt of a similarly crafted praising letter, Holmes responded by writing:

"All I can say in reply is to send you my affectionate thanks – my rather fearful hope that I may never fall from the place you have given me and expectation that always while I live, as now, I shall have great cause to be proud of having counted of something in your life."

Such exchanges may compare badly with the more understated and, in my view, elegant letters written during this period; but it was all part of the carefully planned strategy of Frankfurter to "break the bounds of his culture – he had already rejected all religious forms of Judaism – and gain acceptance – of a certain kind – from the American [Brahmin] establishment" (21) to which Holmes so obviously belonged. This was not going to be easy for, as is biographer puts it "Frankfurter continually tried to resolve the question whether he was an insider or an outsider." (23) We are back, in short, to the social complexes which tend to accompany Jewish people more, I think, than other émigrés and can lead, in Berlin's words, to becoming a little too "accommodating' in order to become "accepted".

Yet Frankfurter's constant flattery of persons of influence – Holmes and Brandeis in particular - was not as one sided as may appear. For there is a very cynical twist to this mutually admiring exchanges of epistles which reveals the "hero" – not much nobler – that his "flatterer".

For Holmes - about whom more recent authors have been slightly less reverential than the older generation – was cynically busy making his own posthumous reputation by himself bestowing his friendship on two young and ambitious colleagues, an American – Frankfurter – and an Englishman – Harold Laski – in the hope and belief that they would eventually sustain, even elevate, his reputation to Olympus. The strategy worked and the disciples did what was expected of them. The myth of the great judge only now is beginning to crack in times when all our institutions and heroes are subject to the onslaught of contemporary revisionism. Grant Gilmour, the distinguished Yale Law Professor who was asked to act as Holmes' biographer gave up after some years of reading himself into the Holmes archives and coming to the following very damning conclusion which supports the point made earlier on. Grant thus observed: [22]

"Holmes is a strange, enigmatic figure. Put out of your mind the picture of the tolerant aristocrat. The great liberal, the eloquent defender of our liberties, the Yankee from Olympus. All that was a myth, concocted principally by Harold Laski and Felix Frankfurter, about the time of World War I. The real Holmes was savage, harsh and cruel, a bitter and lifelong pessimist who saw in the course of human life nothing but a continuing struggle in which the rich and powerful impose their will on the poor and weak..."

To conclude we must again ask, even if the question courts by its nature inconclusive answers, whether such psychological investigation of great achievers serves any legitimate purpose. I think understanding people and their motives and characters is enriching in itself quite apart that it may accustom us to test our contacts with

---

22. *The Ages of American Law*, (1977) pp 48-9.

people who approach us with similar motives. But in Frankfurter's case the need is even greater even though this cannot to be demonstrated in detail in a book which is not aimed at lawyers. Yet for lawyers understanding his character - indeed that of his character as judge - can be immensely useful if one is to have any idea of what lies ahead of him in any professional encounter he may have with such a judge.

This is particularly true in the case of Frankfurter for, as his biographer who is himself a law professor remarked, the need was doubly great. For "this need to examine judicial personality seems especially acute for the analysis of periods of transition within the Court, when constitutional precedent gives way to doctrinal confusion. It is during such periods of uncertainty that personality may become a particularly important determinant of judicial outcome" (4). Frankfurter's involvement in the so-called "flag cases" which occupied the Supreme Court from 1940 onwards,[23] provide ample illustration of the point made above.

Dual backgrounds, dual visions, dual values and making choices

So let us try and wrap all of the above into some plausible summary of what I attempted to do and what may be the conclusion of this effort.

In this book I have tried to convey observations of a life time concerning various nations with which I have had the privilege to be closely associated. I have tried to describe how they see each other and, indeed, how they – I – see others with whom my life and work brought me into contact. Since I wished – and still do so – desperately to converse mainly with my ordinary, normal, non-lost in the haze of abstractions and theories fellow citizen, I tried as much as any academic can do, to write simply and, wherever possible, with a touch of humour.

Yet even if the apparel was designed to look simple it is functional only if what holds it together is well grounded to reality and corresponds to basic behavioural patterns of human beings, especially the

---

23. Starting with the *Minersville School District* v. *Gobitis*, 310 US 586 (1940). The issue in that case was whether the children of a Jehovah's Witness could be required to salute the American flag at School. The most important of the flag cases, with facts similar to *Gobitis*, was *West Virginia State Board of Education* v. *Barnette*, 319 US 624 (1943). Justice Jackson's magnificent speech affirming the individual's right to decide whether to salute or not is one of the classics of American judicial literature. See ibid, pp. 638 et seq.

most complex kind, i.e. those belonging to different cultures. There thus comes a point, even in a book aimed at the general (educated, I hope) reader, where one has to explain to him how one reached the conclusions about people, their habits, and characters, described in this book and how, in turn, they were themselves influenced in their decisions by factors which affect them and their behaviour but which are not always easily discernible. My main thesis is that you understand these background factors and then your understanding these peoples' works better.

The explanation is best done by "closing the circle" that is by completing what was said in the other somewhat theoretical chapters of this book - the first - where I talked about observing people and events from changing angles and tried to understand the multiple factors which shape or distort their minds and thus how they express themselves in their daily lives and through their works. Providing a theory to serve as the backbone of the whole project is one way of doing this and then asking the reader to reflect whether the details given bear it out or not. In fact, in writing this book the reverse occurred for it has been developing slowly and in an unplanned way over a period of close to fifty years (which has more or less been the duration of my peripatetic life) as moments of my life were noted and preserved to be put one day to some use. That day has arrived!

The first point to note - and it must be obvious by now - is that I lived my life with many people, in different lands and progressively came to see them differently than I had before I embarked on my life's journey. The result? I feel that I now know them better so that I can talk about them with enhanced understanding and, I hope, objectivity. In this way, what I say may be of interest to others but also say something of the transformation process which makes such enhanced vision/understanding of people possible.

All of this occurred because, as I explained in my first chapter, *I* changed with the passage of time. But this change, in turn increased, because I lived and worked with different people and did so as a fellow human being: curious, inquisitive, prone to teasing and willing to be teased, ready to learn and, above all, inclined to see the lighter side of flaws and human peccadilloes but, nonetheless, always well disposed towards all. Adorno's learning may have not been mine; but neither was his constant willingness to be critical and quarrelsome. I have admired many colleagues whose abilities I could discern even if I disliked their characters and I am not going to change at the end of seventy one!

As the title of the subsection states this was made possible by the fact that my vision of people, characters, and events was doubled – if not tripled and quadrupled - by spending so much time in different countries searching in each what I thought was attractive and useful and then making it my own. Above all, trying to discover and understand what provided all these people the urge to succeed. This last word also made me realise the true meaning of success. For success was not, as so many in our times feel is, making money; nor does success mean getting worldly recognition for one's work, pleasing though this may be in moments of weakness of self-doubt. True success, however, can only be gauged by discovering how *'useful*, to others and society, one's life has been." My yardstick at first instance was thus defined by my pupils' reactions; and since they came from countless countries and regions the wider the utility of what I tried to do for them, the better I might feel my chosen profession was practiced.

In teaching in nearly thirty universities in three Continents my vision was also sharpened without it being accompanied, in Edward Said's words, by "rancour", "regret" and I would add "envy" which, I believe, were feelings more prominent with him than they were with me. That my reaction was more "mellow" was almost certainly due to chance. For, unlike Said, I was not an exile or refugee, but a citizen of two countries - three if you add my Venetian ancestry - and from the outset of my life lucky enough to be taught by my parents to be proud of all three and respectful of all others. Indeed, as far as my mother was concerned I now see how she conceived the guidance she gave me in my youth while still in Greece as a preparation for my adult life in England.

This was, essentially, the education which she had received at her Convent and it was built around the biblical word of "charity" which in modern parlance becomes love (loosing, I think, much of the breadth of meaning of the old term.) This was opposed to hatred and revenge; it favoured forgiveness – άφεση not the less Christian συγγνώμη; it emphasized self-sufficiency and not dependence on others nor greed'; it constantly made me reflect on the lives of the poor and the suffering; and whenever I felt miserable or was affected by the 'blues' she would teach to me look at others less fortunate than I and recognise how lucky I was. Above all, she thought the environment I was brought up in – Greek politics - was the least appropriate for bringing up any boy so she resolved from early times that one of her missions in life was to *snatch me* - her word not mine - out of the jaws of politics. I owe my education to my father but my character -

notwithstanding its flaws – and my family happiness to my mother. May God rest their souls. For my part all I can add is that as their son I worked hard to prove worthy of the confidence and support they both showed towards me.

Thus, there was no rancour bur friendly feelings; no envy but pride that I shared in the strong points of two (or three) nations with which I was intimately linked; no disappointment for lacking what others might have earned or inherited but gratitude that I had from birth been endowed with the ability to appreciate the good fortune of an incessantly caring family. My view, in short, of the world was much rosier than Said's; and probably it is this extra hardship which he experienced (unlike me) that gives his writings their extra "punch" – literally and metaphorically – contrasted to my own more serene sentiments of marvel, amusement, contentment and – not infrequently – a simple sense of sadness at the way people around me behave!

Those, then, are the first two lessons one acquires from benefiting from dual or even triple nationalities and the next logical question that arises is "how do you cope if/when the two of them clash?"

Said ground here; yet my character and professional training always assures me that clashes can be resolved, indeed if one is intelligent enough, they can be anticipated and stopped early enough before they cloud one's reasoning powers and lead to conflict. So the question of possible clashes never bothered my mind and was thus, in effect, left technically speaking unanswered. Conciliation, compromise were all words beginning with 'c' and much better than the ones which reminded people of clashes and conflicts.

Yet clashes do arise in an increasingly quarrelsome world and the question of dual allegiance can then come to the fore much more acutely for the dual national than it does for the exile or émigré who finds himself confronted with a similar dilemma. For where *the latter's* loyalties will lie, in most cases, will be clear.

Adorno and Said's life and work made this abundantly clear since the first returned to Germany and the second remained a proud Palestinian to the end of his life in New York. The same, I believe happened to most of the foreign comparatists who settled in England or the USA, even though their sojourn in Anglo-Saxon environments instilled in them a healthy respect for the Common law. It is thus natural to expect that such "displaced" people will retain a special kind of longing for the land they were forced to leave behind. It is different, however, with the true dual or triple national, the one who treats his two (or more countries) with equal affection and admiration and accords them –or so he believes until the crisis point arrives – equal loyalty.

So, my first way of treating the question "what happens when there is a clash of loyalties?" was to treat it as a non-question and, as such, it had to be modified to make sense. Norman Tebitt, later Lord Tebitt, a politician whose pugnacious temperament and personal bravery in the face of adversity I often admired - more so - it, has to be said, than some of his political ideas - in a well-known statement about the Englishness of immigrants argued that you can detect the *true* Englishman for he is always "cheering for the home team". I thought of this in the context of the question set out above and found true as a fact but intellectually unsatisfactory. For should I not cheer the opponent if, for instance, while playing football or tennis, he scores a goal or hits an ace incomparably well so that it makes the scoring of the goal or the success of the serve unstoppable? Patriotism should not deprive me of the chance to judge freely, admire earnestly, and applaud loudly the opponent who plays better than me or my side. Merit must thus not be limited to nationality but attributed to anyone who had shown clear signs of it. Being part of two nations and not one gives you the chance to compare the attributes of your two halves over a wide range of issues and admit – if you are honest – that in some cases A is better than B and in others it is the reverse.

The above is a pleasingly balanced stance. But what if the question was changed, narrowed to the most awkward of situations, and thus made more difficult to answer? "Would one", for instance, "be willing to make the supreme sacrifice for one's country?" Speculating on hypothetical questions is always dangerous for it is possible, indeed humanly very likely to give a theoretical answer which would then be overturned at the moment of real decision. Yet it is perfect possible to reflect on such questions and try to guess what the sense of duty if likely to demand of one.

Reading and re-reading Said's thought-provoking works leaves me with the clear impression that my reaction is perfectly normal; for I understand him and give him credit for having the courage to use word "rancour" and indirectly admit to his psychological wounds. It is entirely normal for those who have suffered mentally and experienced the feelings he did so to feel. Had I suffered as he did would I have been able to write in the balanced way he did? I never sat such an exam; he did, and passed it with flying colours. If the need ever arises I hope I will pass mine in an equally meritorious manner and show that my training has taught me never to forget my debts.

For my Greek compatriots the extent of this dual affection may sound surprising; I would not be surprised in the least even if some condemned me for writing as I do. They should not, however feel in this way since, after all, English was my mother's citizenship; and it was so unashamedly declared by my father when he registered my birth in July 1944. This is also the nationality of my wife and children. England is the country in which they spent all their lives; and I three quarters of mine. It is this environment which enabled me to complete and enrich the education I received at home; and it is this State which offered recognition to me to my work over and above all which I or it deserved.

It is only natural that I feel indebted to it and for a long time now made it clear that I wish my ashes to be scattered at the root of a tree in Grantchester overlooking the Cam where I used to walk and admire the Spring sunsets with the woman I have loved more than any other in my adult life and whom I convinced to become my wife. I have never asked her if she would ever join me there for, whatever her decision, I know that I will remain a free spirit even in the other world so I will catch up with her wherever she may be!

I said I cannot answer hypothetical questions; but I know I have been entirely honest in proclaiming by feelings for only honesty enabled me to write in public, time and again, that I never, for one instance, subscribed to the strong anti- Russian, anti-German, anti-Dutch, anti-Turkish feelings often voiced by Greeks. My disappointment with America has been just that – disappointment for mistakes done on the foreign policy and human rights front but by no means dislike let alone enmity; for I owe much too much to my American Law Schools and my American colleagues during the thirty four years I spent in different parts of their country teaching but, above all, learning. It makes no sense to criticise a whole nation especially if among them are countries such as America, Germany and the Netherlands where I spent much of my life and learnt much from their ideas, customs, and their inhabitants.

My beloved Goethe, in his most remarkable *West-Ostlicher Divan*, advised as much even though his "orientalism" was intellectual rather than acquired *in situ*. He thus wrote convincingly that:
"Who the song would understand
Needs must seek the song's own land.
Who the minstrel understand,
Needs must seek the minstrel's land."
This is not just a love poem in the sense that it is erotic; this a chef

'd' oeuvre where love symbolises sameness, conciliation, *rapprochement*. In my life I did just that; taught that, wrote that (without hiding shades of disagreement where such existed) and lived influenced by this feeling of sameness. Such knowledge as I acquired from different people I acquired it precisely because I was able to do what Goethe in the end preached under his momentous attempt to lay the foundations of a *Veltliterature*. I tried hard to start a similar move for law but failed; but that is not surprising for how many people aspire to think like Johann Wolfgang Goethe - *Herr Microcosmus* the term he used in Faust – but simply cannot reach such heights.

The advantages of a double and sharpened vision of life given only to true "outsiders"[24]

In these remaining sections of this chapter I will now shift my attention away from the possible drawbacks of double backgrounds and geographical displacements to the advantages which "outsiders" have over "insiders" precisely because they differ from the latter. By "outsiders", here I mean all of my above categories –exiles, émigrés, expatriates, double citizens, and the like.

Three of Said's advantages deserve to be stressed since they have already appeared subliminally in various parts of this book. I reached these conclusions independently and did so a long time ago. My way of reaching them was through my work in law; his were the result of his capacious mind devoted to literary and cultural matters. Though the beginning and ending points of our views are similar, I will use his words rather than mine, not least because my directions have been couched in the more grey language of the law.

First, is the advantage of double vision. Said writes:

"Because the exile sees things both in terms of what has been left behind and what is actual here and now, there is a double perspective that never sees things in isolation. Every scene or situation in the new country necessarily draws on its own counterpart in the old country. Intellectually this means than an idea or experience is always counter posed with another, therefore

---

24. Again, much use has been made of Edward Said's 1993 Reith Lectures published by Vintage books in 1966 under the title *Representations of the Intellectual*. To avoid inserting too many notes, the pages where a quotation appears will be indicated by a number in parenthesis at the end of the quote.

making them both appear in a sometimes new and unpredictable light: from that juxtaposition one gets a better, perhaps, even more universal idea of how to think, say, about a human right issue in one situation by comparison with another..."(60)
Secondly, Said continues:

"For the intellectual an *exilic* [sic; and I hate the word he has made up] displacement means being liberated from the usual career, in which "doing well" and following in time-honoured footsteps are the main milestones. *Exile* means that you are *always going to be marginal*,[25] and that what you do as an intellectual has to be made up because you cannot follow a prescribed path. If you can experience that fate not as a deprivation and as something to be bewailed, but as a sort of freedom, a process of discovery on which you do things according to your own pattern, as various interests seize your attention and as the particular goal you set yourself dictates..." (62)

Personally, I see in this statement an exaltation of the freedom to think laterally, unrestrained by the usual conventions. Said describes this as "a unique pleasure" but I see in it also – or mainly – as a unique opportunity of being original, precisely because you are forced to think "out of the box".

Finally, Said notes an advantage which, in my view, brings him even closer to the thought just expressed, for he writes:

"Even if one is not an actual immigrant or expatriate, it is still possible to think as one, to imagine and investigate in spite of barriers, and always to move away from the centralizing authorities towards the *margins*, where you see things that are usually lost on minds that have never travelled beyond the conventional and *comfortable*" (63)[26]

Taken together these ideas also suggest further and welcome side effects which flow from this double vision.

First in that they show seeing matters from different angles and applying different reasoning processes may still reach similar conclusions, albeit via a different reasoning process.

---

25. Obviously here the statement refers to exiles proper and should not be extended to other types of displaced persons.
26. I have italicized here two words for, though what is said here is not limiting his view to exiles proper but is using the words which are particularly appropriate to his own traumatized position as an exile: margin and marginal and (un)comfortable. Note that these also appear in the previous quotation. My expressions, thinking "out of the box" or "laterally" convey the same feeling of lack of orthodoxy in the thinking process but, as words, they do not allude to trauma or pain. As I explain in other works of mine, the way we think – even subconsciously - often dictates the words we chose to externalise our thoughts.

Second, this gives one the possibility of discovering that the "different" is not really "different", as one has traditionally been led to believe, but merely formulated through different concepts or notions which are more suitable to different cultures.[27] This point, finally, could be formulated in yet another way namely, that the "truth" can appear differently to different people even though every image of it can be as real and as correct as any other.

Discovering similarities

Thinking thoughts such as the above started me in my career as a student intent on understanding different legal systems and then discovering how to present them to "foreigners" and my English judicial friends with a view to facilitate mutual inspiration. Despite or because of my double background, it fell upon me to help play a small part in assisting law students bring European legal systems closer together in their minds. Strangely colleagues who because of their national background – for instance because of their Canadian origins – should have been 'doubly oriented' that it is open to the thinking and the languages of two cultures – were opposed to my constant attempts to bring them *openly* closer together.

This idea of discovering a way to achieve an intellectual *rapprochement* excited me so much that, with the arrogance of youth, I semi-convinced myself that this was my calling not just my way of approaching foreign law. I was thus able to spend hours on end in "European" universities teaching not the Common law but its common sense and rational strength, while gently - and when back at my base in Cambridge - introducing generations of common lawyers to the sound theorizing of their Continental brethren admiring it to be sure but then also comparing it with the English pragmatism. In my view, then and now, each had something valuable to contribute in the construction of a more unified legal culture.

Most of my colleagues thought I was crazy – crazy to be doing so much travelling; crazy to be advancing novel theories about *convergence* of the legal systems instead of sticking with the established dogma of unbridgeable gaps. This was the intellectual climate in the

---

27. On this see my contribution in *The Search for Principle. Essays in Honour of Lord Goff of Chieveley*, ed. By William Swadling and Gareth Jones (OUP 1999, pp 59-77) under the title "The Familiarity of the Unknown".

mid/late 1960's in my second country there was only one Professor - Dominick Lasock a Hungarian refugee if I am not mistaken – who was teaching Community law at Exeter.

Yet for me my self-appointed task was fun, not least because I could *effortlessly* find good things to say about both legal worlds as well as recognize that behind homonyms and synonyms, concepts, and notions, lay similar judicial and legislative attempts to address identical problems. Given this, how could the answers found in the different systems not be analogous if not often even similar? But there is no denying the fact that what I was attempting to do was a solitary exercise, since each system vigorously claimed that it was different and, of course, better than the others. I once even turned by English tort class into a comparative methodology discussion, aided and abetted by my two close friends – Professor Hein Kötz at the time Director of the Mac Planck Institute of Hamburg and Laurent Aynès, a very productive author and Professor at the Sorbonne. The large auditorium in the Saint Cross Building was packed to the rafters with students even sitting cross-legged on the floor surrounding the three lecturers and my recollection was that it was widely appreciated. Young people are always more willing to experiment; older colleagues on the other hand tend to dislike innovations for they take them out if their comfort zone!

So in practice this work showed that many differences were just differences in classification and terminology not function. Large chunks of our law of torts in France and Germany and found in the property sections of their codes. The tort of "nuisance" in the eyes of Common law practitioners is a "wrong" – hence a tort, discussed in tort classes. For the Europeans, by contrast, what is at stake is a right, "lesser" than ownership, which may confer immunity from action even to a person who uses his land in a way which interferes with the use and enjoyment of his neighbour's land. Why this difference in thinking and arrangement of the material?

Harry Lawson, who knew European law backwards, was one of the few who addressed the problem making full use of his usual history-oriented erudition in his pioneering *Negligence in the Civil Law*. The bulk of English lawyers – even the bulk of the tort teachers - remained uninterested in such early but brilliant attempts to bring two worlds closer to one another by stripping them of their different apparel and studying how the accidents of history had created the modern differences. I, like so many others, learnt an awful lot from Harry's erudition; and I am one of those – many I hope – who still remember him fondly for his ability to make his pupils think. I also feel grateful to him for entrusting in my care a new edition of one of the above-mentioned book of his which set me up to follow with a number of volumes on the *German Law of Obligations* presented from a comparative point of view.

So I resolved that if I were to be different from my predecessors who taught the subject and, above all, I could manage to increase the size of the comparative law classes from two or three to, say, thirty or more (which I managed to do my with my Cambridge LL.M. class and, later, with the much smaller intake for the Oxford BCL degree) I felt increasingly obliged to preach heterodoxy; for orthodoxy is not the best way to make young people think laterally. In short, I was to use to the advantage of my double vision as described above by Said and pray for the best.

On the surface of things this was hardly the best way to begin a career and survive; but luck was on my side. In 1975, in the presence of Otto Kahn Freund, Jack Hamson, Kurt Lipstein and Pierre Lalive,[28] four of the four most prominent comparatists in England at that time, I dared this approach in a public lecture in Cambridge. In European speak, literally translated, this was my "virgin academic speech." The class, around twenty five – plus the four professors - assembled only because it became known to the Cambridge students that these four "giants" would attend the lecture of an unknown newcomer from…Greece who had just been elected to an Assistant Lectureship.

The students behaved impeccably though my vivid recollection is that they were unimpressed and unconvinced. The four "giants', however, at the end of the lecture took me aside and openly gave my effort their full blessing and urged me not to abandon this effort of trying to bring the legal systems closer together whatever the opposition such an attempt might attract. I was delighted but it took years for me to realize that during that single, nerve-racking, hour in Room four of the Old Schools in Cambridge my brand of comparing laws and cultures had given me my *venia legendi*; for a few months later the law faculty gave me tenure and promoted me to a full Lectureship.

Oscar Wilde said somewhere that "behind every successful man one finds a surprised mother in law." The saying, in modified form,

---

28. An eminent comparatist and practitioner who, at the time, was Arthur Goodhart Visiting Professor at Cambridge.

applies to academics as well; and in my case, the luck was plentiful for not only I was fortunate to acquire superb academic mentors but also some of the most learned judges from the Supreme courts of many countries *who felt the need and not just an idle interest to learn how to look at European solutions in a world where exchanges and collaboration were, by the mid-seventies onwards, beginning to be seen in a more positive light.* There are some clear hints in some of the judgments of the judges I have in mind but I earnest ask my readers to try to appreciate the extent of interest that these highly imaginative minds were displaying in what once would contemptibly been described as 'foreign'. My "alien" legal thinking as someone already trained in the Civil Law came of use – to me but also others.

The way of re-shaping the raw material from other lands for the purposes of it being used by lawyers of Anglo-Saxon legal systems was to be the kind of work that kept me busy for forty eight years of teaching. Focusing on a number of specific problems and seeing what could be learned from different worlds and different experiences was not easy but had its rewards. The number of people interested in such ideas grew and for good reason; for the problems being addressed by lawyers all over Europe and the USA were similar of not the same in all these countries.

For instance, take problems related to criminal law and criminology such as methods of treating young offenders, the running of private prisons, the range of permissible intrusions in the private lives or private and public individuals, the measure of damages in accident cases, the effectiveness of alternative methods of dispute resolution to reduce recourse to our over-worked courts. Or, to move to another subject, see how systems which allow controlled euthanasia work in practice and avoid abuses. I am not saying that courses on these subjects can never be found, especially in the better faculties; but I am saying that this method of *practical* comparison can help enhance the effectiveness of university teaching but also assist administrators occupied with such topics in finding better solutions and, where it is deemed desirable, harmonizing the laws of closely collaborating countries.

Yet none of all this could have even begun were it not for displaced people of all kinds helped by indigenous lawyers who were increasingly infected by the curiosity to find out how colleagues elsewhere had handled these same problems. The South Africa's Constitutional court, a mere twenty years old, has proved a pioneer in this kind of work; and so did the Israeli Court, especially during the years when

Aaron Barak was its President. On the other hand, as the American Supreme Court became more and more conservative and thus less able to inspire other courts to use its ideas, other courts stepped in to fill the gap: Canada's, South Africa's, Israel's, Strasbourg's Court of Human Rights. In the emerging European democracies of the 1980's and 1990's the American courts had once found willing students and imitators. By contrast, American scholars continued to show their ability to use material from other countries, even in the very area – constitutional law – in which their own court was showing such timidity. In doing this they were not just being innovative; they were, without perhaps knowing it, following Said's which I site with a minor alteration: "the proper attitude of the intellectual ... is some sort of *defiance*."[29]

I have italicized the word defiance for I believe it can be ascribed inspiring connotations if practiced in the teaching of subjects which stress the human mind and lead it to think. It is thus in this wider sense that I use it here, influenced by what I have seen and learnt from California and Texas, Cape Town and elsewhere. All pushed me to urge even further the new ethos both in education and business.

This is the kind of thinking I would like see established from the College years of my Continent instead of memorizing, pre-occupation with grades, aimless dissipation of talent allowed to study modern trendy subjects with a minimal intellectual and mind-stretching content. In short a way of thinking that would not only penetrate the world of business encouraging innovation in the ways just mentioned; but also in a way that would strip modern capitalism of some of its deeply anti-social tendencies. Thus, through practice but, if need be, even legislation, I would praise profit but ostracize greed; try to tame the bonus culture; give an economic interest to managers and workers in the affairs of corporations to encourage hard work, and enhance loyalty to one institution or company which, unlike in traditional capitalism, has been so weakened in modern times.

Dissent in other words, defiance, and challenge of existing practices which all but the most blinkered must see are not helping us come out of a prolonged and unprecedented educational and economic crisis. It is a source of surprise but also a reward of sorts to acknowledge

---

29. The alteration consists in removing his words "outside the academy" which in his text – "On Defiance and Taking Positions" was originally published in *Beyond the Academy: A Scholar's Obligations*, American Council of Learned Societies, Occasional Paper No 31, Winter 1996.

that the ideas to which I have alluded in these last sections were all brought about by displaced people of talent and determination which remained true to the greatest value of all institutions of learning. And never forget that the greatest value in academe remains the pursuit of excellence; a value which can never accommodate attempts, even with the best of motives, to water it down.

Chapter Eight

MAJOR PROBLEMS OF OUR TIMES

The problems of soaring immigration

This chapter will look at the immigration debate, how it has been handled thus far and then compare these first approaches to our own suggested responses. One can state from the outset that our aim is – or appears to be - different from that of the EU officials; for *we* are concerned with the *causes* of the phenomenon and how it should be stopped from increasing whereas they – the European officials are mainly interested in hurriedly devising responses *to its consequences*. The concluding sub-sections of this chapter will therefore switch to a multitude of divisive problems faced by modern societies – European in particular - and will thus set all that has been said about immigration against this wider background replete with a variety of economic and social problems faced by capitalist societies. Because of lack of space the focus will be on the leader of contemporary capitalism i.e. the USA; but then our attention will switch to the other end of the spectrum and glance at the deeply troubled Greece. Highlighting the problematic features of two very different countries will, one hopes, help show that the immigration problem will actually prove to be a much bigger and unpredictable problem in the wider consequences it will entail in more than one countries.

In chapter seven we mentioned the disruptive consequences of immigration on the migrants and discussed extensively the psychological effects this state of affairs can have on their character. The peculiarity of this chapter lies in the fact that it will not focus on the psychological traumas which one almost takes for granted and suffered by the less well of, uneducated, traumatised immigrants but by those who were both exceptionally intelligent and ended up very well treated by their host countries. Yet they, too, ended up being 'marked' for all their lives; and if this is the case for the better off or, 'lucky' ones one can only begin to imagine how deeply affected must be – literally – the 'hoi polloi'.

In the present chapter we will, by contrast, look at massive immigration movements and the way these vast displacements of humans can affect, not them, but the countries in which they move to. Though, to start with, this will be our main concern we must throughout this discussion bear in mind the huge *physical* problems which immigration poses for the moving masses. Finding them decent housing; feeding them adequately; providing them and their infant children with a minimum of medical coverage and, of course, understanding – and this we stressed in some detail in chapter seven so it is omitted from the list of sufferings given above – the often unfathomable consequences such experiences will have in the future on their psychological wellbeing. All these aspects of the problem can only be considered with the use of ample figures and statistics and this is not the kind of book that can or wishes to go into reviewing this material.

The main discussion will thus focus on the ways of handling the causes of mass immigration movements: what (little) has been said or done thus far, and, more importantly, how its *causes* (rather than its *consequences*) could/ should be addressed. Dealing with the very real problems which the migrants will face once they end up in their host countries will come later; and as stated is left for another book. Suffice it to say, however, that this is not going to be a short-term problem; and it will raise different kind of issues related to employment, temporary apprentice schemes, social difficulties in cohabiting with the natives. Important though all these issues are they will have to be addressed by the host countries in their own ways and in the more distant future so they will not be the object of this chapter.

It is best to begin by stating our belief that mass immigration is an issue where major human values clash and in trying to cope with it one has to discover a workable compromise between them. Lawyers, more I believe than politicians, know the sensitivity required to address issues which involve competing values. In some instances – for example the clash between the value of human privacy and the equally important value of free expression – British society has gradually managed to move forward towards a more balanced position than the one it accepted less than one or two decades ago. The position, in my view, remains far from perfect; and the Press and those who are used to see it hound ordinary citizens or hack into their private phones of others and still enjoy immunity will sympathise, perhaps, with my view that the perfect balance has yet to be adopted in England. Indeed, the fact that in the complaints made against the Murdoch Press the general discussion also involved accusations that members of the police force may have been bribed to remain silent or 'close their eyes' to illegal hacking shows, in my view, how more wide-spread and dangerous the problem is.

This problem will soon re-surface in the form of giving the Government and its official agencies greater rights to snoop and hack our private communications in the context of contemporary terrorism. The problem is a growing one; and in terms of reconciliation, possible proposals concerning privacy rights will be the acutest faced so far as far as this issue is concerned. For though protecting the country's and its citizens security is the prime obligation of the state, doing so without riding rough shod over privacy rights will not be easy. For me the right balance will only be found if we identify the right methods of controlling such activities *before they are authorized* as well as the way and extent to which the courts will be allowed to control then *ex post*.

In the immigration context the clash of values are as important as those alluded to above – probably even more serious still for the scars they will leave on affected people – immigrants and hosts alike will run deep. The weak, the hungry, the unjustly persecuted by inhuman gangsters or intolerant governments, those condemned to live though vicious winters in cheap tents, cannot be left unprotected. It is also shocking to modern sensitivities to have to fish out of the sea the dead bodies of young children drowned while attempting with their parents perilous crossings of the sea in totally inadequate vessels or simply overcrowded inflatables. How one prevents these things from happening is, in my view, just as important as finding the right ways of reacting once they have happened. Yet translating this anger into action is difficult; for thought it is easy to condemn the merciless immigrant smugglers, it is near impossible for countries to condemn other countries who are just as responsible for the problem at hand without endangering their own commercial dealings with them. This last sentence touches upon a very sensitive issue for even 'model countries' are more often than not willing to close their eyes to gross illegalities if by doing so they hamper their ability to export to these countries their expensive military technology. Frankly, this hypocrisy of the 'goodies' may be 'politically understandable; but morally it remains totally condemnable.

In the light of the above let us then begin by stating in a categorical manner that opening one's frontiers to all of the above without more and condemning them – as we will be - to squalor in the host land is not an option. At the beginning of the present crisis Chancellor Merkel *appeared* to favour an unrestricted acceptance; and those with inquisitive minds, always searching for the true motives of statements made by politicians – dare one say a futile task - wondered whether hers stemmed from the fact that she was once a pastor's daughter or whether as a politician she was trying to project her country's humane image in view of disgraceful past behaviour towards various minorities residing in her country – Jews, mainly, but also gypsies and homosexuals. Probably the most important but, for obvious reasons concealed reason behind the original Merkel generosity to offer asylum to all was the pressure placed on her by German industrialists to admit immigrants since they desperately need cheap labor.

Despite this declaration or, arguably, because of it, the number of immigrants grew rapidly and has only in recent weeks slowed down somewhat as a result of other countries closing down their borders to the immigrants using the 'immigrant highway' which takes them from Athens to the German borders. Television began to show unattractive scenes occurring in Bavaria's main railway stations or at the boarders of Hungary and other central European countries. The Chancellor was forced by reality to modify the original position; and a more cautious approach was voiced on television by some of her most senior lieutenants who were, tactfully, asked to do the back-tracking Already, Germans are *attempting* to calculate the cost of hosting the hundreds of thousands *ante portas* and 'imaginativelly' trying to invent reasons which will justify the working entrants a lesser wage than the local citizens.

The figures I receive from Germany keep varying. Originally the cost of 'absorbing' – a deliberately unclear term – of 800,000 refugees – was estimated as being in the region of 16 billion Euros. The more recent figures have risen to 29 billion Euros, 8 of which would come from the Federal Government. To me, these are only guestimates for it is not clear what exactly do they include – e.g. costs of housing; sorting centres; social security payments, the cost of apprenticeship schemes, medical care, unemployment benefits – at what level and for how long. And what about payment for those employed – including those temporarily enrolled in apprenticeship schemes - bearing in mind that many if not most will hardly be able to speak any German and may well be devoid of any special skills? Then we have the question of the minimum wage which in Germany, if I am not mistaken, at present stands at 8,50 Euros per hour. This means for eight hours of work per day 68 Euros per day or, if working five days per week, a weekly sum of 340 per week or 1360 per four week month. The German Conservatives have – understandably - already objected to this and have argued in favour of a lesser sum; the Social Democrats, as most Lefties do, disagreed at the discrimination and were quick to give money which may be hard to find. In my view and in the light of the above it is likely that the most cynically minded Germans are planning/ hoping to acquire 'cheap labour'[1] by underpaying even the abler of the immigrants to fill the vacancies which exist in their labour market as a result of reduced births in contemporary Germany.

Worse, still, Europeans – officials and ordinary citizens – are in the dark as to how many immigrants still remain to reach them, *first* via the Turkey *autobahn* and *second*, from North Africa. The estimates I have seen simply do not seem to be realistic and that means that no one has really even begun to contemplate the social consequences/ upheavals that will follow in the countries these poor creatures will settle. I predict these problems will sink in more deeply into the Germans consciousness and as this occurs German and, indeed, European attitudes will harden. As I write – early winter 2015 – both the *Spiegel* and the *Financial Times* are speculating whether Mrs. Merkel can survive the storm that lies ahead. Most certainly she will; unclear, however, is how will the German react.

Whether wise or precipitous the Chancellor's original statement, though still shared by many in her country (and lefties and genuine liberals across the world), no longer appears to represent the majority view even in Germany. It remains important to point out how quickly the mood of many others changed in Germany as the full extent of the problem began to be digested. Human sympathy has not evaporated. Many like to portray the Germans as a being a harsh and uncaring nation but my experience – inside their country and outside – is the reverse. I never tire stressing that the German humanity is real and it is there; and it appeared in its full glory in 19th century German humanistic thought. Also there, however, is a strong sense of guilt for

---

1. This is only one step away from 'slave labour'; and if this term appears to harsh let the reader investigate and reflect upon the state of the illegal immigrant from Mexico who enter Texas with the connivance or silent consent of rich farmers who then treat them as slave labourers.

their past sins committed by the very same Germans between 1933 and 1945. Memories from the *past*, however, can never determine how *current* suffering will play out politically. Ideology and romanticism always succumb to realities on the ground; and if over the centuries the capitalist system has showed a greater degree of success and endurance it is because true capitalists were hard-nosed pragmatists.

It is only just and reasonable however that our feelings about these poor creatures before our gates is combined with concern over how any one country – indeed Europe as a whole - can cope with the anticipated numbers. For nations, especially those who have some experience in such matters know that such unrestricted 'welcome' simply may push – should I be bold enough and predict *will* push - many of the displaced persons, to destitution, despair, and then even the possibility of some of them opting for the whole gamut of criminal behaviour from petty theft, drug dealing, prostitution, and – for fewer still but some nevertheless - even to forms of racial militancy. Incidentally, when talking of the likelihood of increase in criminal activities I am not thinking or even trying to estimate the possible effect of the coming human destitution may have in radicalising some at least of the immigrants thus enlarging the number of European situated potential terrorists.

I make all of the above points since, in my view, it is not enough to call for the severe punishment of those who robe the desperate immigrants of their remaining savings in order to provide them with unsafe boats to escape their lands. The dignity of those who 'make it' to our lands must constantly be considered and respected; *and it is not, if we even indirectly and even with the best of motives make them believe that they can all be accepted in Europe as a matter of course, condemning them to the above-mentioned state of affairs.*

Also necessary, as I will explain below, is for Europe as a whole to push the Arab countries – such as Saudi Arabia or Qatar - to do their duty; and their duty is not to aid and abet rebellion in Syria and parts of Iraq of the kind that only increases the number of displaced and suffering people. More about this dereliction of humanity on these countries below; at present I must return to the need to respect the dignity of the migrants as human beings.

In my Texas days I heard the same voices of compassion. There, too, *as everywhere in the world,* one finds caring people. Yet, as already stated, in Texas I was also made aware of the exploitation of the illegal Mexican immigrants by the wealthy Texan landowners. For often, those who helped them enter illegally in Texas were also those who then profited from the fact that, by necessity, they ended up as cheap labour. Cheap - or why not call it by its true name – slave labour? This phenomenon also exists in Europe though it has not been publicised as much as its Texan part has been; nor has it yet reached the high levels I believe it will.

Texas toughness is well known. Alas, however, we have seen similar exploitation of impoverished immigrants happen in Greece even though this small country never had the experience the US had on the dark practice of slavery. The result represented, and to this extent that it still happens, still represents a public scandal. For many a Greek village squares have since the 1980's been daily filled by Greek famers sipping their pastiche and profiting from EU subventions received to help them in their agricultural activities. The bulk of that money was – to put at its most blunt and simple terms – pocketed by the farmers, while a tiny fraction was used in the summer and later the autumn months to pay travelling immigrants to collect the grapes and then the olives and do the most menial of jobs the farmers would not touch. In those days, the Greeks loved the EU. Greece, too, had it "Grapes of Wrath" though not a talent of the kind of John Steinbeck had to describe the inhumanity of the practice. *For Greece is not only to be found in the beauty of its ancient civilisation but also in those darker recesses of the northern suburbs of Athens where the capital's mega rich have been guiding the country's gradual decline with one aim in mind: how to get richer themselves which they have while the bulk of the Greeks got poorer.*

Such pictures bring no credit to anyone. The EU suffers as well for its subventions are being put to wrong use since the farmer, by his action, is exploiting the EU, his state, as well as his workers. These labourers are treated in ways which those who knew Greece of my youth would hardly find believable.

This is a sketch of how immigration worked in the country side. In the capital city itself, it took even more demeaning forms. Not long ago I recall seeing late in the nights black immigrants selling the sexual favours of teenage girls in their 'care' A prostitution market was, almost every night, set up in Athens' in its most famous boulevard which is surrounded by the beautiful neo-classical buildings of the Othonian era. Athenians bore is silence this degrading behaviour but did nothing. Less than I mile away – as the crow flies – in the affluent neighborhood of Kolonaki the better-off Greek youth enjoys every night a life of comfort oblivious of the suffering nearby.

And what can the police do? Well, in recent years, the prevailing 'democratic spirit' has cowed them into a form of forced passivity under the influence of those liberals who had accumulated over the years

– it must be admitted in some cases justly so – a considerable amount of complaints and antipathy against all forces of law and order. Antipathy is the first stage towards animosity; and then comes revenge. Though revenge was the theme of many ancient Greek strategies the one thing that has been proved is how it burns in the heart and soul of those who feel it.

Notwithstanding official statements to the contrary, accepting immigrants under such conditions does *not* amount to charity, hospitality, civilised behaviour or magnanimity on behalf of the Greeks, the Americans, the French or any other nation. The invocation of high motives – even if genuinely shared by some – does not amount to civilised behaviour towards unfortunate immigrants if not accompanied by the right acts and society can absorb the resulting shock. Charitable declarations often represent a screen that hides their 'acceptance' under conditions which breed worse things to come in all the countries which end up hosting immigrants in uncontrollable numbers. I mentioned some; and more could be said but this is too sordid a subject to dwell on for too long.

Free and unplanned immigration is thus as unacceptable to the immigrant as it is to the inhabitants of the host country. It is hypocrisy disguised as humanity. It amounts to short-sighted politics by politicians who are not statesmen and, of course, by no means true leaders. The reasons for all this are as obvious as they are real; and growing numbers of European are dissatisfied with their governments as much as with the Brussels bureaucracy for, despite many warnings, not acting earlier to anticipate the crises and prevent it from getting out of control. But those in power do not see the tidal wave sweeping them off their pedestals for continuing policies which are half backed and simply no longer represent the concerns and interests of their citizens. Yet what is happening as we write may well achieve this unbearable result if it is left unchecked.

The refusal to admit numbers which cannot be humanly handled by the host country raises other problems besides those sketched above. Once again their severity must be noted and not concealed by invoking sanctimoniously philanthropic ideas. One argument is the very opposite of being called racist. Most European countries are getting used to becoming multi-racial societies. As I have been stressing from the beginning of this book is one of the great achievements of post War Europe. This, however, does not mean that the 'internal balance' between races can be *distorted in an unplanned way which will happen if the current human displacements are not halted.*

Take Britain for instance which has greatly changed since the days when Enoch Powell made his famous speech about 'rivers of blood' flowing in England's streets if immigration was not stopped. I do not believe that these days, *within limits*, the majority of its citizens is opposed to their country being a multi-racial community. There is, however a great danger of today's happenings moving the country in the opposite direction if the floodgates are opened and a significant increase in numbers destroys all ideas of a *planned and controlled* multiracial society by placing unbearable economic demands on limited state resources. To put it differently, I am among those who strongly believe that an unlimited admission of immigrants, who will unable to maintain themselves and thus end up dependent on charity and the ever-reduced social security payments will increase racial tensions and darken England's image as a modern and enlightened country on matters of race. The painful rehabilitation of the country's economy in the recent past could thus easily be destroyed by an unwise submission to the wishes of those who would welcome even an unplanned and uncontrolled migration. Such a policy could, indeed, revive the kind of biased hostilities which most of us hoped the country had buried for good. So, not only do I understand but welcome the British government's tendency not to jump on the bandwagon of pure sentimentality and try to think in terms of (a) restrained numbers and (b) identify carefully from where those who will admitted to come to the country will be recruited.

In the long run ethnographically the consequences of a significant inflow of immigrants would also be serious since they would alter the ethnic composition of Britain given that other races tend to have significantly higher rates of procreation than the locals. The same would be even truer and even more dangerous in the case of Greece which is frontier country at the most eastern part of Europe and thus an ideal entry point for illegal immigrants. The internal population of a nation would thus be suddenly unbalanced both for the immediate influx of foreigners – ethnically, religiously, and, in terms of customs and habits, entirely different from the locals – but, just as importantly, posing different kinds of dangers to the social stability of the nation in the long run as well. It would not take long before a country with a population of about 10 million would lose its ethnic and religious identity. Social divergences between the different sections of the population would grow rapidly into street confrontations and the country, socially as well as economically, would be plunged into an even great chaos than the one currently experienced. In days of economic hardship, the strained state resources might also be deflected towards unplanned purposes such as guarding more efficiently the borders, maintaining law and order in the streets, battling increased incidents of robbery and drug dealing, providing minimal social services for the new comers when the current and local population is already facing a vastly deteriorating level of medical care and services.

The list of problems flowing uncontrolled migration is not over! Massive human invasions also tend to increase the pressures to adapt or influence local politics and the way they are conducted by certain parties. As a general rule, therefore, one might speculate that a substantial increase of such entrants will, in the fullness of time, generate pressures to increase their political rights, including perhaps, acquiring the vote or the Greek citizenship. We already mentioned the dilution of ethnic consciousness this would entail. Such a move would almost certainly favour the left or extreme left parties who tend to adopt – out of self- interest, liberal ideology, or both, a much laxer attitude towards immigration.

If Greece (and its allies) wishes to see the country swing to the Left this is perfectly in tune with the notion of true democracy provided the electorate so decides after due deliberation. Twice in the recent past the Left won the general elections and formed a government. Whether one agrees or not with its policies is not an issue here to be discussed; but a general political shift of the country toward the left or the right should be decided by its inhabitants openly and by means of a public vote and not brought about indirectly by an unplanned acceptance of everyone who lands on its shores.

For the above reasons – and my list is by no means complete - a total open policy of welcoming foreign immigrants would, I repeat, be as unworkable as a totally closed attitude towards these lost souls and their hideous problems. The solutions I envisage should be discovered on what one might call the 'foreign' and 'internal' fronts *but I do not include among them the currently favoured view among some European countries idea of obligatory quotas.* Such as approach so totally ignores local sensitivities and different concerns that would only land the EU and its organs with a renewed accusation that their mentality is too centralising and this would provide yet another sign, along many others (notable on the economic front), of the EU being rudderless, increasingly out of touch with its citizens, and unable to meet their aspirations since they are no longer accurately reflected by the Brussels *nomenclature.*

It is saddening to express the above doubts about the EU for once I was a strong advocate of deepening harmonisation of European policies. Now, however, I have joined the ranks of those disillusioned citizens who see little merit in policies invented by international bureaucrats who hardly echo prevailing views of the member states not least because the Union has grown too big and the lack of homogeneity is becoming increasingly obvious. The massive immigration problem – which I predict will grow more acute in the years ahead – thus CANNOT be solved by public officials or civil servants however intelligent and well-educated the may be. The solution will come – perhaps I should remain a pragmatist and merely suggest it *may* come - when politicians abandon politically correct language, unconvincing moralising, and move forward quickly and on the basis of a well thought out plan. Success in politics is rarely linked to sentiment and is hardly well externalised taking the guise of sentimentality for Europe simply cannot absorb such numbers of immigrants, be they technically speaking refugees or fugitives of economically suffering countries which can no longer support them.

How does one face this problem?

1. Existing ideas and reactions

Various suggestions have begun to appear in Greece and elsewhere to face this new crisis. Most suffer from three faults; and can only be taken more seriously once these have been cured or at least their generality is replaced by greater detail. A rapid classification of the commonly repeated problems of these solutions includes the following.

(a) Expression of obvious generalities
A recently submitted plan by PASOK – the formerly major socialist party of the Papandreou family – starts with such a declaration: "The immigration problem is a world problem not only European." Trite but entirely acceptable; but as a statement this can begin to look as something potentially useful if and only if world organisations or major states accept it and take *immediate and meaningful* steps to turn the statement into something resembling a plan. At present it is, at best little more than hot air, at worst meaningless for reasons which will become obvious when we look below at what else has been proposed.

(b) Expression of broadly phrased proposals demanding funds but nowhere making it clear where they will be found; to whom they should go; whether the agreed sums will be adequate; and for how long such funding can and should continue?

Another academic proposal which will need time, details, itemization of sources of funding; full justification as to who should be their recipient; setting up of small, fast-moving bodies of competent people who can turn the wish-list into something real. Pasok's proposal no 9 thus claims "adequate funds" to support areas directly affected by massive displacements. The Greek islands of the North Aegean are mentioned as examples. Nice wish but it again presupposes the creation of more committees properly staffed and not filled by party supporters, able to procure such funds. The whole text reads like the product of party activists sitting in a committee asked to invent out of thin air ideas which sound appealing; and this is not the end of the matter. Who should get the funds is just as important as is the need to ask for them? Greece; its island and the mainland, currently suffering from the invading masses should be among the first recipients. The amount of money promised to this country is miniscule; and even smaller is the amount actually received. On the other hand, 3 billion Euros were promised to Turkey to set up sorting centres – hotspots according the current terminology; and since this clearly did not satisfy the Turkish greed it had to be accompanied by promises of expediting Turkey's negotiations to join Europe which few European citizens – it is different with European officials – even wish to contemplate. Needless to say, the Turks have done nothing in exchange for this promise for being oriental bargainers by tradition they will do nothing until they see the colour of the buyers money and then, if possible, cheat then by offering them second or third rate service of whatever they promised.

(c) Increase of numbers of immigrants beyond those already planned to be hosted in Greece for limited (?) periods of time to be stationed in Greece during the periods of their relocation

Presumably those placed in such camps – hotspots - would be expected to spend a longer time in these 'temporary; accommodations until the places of the final destinations were agreed. A disastrous idea which would increase hugely the problems of Greece but could well emanate from some Brussels based body simplistically believing that such centres (and enhanced number of transient emigres) should be placed in the countries of first visit which in practice could mean principally Greece and Italy. This will be an economically particularly costly operation and also runs the risk of being socially explosive. The figure originally banded for Greece was 50,000; the one more recently mentioned by the Greek Commissioner spoke of 100,000; the number, at the time of correcting proofs, has risen to approximately 200,000 with most commentators expecting it to rise significantly further in the future. In reality – and this counts much more that the 'invented' figures of the EU officials Greece now has many more immigrants within its borders, especially since the former Yugoslavian Republic of Macedonia made it difficult for immigrants walking toward Germany and neighbouring countries with the result that the immigrants take the road back to the South of Greece.

(d) Europe desperately trying to hide its divisions and its lack of long term planning

My heading here will irk the European officials but an independent author (unlike a hired gun) is not meant to aim to praise and defend or annoy and kill individuals but to make his readers think beyond what they find in the daily press fed to it by European propagandists. The old Greek daily *The Vima*[2] thus summarized the recent announcement made by the Commissioner for Immigration. The Commission is a Greek - Mr. Dimitrios Avramopoulos - known for his charm and smooth talent to please politicians from all parties.[3]The Commissioner's statement suffers from three major defects.

The first is contradictions. He thus kicks off by saying that "*substantial* progress" has been made by the EU's handling of the crisis though he then adds that he regrets that the "desired results are still *not* obvious." But can progress be substantial and yet not obvious? Later Reports – all summarized in the recent press[4] - by various EU officers or specially formed Committees repeat the same story suggesting that greatest 'growth' - if that can be equated with success – appears

---

2. I am relying for what following on the papers report of 10 November 2015 and not on an official document so if inaccuracies appear I my account not only I apologise to the Commissioner but also pass the responsibility for what is written to others.
3. On the strength of this talent – and I suppose this how this tendency must be described – Mr. Avramopoulos almost managed to be elected to the ceremonial post of President of the Hellenic Republic nearly one year ago, a post almost promised to him by the Greek Prime Minister Tsipras but then suddenly taken away from his grasp, literally at the last minute. So he is now in Brussels in charge of a problem which, so far as I know, was never included among his special interests.
4. For Greece see: *The Vima*, 13 December 2015; 16 December 2015; *Kathimerini*, 17 December 2015. Rarely have I read more vacuous documents.

in the formation of committees which report on progress made (or not made) or recommend to the 'disunited European states to show great cooperation and collaboration. Certainly the countries from the old eastern European block are not co-operating but, on the contrary, showing an admirable inclination to put their own interests first and in many cases erect barriers to keep the immigrants out. The result? At the last European meeting agreed to address this issue eight European countries (out of twenty eight) were present while Turkey – always pleading for more money and an expedited procedure to join the EU – was there to do just that. It earlier promise to set up 'hot spots' to decide who was allowed to proceed further into Europe and who had to be repatriated remained on the drawing board until, as stated, the Turks had 'seen the colour of the European money', i.e. their promised 3 billion Euros!

The second, in the details the Commissioner invokes, undermines his own claim that the progress made is "substantial" by claiming, for instance, the appointment of 400 extra policemen in Slovenia while other member "states" – note the plural – have agreed (presumably because of EU requests or pressure) to appoint "250 officers to deal" with the problems arising. To offer one more of the Commission's amazingly important actions already taken by the EU officials handling the crisis he states that the papers of 147 émigrés have been sorted out in Italy and Greece with the result that they have been given permission to settle in the countries of their choice. For goodness sake: this crisis, in medical terms, resembles a major life-threatening illness requiring drastic treatment and not the display of pride by the hospital pharmacy for administering to the sick person (state) a few aspirins!

One last addition promised to illustrate the Commissioner's use of the word 'substantial progress". Since the summer explosion of mass immigration only nine states offered 305 places for immigrants to re-settle within their frontiers while a further fourteen states have agreed to appoint officials to co-operate with those from other countries in order to *discuss* [sic] the problem. Even in Italy, which was the first southern European country to fall victim of mass human displacements, has barely managed to move some one hundred and thirty people to permanent relocation.

Finally, the Commissioner admits that *immediate* action needs to be taken and based *on the collaboration* among the member states. Has Europe's reaction been *immediate*? The answer must be anything but, which in turn means that it had no plans ready for what happened.

As for *collaboration*, where should one seek to discover the signs of collaboration: in Hungary, Slovenia, England, countries of the European South, or Turkey, which is one week demonized for the way it treats it minorities – Kurds, Alewites etc. - and the other treated as an indispensable ally for being able to save Europe in exchange for … billions of euros. If Mr. Tsipras sentimental ideology places him in the clouds of politics, Mr. Erdogan's money-grabbing instincts and treatment of his journalists may well have earned him a very special position in Dante's deepest and frozen cycle of Hell.

To be sure, European leaders even more recently at their Malta meeting with African leaders, promised further substantial funds - 2-3 billion euros - to handle the immigration *problem originating in Africa*. Who will pay such money? Or will Mr. Draghi continue printing it without even he, one of the most intelligent European operators, being in a position to estimate future costs from the further development of this crisis? Nor do we know how much money will actually be raised and how it will be used? Has anyone in Europe tried to calculate how many more immigrants are likely to come and seek cohabitation with us? If these figures are, at best, estimates, how can the total cost be covered? And what about the arriving in immigrants in Greece who, as a result of the recent terrorist activity in France may end up being trapped in Greece for an indefinite period of time? Will the proclaimed charitable disposition of the Left be able to cope or will it finally "sell" its services to Europe? And if it does, is this the right way to serve the interests of Greece? And, finally, have the intelligence services of some key countries been in a position to work out, even approximately, how many potential terrorists are slipping in through this highly inefficient net?

(e) The true reasons why Europe lacks long term planning

My desire to speak my mind forces me to confess, once again, that there may be something rather arrogant in this subtitle. Indeed, the use of such a title may be due to my own ignorance as to what precisely is in the minds of the EU's top leaders. Yet I dare ask the question; and do so because I have stressed the plural – minds not mind – in my previous sentence; and this word conceals one of the difficulties which plural structures are faced with. This means that if one leader in one country has been thinking of future problems about to hit the EU may have a perceptive and restless mind but that is only one out of twenty eight. So, even if only one (or even a few of them, have been doing some long term thinking) it is not enough since the majority and in some cases all of the twenty eight states must agree (a) what the root of the problems may be and (b) how to face them.

The immigration problem must have been such a problem which, though the indications were growing by the year as one likely to hit Europe in a big way no one leader seemed to have taken it seriously enough to *start thinking if not planning their reaction to it in advance of it becoming a full blown crisis*. And yet the dinghy crossings started from Libya to Italy well before they began their journeys from Turkey to Greece. I do not know *when* the next phases of such 'invasion' will come' – and the word I used was deliberately italicised - but it *will* come. Moreover, though this is currently denied – laudably but not believably by Mr. Tsipras - it will also soon begin to take the form of land crossings at the Turkish/Greek border in Thrace.

So let us assume for structural reasons that *the EU is not an ideally designed organisation for collective anticipatory thinking*. But once disaster has struck what prevents the institution's the next weakness from arising? This is its unwillingness or inability to discover the deeper causes of the problem and build its responses around these true causes? I ask this question because, judging from the little said above, I see both the slowness of the reactions of the EU but also the superficiality of its proposed solutions. To put it differently, what prevents a deeper and more global appreciation of the problem and, correspondingly, an answer sufficiently radical to address its causes? Is it lack of imagination or is it lack of courage to admit the inadmissible?

Perhaps let us assume that this too is a statement that lacks imagination, foresight or, to put it in one word – as I will in the next chapter [5]– lacks the vision of a true leader. By levying accusations against the EU in its recent phases perhaps one is excessively stressing its structural inability to address the problems appearing before it. Yet let no one doubt that the problems I am hinting at will continue to appear in the months or years ahead; and they will increase as much in numbers as will the seriousness of their consequences become more difficult to overcome. If Europe continues to act towards these major problems as it did with the post-2007 economic crisis or it is now doing with the looming current immigration disaster then, unbelievable (or unacceptable as this may appear to some or even many) the Union may simply crumble.

So in what follows I offer some possible solutions that Europe ought

---

5. This topic will figure prominently at the end of the last chapter for it represents one of the EU's greatest deficiencies.

to be considering now as well *as the tailor-made responses* designed to address the true causes of the crisis. To put it differently: *should we not be trying to eliminate the causes which gave rise to our current problem rather than just try to cure its consequences?* Here then are some of the answers I find worth considering instead of just planning to create a few more low to medium ranking bureaucrats who will deal through un-ending committees how to employ their rather unimaginative solutions or simply see the Union pouring money down bottom less drains.

2. Proposed ideas and reactions

(i) Putting an end to America's oversea wars which fuel immigration

The modern problem of immigration is to a large extent the result of the modern expansionist greed on the part of the West which has prompted armed conflict in, among other places, Afghanistan, Georgia, Pakistan, Iraq, Syria, Libya, the Palestinian territories – not to mention the Ukraine (by triggering off the pro-European demonstrations which toppled the then President and led to the occupation of the predominantly Russian inhabited Crimea). In all, in one way or another, it was the USA who prompted the conflict, partly at least financed it, and in at least two cases led a prolonged military campaign followed – unfortunately - by England and France. France, at the time of writing – 13 11 2105 – has been the first to pay the price of this close military association with the USA; I pray the feared turn of my country – England – does not follow suit.

So in my view the *modern* massive immigration problem is closely linked to the *very old tendency* of solving disputes though military campaigns.[6] Let us then briefly look at all the above stressing the obvious namely, how different our analysis (and thus our recommended reactions to the current immigration disaster) is from what little the EU has done so far. Before we look at these points in greater detail, however, let us dispose of a preliminary point already raised but not adequately stressed.

---

6. As far as I aware the only politician to mention to stress the above as a major if not the major creator of the current immigrations crisis is Mr. Tsipras in his speech at the Greek Parliament of 30 October 2015. His phrasing, however, implies that had these wars been aiming at the installation of democratic regime in these Middle Eastern States then their consequences might have been tolerable. With respect this thinking is unconvincing for democracies can never be installed from upwards but have to grow from the local soil upwards if they are to survive.

Wars form a part of the history of mankind. Some have argued that they are not an inevitable part of such history in the future. Such an approach is not novel;[7] but in my view it remains utopian. The inevitability of wars is a fact of life. Learned scholars still go on arguing this;[8] what they have not done, however, is to explore their links with the theme which concerns us here: mass immigration. *This is ripe for discussion since the interlinking of these two phenomena[9] must be acknowledged and studied.*

With the above in mind let us return to the particulars of the recent outbreaks of wars or military confrontations in North Africa and the Middle East and ask the controversial if not difficult to address openly question: is America's presence in this part of the world an important destabilising factor? In my view it is as, indeed it is harmful to America's own economic situation.

Let us begin with the relatively recent past.

In Libya the USA, France, and England destabilised a brutal dictator whom they had, just a few years earlier, semi-tamed in the interests of their oil companies. Then the policy changed, hundreds of missiles were rained down on Libya, the dictator was finally killed – as brutally as he once used to exterminate his opponents - and the question still unanswered is what did the West gain? The country effectively was split into two; different terrorist groups gained the upper hand in each part; further consolidation of terrorist infiltration took place in the southern, mountainous regions of Tunisia and Algeria; American diplomats were assassinated in the Benghazi region, an act which the US government was unable to prevent though warned that it might (was likely?) to be attempted. In short: disaster not victory all round. All that is left of a once rich oil-producing state is a country with a long shore line suitable for launching unstable rubber dinghies or other small boats to take impoverished and on the whole untrained immigrants over to Italy risk-

---

7. One of the first to argue this as far back as 1795 when Immanuel Kant who published his Enlightenment views in his elegant essay *Towards Perpetual Peace*. More recently the thesis was advocated by authors such as John Mueller (in a somewhat utopian - one is tempted to suggest - *War and Ideas*, (2011) and John Horgan, *The End of War* (2012.)
8. For instance, Christopher Coker, *Can War be Eliminated?* (2014), a concise but eminently readable and tightly argued thesis. For more details see: Michael Howard in *The Invention of Peace and the Reinvention of War* (2002); Edward Luttwak, *The Rise of China versus the Logic of Strategy* (2012) and John Gittings, *The Glorious Arts of Peace* (2012).
9. Naturally, it was picked up by the Ancient Greek Tragic Poets such as Euripides. See, for instances, his *Hecuba, Andromache, the Trojan Women* and others.

ing their lives *en route*. Who gained from this policy? ONLY the migrant profiteers and various terrorist groups is the obvious but not exhaustive answer. The recently signed accord among *some* of the tribal leaders of the country has led optimists to argue that the country is on the road to recovery. I fear there is far too much evidence to suggest that this is willful wishing and that the African Continent, East, Central and Western part is increasingly infiltrated by Islamist terrorist groups.

Libya followed the destabilisation of Tunisia and Egypt. It is early days to make predictions, but I am willing to hazard the guess that it will, once again, facilitates a possible return of hard line Islamist in Egypt by toppling the regime of President Sissi.

What is particularly interesting about Egypt is that, for a long time, the country was an American stronghold second in value (and cost) only to Israel. Its poor civil rights record did not worry a single senior American policy-maker so long as the Egyptian leader of the time behaved as he was expected to behave in Washington. Yet such subservience was not playing out well with the growing poverty and religious restlessness of the poorer Muslim population of Southern Egypt. During the first disturbances some four years ago America visibly prevaricated on the question how it should react to the gathering clouds. Different high ranking officials aired their differences in public while the President of the USA tried to remain quiet. No longer the inspiring motto "Yes we can"; instead the limp whisper "no we will not speak".

Commentators such as myself have been complaining about America's polyphony as being a source of confusion to its allies in the region. This had already been demonstrated very visibly during the dying days of the Shah's regime in Iran when Dr. Brzezinski and Ambassador Andrew Young were unable to synchronise their advice to President Carter;[10] and, worse still, he did not succeed in keeping their differences out of the public arena. This polyphony helped loose the Shah's regime and Persia for the USA.

Be that as it may, America's treatment of the Mubarak regime annoyed another key American ally in the region: Saudi Arabia. What must be understood, however, is that America's prevarication is institutional not personal. In other words, it largely stems from the constitutional and legal allocation of powers to different people and agencies. It is thus unlikely to disappear since it finds its roots in key legal documents of the state which divide the decision-making pro-

---

10. The first favoured strong support, the second the encouragement of liberalisation. The deposed Shah, in a later interview, admitted that he found America's contradictory signal very confusing.

cess among the three major powers of the state: The Executive, the Legislative and the Judiciary.

The loss of Egypt represented a huge irony; for Mubarak's abandonments was largely decided on the grounds of America's support for human rights, a concern which – it merits repeating - was hardly whispered let alone loudly proclaimed when the going with Mubarak was good. Polyphony in other words, combined with hypocrisy – a well-known feature of American foreign policy for decades now – such combination can hardly be a good way of conducting foreign policy.

America's prevarication was given one more chance to manifest itself; and as most commentators in American newspapers commented at the time of the first Syrian crisis – for I am referring to the one preceding the international agreement to destroy its chemical reserves - revealed America's divisions in public every day and every night while TV stations were on the air. The President – rightly I believe - was clearly not keen to become too involved. At the other end of the spectrum a section of Congress wanted boots in the ground. Yet others – probably forming the largest group in the USA, disagreed but were also unclear what exactly they favoured. A truly ridiculous compromise finally emerged based on the idea of sending four missile-equipped destroyers (!) off the shore of Syria ready to pulverise their chemical installations with their missiles.

Mr. Putin's surprise appearance out of thin air saved the American President from further ridicule and earned the Russian leader many 'brownie points' in the Middle East for being imaginative, determined, and knowing when to act. Even the conservative section of the Greek press always over-anxious to demonstrate the country's subservience to its great ally – the USA - was quick to claim that the American President had lost the last remnants of prestige which he still had.

Was peace now around the corner? No, not quite; for the war against Iraq which President Bush had boasted so unwisely and prematurely that it had been successfully completed, was not over even though the American troops, after a prolonged and bloody stay, had been forced to leave the country. The 'liberated' country, however, was and is now crumbling as Afghanistan – another American 'success' story – is following suit. *Villainous* states had now become *failed* states; and militant Muslims love a vacuum just as nature abhors it. So, bit by bit ISIS began to emerge and spread making Al-Qaida pale into insignificance if compared with the brutality of the new version of Muslim fundamentalism which, this time round, also seemed better financed and run not from with mountain caves but towns (and important centres in the Gulf states). America was on the brink of sending troops overseas though, as usual, bombing from a safe instance was the wiser (though widely admitted less effective way) of waging war.

Blood excites hawks; more blood is irresistible to the Arizona variety whose Senator Chairs the Senate Armed Committee. For hawks, swooping attacks from the air, is a safe way of dismembering opponents while they are out of harm's way. It works in nature, but not as the Americans think, in politics or wars. For in the case of the latter, success comes not through bombing alone – often killing innocent people – but through battles won by mechanised infantry units operating on the ground closely aided by air support.

Despite such a long history of miscalculations Americans remain ambivalent and thus inactive. President Putin, on the other hand, has once again proved that he has learned these lessons. For a second time he has caught America's information services napping when he surrounded the Syrian coast with twenty warships of different kinds, landed aircraft, armoured cars and personal carriers on Syrian soil and quickly turned Lattakia and Tartus into modernized bases (which, as I write) are still being improved. Freedom fighters and 'interest' fighters are now fighting with Russian forces and may soon be joined by Chinese and Iranian, not to mention local contingents of Hezbollah, apparently equipped by Russia. On the ground, ISIS is in retreat; though personally, I belong to those who believe that even if they are defeated, another militant group will replace it. This is inevitable for as long as those who finance such barbaric groups are doing so to protect – or so they believe – their own unstable regimes in the Persian Gulf.

If the predominantly Russian forces were to succeed in putting an end to the ISIS fundamentalist movement and checking Turkey's constant self-interested threats to Syria's North-Eastern borders, their success should be seen as progress by most fair minded people. And if it is progress it will be one which, once again, has resulted from Russia's decisiveness and not Western bombing from huge heights. What happens to President Assad can then be sorted out by a later international conference and my personal guess is – and it cannot be more than a guess – he will be given a face-saving way out of active politics but not before Russia has gained what she really wants in the Middle East.

Who has thus far proved the biggest casualty of all these intricate manoeuvers? The average local citizen – often a fellow Christian or Kurd - ravaged, whenever possible by the Muslim fundamentalists. And who comes next? Europe, of course, since it now has to face new waves of immigrants who, thanks to Turkish courtesy, will be shipped off to the EU by crossing Greek waters and arriving at small Greek islands totally unable to cope with immigrants arriving at 2 or 3 or 4,000 per day.[11]

And what about America? I suppose her main if not only hope must now be that the Russians exhaust themselves in Syria as they did decades ago in Afghanistan. Until that 'happy day' (for the Americans) arrives – if it ever does - the Americans will have little more to do than move around their aircraft carriers or contemplate – as the hawks are currently urging President Obama to decide to send into the Syria region a small specialised force. When these lines were written it looked as if something in the order of 2- to 50 specialised troops would be sent to Syria to advise those who oppose President Assad. Still, the scenery changes in the Middle East in a very fast way; and the recent – 13 Nov. 2015 massacres in Paris may change the mechanics on the ground.

So, boots on the ground? How would such a move tie in with an early explicitly given assurance by the American President that he would not put boots on the ground in that part of the world? The explanation offered is that if small numbers of soldiers are sent, they will not be fighting troops, just advisors. But if 50 go today what is there to stop the American increasing them to 500 tomorrow if they prove inadequate to do what they are meant to do. Besides, what precisely would such a belated move aim to achieve? To claim that they, too, were in Syria and thus shared in Russia's success if/ when the latter manages to defeat ISIS? That would be seen as a cheap way of trying to steel someone else's triumph. So, could the aim be to protect the anti-Assad rebels, whom the Americans have unsuccessfully thus far, been using to help to unseat Assad? Such a small contingent is unlikely to achieve what American, English, and French bombing has failed to achieve thus far. Besides, the larger the American presence in *neighbouring* regions of one and the same country the greater the risk of Russian and American troops accidentally harming one another.

11. 30,000 crossed over to Greece during the weekend of September 16th-17th and not an item appeared in any of the major papers apparently anxious no to exaggerate bad news now that Greece is, as the papers tells us, doing so well with the newly negotiated plan with the EU.

Happily, by warning each other about flight paths and other such information this risk has been averted; but accidents can always occur. Surely, this is a risk that not even the most fanatical American hawk would even wish to contemplate. If such unthinking planners do exist among the American military, then let Christians and Muslims pray together that such sinister ideas do not materialise into a major military conflagration.

To be sure, anyone in the United States influenced by the virulent anti–Putin propaganda of our time will feel annoyed that commentators like me – traditional pro-West Europeans - are daring to proclaim in public. More important, those who consider American intermeddling in the Middle East as blighted from its inception may begin to worry about the corollaries of such a strengthening of the Russian presence in that region. Yet the question is not whether one likes my speculation but whether it is wrong and, if so, to what extent it is wrong? This naturally means that we must switch out attention to what I called the 'corollaries' of this basic thinking and also recall that it is the American who either abandoned the region to its fate or lost in in the last two to three years through the ineptitude of their policies.

What I call the corollaries of further American set-backs in the region refer to the future of the Gulf States? Yet who can deny that at present it is uncertain to say the least? And are these states or are they not dead-scared about their futures? More importantly, have they or have they not made their own position worse by financing ISIS in Syria thereby bringing themselves into an even deeper confrontation with Iran? If so, and their survival is what is at stake, which country would be in a better position to defend them better: America or Russia? Yet after seeing how America's handled the crisis in Egypt two years ago should they not rightly doubt America's resolve and ability to defend them? Has the prolonged war in Yemen shown Saudi Arabia's ability to quell a rebellion by a relatively small group of determined fighters? Is the fact that all in the region – including the Israel – are periodically offering to purchase Russian armament sufficient proof that most wise statesmen in the Gulf are nowadays wondering who is in a better position to keep afloat their unstable regimes which many - including the Americans – have openly described as corrupt and, at one stage, even Condoleezza Rice wished to overthrow herself?

The above is a frightening list of questions but most assuredly not a precis of anti-American propaganda. It is a summary of facts that demonstrate conclusively the key role which America has played in encouraging military conflict in the whole region, losing almost completely all the influence it had over North Africa and the Middle East, less that ten or so years ago.

More relevant to the theme of this book such behaviour has created through this military upheaval, the single most potent reason for hundreds of thousands of people to become desperate to leave their home lands and seek refuse elsewhere. Add to all the above America's sole responsibility for the prolonged wars in Iraq – historically never fully justified nor successfully completed – and Afghanistan – once again tottering on the level of a new instability – and what do we have? Disaster brought about by good intentions, bad planning, or both. All of this is accompanied by a doctrinal foreign policy, made as one goes along, out of touch with realities on the ground, and unable to get the true measure of their greatest self-made opponent – President Putin.

This return to the refugee flood crisis raises the final question: will it/ might it/ could it even bigger? Of could it finally shake Americans and Europeans out of their lethargy and make them treat foreign policy as the serious planning endeavor that it is and stop seeing it as an instrument for promoting their states' economic interests in different parts of the world at the total expense of local interests?

If the proper answer is given to the above question *the time has come to ask some serious questions. Here are five.*

If Americans are a major cause of this problem why should they not carry at the very least the bulk of its economic consequences? And if the bulk of the immigrants are Arabs why should not the Gulf States - so conspicuously absent in offering any assistance to them – carry their can? (more about this below). And if the Americans fail to accept the logic of the above should we not review what American *exceptionalism* means. If it means, as I suspect Americans interpret the term, that America as a country is *exempted* from all responsibility for what harm it causes through its foreign policy then the time has come to review this doctrine. As for the Europeans, the time has come for them to learn their lesson and drop all the subservience they show towards the USA in a host of others matters – the squabbling over the Ukraine is one example – where their own financial interests dictate different attitudes and policies.

Will any of the above happen? No. Not, at any rate, soon nor easily. The situation will have to worsen even more within Europe for its political elite to realise that they must show some spine, appreciate the problems facing their countries, digest the fact of how quickly Europe – that is the EU – is losing the support of its own citizens – and change policy.

And how about America? Well maybe - just maybe – 'confrontation fatigue' might help influence the forthcoming general election and bring to power a new face free from the ghosts and thinking of past times and able to steer this great country to calmer waters. It is easy to suggest who could not achieve such a re-direction simply because he or she belongs to the world of yesterday. It is more difficult to name the innovator who could review the record thus far and give a completely new meaning to the sentence: "yes we can".

(ii) A new approach towards the ordinary Arab

In this and the next subsection we continue the proclaimed necessity to study the true causes of Europe's current nightmare and not to be content with taking patchy and (relatively) insignificant steps which deal with the consequences, not the causes, of the crisis.

The West, with a few exceptions, has enjoyed privileged links with Israel and has cultivated personal connections with rich and powerful Arabs leaders. In practice this meant kings and princely leaders of the Gulf States. The motive was mutual enrichment which meant that the lesser Arab citizen or simple worker in the region was ignored. Be he a Palestinian, with his own legitimate and long-standing and unaddressed problem, or a Shia Arab worker in Sunni lands, both were treated as second if not third class citizens. Even labour legislation intended to create the impression of liberalising the legal regime has not worked in the proclaimed way.

The Arab, as a race, was always compared unfavourably to the Jewish or the Arian race; and in the mind of the ordinary European, he is constantly downgraded, insulted, treated as being by definition less inventive, less shrewd, more lazy that his Jewish counterpart. His education at home is, with few exceptions, less good than that received by the internationally accepted Jews and, for all these reasons, *he is turned into the most difficult immigrant to absorb in the West unable to be self-supporting.*

Such beliefs suffer from a mixture of gross generalisations and self-serving Western propaganda and must thus change and change quickly. The Westerner must sense the day of the dominant Arab rulers may be limited and a new era may be about to start in which the neglected Arab citizen could be helped to move ahead. If the Westerners believe in democracy and humanity – as one would like to believe they do – as well as wish to preserve their own interests in the region they must support such efforts at modernisation. Democracy cannot ever replace the conservative rulers of the past from the top downwards i.e. by being imposed by foreign fiat. Democracy, however, can be helped to grow roots progressively from the bottom upwards. Instead of spending millions if not billions catering for these people in Europe, they money envisaged should be spent to help them get the Arab populations to receive appropriate education and gradually get established in their homelands; and this goes for those women as well who wish to acquire a professional independence; for if western money and expertise will go into such projects the Muslim gross inequality between sexes must also be slowly faded out for those at least who are willing to accept this change.

The West proclaimed this as a major aim of the Afghanistan War; why should they forget it in the context of a wider effort to stabilise the Gulf States? Money spent in housing and feeding Arabs in German or French suburbs, should thus be re-directed in making their lands democratically governable slowly promoting those elements of western democracy that ere compatible to Eastern customs. The transformation will not be quick; nor should it be enforced on anyone, just made available to those who wished to adopt these changes. Education would be the medium; training as electricians, plumbers, to computer experts or educating then in arts and sciences. Talent and personal interest should be the criterion, though it should be accompanied by assistance and assessment to make sure that the most suitable professions were chosen. It goes without saying that making them work will require a huge effort on behalf of all in the region and in the West. But the West could assist not only by providing the funds which otherwise be spent in building refugee camps or paying for unemployment benefits to gradually building in infrastructure to truly modern states for all its citizens and not just exceedingly luxurious hotels for its few tourists. In this planning the Westerners could provide planning expertise, organisational expertise in setting up such institutions; links with their own centres of higher learning for those who did well and were deemed able to rise further up in their chosen professions such as medicine, engineering, high technology and so on. The Arab states but even more so the currently less educated or less well paid Arab population would instantly see the advantage that such method of improving their future chances presented. For in this way they would acquire much of what they are seeking for in Europe but continue living in their own favoured environment which the vast majority leave not out of choice but because of necessity.

With time, *if the Westerners behaved reasonably*, new and close links could be developed in Arab lands with precisely those whom we are now facing as disruptive refugees. Such initiatives, if believed by East-erners to have the genuine support of the West, could end up achiev-ing the prerequisites for a future cohabitation and not endless local di-visions. These would be constructive moves, not temporary solutions; and if they succeeded they could bring greater peace in the region than the upheaval which the Americans invasions provoked.

To be sure, those who only see problems in life and are not in-terested in answers – especially if they disturb their own privileges - many well retort to my suggestion that money funneled in the direc-tion for these states would be siphoned away to private accounts held by local corrupt officials (with or without the help) of equally greedy westerners. *We must plan with idealism but not naivety* and thus make sure that trustworthy people are placed in the position of administra-tors of these funds and that they are regularly controlled by suitably selected firms of accountants; and we must link such rules of manage-ment with severe criminal penalties if they abused by those entrusted with the task of applying them to the new lands.

We must thus lay the foundations of a new world knowing that it is in our interest that it succeeds and not that it simply continues its subordination to our own economic power. The risk of failure cannot, of course, be excluded; but then who can put his hand to his heart and assure me that the famous "Quartet", which for years has been meant to be supervising the resolution of the Palestinian-Israeli dispute, has not cost us all and arm and a leg for, apparently, no better reason than to keep notable individuals well healed, but has achieved nothing of note let alone distinction as far as the Middle East is concerned?

In short, the refugees are threatening Europe with a major disaster; indirectly this upheaval may also weaken further the position of the Gulf States who have done nothing constructive to help the refugee problem except to increase its size by financing so-called liberation fighters in Syria. It is thus up to European leaders, to come up with constructive ideas to diminish the crisis simply by managing it on a temporary basis and hope that this storm will blow away. I sketched out above one idea; others could be advanced and, no doubt, be much better. But ideas we need not inaction or simply throwing away mon-ey on the patch work pattern that always seems to figure in the minds of EU planners.

If the chance of peace, even in some not all at once areas of the Middle East, was genuinely established I am prepared to bet that most of the untrained immigrants would be happy to go back to their countries, re-settle, improve their skills and their education with the new educational schemes I suggested we should set up locally and, eventually, become more active in the administration of their home-lands. Their current princely lords and masters should welcome and promote such ideas, not necessarily because they will like them, but because they may well prolong their own political survival. As for the variously trained able, adaptable, people, their continued presence in the countries which granted them asylum would - again I would bet - through their talent and working ethos have more than a good chance of having their wish to a permanent permission to stay granted.

One last point: who might not like the above ideas? The answer is odd but not unexpected for in my view those mainly opposed to such pans would be the ruling elites, fearful of losing the cheap labour poor Arbs from other parts of the Middle East supply, scared that liber-alisation methods of government might end up toppling them from their privileged positions and religious fanatics. These sources of pos-sible opposition can be addressed if the West is willing to convince them that these changes will be to their advantage and, in any event, the West will cease supporting corrupt regimes unless they play their part in modernizing their states and gradually removing some of the sources of local instability if not wars. So how does one persuade the Arab Kings, Emirs, and Sheiks that it in their interest to adapt rather than be toppled?

(iii) Persuading the Arab states that Muslim migration is primary their con-cern

The EU's negotiating techniques hardly measure up to the tradition of diplomacy in Europe. For in practice Europeans 'bully' those whom they regard as weak and of no present utility to them – for this see the attitude shown towards Greece during the last few years though, in fairness, one must not omit to mention that the Greek have, themselves, contributed to the image of unreliability they widely have in Europe. By contrast, Europeans grovel when facing Turkey, a practice which can be explained but not justified by the fact that Turkey is an impor-tant country in a region where the Europeans have a history of proven incompetence. Indeed, the Europeans are good at groveling when their own economic interests are at stake. We in England did this with China with great success, setting aside as is always the case worries about their standards in observing human rights. Indeed, in contemporary diplomacy there is no principle more often declared as sacred as that of respect from human rights and more frequently forgotten when eco-nomic interests dictate the desirability of such amnesia.

The American attitude towards Turkey reveals, once again, their institutional inability to set a clear course and keep to it. Readers of the serious American Press and geopolitical journals will have thus noticed how critical American writers have become towards Turkey in the course of the last two or more years. The blatantly autocratic behaviour of the President of Turkey is one reason. His quarrels with his former religious mentor the very powerful religious leader Fethullah Gûlen is another - at any rate for those who have followed it in some detail.

Turkey's traditional ferocity towards their restless minorities – Armenians, Alevites, but, mainly, Kurds – is another blot on their landscape as indeed is the way the Turkish government treats even their mildly dissenting journalists. Turkey's ambivalent relations with Syria add to the confused picture and this blurred vision has been enhanced in recent years by the fact that they are no longer the country America once believed to be a reliable ally. Still, the mess in Syria is so deep, that many in the USA believe that they still need Turkey's support. So, the pampering continues with the Turkish coffers receiving generous but undeserved periodic subventions to stop them from complaining. Three cheers then for Turkish diplomacy, one of the best in the world – and the compliment is honestly paid to this very professional service which they – not the Greeks – inherited from Byzantium.

Congratulations to one side, of course, entails commiserations to the other - the Americans - for being unable to give a strong and fair leadership to the many problems festering in the region – Palestine, Cyprus, Armenia, Nagorno-Karabakh, Kastelorizo, a Kurdish state, the EEZ with Greece, Egypt, Israel, and, of course, Iran – which have nagged the entire world because of Turkish negotiating techniques which never believes in quite solving a dispute but prefers to keeping a small part of it alive but unresolved so that they can return to it at some later and more opportune moment.

Still, the above is not success but an irony. An irony, indeed, a sad one with which no one – especially Turkey's neighbours - should rejoice. For to see Professor Ahmet Davutoğlu's theory of 'zero problems with neighbours' be transformed into 'increasing problems with the totality of our neighbours" during the premiership of the learned Professor is a disaster for the entire region not just for his country. I thus repeat look at Turkey's current relations with Iran, Armenia, Greece, Syria, Israel, Egypt and Russia and note the totality of the collapse of a once brilliant professorial thesis which proved unable to survive outside the academic laboratory.

As for the Gulf States, the other part of the Muslim world which must be convinced to collaborate in solving the immigration crisis, let us not forget the reason which makes so many great European's powers succumb to the charms of the regions kingdoms and emirates. Quite simply, it is the greatest of all (political) aphrodisiacs: money, especially in the form of armament sales. The human rights beliefs of the European nations evaporate into thin air when the local Emirs wave the magic wand which conjures up images of more purchases of war planes.

Again, my humble but honestly-held view is that if the West were to gently but firmly remind these states how precarious their position is and encouraged them to support the kind of controlled extension of democratic rights to their lesser citizens in the ways envisaged above they might find their (European) positions strengthened not weakened through a series of planned and negotiated compromises. Surely, this proposal is worthy of some consideration rather than a life of progressive political degradation of their bases as the Arab Spring, now about to become an Arab Summer, will turn the local rulers into (very rich) emigres themselves. I would like to hear from anyone who wishes to bet in the opposite direction predicting, for instance, a long political life to the Kingdom of Saud.

One last word concerning the religious groups functioning in the Gulf States. They would, one suspects by definition, oppose the liberalisation plans which improved the levels of education and freedom of the ordinary Arabs in the region and excluded the applicability of Sharia law in the daily and commercial life of foreigners and those of the local citizens who opted for a more relaxed and liberal regime. The emphasis here should be on the fact that all sections of the population would be free to choose how to pray, dress, and conduct their lives. The same freedom would be given to those women who wished to be applied to them. Refusal to accept such changes should be accompanied by the pressure of economic sanctions and cutting off all local access to advanced forms of aid originating from the West. If the Emirs accepted such an adaptation of their societies as the cost of their survival and ordinary citizens welcomed the educational and economic advantages which such changes would entail for them, the organised and fanatical religious cells opposed to them would soon find themselves without a proposer base.

(iv) Building sorting out centres and refugee camps and improving existing ones but outside Europe's frontiers

Changing American or European foreign policy is like bring one of the modern super tankers to an instant halt. It simply cannot be done. Are, there, however, other things which can be done and done more quickly? Yes and here are some on top of the above which are truly essential if the Westerners seriously wished to put an end to the reasons which pushed most citizens of the Middle East to seek refuge in Europe.

In a previous chapter I stressed the need to sort out refugees, whose acceptance by foreign countries may be relatively easy, from economic immigrants who will have to be sorted out and, almost certainly, end up being repatriated. This will need time and money; and Europe is slowly – what is new about this? – realising that it will have to foot this bill in order to avoiding paying this money in Bavaria, Cologne, or the suburbs of Paris.

The gross mistake, however made at present is that these centres are being envisaged to be built *within the EU's frontiers* and not outside them. I already explained why this is a grave error and an unacceptable burden on the frontier countries concerned such as Greece and Italy. Such attempt will only make local conditions more unbearable and cause their societies enhanced social dislocation of the kind which would, eventually spread back to them. With some delay – mid November – the Greek Ministry of Foreign Affairs seems to have espoused this idea though for those interested in how Greek Foreign policy is formed the delayed acceptance of this obvious idea makes one wonder as to who or what reasons prevented this clarification was not mentioned earlier on.

Yet the Europeans are still giving the impression that their thinking is vindictive and not magnanimous; mundane and not imaginative. So, at least, I interpret their latest decision to force on a mentally exhausted Mr. Tsipras their decision to force Greece to open a reception camp for up to 50,000 refugees. Can the Greeks carry such an extra burden, even with the allegedly promised sweetener that the Europeans will lessen – how? by what means? to what extent? – the economic burden of the economic deal they forced onto Greece last June and the Greek Parliament has had its arm twisted to accept. This idea is so balmy that I will not discuss it further other than to say that it will have to be constantly modified – at the expense to Greece – as immigration gets worse and the Europeans pass the can on its weakest member.

Émigré camps must also be built outside European borders – the Turkish western borders for instance in exchange for the huge amounts of money demanded by that country. *If they want to take European money they should in exchange do something for Europe, especially since they are constantly attempting to join it even though they do not satisfy the required criteria.* In my view one should begin by restoring and improving those already crumbling under the weight of numbers and currently situated in Jordan; and others could be set up in other Arab countries in accordance with the above mentioned more general plan to improve the living conditions of Arabs working under adverse condition in countries of the Gulf. If money is to be spent – and it will be - why not spend it (*under constant control that it is sued for the intended purposes*) in the location where it is most suited to all concerned? Some, of course, will not accept such terms until the Europeans make them bluntly aware of how much they depend on European and American money and constantly reminded of the constant need of the Western protective umbrella against threat posed locally by bigger and potential expanding opponents. In short the West should insist on such an approach which essentially adapts Condolezza Rice's views in the early part of this century but, unlike her, insist that the local liberal ideas should be aided on condition that they grow upward and with the willingness of the bulk of ordinary Arabs who live as second class citizens in the unstable lands of the rich Emirs.

(v) Finally, equipping Greece with the proper means to patrol its waters and prevent (peacefully) further immigrants from approaching the Greek shores

Two words in this subtitled have been printed in bold font and for a very good reason. The aim of this suggestion, unlike the previous one is not to aspire to provide a long term and more durable answer but to attempt to restrict the current bleeding into Europe. Again the Union's reaction was to mishandle the problem by trying to use the crisis to favour Turkey's long term ambition to share the Aegean with Greece. This is a huge problem which one day will have to be solved in accordance with the rules of international law and not in a way which flows from Turkeys constant violations of Greek air and water space or nagging Europe to take its side and take measures which would promote new conflicts and not bring peace. Such moves call for imagination and courage on both sides. At present, I see nothing but suspicion and enmity and, what is worse, political instability in *both* countries, for though Turkey's style remains bombastic, its internal political situation is seriously weakened by the growing opposition towards its President's authoritarian rule notwithstanding his recent electoral victory.

The turn for the better will come only when the time is propitious. This will be the occasion to settle the cluster of disputes which are concealed behind the respective claims of these two neighbouring countries behind the words "The Aegean" Sea. Trying to produce *de facto* situations that would favour possible future Turkish claims by giving to the two countries co-responsibility to police GREEK waters – or even entrusting this to Frontex with the ultimate right to take the final decisions - would amount to an unacceptable violation of Greek sovereign rights under the pretext that the European interests should come first and trump such local rights on such a sensitive issue for Greece. No other European country – certainly not England – would accept such an intrusion on vital national rights. Moreover, one should not allow oneself to be kidded by a cunning way of exploiting the current Greek weakness. One would expect from traditional oriental bargainers who make their living by cheating each other and, especially foreigners, in bazaars but should treat it a shoddy imitation which would not flatter European diplomacy.

The second word in this proposal – *peacefully* – needs no elaboration. All it is meant to do is to negate categorically the often quoted stupid argument: "what do you want us to do to stop this continued influx of refugees? Kill them in their dinghies?" Of course not; no one would even imagine such a possibility. What I would like to see happen is to see Greece be given sufficient coast guard vessels to patrol its waters and gently but firmly persuade/ help these immigrants in their shabby dinghies to return to where they began the perilous journey. Frontex officers might be allowed to be present but NOT to have the final say for reasons already explained. In the beginning it may prove difficult to convince them to do that; but if, at the same time, these sorting-out centres and hospitality camps had been set up in Turkey and other Arab lands nearer the 'clash spots' with European aid, I suspect a fair number of those trying to flee might be willing to return to safety on land than remain exposed to the perils of the sea. Once again, however, the final result would depend on how much Europe's intention to help life improve in their lands was believed by the Arab immigrants.

Equality of wealth is impossible; growing inequalities are socially dangerous

I firmly believe that people must be encouraged to dream and made to believe that through their own efforts their life styles and prospects can improve. Nothing – neither religion, nor ethnicity, nor political views, nor sex, - should stand in their way to success. But this success is never going to be the same for everyone; the level achieved will be determined by the abilities of the rising young man or woman as well as luck (helping his aims) or bad luck (frustrating them). Encouraging people to believe in unattainable results is neither healthy nor a recipe for peaceful existence since it generates in the affected person a state of constant anxiety.

Equality of result is thus a utopian dream and citizens should be made to realise this early in their lives. Some preach it but it is no use to pretend that it is attainable in this world given that the abilities of people are vastly different and the way fate operates remains totally unpredictable. *Equality of opportunity*, on the other hand is a noble aim for any society encourage; and the best way of moving in that direction is offering the inhabitants of all societies the opportunity of a sound (and not fanciful) education.

The West, of course, has for years now prided itself for the equality which its market-oriented economic system can help produce in the form of enabling poor people becoming rich. Certainly, it outdid whatever the old fashioned Soviet or Chinese communism could throw at it in return. In practice, however, inequality has remained the prevailing result; and nowhere does this manifest itself more clearly than in the ability of humans to earn money. In this realm more than any other human endeavour, inequality reigns supreme *and will continue to do so for as long as one can predict the future.* The simple and widely accepted proclamation of faith by the Western economies in the opposite result calls for two responses.

First, the Western economies have not *agreed* on program for economic growth for tackling economic crises whenever or wherever they arise; for the available blue prints are based on two very different approaches? The first is the 'growth' (or neo-Keynesian) approach which involves spending money on infrastructure works to make money in the future and thus generate new jobs. The second finds its answer in 'austerity' i.e. cutting salaries, pensions, and (often and mistakenly) instituting *horizontal* cuts affecting the low or middle incomes but not the wealthiest (whether they generate new income and jobs) or just live off earned income, for instance, from capital earned by their late husbands! Europe and American disagree over these dilemmas; and Europeans are also increasingly unsure themselves as to where the right answer lies. This is a huge issue having already attracted a voluminous literature of its own which may have informed people better about the problems each approach has but rarely alerted them fully to the very real dangers of failure found in both approaches.

Second something more has to be said about the Western/capitalist systems' failure not only to achieve 'upward' equality but, on the contrary, for helping increase *inequalities* in wealth. The sad truth thus is that everywhere in the West, especially in the course of the last ten or twenty years, its rich people have become *infinitely* richer, its poor people have been become poorer, while, finally, probably something around 40% of the population in the (lower) middle ranges, have not moved at all from their earlier position which, indirectly, means that comparatively speaking they, too, have become poorer. I do not call this equality. This the myth of the non-existent but – allegedly attainable – equality or at least 'up-lift' which the capitalist system can achieve has been a shrewdly cultivated myth but has not be reflected in the actual results. This myth that playing the market enriches most people must be treated for what it is – a myth – and the way it misleads the barely well to do to invest the money in the market must be condemned as highly dangerous unless it is accompanied by detailed rules which protect the unwary. Such rules, of course, do exist; the problem, however, is that the more such rules are multiplied the more the market system is diluted. Excessive regulation of banks, for instance, can help protect investors; but it may also drive the banks to less regulated locations such as those found in the Far East.

The electorate must thus be told the truth of how the totally unregulated market system works in practice and how often it cheats its own members. For fashionable though this system is among its *aficionados* – mainly those who operate it - it has given to those corporations who operate in different parts of the world the chance to exploit different tax regimes, different accounting techniques, and often end up paying little or no tax while their shareholders may actually be losing money. Likewise, many of these companies which operate in underdeveloped countries have for years now operated in ways which have allowed them to cream of the top profits emanating from the exploration of the local wealth – be it food stuffs or minerals. The inevitable is thus being repeated: corporations and their shrewd manipulators, along with mangers of (relatively) unregulated funds – e.g. the so –

called Hedge Funds – can, indeed, get richer while the poorer countries or individual investors in such companies remain either stable or even, lose money. The idea that the market is a place anyone can make money must not be understood that everyone will. The idea that the majority of small investors can, even with the help of 'advisors' make money playing the market is a myth and thousands of innocent people every year end up losing their investments.

America, once again, finds itself in a commanding position in this game. A brief glance at the United States markets one makes one marvel at how almost all of its major corporations manage to 'play the system' and exploit the highly complex accounting laws ending up by paying zero taxes in the USA.[12] As these results filter out of the country thanks to increased communication and the social media one begins to wonder how such practices will affect America's image. For fiddling with taxes – to express the idea in common parlance – is as much a game played in the USA as it is in Greece though in the former it happens in a much more sophisticated manner. Thus, if a century ago it was easy to cultivate the image of America as the land of the free and successful, nowadays rapid transference of information can - and does - easily demonstrate how many in the USA many become richer by not paying taxes while many more live near the poverty line or are totally unprotected by any social security system. My guess is that America's negative image is in this respect growing. Even populist slogans, like the famous, "let us look after High Street and not just Wall Street" have caught the imagination of many inside and outside the USA. To be sure, 'slogans' can be dangerous'; but they can also help spread ideas which would otherwise not reach the masses; and the one just quoted reflects the view of an awful lot of Americans that the Wall Street American is far removed from the one living far removed from the neighbourhood in which money *and only money* counts. It is thus equally interesting to give even the average reader of a book such as the present some indication of the extent of the myth of equality and easy enrichment which one finds assiduously cultivated by modern capitalism.

All these uncertainties or changes for the worse have altered American habits, attitudes and feelings. The extent of the change

---

12. The wonder is dispelled once the *system of American tax exemptions is seen as being one of the most widely used ways for allowing corporations to evade taxes by calling what they do legal tax avoidance.* This is achieved by means of legislation passed by lobby pressure from individuals favourable to big interests who introduce complicated tax regimes which benefit the richest, usually multinational, corporations.

is, as I have stated, debatable; but its reality is not in doubt.[13] Many commentators thus feel that the majority feeling in the USA is now one of gloom and this despite the economic recovery which has occurred since the 2007 crash.[14] Egocentricity, selfishness, double-faced attitudes to life, isolation, loneliness, loss of purpose - all seem attributes which *a growing number of modern Americans, themselves,* see as prevalent in *their country* these days. To those concerns we must add worries about immigration – their own version from Mexico for instance– and the rise of terrorist militancy in the world which in their heart of hearts they know they have not stopped from reaching their shores. This last point is of great importance not only because of the dangers it raises and the concern it causes but also because, as time passes, it proves the failure of the prolonged military engagement in both Iraq and Afghanistan haled contribute to this contemporary atmosphere of anxiety and insecurity.

The result of all this turmoil and the economic crash that followed in 2007 has enhanced the image of Americans as, cynical, jealous of those who have succeed, easy critics of what they do not like, mistrustful of those around them, and in very recent time whipped up into an unthinking paranoia against Russia simply because this suits a section of the governing establishment. These massive changes in the American character are reflected in figures. For instance in 1960, 58% of Americans believed that "one can trust most people". By 1994 the figure had dropped to 35%; the figure is now even lower.

I repeat, I am not the one who makes these assertions; reputable American authors and organizations periodically voice these concerns

---

13. To avoid the frequent use of inverted commas, much of what follows draws from the works given in this note and my indebtedness, especially to the erudite work of professor Alschuler is not lessened by this general acknowledgement. For more specialized issues I have added particular references. Here then suffice it to declare my awareness that for everything I say there is a counter-argument and much literature to support it. What I have chosen to cite thus corresponds to my own experiences within the USA for over thirty years. Thus, see, Albert W. Alschuler, *Law without Values: The Life, Work, and Legacy of Justice Holmes* (Chicago: University of Chicago Press, 2000)· Albert Borgmann, *Crossing the Postmodern Divide* (Chicago: University of Chicago Press, 1992)· Robert D. Putman, *Have We Become a Generation of Loners?* (Arizona Republic, 16 Ιανουαρίου, 1996)· International Monetary Fund, *Balance of Payment Statistics Yearbook*, 2° Μέρος, World of Regional Tables, A-2, vol. 48 (1997)· The Council of Civil Society, *A Call to Civil Society: Why Democracy Needs Moral Truths* 3 (Institute for American Values, 1998).
14. Most of what follows is taken from American books and reports. I thus repeat the warning so that the views here published not seen as those of the unfriendly outsider.

and I have cited some in my (deliberately) limited footnotes. In 1998 for instance the Council of Civil Society remarked, and I paraphrase, commented that

«our democracy is weakening daily since it is no longer able to replenish its moral and societal reserves which are used to maintain a democratic society."

These mutations in American society are, in one sense, inexplicable given that the indices of material life – health, longevity, financial comfort, opportunities for education, health (if one can afford it), even employment (if comparison is made with the pre-War years) are, on the whole improving (though, as stated, we are also seeing recently some negative trends in other, important, indicators). On the other hand they do suggest that many attitudes, views, and even values are changing in America as we write.

How do these developments affect American political life (and, indirectly, that of the inhabitants of countries which belong to the so-called Western world)? In my view we are again faced with a paradox: the American political life is over and over again displaying serious incidents of foul-mouthing; deep envy towards the wealthy; abuse the social security system (such as it is) by the needy; gun violence; animosity towards the successful (but often dishonest) middle classes (such as bankers, lawyers, doctors) and the insurance companies and fund managers (including banks) exploiting their own clients; anger towards the house owners (constantly asking for rent increases); hatred towards the immigrants adulterating a "pure society" – even in a society which traditionally was made up by immigrants; annoyance towards the illegal immigrants, whom the rich Texan farmers often welcome in order to exploit; tolerance towards the often brutally acting policemen towards a citizen simply because the latter is black; horror at the increased cost of the prison population; Bias towards homosexuals (for debasing American morality and spreading diseases) at the same time as many others are fighting successfully to legalise their presence in society; Persecution against the ever-increasing numbers of prostitutes who, by their numbers, can even bring down the value of entire neighbourhoods. On the purely political front the end result is not any better given the decreasing effectiveness of American foreign policy, a decrease which stands in contrast with the increase of costs in mounting such operations.

Also noteworthy is a climate to gain "quickly" and to "rise socially" (in a society which, in theory, does not tolerate social differentiations), even if it entails treading on others' rights, are constantly nourished by personal interest. Uncontrolled sexual gratification (accentuated by the stress in daily life) also leads to a growing number of broken marriages, increased drug and alcohol abuse, and even contribute to the increase of the prison population as a result of crimes which the above commit to satisfy these urges.

Gun abuse - I repeat this for here I wish to link its growing presence to America's romantic attachment to a constitutionally protected "right" to carry arms – is another example over which society is – guess what - divided. Homogeneity in views is not a requirement of democracy; but it can become a serious problem if, because of constitutional provisions, the rigid and legally absolute respect for divided views can, in practice, bloc reforms which may well enjoy the support of a majority. Repeated and admirable initiatives on this issue from the current President have totally failed to address this major weakness of American democracy which hides behind an antiquated constitutional text which a highly modern method of media propaganda by the interested groups knows how to exploit.

The violent massacres which periodically occur in schools are an aspect of this phenomenon and a particularly dangerous at that since they tend to be difficult to predict given that they often stem from psychiatric disorders which the broken families or the underfunded social security system either fail to detect or treat. Thus, between 1985 and 1997 the number of such incidents over doubled. More precisely, three such incidents, in the space of two years only - 1997/1999 – resulted in twenty nine deaths (26 pupils and 3 teachers) and over 69 injuries, some serious.

If the social/medical systems cannot together prevent all 'nut cases' slipping through their nets, those who sell guns could do a better job by seriously being forced to restrict the type of guns they can sell and also be giving them the right – or better still imposing upon them the obligation - NOT to sell to those who do not provide 100% proof that they pose no danger to society. The number of schools attacked continues to rise; the numbers killed get bigger; the ability to react remains at a zero level. No use offering more statistics for these figures – alas – continue to increase. That is NOT a sign of a flourishing democracy; and a huge increase of immigration might well increase such incidents in our Continent as well.

This, of course, is one aspect of the growing climate of criminality which is aided by an abundance of guns and drugs, alcoholism, and family violence. One consequence has been the rise in the prison population from 196.000 in 1972 to 1.726.000 by 1997 and today exceeding 2.000.000.[15]

The number of criminal convictions of black Americans is even higher approaching one in third of the population.[16] I have already stated that the way the police has handled black suspects has also attracted growing criticism. To be sure, in a country where racial prejudice is still very much alive – the continuing defamatory statements made about President Obama provide a nasty, indeed, totally unacceptable reminder – one can also find many, including scholars, arguing that this difference is due to the greater propensity of blacks to offend. I belong to those, however, who remain unconvinced and tend to associate criminality mainly to environmental and economic factors or, even, to the abysmal conditions of life of illegal immigrants.

The collapse of normal family life is also a contributory factor to this phenomenon.[17] Statistics thus show that one in ten young women between the ages of fifteen and nineteen have children outside wedlock, a percentage which surpasses the English and Canadian equivalents by a factor of two while this American figure exceeds the comparable Dutch and Japanese by a factor of ten! In their vast majority these children received no support from their parents nor, indeed, do they maintain any social relations with them.

More precisely, in 1963 and estimated 240.000 children lived with their mother in single parent households. The figure was up to an astonishing 3,7 million by 1983 only to reach 6,3 million by 1993. It has been rising ever since. It goes without saying that these children all suffer physical and psychological deprivations compared to those growing up in proper families which may also explain why the number of suicides has tripled during the post War period with the figures maintaining an upward trend.

Contemporary American consumerism calls for a chapter if not a book of its own. Here suffice it to mention that easy credit – urged on the young from later school life through the easy provision of credit cards – has transformed this country into the greatest world debtor

15. See Marc Mauer, "The Sentencing Project, *Race to Incarcerate*" (New York: The New Press: 2006).
16. See, Fox Butterfield, «1 in 3 Young Black Men is Caught Up in the Criminal Justice Population», *The New York Times*, 8 October 1995, §4, p. 2.
17. Again, the bibliography is endless. I draw the information given from: Karen Brandon, «Teen Age Girls are Wising Up on Having Children», *Chicago Tribune*, 3 Μαΐου 1999, §1, p. 1· Roger Worthington, «Adding Father to the Family», *Chicago Tribune*, 14 February 1994, §1, p. 1.

with a public debt of well-over $16 trillion at present and reliably esti-
mated to rise to $20 trillion by 2020 if not earlier.

This unending list of growing trends of a malfunctioning society
can be brought to a conclusion with one short observation. In the USA
of the 21st century complaints, jealousy, political rivalry, financial
greed of biblical proportions, leave no profession, religion, or political
party out of their sights. The consequences of such trends go beyond
pure financial results and make the United States of America, a country full of talented and inventive people who, nevertheless, appear as
a very disunited society living in a state of semi-permanent anxiety
and confusion.

The preceding paragraphs have also failed to refer to the political squabbling which delays or fragments America's ability to react to
foreign crises (though we have referred to this phenomenon in other
parts of this book). Infrequent has also been the discussion of the importance that the dollar has as a common reserve currency in "saving" the American economy. This is something which the geopolitical
sleuths should investigate further in order to determine whether part
of America's foreign policy may not, one day, be determined by the
widely rumoured desire of many Middle Eastern countries, China and
Russia to shift (by means of carefully planned moves) their reserves
to another currency or, at least, agree to conduct financial transactions
among themselves on the basis of their own currencies and not the
dollar as the five countries known as the BRIC (Brazil, Russia, India
and China) countries have been threatening to do for some time now.

Dealing with this wide range of problems which are if not generated certainly facilitated to figure in our societies is not a problem that
can be avoided nor easily solved. Enough, however, has been said to
convince, I hope, the reader not tied to particular interests to realise
that though this problem is not new it has reached in our times, explosive proportions. Those who believe in peaceful societies must at
least address some of the issues briefly touched up above; for problems such as the above, if allowed to fester, will inevitably enhance the
chances of social unrest.

Problems particular to Greece: un-ending disputes instead of in-ternal harmony

In Greece as in most other European states politics was once seen as
vocation. Service, not self-publicity, even less so, personal enrichment,

was their aim. Even in Greece which had suffered from four centuries of Turkish yoke, an environment which encouraged immoral or illegal behaviour as a way of survival, lack of the gradually-formed middle class attitude towards social life had to be conducted – notwithstanding occasional aberrations – correctly. That is what these new ruling class hard learned, often from they stay abroad or their study of model societies as England for was long considered to be. What was considered to be appropriate by them was invariably followed by the newer countries such as Greece. The early heroes of the Greek Revolution who turned politicians were people who, on the whole, became involved in politics because of their desire to serve the recently established state. In the beginning this spirit was helped by two events.

Chronologically the first was the character and personality of the first elected governor, John Cappodistria. Few can doubt he was the greatest politician Greece ever had. For years he had served as Russia's Foreign Minister. He was a true cosmopolite and his international experience and far sightedness was proved at the treaty of Vienna where he was not one of the fanatics who wanted France's total humiliation. In Vienna he also fought and succeeded in the creation of another new and independent state – Switzerland; and visitors of Geneva, where he lived for a time, recognized hiss services in many ways.

In Geneva he also met and befriended Count Eynard, a wealthy banker. These days eyebrows will be raised if we here politicians getting too close to businessmen or bankers. Cappodistria did, in fact, ask the banker for a favour but one which revealed his true character. For he asked the banker to donate to the new state he was about to lead any books in his library of which he had second copies; for he saw his job as including the obligation to educate his people just emerging from four centuries of Ottoman occupation. During the few years he was destined to live after his election he worked tirelessly to set up a structured state, establish the first Mint, the first orphanage in the island Aegina and lay the foundations of other state institutions In this tireless task his soon made his political enemies. Disputes often had localized differences; in his case this led to his assassination as he entered the Church of Saint Spyridon in Nafplion which was made by him the first capital of freed Greece – incidentally a state only about one third of the size it now has. Throughout its history Greece has shown a sad talent of combining grandeur with disgraceful and condemnable behaviour.

The assassination of a great man marked the sudden end of a promising start. But the king who was elected to succeed him, though young, of sickly disposition, with weak concentration powers, and inexperienced, was good looking, had a kind heart, was well trained in foreign languages – including Greek in which he continued to receive regular lessons even after he arrived at his new kingdom in January 1833 for he came from a true Hellenophile Bavarian Royal family. So if he had a notable attribute it was his undoubted love for the country he was asked to rule. He also had the good fortune to arrive in Greece with a bevy of learned Bavarians: military officers, a regiment of some 3,000 Bavarian troops (to replace foreign forces already in Greece from the later days of the Independence War), jurists, architects, and able administrators. This minority of legal and originally welcome arrivals was what Greece most needed at that time.

It was not long, however, before this variety of nationalities became unpopular with the locals. Worse still, they became suspect to the foreign powers – known as the Great Powers namely Russia, England, France and Austria – Germany was added to the list at the end of the 19th century - who never ceased to fear that Greece might steer too much in the direction of one of the Great powers rather than one of the others. England, proved the best at this game through a shrewd selection of Ambassadors; but the Russian pull could never be underestimated because of the common religion – Orthodoxy. To this day Greece must avoid Mrs. Merkel's embrace, President Hollande's courting, America's crude courting, England's occasional flirtation, or the Bear's scratching hug. All, must be flattered; but all kept at a decent distance. It is hardly a joking matter to suggest that studying the life of Juliette de Recamier, one of France's most famous *Salonière* of the early 19th century could teach one how to encourage courting but also keep it under control!

Notwithstanding the suspicions and rivalries between different nationalities the Bavarians did not stop progress on the work already begun by Cappodistria. Until Otto's formal coming of age a Regency staffed by three Bavarians took charge of economic and foreign affairs, military organization and education and culture. Athens had, by 1834, become the capital of the new State though its population of the time hardly rose to about 10,000 many of whom many were living in old if not dilapidating buildings – a far cry from today's conurbation of over 4,5 million (if one includes its nearby port of Piraeus) and the sprawling Athenian suburbs.

Many have, at times, expressed mistrust or dislike of Germans. In some cases the reasons for the resentment are understandable. But no one has ever doubted their abilities; and the Bavarians turned the village into a true if small capital during the twenty odd years they worked there. In any event, the all knew they were starting from scratch and that time could not be wasted.

To begin with a home/come Palace had to be found for the King and, in due course, his Queen so two private homes were leased and decorated – *all financed by the King's private purse* - to serve as his Palace between 1833 and 1843. (The two building now house the Museum of the City of Athens and merit a visit.) The emerging city got in the 1837's its first University, housed, to begin within the home of a famous architect, on the western side of the Acropolis mount, and later - in 1841 - moved to a more central position of the slowly expanding city in a building designed by the famous Danish architect Christina Hansen.

The first urban plans also took shape at the time, the city being constructed around a triangle, one side of which consisted of shops since it was to be for years treated as the main trading street of Athens (and was thus duly called Hermes Street); a wide avenue subsequently named Panepistimiou (University) Avenue, since on one side the Bavarians commissioned the erection of three neo-classical buildings to be used by the newly founded Academy of Athens, the central building of the new University and the National Library; the last side of the triangle swept south and joined Hermes street and was given the name of the God of winds – Aiolou Street.

Other institutions' were founded. The National Bank of Greece received a splendid neo classical building at the beginning of Aeolou Street and what is now the national Parliament began life as the King's intended and larger Palace which began being built in 1836 and was completed in 1843. *Once again, its building was financed by a loan obtained by Otto's father – King Ludwig of Bavaria - so the new state was not burdened* [18],tough oddly (and improperly) neither Otto nor his family were ever compensated when it was nationalised upon their dethronement in 1862. While these building were going up the Queen laid down the first park in the center of Athens and insisted that it should be not just a green space but a true botanical garden full of different species of shrubs, plants, and trees late to be enriched by the addition of various exotic birds, including male peacocks which greatly fascinated the Athenians.

Politically, the first phase of the Othonian years were years of royal

---

18. Such frugality, honesty, and generosity were never demonstrated by the Danish Royal family who was given the Greek Throne in the 1860's.

autocracy with the members of the Regency often getting criticized for decisions taken without proper consultation with the Greeks, While such squabbling continued, foreign Ambassadors and their masters squabbled over the more serious matter whether it might be a good idea to turn the monarchy into a constitutional one by equipping it with a constitution that would – at the very least – confer a semblance of democracy. Their planning, however, was pre-empted by a mini Revolution which was staged in Athens with its leader, Colonel Makryannis, extracting from the King in September 1844 the first Constitution of the free Greek State.

Though not far removed in style and content from the French Constitution of 1830 it marked a symbolic rather than substantial move towards the kind of liberal documents being discussed in Europe at that time. The earlier charters, espoused as temporary 'basic laws', and prepared by revolutionary assemblies meeting during the Independence Wat at Epidaurus, Argos, and Troezena and often inspired by the thinking of the likes of Bentham and in some respects were more liberal than those that followed from 1844 onwards. All, however, were set aside after the death of Cappodistria and the arrival of the new King.

The democratic, individualistic, even anarchic features of the Greek character, however, were never snuffed out either by the Turkish yoke or the early attempts to devise a liberal constitutions which coincided with the ideas and ideals of the liberal middle classes making their mark in Europe despite many and varied attempts to suppress them by Europe's most conservative states namely Austria, Russia, and Prussia. Liberal ideas, however, continued to filter into Greece thanks to the Greek intelligentsia of abroad, most of whom were living in the same Italian, French, Russian, Romanian and even Austrian cities which had served as the centres of Greek traders abroad and espoused the cause of the local liberal, at times quite revolutionary (such as the earlier Italian Carbonari) movements or secret societies.

The 1844 type of Constitution was thus more of symbolic than the source of real popular power if the wish of the majority of the people was – which it really was not – to curtail royal powers. This point in fact was never effectively reached in Greece, with major constructional crises erupting in 1915 and 1965, and the monarchy always somehow being caught in the middle of them. Its position thus progressively was weakened and its true role was never resolved until finally, in 1976, a referendum held by Prime Minister Constantine Karamanlis, formally put an end to Greek monarchy which in some important areas of the

Country – Crete for instance – or major cities such as Athens or Salonica it did not manage to obtain more than 12% or so of the public votes.

The Bavarian Royalty's affection for their new country cannot and, on the whole, was never denied even by the most rebellious of its citizens; but their popularity took a further dip from which it never recovered and that occurred when it became obvious that the King and Queen were bound to remain childless. Thus in 1862 a second and fully blown Revolution took place and the romantic first King and Queen took the path back to their country and, finally, their lonely and unjust – I feel - internment in the *Theatinerkirche.*

The establishment of a full Republic remained alive as an ideal, for a brief moment at least. In the Seven islands – which included Corfu and Cephalonia, and did not belong at the time to Greece but were a possession of the British Crown - an attempt was even made to convince William Gladstone to become their first President. But these were not propitious times for such innovations; and, in any events, the Greeks were never allowed to decide about the future.

Once more, the important Royal families of Europe got together and appointed a Danish Prince to be the next King. He was an intelligent, remote as a character, but cunning and fully aware of the pitfalls of being Head of State in Greece. Though he never attained much popularity in his new home his son, a military man, became something of a hero, not least because he personally led his troops during the Balkan Wars of 1912/ 13 which freed large chunks of Greece still under Turkish rule.

Being married to the Kaiser's sister did not, however, help royal popularity as the clouds of war began to gather; and the royal court, though staffed by exceptionally able people, never hid their sympathy for Germany nor managed to avoid a direct clash with the most popular and notable liberal Greek politician since the days of Cappodistria – Eleftherios Venizelos. The dispute was over Greece's position during the First World War: siding with the Germans – the least popular view – remaining neutral – a view with wider appeal – or siding with the Entente as the westerners were called. In academic terms this was not nor is it now judging ex post fact – an easy question to resolve. Small countries situated in trouble areas, have – in theory – every reason to stay out of the quarrels of major powers. Venizelos' view prevailed; for a time literally split the country in two, and ended up gaining a mandate from the Treaty of Sevres for Greece to administer some of their old possessions in the Ottoman Empire including...Constantinople.

Despite this triumph the wavering and temperamentally inclined Greek electorate, voted Venizelos out of office; while his European supporters, French President Raymond Poincaré and British Prime Minister David Lloyd George were eventually voted out of office as well. The continuation of the military occupation of lands once part of the Ottoman Empire thus became a growing problem for the new Conservative government in Greece bereft as it now became of the support of those who admired Venizelos. This must have been obvious to all those in the new government (all, it must be said able honorable politicians) but who had never believed in the expansion into Asia Minor authorized by the Treaty of Sevres. It thus remains something of an unsolved mystery that they decided that in order to strengthen – or so they believed - their grip on the situation the new government decided to expand its military occupation of Turkish land further eastward. The further east they moved, however, the weaker their lines of communications became, while the Turkish decision that enough was enough and the time was ripe of them to regain control of the core of what was once their empire, found in its charismatic leader Mustapha Kemal Pasha, later to become known as Ataturk – father of the Turks – a determined, authoritarian, original mind that led them to victory and – most surprising of all – to a most sincere attempt to Europeanise Turkey, its costume, its alphabet, its international orientation. During his day in power it became even illegal to teach Arabic!

The Greek defeat in 1922 was the greatest political, social and economic set back the new country had suffered since its re-creation. Six of its top officials, including the Prime Minister, the Minister of Defense and the Head of the Joint Chiefs of Staff were executed in a farcical trial over which the former Prime Minister Venizelos may have played a shadowy role. Prince Andrew, Prince Philipp's father, who had, as was customary in those days, participated in military campaigns as a Royal Prince, was snatched by the British Ambassador to Greece from death's claws just in time. The Greek Royal family once again took the road to exile while in Greece a succession of operatic coups took place. Not for the first time, a small country with able and educated persons within its borders was unable to govern itself properly. The interregnum of Republicanism, not without some successes to its name, came to an end in 1933 and the monarchy returned soon to make a flawed – but necessary many believe - move by suspending the Constitution and nominating in 1936 a famous general from the First World War as dictator. Such tolerance as this move received came from the widely held belief not only that it had the support of foreign governments such as that of Britain but was also deemed necessary to prepare the country to stand up against the emerging threat which Hitler and Mussolini posed in its West and North. In the war that came Greece thus stood, once again, on the side of French and the English and fought valiantly first against the Italians (whom they defeated in Albania). For this the country earned public praise from Churchill but little more since it suffered even more from this War which ended with a Greek defeat in the hands of the superior and more efficient Germans forces.

When the War ended in 1944 Greece was in absolute tatters. One might have hoped it could now finally begin making a slow return to normality. But it was not to be. Old scores had to be settled. A disastrous period of Greek in-fighting began; and the marks of that Civil War are very much with us to this day. That is why we spent the preceding few pages explaining to the readers who may not have followed Greek history something of its immediate background to which most of its contemporary problems find their roots.

When Greek fights Greek who will pay the price

The Greeks are an amazing race for in the three thousand year history they have repeatedly shown the heights and lows they can reach. Heights of the like which Achilles reached; for his ambition to kill in mortal combat his heroic opponent Hector was so great that he pursued the dream even if he was made by his mother the Goddess Thetis that the price would be imminent. In the Odyssey we discover another admirable yet rare human characteristic: the ability to wait and bide your time until the time to strike is propitious. Finally, Euripidean men and women where characters which were neither entirely bad nor entirely good: humans, in short, suitable to strive in a human world, suffer, and not infrequently lose.

Those who dragged their country into the sewers were just as remarkable. Alcibiades was intelligent, inventive, charming and very good looking; but he destroyed anyone who relied on him simply because he was utterly unreliable. The archetypal populists was also born in Athens and though constantly lambasted by Thucydides the Athenians often listened to them and duly paid the price. The species still exists; and the harm they cause remains notable though, in theory, it could always be avoided. Finally, were the traitors, who would switch allegiances, and give advice and succour to the enemies of their country once they felt that their carriers at home had run their course.

After the end of World War Two Greece took another four to five years before it could start healing its wounds. During the War the Communists had been more active in their resistance to the Germans. Their opposition to the dictatorship imposed upon the country in 1936 had galvanised the endurance to state oppression. But at Yalta, the Russians ceded Greece to "the Allies" and in exchange took control of Poland. Could the Greek communists acquiesce to losing the power they had gained in the country side and the towns?

Well if they could they did not; and they came close to winning. If they did not, it was partly because, being Greeks, they lost all sight of the medium and pursued their fighting with incredible brutality. Arguably a more significant reason was that Field Marshall Tito finally fell out with Stalin and closed the border between Yugoslavia and Greece through which the communist guerrillas received the supplies. English help in the form of troops and American support eventually in the form of much-needed fund provided through the Marshall Plan in the end combined to put Greece on its latest and most modern course.

In casualties, human and material, however these five years of civil strife cost Greece more than four years of German occupation. Magnanimity in victory is a virtue. Nowhere is it more beautifully portrayed than on a canvas painted by Diego Velasquez entitled "The Surrender of Breda". I it is a true masterpiece, not least in the way it depicts the Genoese General Spinelli stooping forward with immense grace and style to take the keys of the surrendered town from his defeated opponent.

But no, this was Greece not the world of gallantry of the 17th century. It was the victors turn now to show their venom even if this was to the disadvantage of the entire nation. Thousands of active communists were banished on two island which from Roman times were known for their inclement weather and their isolation where their survived undernourished, un cared for medically, and often tortured during thirteen years of Conservative Government (1951 to 1963 led by Field Marshall Papagos and Mr Constantine Karamanlis)) and even two years of socialist government (1963-5 led by George Papandreou). Isolated calls for a complete 'oblivion' policy - not just an amnesty - were totally ignored and not even considered.

As for those who were only 'lesser' supporters of the Communist hard core, they had to live for all of the fifties and most of the sixties through hell since employment, medical coverage, even the right to acquire a driving licence required a certificate from the police, the Church, or a public official that the applicant was of a human of 'proper political beliefs.'

This inhuman phase of Greek history did not cease until 1974 when the Junta fell. It is, however, mentioned here because I believe that the scars it left are still alive and extremism, in its contemporary form, rising by the day, may return to haunt the country with a vengeance. This revival is in part due to the existence of two small parties representing the extreme Left and Extreme Right but mainly, in my view, because of the way the major so-called 'constitutional parties' are cultivating extremism in the hope that polarisation will give the benefit of electoral victory to one of them.

This policy which feeds extremism came to a peek when a Right-Centre governments of Messrs Samaras and Venizelos a witch hunt against both Right (and to a lesser extent Left) began which in many respects was technically illegal, keeping the leaders of the neo fascist party incarcerated without a trial for over one and half years, confiscating the state money allotted to them as a popularly elected party who had obtained some 500,000 plus votes, and daily using the media to condemn their conduct and defame their policies. Accusations form part of politics; exaggerated political discourse is entirely Greek. Whatever they may be or characterised they have contributed to the current polarisation and contribute to making Greece's future unpredictable. The immigration dispute will play straight into the hands of such extremists.

Now the 'Golden Dawn' –as the Greek neo fascist part is called – has little that makes it attractive except to those marginalised by society. The speeches of their members tend to be full of platitudes; their tone is pompous in the extreme; their content is vacuous. Had they taken a leaf out Madame Le Pen's book sharing her modernising spirit the overall presence of the Right could have become a force to be reckoned with in Greek politics. For patriotism, the repetitive attacks on the role of religion in Greek public life by the modernisers and, above all growing immigration, could all have been topics which could have been 'exploited' – I prefer the word 'addressed' – without stooping as low as the party has in praising Hitler, adopting many of the symbols of the Third Reich, and even heaping praise on some of the deceased thugs which served the 1967 junta.

Similar condemnation could be levied against the far Left party – the true communists – for they too are extreme to the extent that un-ashamedly they describe themselves as a Stalinist party. It is interesting – maybe even good – to find one political party in Greece which remains true and unchanging in its beliefs; but Stalinism is forgotten, dusted away with cobwebs of the past, even in Russia. Is it really a tribute to the Greek inventiveness that in Greece some still believe it to be alive and are willing in the 21st century to name their party after a brutal, dead, dictator?

This state of affairs could, in my respectful view, get out of hand if the current policy of economic austerity is not relaxed and the Prime Minister – a young, charismatic, leader but not the intellectual heavy-weight which the preceding model – Andreas Papandreou – was, manages to turn around the prevailing crisis in Greece. At the time of writing this remains doubtful; and the doubt could grow if the im-migration crisis grows still more for among those on the Left the topic brings to life the kind of sentimentality which is understandable but not appropriate to the problem Europe's is facing. Worse still, if the whole atmosphere in the region takes a further turn towards conflict, Greece could find itself attacked by neighbours and such a horren-dous eventuality would push the country further deep into the quag-mire it has experienced since 2009.

To conclude Greece has before her an uncertain future. Its geo-graphical location suggests – I hope only to me – reasons which could enhance the internal crisis and instability. The Greek temperament is both a source of hope and despair given its volatility. And then there is the past, the past I tried to sketch above; a past full of divisions, often enhanced by Greece's so-called friends for all of them wanted a slice of wealth, its mineral, the military advantages of its position but true friends they could hardly be so described.

The surface wounds caused by the Civil War may appear to have healed; yet under the surface the micro-organisms that lead to the spreading if infections are still there. All of the above could, just as suddenly, be seen in a brighter light. But this would to a large extend depend upon what we shall discuss in the next and last chapter; and here the problem of the unexpected appearance of a *true leader* comes into the picture. The word I place in italics is what worries me. Study-ing the tea leaves gives little ground for hope.

Epilogue

America and Greece: two very different and yet in other ways to fairly similar modern societies, both riddled by anxieties, faults, biases, and injustice as well as numerous strong points. Into this word the ethnically and religiously different people, persecuted in different ways in their own countries, and physical exhausted from their escape, may eventually be transplanted. Will the transplant take or will it be rejected by the host body?

Brave I think is he who can guess, especially the indirect and distant consequences which will flow from this operation. But unpredictable consequences they will be; and they are the ones which we can only partially predict. I am not one of those who can even attempt this task; but at the very beginning of the book I mentioned some 'guiding principles' which have inspired me in my seventy two years of peripatetic life and which some might find useful to them as well.

Chapter Nine

SAME OR DIFFERENT?

Words and notions which clearly suggest divisions; but could they also provide the basis of coexistence and union?

When deciding the possible topics of this first subsection I came up with a few words which, I felt, had to be included for consideration. They were: religion, ethnicity, differing political and economic ideologies, wealth and the lack of it. In the first part of this sub-section they could all be put to the reader in the form of questions leaving it for him to evaluate their importance and place them in such an order as he felt that they most contributed to divisions and quarrels. The assumption often if not usually is that all these words describe or lead to divisions. I will adopt this way of looking at the problems which arise in the first part of this subsection.

I have decided, however, to include a second part in this same subsection where the working analysis will turn on the question whether the existence of many and different religions, ethnicities, political ideologies or varying states of wealth have *co-existed* in the past in given geographical regions and could, in fact, be seen (or turned into) blessings and a source of unity and strength and not division and weakness. The reader in this (second) part of the first subsection will be asked to reflect whether he can think of historical examples in which coexistence became possible as did mutual progress despite *ethnic, religious or wealth*, words treated in the first part as found in cases of divisions. The second subsection will thus give scope to different readers to understand these words differently, turn them as it were on their head, and see if they can treat them creatively rather than as words which can only and always lead to divisions.

There is no doubt of course that the tolerant or enlightened among my readers may instinctively move in the second direction; and I can state as a fact that there have been times when in certain geographical areas such state of affairs existed and human creativity flourished as a result of such inter-mixture of backgrounds. The crux of the matter here, however, is whether it is realistic for us to expect such a state of affairs to exist in times such as ours when a return to fanaticism, ferocious competition for the world's resources, and the complete de-humanisation of contemporary capitalism, have led the bulk of those who work in one and the same company to declare in official questionnaires that their prime loyalty is to their own personal gain and not the success of their corporations.

Notions leading to divisions and conflict among humans and states

Religions have through the centuries been the causes of wars, massacres, violence and oppression. Reading the Old Testament we are constantly reminded of the wars waged against the Jews or by the Jews and their neighbouring rulers who subscribed to different – invariably polytheist - religion. The same applied to wars among the older Mesopotamian Kings until Persian dominance put a temporary halt to such disputes.

The story of Rome is also full of wars; and those associated with the East – the Zealots in particular in Judea – acquired much of their extremist elements from the religious devotion of the most religious of Jews – the Zealots. Byzantium, too, was also constantly at war, first with the Persians – always a formidable nation - then with the Arabs, finally with the Turks. In many of these battles the religious element was prominent; and, indeed, it became the core, the symbol, the purpose of the Crusades which was nourished on the fanaticism of hundreds of thousands of simple people who naively believed that their pilgrimage to Jerusalem would restore the holy lands to Christianity. It did, but only for a limited period of time.

The ferocity of the Catholic Church became obvious in the way it supressed the Albigensian heresy. The massacre in the Church of Saint Magdalene at Beziers is all the more remarkable in that it was ordered by one of the greatest Popes of the Middle Ages – Innocent III. Violence breeds violence and approximately three centuries later the Catholics returned to violence, this time killing approximately 25,000 Protestants during the Night of Saint Bartholomew. It took an imaginative Protestant King to be baptised Catholic, and issue the famous Edict of Nantes proclaiming full religious tolerance in his country before he was crowned King of France as Henry IV.

Christian religious fanaticism of earlier days has now passed on the Muslim fundamentalists. Personally, I think, their atrocities which consist of killings, beheadings, mutilations and the destruction of priceless antiquities in both Afghanistan and Syria – e.g. Palmyra – hardly serve their purpose. The spread of misery to thousands and the enlargement of the immigration movement help neither the fundamentalists who cause the displacements nor their innocent co-religionists who suddenly find themselves on the run.

The same fanaticism is shown when Danish or German citizens, making use of their constitutionally protected rights to free speech, stage plays or publish cartoons which, a fraction of the Muslim population takes so much to heart that it demands that the foreign lands in which they seek refuge adapt their customs, habits, and constitutional rights to meet those of the invading *desperados.*.

None of the above makes sense and none will be tolerated for long; and those who through their own barbarity help enhance this crisis will, eventually, carry a big portion of the blame for the train of events which a fanatic minority starts by defaming the bulk of law-abiding Muslim citizens.

Race and culture can be taken together; and they, too, can and have historically provoked enmity, discrimination, in-fighting, conflicts of different kind. Muslim and Jews have both suffered because of their race as Spain experienced – to its loss – following the Christian *Reconquista* of 1492. Some of its best talent and most of its merchants fled ether to Morocco or Leghorn or other more hospitable parts of Europe and their arrival enriched the foreign lands and correspondingly impoverished the Eastern shores of Spain – Valencia and Barcelona in particular – where most of these different – not Castilian minorities had existed for centuries.

We have already mentioned the expulsion of the Greeks from the shores of Turkey and today we see growing signs of ethnic restlessness being deliberately cultivated by the Turkish state in Western Thrace. This is a huge mistake for ethnicity is, in practice, raised as an argument by the remaining Turkish origin Muslims of Thrace against fellow Muslims who, however, are *not* of Turkish origins. These latter are the Gypsies and the Pomacks who, despite their religious beliefs, actively desire close relations with the Greek, not Turkmen population. Actively encouraging ethnic rivalries may appeal to Turkish irredentists; but it represents a backward step since the Treaty of Lausanne of 1923 proclaimed religious tolerance in the region (but was totally silent on ethnic identity) since on this issue its main ruling had been to exchange populations between Greece and Turkey at the time. Ethnic homogeneity or diversity in Thrace had not been within its remit.

Not many in Europe may realise what is simmering under this surface; yet most Europeans know that Balkans remains a powder magazine ready to explode and all because historically the entire region was always riddled by religious – Muslim, Orthodox, Catholics – and ethnic – Turkish, Albanian, Serbian, Slav, Bulgarian, Greek - and political – western capitalists versus Slav communists - differences. How ferocious these differences could be was shown in the not so distant past when the war in Yugoslavia was fought. The abuse that preceded it and the rumblings still present remain alive in the minds of locals.

It is essential to appreciate that no one gains from such clashes; and the locals suffer more than most. They enmity and mistrust, however, continue; and the big powers cannot always claim with conviction, that their 'humanitarian' interventions are devoid of their own political motives nor, indeed, that they always achieve their aims in a genuinely honest and bi-partisan manner. The truth of the matter is that they do not.

The reader will have noticed how my account has moved from God to Mammon, from religious and other abstract ideas connected to material disputes, which in turn are all lead to the acquisition of power and its fruits. Could this mean that, at the end of the day, all our words boil down to one sentence: power in pursuit of money? Or could it suggest that the causes of our divisions do not stem from one source but can be attributed to one word only as a result, however, of interlinked forces? If I wish to take such theme to its most cynical extreme one might even say that the advantage of using religious, cultural, or ethnic words is that they make it easier to mobilise the masses to stand behind the ruling elites who operate with only their self-interests in mind. They, however, know exactly what they want but just as importantly they know how to package it and thus make it more sellable by mobilising masses to do the work for them.

Political disputes, by which I mean, diverging views which barely conceal the political motives of the large powers, are the flavour of our times. A major reason for their increase is the sudden collapse of the Soviet Union. The 1990's offered a major opportunity for reconciliation between the old Eastern bloc and the now victorious Westerners on the other side. Never before in its modern history was Russia and its youth so open to American tastes, fashion, style, music, fast food, ideas in general. Many Americans, I venture to suggest, would have reciprocated such calls of co-operation and friendship were they the ones who decided the future of the country. The USA, however, is only nominally governed by its ordinary citizens; in practice its foreign policy is determined by extremist groups – these days the neo-Cons have once again the upper hand - the military industry, the intelligence services (often competing among themselves), the bankers, and its Congress which is notoriously divided and susceptible to lobby pressures.

The attempt for East and West to get closer together was scuppered by the generation of neo-conservatives. Many fine minds among them felt convinced that the weakness of the post –Cold War Russia gave America the chance to 'finish it off' and become the sole major power on the planet. Nothing that has happened since 1991 suggests that this thinking was even remotely correct or feasible. Even those who wrote much discussed monographs under eye-catching titles such as "The End of History" to celebrate the triumph of the Market Economy are now semi-forgotten. On the contrary, the indications were - and have become stronger since Mr Putin's advent to power in 1999 - that we have entered a multi-polar world with China, the USA, and Russia, all vying for a decisive role in the years ahead. Naturally, we should also be prepared to see soon – maybe during the next five years - India joining this club of super powers. Foreign policy dictated by American fiat is thus bound to become a phenomenon of the world of yesterday. The world of tomorrow will call for a different set of alliances which, of course, does not mean that America's amazing technology will not continue to give it a pre-eminent place at this table; but it will only be one of four.

What is even more crucial for our present sub-heading to note is the fact that its policies will no longer turn on rigid definitions of what is expected from a market economy versus a communist state. These summary labels, appropriate to the fifties and sixties, will no longer give an accurate picture of the principles which really guide the major states vying for dominant positions. States which thus operate under communist banners for some purposes will also be moving towards market ideas and even the partial adoption of aspects of the rule of law in those areas will have as its main aim the attraction of capital inflows and know-how and no generalised belief in human rights.

That is already happening in China more than most people suspect; and it is a process which will continue since the latest economic plans issued by the Chinese leadership show that amazing country wishing to transfer to other entities decisional powers once exercised by the centre or local authorities. The central government's concerns are likely to shift more than ever before towards battling corruption and pollution but not abolishing the central role played by the Communist party which is unrealistic even to envisage in a country of the size of China. I gave a special paper on these issues in Beijing and Shanghai to Chinese officials and judges over one year ago; and 'censored' versions of it have been published in English, Italian and Greek.

In these days where communications and gossip about celebrities of all kinds flourish over the social media, their wealth and life styles receive wider publicity than ever. At the same time, hunger, and disease in Africa, civil strife and maiming in the Middle East, and massive movements of boat people in search of simple survival - not much more – in the eastern Aegean also make the headlines daily. Such contrasts enhance the appeal that power which wealth brings (and vice versa) and make more people wish a bigger share of the available wealth. For some this will act as a stimulus; and the stories of those who made it from rags to riches will increase; those who never made it – for whatever reasons – are only likely to enlarge the size of the jealous and the malcontents. Calvinism was, traditionally, one of those religions that believed that the display of economic inequalities was socially destabilising. In what I described above, we are likely to find the same reactions and results. The distance between the 'haves' and 'have-nots' will increase; and the phenomenon – discussed above - about decreased equality among citizens despite the fact that they are doing all they are meant to do to improve their situations can only jar many among them. There is room thus to argue that the difference between wealth and poverty may be more destabilising in our societies that the differences based of religion, ethnicity or political ideology.

This result, if true, may well change the hierarchy of 'dividers' which put one section of society on a collision course with others. This was most certainly true during the early phase of 19th century capitalism which created the steel and steam barons; but today's greatest publicity given to those who have and those who have not must, per force, increase envy and the desire to catch up by all means, even *illegitimate*. I italicised the last word simply because in a society where the traditional devices which controlled human behaviour – the law, the church, the family, the neighbourhood – nowadays all play a weaker role in keeping people on the straight then the result must be increased envy and confrontation.

This thought calls for some deeper reflection. I am not suggesting that humans have become by nature more dishonest. Though there may be some truth in this idea, as well. What I am, however suggesting is that modern electronic technology, modern ways of operating across state borders, must be giving people *more new ways to deceive* in the search of faster, ill-begotten gains. The factors to choose to stress in the subtitle of this chapter are, once again, interlinked though this time this interlinking is less to promote divine teaching, attractive ideals, or the interests of a persecuted race, but to enhance the chances of the most cunning, the most ruthless, and the most inventive among us to become rich quickly but in violation of the basic rules of law and morality. The people who make money cramming scores of hapless people in dinghies in order to cross rough seas are the kind of example I have in mind and deplore. It is modern, it is despicable, and it interlinks with issues which have figured in these essays but in each chapter reveal aspects which merit their own discussion.

The reverse picture: the 'dividers' generating creative co-existence. Has it ever happened? Could it happen again?

Could we now move to the exact opposite situation and envisage divergent religions, ethnicities, and political ideas, working together in harmony to promote the common good? Constructive thinking is always more difficult than the destructive variety; but history offers some notable examples so we must try to discover what brought about such a state of affairs and see how we can explore this positive way of thinking.

Our first example must be linked to the unique cultural achievement of the wars – yes, wars – of Alexander the Great. I stress the paradox for huge it is without any doubt; yet, nonetheless, the coexistence of races, religions, and very different ideas was brought about by military means. All of this flowed from the unique mind of Alexander the Great which turned the crushing of the mighty Persian Empire into the birth of a new world of 'mixture' 'cohabitation' 'inter-marriage (of people and ideas), and of a combination religious practices and national languages.

Alexander's epic campaign all the way from Macedonia to India was thus constantly accompanied by gestures of reconciliation to the people he had just beaten. *His was thus the only military campaign in history with a civilising purpose in the sense of spreading Greek culture else-*

333

where but also in combining it with what good he found in his ceaseless travels. To implement this belief of his he favoured mixed marriages; gave the example himself by marrying a 'barbarian princess' – Roxanne who apparently bore him a son but who was murdered along with his mother upon their return to Macedonia after Alexander's death in Babylon.[1] Whatever the set-backs, the seed was sown; and the first shoots appeared after the death of the chief gardener when his vast lands were divided among his senior Generals who retained for a long time the strong ethically and religiously mixed character Alexander's reign had, from its outset.

Indeed, in the mind of Alexander the idea of contact and influence through marriages and other forms of closer exchanges was so firmly fixed in the young King's mind that he was determined to ensure that his heirs continued with the practice. Evidence thus exists which suggests that in his testament, read out to his troops by one of his Generals – Perdiccas – a member of his personal guard. In it, Alexander advocated inter alia the transplant of entire populations from Asia to Europe and vice versa in order to bring about greater unity among the largest Continents and friendships among their people. It is safe to say that the idea was unrealistic though, one could counter-argue, that Alexander's entire military campaign was unrealistic and yet it was realised in the full. So maybe we should not condemn his idea out of hand the way I did[2] but simple stress its weakest point which was that he was not destined to live long enough to force his plan on his soldiers who remained obedient until he asked them proceed beyond India into South East Asia!

It does not, however, call for much searching in history books to discover states or wide geographical entities where such state of affairs became a reality. Historically, and for the reasons already given, starting with the Hellenistic kingdoms which sprang into existence after Alexander's offer good examples. Egypt under the Ptolemy's is, for me, the best, showing the peaceful co-existence of Hellenic, Oriental (by which I include Jewish as well) and local Egyptian-based populations – heirs of a great past – coexisted in a way that showed in the flourishing of cultural achievements of the era.

---

1. Such information as we have, however, suggests that these marriages did not last long though his own, despite much speculation, lasted until his death and his pregnant wife even bore him a son upon their return to Macedonia where, however, both of them were murdered thus bringing to an end Alexander's direct line.
2. Robin Lane Fox, the author of the most readable and scholarly account of Alexander's life available in English, describes his idea "as memorable but not impossible": see *Alexander the Great*, Allen Lane (1973) at p. 476.

For how many empires or states can we imagine where such a variety of talent on subjects such as mathematics, geometry, astronomy, geography, history, poetry and many other areas of intellectual activity received so much attention and, indeed, were encouraged by the state not only to assemble in Alexandria but to be centred in the Royal Museum – pat of which was the great Alexandrine Library – an early forerunner of the Modern Interdisciplinary Institute for Research? The peaceful coexistence of cultures flourished in such an environment; and the first King's own gesture – Ptolemy I, Sotter (the Saviour) – to add to his titles that of Pharaoh showed that he was a true disciple of his former boss who believed in bringing together different cultures and not allowing them to waste time fighting each other.

How Hellenic, Hebraic and other cultures mixed and, indeed, could come together in peaceful coexistence was demonstrated by Philo of Alexandria – an utterly Hellenised Jew (as indeed was the (Apostle) Paul – who tried to bring together Plato's and Moses ideas and with the help of Stoicism prepared the ground for the reception of the new religion in the West.

The same re-birth appeared in literature, Epic poetry in particular. In terms of continuity his cultural policy of co-existence of cultures met its greatest success in the kingdom of the Ptolemy's in Egypt. For there, under royal patronage by the first three Kings all of whom acquired Greek names to describe their characters, the presence of the famous Library, and a significant mixture of Greek and Egyptian populations – especially in flourishing cities such as Alexandria – the Greek elites helped organise the preservation of most of the learning of classical antiquity and even the flourishing of the locally invented and cultivated Bucolic poetry.

This, too, was an achievement of the age; for it drew heavily on ancient metric styles and myths – Apollonius Rhodius' *Argonautica* is a perfect example of a Romantic Epic about the recapture of the stolen Golden Fleece. It borrowed much from Homer and Euripides but also gave expression to the tastes of the inhabitants of Alexandria – Greek and Egyptian. These inhabitants loved stories of exploration and discovery; showed a predilection towards a poetry that idolised nature; meticulously studied climate and the environment in general; and provided, in the end, the immediate and necessary inspiration to the Roman poetry which followed from about the end of the first century BC onwards. Ovid and Virgil are unimaginable without these predecessors. Civilisations thus blended as tastes did, as were methods of poetic composition from much earlier times and in turn procreated worthy successors. The past was kept alive in the present and in turn lay down the foundations for the Rome's poetic future. This, in itself, is a unique example of how the careful mixture of influences and ideas can give rise to subsequent civilisations, different and yet continuing to a large degree the basic ideas of the predecessors.

Volumes – historical, philosophical, and theological have been written on this subject so, for present purposes, it is best to move to a completely different era and part of the world to show that the Hellenistic miracle of constructive intellectual coexistence in Egypt was not – and should not be – seen as an isolated phenomenon though, admittedly, it needs luck and perseverance to help bring it about.

So I turn my attention to Medieval Cordoba and Granada, always in search of those factors which help achieve symbiosis and avoid conflict. The intellectual coexistence was achieved at a time when the religious competition in what is today's Spain was deep and strongly felt; and the local princes externalised the competitive clash which existed between then in the battle field throughout the 12th to 15th century (if not even earlier).

This is the 'Andalusia *phenomenon*', alluded a few lines above, and no other expression than the italicised word can, in my view, explain its contradictions – which on the intellectual plane resulted in Muslims, Jews, Spanish Christians, showing such a unique measure of tolerance towards each other's intellectual ideas and achievements.

To be sure none of this happened over night; and this is a key point to bear in mind. The start was, again, characterised by an expansive military campaign in which the Muslim world nearly swallowed up the whole of Spain and a good part of the French South. But after the expansion was halted in the middle of the 8th century AD, invaders and invaded *learnt* to coexist in numerous ways which often were inexplicable but helped produce the amazing climax we find in Cordoba and Granada in the 14th century.

For first the Catholic, Spanish, princes once defeated retreated to the only parts of the Iberian Peninsula which remained Christian – the North-West corner of the peninsular. Then, roughly from about the 13th century onwards, they began the (very) slow process of the *Reconquista* which finally freed Spain in 1492 from an eight centuries Muslim domination. Like most great achievements it came with a high price – in this case racially, culturally, and economically for it brought back division, barbaric prosecutions, contempt for different religions and ideas and ethnicities.

In the Andalusian region – around Seville and the Caliphate of

Cordoba – the great years of the 14 and 15th centuries, though the remained years of internal conflict among Muslims Caliphs, they did not end the intercultural collaboration and co-operation with other sections of the local communities. They thus coincided with the reign of Arab princes who, through their love for education and culture, promoted the art of coexistence with other races, deliberately filled their courts with sages irrespective of the religious beliefs or ethnic backgrounds, and left so many varied treasures behind them which make visiting this part of Spain such a unique aesthetic experience. Another indication, found often in history, is that strife or coexistence is determined not necessarily by the words we considered above – religion, financial greed, cultural ego-centrism - but by the presence of 'leaders', 'unifiers', 'saviours' - the exact name does not matter – imbued in the idea that mutual learning brings with it *varied and multiple* benefits.

What matters is to note that, *first*, all of these people were unusual if not exceptional and that their approach to life and its treasures was positive not negative. *Two*, though many of them were Muslims, they are – or seem to me to have been - light years away from the contemporary fundamentalists who thrive in destroying the treasures of the past, for instance in Greek Palmyra. The *Third* point should lead us to consider whether it is the religion which divides and destroys or the spirit and the mind of *organised minorities* acting within such groups. No one should be surprised with such a formulation; for, as Disraeli nearly two hundred years ago, rightly observed the history of the world has been the history of organised minorities. *Finally*, and most important for our times, we must note that this spirit of tolerance of coexistence happened gradually and, to the extent that one can even use the term, planned carefully. By the 13th or 14th century this spirt f intellectual tolerance and co-operation lacked the kind of elements of 'suddenness' and 'destructiveness' which accompany 'storms', be they cultural or of the other kind which nature whips up herself. I stress this last point for I honestly believe the current mass displacements have all the frightening and destructive characteristics of natural Tsunamis and may thus destroy decades of carefully planned – timid perhaps, but enlightened nonetheless – steps which occurred in post War Europe and assisted the wider ability to co-exist which was unknown in Europe in 1945 but which could be found in the Europe of the twenty first century.

The Spanish invaders were also, in cultural terms, unique for they were by nature borrowers and givers. From them Spain (and the rest of Europe) thus got the introduction of figs, sugar cane, dates, ginger, pomegranate, apricots and – mainly - their wonderful citrus fruits. It was they who also first brought to Europe – via Spain –a device for measuring the stars and planets called the 'Astrolabe'. From China, curtesy of the Arabs also came to Europe the compass; and it is this latter race which helped make huge progress in the sciences of Astronomy, Chemistry, Physics, Mathematics, Geography taking a step further the work begun by ancient Greeks and Alexandrines. They also built cities – the first in Europe – with raised paved sidewalks, illuminated them with lamps decades before street illumination even appeared in London or in Paris, and even cultivated music to high levels inventing, among other instruments, the guitar which became synonymous with what these days we clearly identify as Spanish guitar music.

How did they all - Muslim, Jew and Christian - coexist with each other especially in Andalusia, learning from each other, respecting each other, using the learning of each other in the *seventeen Universities* (!) which Muslim Spain has acquired (and I am including among them Cordoba, Granada, Malaga, Seville, Toledo and Almeria) *at the time when the rest of Europe had merely two*? Must we repeat the importance of exceptional individuals in the development of history – Carlyle, somewhat dated these days, would have called them 'heroes'; or should we leave this for the very end of this chapter and, in the meantime, remain faithful to my earlier aphorism about the destructive but also constructive powers of organised minorities. I must, however, return to one further Arab legacy in Andalusia: architecture of buildings and architecture of gardens, or simply put, garden design.

Granada's cultural heritage is mind boggling. The divine palace and water gardens of the Alhambra (literally: "the red one") has amazed millions of visitors over the centuries. All who have seen its gardens have admired them; and the discerning also noticed that the Arab garden is superior to the later one which King Charles 1st of Spain (and 5th of Germany) attempted in the part of mount which he briefly inhabited when a very young King. Cordoba's Great Mosque - *La Mezquita* - possesses a golden roof supported by 1000 columns of marble, jasper, and porphyry and was lit up by thousands of brass and silver lamps. It is beautiful; and its beauty is in no way affected or diminished that it was designed and built by people who adopt a religion different to mine.

One can admire the simplicity and mathematic complexity of the Parthenon for days on end; you can feel a tingle in the body as you wonder through the endless beauties of Rome – whether outdoors or indoors (e.g. the Palazzo Borghese); but you must be in love holding hands with your loved one when near one of those magical ponds of Alhambra – those constructed by the Muslims - not the later ones designed by Charles V - saying nothing but just taking softly in that unique calmness which only the *still water can generate*. And, by the way, let us not forget that the beauty of still water was first discovered and exploited by the Persians, another great civilisation of antiquity, and was later taken over by the Arabs. This was a case where beauty procreated beauty; not ugliness succeeded beauty.

I will, however, pose and look at the even more inexplicable reaction of the Christian *Reconquista* which brutally put an end to this human cohabitation, converted forcibly or forced into exile Muslim and Jew, scientist or philosopher, able tradesman, rapidly impoverishing the Eastern cost of Spain where these minorities were principally established. We say enough - I among them - criticising the unpleasant aspects of contemporary Islam; but one must bend the knee with respect and admiration before those who created the sights I just tried to sketch. Contrast and admire and wonder on how could the battling Caliphs combine such sharing, collaboration, co-operation, co-existence, with so many able people from different ethnic groups and religion - including my religion, my race, which a couple of centuries later invented slumped to the depths of inventing the *auto de fe* (the burning at the stake of heretics after conducting a humiliating public penance) and the Spanish inquisition simply to enforce uniformity of ideas and beliefs? If I were asked who were the real great personalities: *Los Res Catholicos* or the Califs' of Cordoba I would have no hesitation in my answer (though, of course, history – which is little more than politics of the past – rewards success and offers its praises only to those who know how to move with the flow of events.)

I make my point obliquely through a question (which though rhetorical and thus suggesting the answer I prefer) has at least one advantage. This is because it is best to know how to ask one right question than to find its answer – assuming, of course, that there is one only. So, I was always told as a student – and later promoted as a teacher - the view that as an academic you must first and foremost learn to ask the right questions. The answers come later; and they need not be unanimously accepted.

In the preceding paragraphs, however, I also dwelled on facts, interesting I hope to those who do not know much details about these golden eras of cultural coexistence, for they shows that the words used in the subtitle of this chapter need not be only seen as dividers among people but also as elements that given the right environment and the right leader can move us towards the coexistence of races, religions, and ideologies for the benefit of all concerned.

Too much information too little time to reflect on it

Ours is a culture which spends huge amounts of time shifting paper. The computer revolution is gradually moving us away from the physical paper; but it is not resolving the real problem which is the multiplication of documents, i.e. information of all kinds. Moreover, one thing on which everyone would agree about this information is that not all of it is of the same value. To decide what is useful and what is rubbish you must read it all. Have time enough to evaluate it and cross check it, classify it if its worth retaining or make it suitable for rapid and or extensive use should the need arise. Who has the time to do all this, even more importantly, has time to reflect on the ideas produced and then even decide whether which need to be taken further. Delegation, some might argue, to assistants, PA's, or junior colleagues, is only a partial answer. Partial at best for, unless they are themselves educated, intelligent, and reliable AND know their bosses interests and even understand his mind, how can they separate the documents he has to see from those which should be forwarded to others person to handle or, even those who can only have one destination: the bin. Then, there is another problem. In a world which is rapidly losing its ability to write clearly, to discover the essence of the texts one receives, and then set aside those ideas which encourage further elaboration, is a task that few can undertake. All of the above are tasks which the leaders of society have no time to do themselves; yet they must remain updated on the matters which fall under their remit.

The leader needs time to write to the few that matter and only say what is needed for further action to be taken. The challenge is to slim down the meetings which need to take place and the size of the documents which have to be studied and written. Churchill would take more time writing his terse Parliamentary speeches than his voluminous historical work. Interestingly but not surprisingly it is these shorter texts that made him famous and kept the spirits of the citizens high when they most needed encouragement and boosting of their spirits. Less means more; but you can only satisfy this irresistible lasciviousness for the concise if you have time at your disposal to condense your ideas and give them an attractive stylistic turn.

So, the conclusion of all the above is that all in positions of authority – political, economic, religious, scientific -must have the minimum - requisite is the word I would prefer to use - amount of knowledge about the subject they are responsible for that will forewarn them what the need to watch out for and what can, in principle, be ignored. Moreover, the person in a responsible position in politics, business, or the intelligence world must also be alert fundamental changes slipping by unnoticed. They must also know broadly what kind of regular up-dates they will expect their associates and special advisers to keep furnishing them with. In short, the higher up one is in a particular politico-economic setting, the broader his grasp of the problems must be and greater his ability to delegate. Broader, however, cannot possibly also mean deeper. Still, as already stressed, the boss must be endowed with the key talent of knowing what detailed updates to demand from his advisors.

The above requirements do not represent what actually happens in practice; for Prime Ministers and Presidents often shuffle their senior political colleagues from one sensitive ministry to another without the new occupants possessing wider expertise or even general interest in the subject matter of their new position. The usual attribute of modern politicians to be jacks of all trades but masters of none makes this possible. But in my view there are some ministries – Defence, Finance and Foreign Affairs are the kind I have in mind – which simply cannot be treated in such a manner.

Worse still is the position of the very top leaders- Prime Ministers and Heads of State or CEO's of large corporations. Theirs the problem is different; where do they find the members of their Praetorian guard? The first problem is trust and loyalty, the two qualities which are the most difficult to find in associates at times which are fluid and transitional, when changing camps and allegiances can be the quickest path to promotion. The second but equally important problem is choosing knowledgeable people to assist one. In Greece, political friends or, worse, relatives of the boss often end up getting such posts and the chances are that the service they render may well be sub-standard. This can have *disastrous* consequences since the top men or women also need to be able to be surrounded by exceedingly hard-working and reliable associates who will be able to stand the unbearable heat generated in this kind of offices.

I italicised above the word disastrous. Were I still active in the academic world I would try to find able and perceptive Greek PH.D candidates whom I would advise to write a series of theses showing how most of the chief personal advisors of Greek Prime Ministers unwittingly (no doubt) may have helped harm their boss's legacy, perhaps even the interests of the country itself. If possible, I would then bring in some able your British historians and ask them to compare the situation in England, a country which I think I know better than others, or France known for the high qualities of the highest civil servants and force comparisons. I strongly suggest that men like Sir John Colville (the only one from the three countries whom I knew personally and whose books I have read with much enjoyment) or Sir Bernard Ingram or Alistair Campbell were invaluable to Sir Winston Churchill, Lady Thatcher and Tony Blair. I rack my mind to think whom I would value as highly as the above when thinking of those next to the last four Greek Prime Ministers. I am *implying* – nothing more – than these very sensitive posts were better filled in England than, arguably, in Greece; but then the question is why this difference? I still feel the reasons I mentioned earlier harmed Greece; for, overall, it is a fact that the standards of the civil service in countries such as England, France, Germany and Israel- to give but a few examples –are distinctly higher that those found in other countries. This is not to say that one cannot find among these people intelligent advisors or civil servants; far from it. Turkey's diplomatic service is, for instance, a formidable machine (in most cases at least!).

What the Mediterranean world (certainly I include Greece in this geographical definition) seems to me to be lacking is the solid and long tradition of a fully impartial civil service which has acquired its ethos and its traditions over a very long period of time. This is especially true of what in England are referred as the Permanent Under-Secretaries who often have many years of experience in their jobs. In Greece the so called General Secretaries who head the civil service of the Ministries change every time a new government comes to power and the posts are not infrequently filled by political candidates who were not elected at the general elections or otherwise confidents of the governing party. Had I ever the chance to change this practice in my country of birth I would attempt it.

The pervasive and perverting effect of political correctness

Remaining up to date on facts and new theories is essential; their analysis will follow with the help of specialists; then comes the problem of deciding how the decision reached will be communicated to the world which also includes a decision as to the way it will be communicated to Parliament. Timing, phrasing, emphasis, are all important in these days when 'the media are the message' as the saying goes; and this calls for yet another kind of expertise. That is the moment where political correctness rears its ugly head and can distort if not destroy the decision taken. For in the name of democracy the content of a policy may be altered to please active groups occupied with their own cultural or libertarian hobby-horses caring little as to how these group interests may affect the common weal.

Feminism, egalitarianism, environmentalism, racial considerations – positive or negative - can all thus place obstacles in the development of a policy which may otherwise need to be pursued by a particular state. It may sound provoking to assert that this is a problem that affects more liberal and not authoritarian oriented regimes; provoking, yes; but also true. To put this idea in the simplest of ways: the problem just mentioned must come before President Obama all the time; I doubt that it does with President Putin. Different systems one will retort. Correct; but on this score the latter's system gives the leader more room for rapid reactions to crises; and one cannot dismiss this advantage lightly.

Can such a state of affairs be modified if not altered for the liberal and more open regimes? A survey of how these pressure groups of schools of thought exploit the growing variety of media communications suggests a negative reply. Still, it is the duty of this commentator to identify a problem area, - academe for instance – in which he has spent over forty seven years of his professional life and seen how political correctness inhibits or even violates the two cardinal principles of any promotion of knowledge: freedom of expression and the pursuit of excellence; values which must *never* be compromised by the application of sectional predilections. This does not mean that legitimate societal interests – e.g. extending education to all the recesses, nooks and crannies of a society – must be abandoned. It does, however, mean that they ways to achieve it cannot consist of electing to an academic post an 'intellectually inferior' candidate solely on the grounds of the colour of his skin of his sexual orientation or because you do not have enough women (or men) in your department and you are solely trying achieve a balance in the representation of sections of a given society. In our time race and sex equality must be actively pursued; but never through the means of debasing the standards of appointments. That, at least is my view; and I am very probably unwise to state it so openly but I do.

The same, as discussed above in great detail, must never occur in the painful but growing issue of immigration. Human suffering must and can be alleviated in many ways but never in a way that runs counter to the interests and clearly proclaimed wishes and needs of a particular state. Political correctness must not inhibit the free discussion of the conflicting values which have to be accommodated when addressing the issue of mass immigration and, even more crucially, the question of massive granting of asylum. This is already becoming a problem in Greece and the signs are there that the most generously minded people who favour the liberal granting of asylum may, politically speaking, be not just out of touch with realities but plain naïve.

The recent condemnation of Hungary, especially by the so-called liberally inclined electors, is an example of a policy which will spread not be revoked. After all, erecting fences which prevent the unrestricted inflow of immigrants in their lands is a policy entirely compatible with the notion of state sovereignty and respect for the views of its people. Nor, in my view, is the criticism of such policy justified because Hungary, like other European states, has surrendered some basic decisions of the state – for example such as the free movement of people within the European borders - to the wider international organisations it belongs. My objection of using this argument is that such force as it has applies only to Europeans, i.e. existing inhabitants of the Union. To pursue the idea to the very end and argue that once foreigners have penetrated the porous external border of the EU they can then travel without restrictions within the EU will – in my view – have major disruptive consequences on the fabric of the European Union. This disruption will thus form yet another reason among those which are already affecting the views of European citizens and loosen if not hasten the break-up of international organisations which are on this issue, as in so many others, failing to understand that there are limits to which multinational agreements can violate the wishes of the internal public opinion.

If the approach I am advancing in outline seems convincing, it becomes imperative to consider (or re-consider) when permanent settlement in the country of first entry can even be contemplated. To put it differently, I am of the view that even asylum laws, all over Europe and not just applying to the countries of first entry will have to be modernised and addressed. For we are no longer talking of individuals but of hundreds of thousands of claimants of such rights. Nor, incidentally, does the solution lie in distributing such entrants among all the EU states on the basis of some criteria which are yet to be worked out but are often determined by the size of the population of the host country. Nor, finally, is this approach strengthened by saying, "what is two extra million settlers in a Union of over 500 hundred million inhabitants. These are all spurious arguments for a number of reasons.

First because the vast majority of these immigrants are *Muslim*[3] immigrants and we have noted as a fact – and I repeat this should under no circumstances be taken as a racist argument – that *this second or third generation of Muslim immigrants are much less easily absorbable in Europe than the more 'tame'/ well behaved earlier generations*[4]

Second the effect which the quoting of "two million" is meant to have is dangerously misleading not only because absolutely no one can identify the exact numbers of immigrants who will try to enter Europe from the South as well as the East; but also because it fails to mention that the number of Muslims currently in Europe is already approaching 70 million. If one adds to this consideration that ethnographically most of these immigrants tend to procreate more generously than local European one runs the risk – and 'yes' I do see it as a risk – that our continent will soon be inhabited by a disproportionate number of non-Europeans.

Finally, I say nothing of the danger – very real according to the French security services – that at least two (possible more) of the terrorists who caused the recent mayhem in Paris had slipped through the European net by entering the EU territories by landing on a small Greek island and passing undetected. This, as I already stressed does NOT mean that all, even most immigrant will be potential terrorists but it does mean that I am sure – instinctively at any rate – that among those who have already entered our Continent they must be potential terrorists who will initially act as 'sleepers' waiting for the right signal before they are activated into service at the expense of our national security.

---

3. Muslim is here italicised NOT to indicate that all Muslims are potential terrorists for they are manifestly not so inclined but to highlight that it *seems to me* to be the only religion in which a militant minority has re-interpreted its famous Holy Book in order to justify terrorist acts. Nothing similar - so far as I know - has happened with populations entering the USA or Europe and coming from India or China.

4. This point was made in chapter two in connection with Belgium – the suburbs of Brussels in particular - a country and a city which I have been visiting regularly for twenty five years now and is based on (a) my own observations; (b) comments made to me by many native colleagues and (c) an analysis of the recent terrorist attacks in France all of which either began or had some kind of "connection" with the Brussels' suburbs.

It is here that political correctness may inhibit if not distort the proper consideration of practical yet important objections (such as those mentioned above) and thus the free expression of ideas must at all costs be preserved not suppressed by this modern "fad". Indeed, how distorting extreme forms of political correctness is becomes obvious when one studies how it has worked in other areas of human activities such as environmentalism but, especially, the area of feminism. Since this is a book addressed to the general reader I have included here a sub-section for those readers who may not be well informed on the way this aberration *of an originally well-conceived idea* has often worked in practice.

Political correctness and militant feminism

I already noted that political correctness can appear in different areas of life and in this context I alluded to feminism, egalitarianism, environmentalism. It is beyond dispute that all of the above subjects pursue worthy aims though is equally indisputable that all can be taken to extremes.

Environmentalism is such a subject, fraught with problems, in need for sensible compromises and often quick action. Only two of these are raised here because we cannot interrupt the flow of the main arguments of this chapter; but important both are.

Thus, first, one has to force – an ugly but necessary word – the big polluters to offer tangible signs of their understanding to restrict their harmful emissions as soon as possible and not in the distant future when their populations will be even larger and, therefore, by definition causing even greater population.

Second, and this problem is very acute in countries such as Greece which urgently need new investments, is how to invent *judicial* ways to sort-out mischievous objections from the meritorious ones raised against investments with potential polluting effects. Just as important is the question which follows the resolution of the previous point; and this is the need to evolve *judicial* procedures to resolve the serious objections drive the potential investor to other countries which are more accommodating attitudes towards their projects.

Political correctness, however, appears in its most militant gear in the third topic mentioned at the beginning of this sub—section – feminism. This is particularly noticeable in the USA, where I have taught for thirty four years and noted in practice the evolution of militant feminism but also seen some of its most problematic drawbacks. So, for that reason, I have included here a subsection on political correctness and militant feminism not least because of the increased presence of women both in academe and political life. I have no doubt that this phenomenon is to be welcomed; but it must also be watched that it does not fall into the hands of extremists.

I sound this warning for what I dislike most in this movement of 'political correctness in the context of feminism' is both its extreme language (which is also changing the meaning of words) as well as its censorial tone towards all those who disagree with its precepts. I say this even though I remain conscious of the fact that if one thinks about this matter for a while one will soon realize that each era has had its own form of 'political correctness movements' which, though named differently, all tried to ban views not in accordance with prevailing thought.

For my part, whether this sui-generis form of censoring thought and expression took the form of the Catholic Index, Jean Chapelain's literary censorship,[5] the (English) Lord Chamberlain's control over artistic life in England,[6] or the Russian Socialist Realism movement, between the mid 1920's to at least the early seventies, they all remain (to varying degrees) objectionable to plain repulsive. This may be too strong a term yet I, for one, do not like the censorial philosophy to the extent that it restricts freedom of thought, especially when it takes the form of 'prior restraint'. When we move from thought to expres-

---

5. Conscientious but pedantic literary figure of the 17th century who helped frame the newly created French Academy's arbitral decision over (malicious) accusations that Pierre Corneille's masterpiece El Cid had plagiarized earlier works and violated the accepted but over-technical rules considered essential for drama of that period. Corneille was absolved of the first accusation but was forced to make some (minor) amendments to the play which is now available to us in both in its pre and post censorship versions.

6. To this, the highest Office of the Royal Household, The Licensing Act 1737 gave authority to veto – for any reason whatsoever – the performance of any theatrical play. The Theatres Act 1843, which replaced it, restricted the powers to prohibiting the performance he was of the view that "it [was] fitting [to do so] for the preservation of good manners, decorum or of the public peace" but in the 20th century this came to be applied also to films. This power was abolished under the Theatres Act 1968. One of its greatest casualties was the prohibition of public performances of Sophocles' Oedipus Rex because of its incestuous theme. It was thus not until 1910 that license was granted to this play which, until that date, had been performed only in Colleges and Universities. Fiona Macintosh's "Tragedy in performance: nineteenth- and twentieth-century productions" in Greek Tragedy, (ed. by P. E. Easterling), C.U.P. 1997, (2011 13th reprint), pp; 284- 323.

sion censorship for expression *ex post* may be possible if it is for *real cause*. Prior restraint on the other hand I like, as stated, even less. So I disapprove as much the old forms of 'political correctness' as I dislike the current forms, such as that represented by *militant* – and the word must be stressed to make it clear that distinctions must be made – feminism.

'Political correctness' – and I use this term in its widest sense (to include all its *legal* derivatives with which I am slightly more familiar) – poses, as I have indicated, such a threat not just to law and the study of law but also to academe as a whole. For even though it's censorial tone is not (often) translated into legal norms, it is disturbing and widely felt. Five features make political correctness different from older (and legalistic) forms of censorship. Indeed, in my view, in an unexpected sort of way, they make it less tolerable than the earlier ways of controlling and punishing *externalized* thought.

First is the fact that political correctness tries to tell people – implicitly as well as explicitly - *how* to *think* and *how* to write while condemning and attempting to marginalize those who think and write differently. At its height, Russia's Socialist Realism represents one of the most extreme forms of this intellectually castrating practice. These practices, especially the Soviet, differed from ordinary forms of censorship – and I use the term here in a non-technical sense – by telling one what one could not *even think about* by imposing on the Russians in the 30's and 40's guidelines telling then *what* to write about and *how* to write it.

In another book I gave my reasons for believing that Soviet Socialist Realism movement between the Two Wars and immediately afterwards, proved that such interference is not desirable and must be resisted even where it appears to be prompted by an understandable (if not convincing) starting point first expounded by Lenin namely, that a completely new regime – the Soviet one in this case – also needs to develop its own literature. More importantly, the Soviet example showed how the quality of published Russian literature at the time was seriously downgraded. What gifted writers of that period did which was good was either published in the West or appeared much later within the Soviet Union and thus remained unavailable to Soviet citizens. If one needs an example, one will do since the man who wrote it and the work itself was so obviously unique. I am referring to Bulgakov's *The Master and Margarita*. Alternatively other talented authors – Pasternak for instance – ceased writing novels or poems altogether and turned his efforts to translation where he produced an interesting (and original) translation of *Hamlet* (which, alas, does not exist in English).

This *emphatically* does *not* mean that I wish to over-stress the parallel between Soviet Socialist Realism and contemporary of *Militant Feminism*. Any attempt to create an exact parallel would be wrong and totally unacceptable simply because the rules and values which the 'political correctness movement' wishes to impose on us are not (or not yet) *a state-inspired* set of rules and values as was the case with Soviet Realism. Nor, to a large extent (*but not entirely*), are they enforced by legal rules. Finally, their violation does not attract the consequences suffered by Russian dissident writers, especially in the thirties and forties. We thus do not live under a Soviet-type regime, we can and do express different thoughts, and if there is any semblance of state support behind the 'politically correctness movement' it tends to be limited to instances where some redress (well-overdue) of old injustices – e.g. concerning inequality between sexes - had to be achieved through legislation.

Yet, unofficially, the interference is there and felt and, to me, bears a certain resemblance with the idea of "voluntary censorship" that Orwell so condemned in his *(originally) unpublished* preface to *Nineteen Eighty-Four*. Legally enforced or not, there is an underlying similarity with the Soviet attitude of the 1920's and 1930's to control how people think (and write). Yet the interference exists; and the author of a piece is thus obliged to conform to the tastes of a different school of thought. To a professional writer few things can be more annoying than that.

In the US this phenomenon is so wide spread that reputable publishers and Law Review editors will thus often insist that authors use as many "he's" as "she's"; insist that an author employs the word gender (which is a grammatical term) where sex (indicating biological differences) would be the right one to use; and even refuse to publish scripts which are critical of the feminist movement. Law Journals in the USA, as I explain below, are also *under pressure* to accept every year at least a certain number of contributions dealing with politically correct matters; and nowadays the Journals – some old and reputable for decades - are even rated on the basis of how favourably inclined they are towards these current fads. Panels of speakers are also often composed with a racial and sex balance in mind rather than on the basis of who is the most qualified and appropriate to speak on a given subject; and, more importantly, electoral boards strive for such wide representation not, necessarily, because its members believe it to be right (and I know this because I have sat on quite a few myself) but out of fear of complaints if not subsequent litigation if the board is not seen as being representative enough.

Some might argue that all this is too insignificant to cause concern. Others would argue that matters have gone too far. I belong to the second category, for I believe the clouds are gathering over civil liberties as a whole, especially since 11 September 2001 where, to political correctness, we have now added a new layer of 'patriotism' which I find potentially worrying. I thus agree with Professor Ian Ward, a much more sympathetic observer of the Critical Legal Studies movement which spawned all these outgrowths than I am here discussing, when he writes:

> "The early socio-political CLS [critical legal studies] movement began with the very best of motives. Its primary ambition was to educate law students about the politics of law. It has ended, not by reaching any particular goal or indeed identifying one, but by going round in ever-decreasing circles, using up its dissipating energies in a multitude of various internecine disputes, and in the invention of increasingly pretentious and ultimately useless language which, rather than educating, serves only to mystify and then to alienate all but the most fervent of believers."[7]

Second, I am struck at the virulence with which some of the proponents of all types of political correctness – though my impression is that this is particular true of members of feminist militant groups - express their dislike of those who have different views. I often feel that they do not just disagree with those of us who opt for different stance on a particular issue but would *also* like to silence us or, at the very least, reduce our say in academic and political discourse.

In the academic world in particular, 'political correctness,' directly but also indirectly (through the fear it tries to instill in those who challenge it), attempts to banish thought as improper if it does not coincide with its own creeds and precepts. This may to some extent be due to frustration caused by the fact that those who share these views may have felt that they and their views were 'marginalized' for a long – I would even accept too long – a time. This may thus be one of the factors one might have to take into account in order to understand the genesis of the movement and even its partial justification. Still, one extreme position does not justify another. Those who suffered from

---

7. *Law and Literature. Possibilities and Perspectives* (1995), at p. 22

lack of understanding should not now do the same to others but be in the forefront of tolerance and reconciliation.

Yet if this provides a partial explanation it does not, in my view, justify the intolerance towards the views of their opponents nor does it make any more acceptable the strident tone found in some of the writing. Indeed, academics can even be prosecuted if they dare to challenge the parameters that 'political correctness' wishes to impose on university discourse through threats to invoke, for instance, laws against race or religious discrimination. Thus, though 'political correctness' may still not have assumed legal clothes, the chances are that this may well develop as a next phase, at any rate in the USA. For, in addition to the existing statutory framework dealing with race, sex, religious discrimination, and harassment of all kinds which, whether we like or not do restrict free thought and speech - universities are also adding extra layers of local 'rulings' as to what, for instance, amounts to 'harassment' (which may, at present, lie in the twilight zone between law and non-law).

That offensive behaviour – in the workplace or academic halls – should not be tolerated is beyond doubt; that it should also not be trivialized either through the constant multiplication of new and silly rules, making daily life more regulated as well more encouraging complaints, is highly dubious.[8] This has not just made contemporary life in academic environments less friendly and less relaxed than it used to be; it has also contributed to making modern universities, especially in the Americas, excessively regulated institutions when it comes to the 'do's' and don'ts' of today.

Unlike the past, in my times we have come to appreciate the huge importance of free thought. We therefore resent all of the above even more so when it is taken away from us in everyday situations and in cases which do not command wide-ranging approval. We see this 'pressure' to conform to this new philosophy in the composition of electoral boards, in the constant directives emanating from human resources departments (which run more and more universities these days), and we also see it at faculty meetings where academics talk endlessly, nourishing their illusions that they are really running their shops.

---

8. At George Mason University, for instance, "staring at two homosexuals holding hands" is treated as a discrimination and harassment offence. The University of Minnesota School of Social Work has asked its students not wear cologne in an attempt to create a fragrance-free zone. For other examples see John Leo, "PC: Almost Dead. Still Funny," *U.S. News and World Report* (5 December 1994), p. 24.

These pressures are also affecting the editorial policies of University Law Reviews which, in the USA are largely student run and provide the bulk of outlets for legal creativity. I alluded to this earlier but here are some notable statistics.

An article entitle "The Top Ten Politically Correct Law Reviews"[9] thus provides us with insights as to how this phenomenon has spread and shows how influential, as always in life, individuals can be. Over time, the building of an "undergraduate culture" can develop which, naturally, is echoed in the student run editorial boards of these reviews. Journals like the *Cornell Law Review* are thus ranked – marked, graded – badly since they continue "to offer a heavy sample of bread and butter work" [10]– an excellent example of the language that the aficionados of political correctness adopt for traditional scholarship. The reverse kind of 'scholarship' that thus seems to be gaining popularity among such circles, is

> "first person narrative, many law review articles today hav[ing] dispensed with the conventions of legal scholarship – case analysis, statement of a legal problem followed by suggestions for its resolution – in favor of personal anecdotes telling of the author's oppression."[11]

Such a re-orientation of what is being taught and what is being published is all the more remarkable that it is being championed in American Law Schools which, statistically, cater mainly for those students who wish to become lawyers. What the employment chances of such young lawyers who write and study such articles are I am simply unable to gage; but, personally, I would feel seriously short changed to be asked to pay the enormously high tuition fees nowadays demanded by American Law Schools and then receive professional instruction of this kind.

Freedom of expression has also been affected in another and novel manner; and this seems very closely connected with some of the values dear to the 'political correctness movement.' For, it seems the effects of 'political correctness' apply less to those who do *not* belong to a particular persecuted group than to those who do. For in the first instance any intellectual divergence on matters of 'political correctness'

---

9. Written by Professor Arthur Austin and published in 1994 *Utah L Rev.* 1319.
10. Austin, op. cit., p. 1340.
11. Heather Mac Donald, "Rule of Law: Law School Humbug". The Wall Street Journal. November 8, 1995, p. A21. For illustrations see, for instance, Ann Peters and Heiner Schwenke, "Comparative Law Beyond Post-Modernism," 49 *Int. and Comp. L. Q.* 800 (2000).

can be quickly transmogrified into racial or religious bigotry and, if possible, given a legal shape to justify threatening legal action when this may have been the last thing that was going on in a scholar's (or an ordinary person's) mind as he was formulating thoughts relevant to his subject. On the other hand, those who, themselves, belong to these so-called 'persecuted' groups can be given much greater latitude in the form they express their views, feelings, or frustrations; and should they ever over-step the permissible boundaries, any critic of theirs runs the risk of being branded a homophobe, anti-feminist, or – these days in the United States – as simply 'anti-American' because he has dared to differ from the views they have expressed. The last example shows that nowadays in the USA one may encounter 'political correctness' both of a 'right' or 'left' variety. Both are equally oppressive in the sense that they do not tolerate questioning of their precepts. I do not like either.

Third, what is both unwelcome and sad is the fact that the tone in which this 'political correctness' is expressed is one which, I think, takes us away from the kind of scholarly exchange that is based on mutual respect and generates new ideas. For, among other faults, those who belong to this school of thought often seem to make (excessive) use of caricature – at times one is inclined to call it comical – stemming from some kind of human feeling of marginalization felt by those who have recourse to such techniques in order to promote their personal views.[12] Yet this is more than a mere matter of 'style.' In law, current trends such as 'post modernism' can also be seen as shortcut away from true scholarship.[13]

Fourth, and unwittingly one is inclined to suggest, 'political correctness' can also affect adversely some of the worthy causes (such as equal protection of women) which lie at the core of the movement by promoting them in an excessively militant manner that borders on the ludicrous. As I said above, I think this happens in part because the tone of some of this writing is mocking and even strident.

Yet sadder still is the *way* in which that precious commodity – imagination – is made to work (and many of those whom I am criticizing undoubtedly possess imagination). For whereas a lateral, new, and imaginative approach to a well-known subject or problem can bring illumination and stimulate constructive dialogue, imagination run-

---

12. See, for instance, the opening paragraphs of Frances Olsen, "The Drama of Comparative Law", 21 Utah Law Rev. 275 (1997).
13. For illustrations see, for instance, Ann Peters and Heiner Schwenke, "Comparative Law Beyond Post-Modernism," 49 *Int. and Comp. L. Q.* 800 (2000).

ning amok, hardly supported by real evidence or facts, externalized only to be fashionable, cause sensation, or attract publicity, is unlikely to end up being convincing even if it originates from very intelligent people. This is so even when it is dressed up in Freudian apparel, so favoured in our times, in the belief that it, alone, is likely to attract the aura of 'erudition.'

This does not mean, of course, that 'isolated' or 'unusual' thought cannot one day become dominant thought; that a heresy may not one day acquire the status of orthodoxy; that the rebel may not one day become the ruler. I am thus not suggesting that such kind of thought should in any way be banned or discouraged simply because it is unorthodox. But I strongly suspect that most readers would agree with me when asserting that, in practice, for every one time in which this transition from 'heresy' to 'orthodoxy' occurs, a thousand other instances can be given where the 'odd' thought remains isolated, without influence, and, ultimately, becomes forgotten. One must, therefore, attempt (here as indeed in almost all activities), a cost-benefit analysis and decide in each case where the line should be drawn. And one must, at the same time, feel free to throw away some of this writing as rubbish. To accept it, to dignify it with publication because it would be unfashionable to reject it outright, is 'bad.'

Chapter Ten

THE MISMANAGEMENT OF THE IMMIGRATION CRISIS BY EUROPE

Is radical European rethinking needed on how to approach crises?

This is a difficult sub-section to write for one has to include predictions and these are bound to be tentative for they will be based on emerging but not yet crystallised trends. A further difficulty is to interpret correctly and transmit accurately nuanced views, not categorical expressed beliefs or statements, by persons in authority within the European – EU and State – set ups. These difficulties always exist in moments of transition when the old gives the impression of dying and the new is actually is in the process of being born; together these features make the task of the *raconteur* nightmarish. If, however, he senses change in the air he must try to interpret it and describe it as best he can even at the risk of eventually being proved wrong. In such cases his main obligation is to exercise caution while a secondary one is to warn his readers that the writer is conscience of the dangers ahead of him.

The modern world, Europe in particular, is showing signs of emerging sociological convergences[1] not just continuing divergences. The gradual recognition of homosexual cohabitations, even homosexual marriages, is an example. These are now accepted in all of Europe, though the acceptance has not come without some strongly voiced objections, especially by the churches, though the debate must now be considered as closed.[2] In the first six chapters of this book I looked at human habits, attitudes, ideas, where such changes can be

---

1. On the type of topics discussed in the earlier part of this book.
2. What remains particularly controversial since the scientific evidence is inadequate and divided is the possibility of adoptions by homosexual couples – male or female.

detected. These, too, deal with a variety of issues which are not life and death issues but did attract different reactions in different European countries and, often, even more severely differing views when looking at countries across the entire world. I will return to some of these themes and discuss their effects in the next subsection. Here, however, let me note some changes which may be on the verge of affecting traditional (a) political structures which placed most of the real power in the hands of the USA and (b) EU institutional structures which may affected by the immigration crisis and the way it has been handled.

It will not sound novel to assert that we live in a world in which the old major powers and their institutions are being transformed (or are likely to be transformed). In the process, they are discovering that in the years to come they will have to deal with newcomers in the super-league in which thus far they held dominant position[s]. For instance, the last time this super league of one – the USA post World War Two - was suddenly and unwillingly enlarged to consist no longer of just one but two countries American strategic thinking was deeply affected. I am referring, of course, to the moment when the Soviets manufactured their own hydrogen bomb. From that point onwards Americans realized that 'their stroll in the stadium every morning' for their daily exercise would henceforth take the form of a race with one more state being involved in it. These days the USA is daily digesting - I suspect with neither ease nor pleasure - the idea that, with the addition of China, the super league now contains three members; and it will not be long before the number goes up to four when India joins, as it must, sooner rather than later.

A multi-polar world is and will be a very different thing to a uni-polar or, even, a by-polar one and adapting to it will not, as stated, be easy for America. The difficulty will be even greater for Europe since it knows that it neither deserves nor will get automatically any seat at this table unless it appears as an appendage of one of the aforementioned three or four ordinary members. At this stage I have to ask myself the kind of difficult question I hinted at the beginning of this sub-section: Is this going to mean that Europe will have to choose whether to remain an appendage of the USA or might it move closer to Russia, at any rate on economic and trading matters?

No use trying to answer this question by using the terms 'market' versus 'regulated' economy; 'capitalism' or 'socialism'; a world with 'restricted human rights or not', for all of these notions and questions have been diluted in practice by the members of the old divide and no longer mean to states and people what they did, say, in the early fifties. What most states seem to be doing these days is attempting 'mixtures' of their own of these ideas which sometimes work and in others prove disappointing.

Take, for instance, the human rights issue. It is often presented as the flagship of countries of the West. Yet note how blatantly it was pushed under the carpet when the day arrived – a few months ago - when the UK needed China and had to genuflect before its current leader as weaker parties have always done when in the face of a stronger leader. A few days later a similar *volte face* took place when the Prime Minister of India – once proscribed by the British authorities as a criminal - visited England and was given the red carpet treatment. If this has happened with China and India, and dictated by my country's need to trade with these two countries, how can anyone state with firmness that a similar day will not come when the same conduct will not be adopted towards President Putin? Indeed, in cultural terms we share much more with his country than those we have with the great but different culture of President Xi Jinping.

However shocking my speculation may sound, especially to those with a conservative bent of mind who are unable to adapt to changing environments, political behaviour these days is manifestly determined by economic interests and a cynical appraisal of commercial needs. Ideologies melt before the heat of economic pressures, the effect of the growing double threat of massive immigration and international terrorism, just as in nature the appearance of the first rays of the morning sun, melt the fog.

These are days when dogmas on economics or human rights once seen as '*absolute dividers*' are daily becoming ideas of the past as most political regimes tend to borrow ideas – even if in mutated forms – from one another. A share of the future – maybe only a very small one – will only go to those who have sensed this global decline in theories and dogmas and make the necessary U-turns in their thinking themselves.

Many of my readers may, of course, rush to answer my question concerning Mr. Putin with one word: rubbish. They may well prove right in this prediction though not, I think, in the haste of such a response if, indeed, they externalise it without due thought and reflection over the facts. I confess to some degree of admiration towards fellow human beings who at times of such fluidity as ours can still command - or pretend to command - an unbending confidence in the immutability of past political beliefs and ideas. This suggests a certain form of courage though not, perhaps, imagination and adaptability. Personally, however, I feel that the few sentences which I added after the question I set above deserve to be considered and thus I caution against a hurried attempt to negate my predictions. The doubt – my doubt at least - about the kind of future awaiting the European world stems from a number of factors.

First and foremost is its political and economic disunity of Europe, much greater now for instance that it was when the Maastricht Treaty was signed some twenty five years ago. The days of truly inspired EU Presidents – like Jacques Delors – have long past and the post of President has been replaced by three Presidents appointed on the basis of geographical criteria and back-room bargaining among the major states. Moreover, the new Captains of the European vessel have been at the tiller of various vessels for a long time and are used to tack as a way of moving their sailing vessel in a zig-zag manner unable otherwise to move forward. European waters, however, have become stormy and the best way to navigate the vessel must change accordingly. My feeling is that so far no one has discovered how exactly this can be done. If honest, the EU leaders might well accept the fact that they and their divided institution fall into this category of a vessel rudderless at sea.

Lack of Captains – leaders I will call then later on – is one reason for the real or apparent loss of direction by contemporary Europe. The loss of the confidence by passengers and crew in the vessel's officers to cope with these storms is another; and, in my view, a more serious sign of the difficulties ahead. Again, it is easy for those in command – and those who earn their living from them – to decry the expression of doubts such as those expressed above. Throughout history, all collapsing regimes refused to see their approaching demise until it was too late just as they refused to blame their leaders for lack of foresight and imagination. The fact that the EU has a plethora of leaders does not change this conclusion; it just spreads the responsibility more widely.

In Europe such a decline has been happening slowly since the decision was taken in the eighties onwards to enlarge its size rather than improve its internal cohesion as the Germans, years ago, had so rightly favoured. But two recent catalysts have accelerated the feeling that matters are not what they were or should be.

The first was a half-submerged rock that did not even appear well-marked on the Europeans charts since it was so small. Its name was Greece. When the tide was low its small surface showed above water and it was attractive to the 'colony's'[3] sun-worshipers who basked on it like playful seals. Otherwise, however, it was too small to be taken seriously by (political) cartographers and was thus never shown with greater prominence - not in their political charts at least. It was instead treated like other charming little rocks – the Baltics or Denmark - though the similarity cannot be taken too far since the first little rock lies in the middle of much more crucial cross roads for international navigation and thus geopolitically presents quite an exceptional interest.

The double success of the Left at the two Greek elections held in 2015 marked another turning point which has not been easy to digest either in Europe or in Greece. The difficulty was to some extent based on the European indifference to what happens on little rocks and a certain degree of contempt felt towards its leaders. Though Greek by birth I have no qualms in mentioning this unflattering attitude nor, indeed, regard as entirely unjustified. Yet let us not forget that in the famous Hans Christian Anderson story it was a little boy – not a grown up and mature man - who had the guts to shout out loudly that "he King was naked" and led to the named King's disgrace. The semi-submerged and insignificant rock thus proved to have one feature that most have underestimated: not that it had been ignored repeatedly and unjustly; but that it had now holed the European vessel and made more Europeans aware that there were unable to affect their vessel's journey by closing the hole and stop further letting in of water.

This time the mistake was entirely Europe's. In fact, it consisted of a series of mistakes. They all stemmed from the old way that venerable vessel was once piloted. Decisions were not based on the accepted rules of seafaring but political considerations and internal bartering by those on the bridge. Countries which did not deserve to join the Euro were made members of the club – the vessel - purely out of ill-thought political considerations and were expected to behave as told. Greece was one; others even less deserving came later as a result of political planning not a careful consideration of their economic situation and their maturity to integrate into this new club. Completely unfit countries such as Turkey are persistently knocking on the door with Europe responding by promising huge amounts of money but no specific responses. The outmoded way of sailing the European vessel thus continued despite the fact that it was now attracting more passengers who, in the spirit of the times, also began to behave like critics. Its cruises were no longer enjoyable but turned into squabbling that lasted well into each night.

---

3   For that, if one is to be frank, is what Greece resembles these days.

We are now in the deepest waters so far faced by the EU so let us jettison for a minute our colourful metaphor. For how can a common currency work without a preplanned way of harmonising budgetary and tax policy? Can it work well without a central bank which was not, from the start, equipped with real powers and, moreover, was/remains constantly undermined by the central bank of the EU's largest economy? And, finally, how could the navigators – from the captain to the boatswain – hold different views as to what should be done and still keep their vessel on an agreed course if the waters became rough as they did in 2007? So, should one follow the austerity path naturally favoured by Germany which has never forgotten the Weimar years of super-inflation? Of should one follow the American example of printing money, now described so meaninglessly by the acoustically unattractive term 'quantitative easing'? And talking of this, to what extent do all the countries of the EU appreciate the constant (but unsought) advice they receive from the US Treasury? Is this 'friendly' experience that is being passed on? Or is it the left overs of the days when the bossing of Europe was more overt? I wonder how German Chancellors feel about this practice?

"Easy as she goes" is the usual captain's command, which means take no radical corrective measures on your course. President Younker did just that at the time of writing – 15 11 2015 – when he said that the European states should in no way link the Paris bombs with the growing problems of immigration. It is mystery to me how he could have made such a statement when: (a) the immigration is provoked by and linked to the terrorist activities in the Middle East and (b) when the Paris events were linked to the Middle East by the murderers themselves and (c) at least two of them had entered Greece and traveled uninhibited through most of Europe before reaching their destination of horror.

With respect, the President's statement strikes me as a very short-sighted political statement which does not stem from what should be Europe's main concern namely to address the causes of the immigration and not just talk endlessly as to how they should deal with its consequences. Am I wrong? Not entirely for I also note - and so should others - that Mr. Younker's statement was immediately followed by Poland very understandable decision that it would close its borders and only accept those – one presumes few – who had cleared all security tests. I read this as meaning that the 'admission procedures would be seriously and rightly tightened. Other countries have followed or will be following similar paths.

Old captains will face new storms the way they have learnt to face them in the past. They will react in the same way even if they are now faced not by storms but by Tsunamis which they have never before encountered. This is also Europe's way; to sweep problems under the carpet and base its belated and tepid compromises on the lowest possible denomination. They always thought like that when they were seven members only it worked well; so, why should they change now that they are twenty eight? Indeed, we encounter this phenomenon in big business as well; for nothing is more unreliable than a businessman who forty years ago took a key and famous decision which saved his company from disaster. Forty years later if he was asked to advise on a new problem he would probably handle it in the same way though by now the entire economic environment will have changed and his old decision regarded not just as dated but wrong. Thus, what was once the right advice – the one which our old boy still treated as his moment of greatest triumph – was no longer acceptable. Companies have nowadays become wise and force their leaders out at sixty sometimes even much earlier. The same happens even in the City's leading firms of Solicitors; and politics have followed suit. Not so the EU which still enjoys filling its ranks with politicians which have passed their 'sell by date' back at home. Remember Mr. Roy Jenkins? Mr. Neil Kinnock? Mr. Romano Prodi? And do not exclude Mr. Younker who once was Prime Minister of the fairy castle/ land of Luxembourg?

So back to the 'USS Europe' so named after its (former) major shareholder. It is easy for its Captain to say 'do not change her course' even though now she has been hit for second time by two icebergs – very large as icebergs tend to be if one takes into account the part of them which is not yet seen. One might even say that the Paris attacks by ISIS should be counted as the third hit and, if anything, more ominously, since it indicates that at least one of the assassins – possible two - had, as already stated, reached France following the immigrant route which recognises no boarders!

To me it clearly indicates, Mr. Younker notwithstanding, what may yet to come. For is it really sensible to go on separating the terrorist activities from the wars which Europe has conducted in the Middle East? From the neglect it has shown towards the Palestinians for over fifty years now? For tolerating in the name of its own financial interests the support given by Saudi Arabia and Qatar to ISIS? For witnessing unbelievable blood scenes in Paris with one terrorist apparently linking his acts to the French bombing in Syria?

I will not repeat the accusation that the EU, though repeatedly warned - for at least ten years now - about the dangers these icebergs could cause has, once more, miscalculated the risks of such a collision as well as its possible magnitude. Nor will I repeat my view that the answers to the crises now faced do not lie in throwing good money after bad money by seeking the help those who appear on the scene when the sense that the opportunity has arisen for them to make a financial killing out of the suffering of others.

Such signs of mismanagement will not go unnoticed and the change of policy will come when the officers of the Commission are replaced. We will have to wait for this to happen until the next European elections. But unless Europe makes a 180 degrees change in its style of management and realises that it is sinking, the composition of the new European Parliament will have the unique opportunity to influence the change the EU's structures for the first time since its numerical expansion began a few decades ago. Personally I belong to those who would welcome a radical re-think across all areas of EU activity and expenditure.

My penultimate sentence calls for some reflection, not least because the accusation against Turkey, implicit in my preceding words, was made more bluntly (and courageously it must be admitted) in the Greek Parliament by Prime Minister Tsipras on Friday 30th 2015.[4] Thus, when Mr. Koumoutsakos, a Member of Parliament of the main opposition party New Democracy and an experienced diplomat accused the Government for agreeing to set up these sorting camps within Greece *in exchange* [sic] *for opaque or non-existent concessions* from the EU the Prime Minister jumped on the chance he was clearly expecting to arise. So he pounced on the Conservative Member of Parliament who has been asking what benefits precisely had Greece obtained from the EU for rendering these life -saving services by asking him "how do you put a price on human life"[5]. So for the Greek Prime Minister neither Tur-

---

4. Extensive extracts published in the daily newspaper *The Vima* of 5 November 2015.
5. The exercise is neither pleasant nor the amounts awarded either legally or morally fully justified – hence some systems – old socialist systems and religious systems refused altogether to awards damages for loss of life. But the majority of the tort systems of the world do award damages for the loss of life – e.g. the loss of the mother or the loss of the child – and in the USA they have even gone as far as awarding to fathers of killed foetus while in the womb (*and not even viable at that time of their death*) for losing the *hypothetical* financial support which they *might* have received from the foetus *had it been born alive and lived long enough to earn and at that stage been legally obliged to assist his father assuming that he, too, was still alive*. The conditions mentioned in the italicised sentence demonstrate that such awards are truly crazy and justify the view that sums awarded under such headings should –

key's approach (demanding money) was the correct approach to this problem nor Hungary's response (by erecting fences) were "worthy of Europe's tradition and its contemporary ideals." "Greece [by contrast] was willing to display through her actions to true face of Europe".

This was not the end of his rhetorical flourish for his final jab was reserved for the EU as a whole whose key meeting he had attended two days earlier. In the view of the Greek Prime Minister his European colleagues "were shedding crocodile tears for the drowned children in the Aegean" and simply wasting their time at their meetings "throwing the ball at one another". Brutus' dagger finished his victims off verbally when Mr; Tsipras, a novice among so many experienced if often old (in age) EU hands, pointed out that "level of debate [among the European leaders] had been pathetic, demonstrating Europe's inability to defend its values." This part of his statement coincides what I have been stressing throughout this book and thus strikes this reader as a convincing damnation of European hypocrisy. We accuse the President, we excite the Greek people into a frenzy, and then we crawl at the feet of our old friends and allies. There are limits to everything in nature and human hypocrisy is not exempted.

This crass summary of an unusually tense and emotional debate in the Greek Parliament must retain us for a few more paragraphs since it the points made are closely linked to many of those made in this book. Here are four of them.

First is the technical one. It is a lesson on how arguments are won in politic fora. Mr Koumoutsakos, who spoke for the main opposition party of New Democracy, is a seasoned diplomat but, except for a spell as a Euro- MP he is a novice in Greek parliamentary politics. To his credit, he is also not obviously enamoured of verbal pyrotechnics. Mr Tsipras, by contrast, is a gifted (though not profound) speaker who, in the course of his turbulent first eleven months or so as Prime Minister, has perfected his talent of giving his speeches a populist tone which appeal to his gallery. This may not add gravitas to their content; but by common consent and at first glance they can be captivating.

Second, the more difficult question is to what extent sentimentality and rigid adherence to principles have guided diplomacy and politics throughout history? To put it more bluntly and more concretely: which is preferable; the Turkish attempt to make tangible gains out of this human crises or Greece's preference to opt for the observance of

---

at best - be conventional. But to Mr Tsipras' question "how do you put a price on a human life" the answers are numerous and they show that courts indulge in this exercise very frequently all over the world.

humanitarian principles and then, in its private meetings with the EU officials ask them or expect from them to take pity in its tragic financial state and ease the terms of last June agreement which the Greek Prime Minister negotiated in person. Bluntly phrased questions bring the dilemmas into relief. The problem is that, notwithstanding the idealistic – almost sentimental - approach adopted in Parliament by Mr. Tsipras, the Greek Press has been reviewing non-stop during the last few days the (assumed) government desire to exchange Greece's services in return for the EU easing of the crushing economic terms which the Prime Minister himself negotiated last June.

So my suspicion that Greece is saying one thing in public and asking for a different treatment in private is correct, cheap, and an ineffectual way of bargaining since all in Europe know by now how modern Greek governments negotiate one thing in public, turn it – more or less as envisaged by both parties – into laws and then fail to implement them in practice. How can Greeks expect to be respected if this behaviour is now widely recognised to be their natural practice?

All of which brings us to the third point which is the crux of the matter: Can problems of this magnitude *and with such unpredictable long term consequences* be countered or placated by making financial concessions? To put it differently, can one dress up foreign policy decisions with the clothes of morality and humanity and then, behind the scenes as it were, strip off this apparel and adopt a Fagin kind of sliminess and beg for "a penny or two"?

I do not for a moment have any doubt that views on which of these two possible answers is most appropriate will differ. Nor, indeed, do I, for my part, doubt that Mr Tsipras genuine Left wing beliefs will have inclined him to give the answer he gave in Parliament unless he believed in it; indeed, this may be one reason why it sounds so attractive since it is coming from his heart but not from his brain..

Yet, as I already hinted, I am not at all sure that his gesture in public towards the immigrants was not accompanied by some cleaver advisor suggesting that the economic arguments could follow later in the privacy of the negotiating room with the contradiction between the two not being widely noticed. If the planners of government policy believe that the Greeks will swallow any – however cheap – ruse devised by them then they are in for a big surprise.

All this may explain why, in the end, in terms of impressions and newsworthiness, the speech in Parliament was so sentimentally phrased which the talking in the smoked filled negotiating room was – or appears to have been – so blatantly disturbing. Following this line of reasoning thus suggests that one first conclusion stated above, namely that Mr Tsipras won the first round of his match with the Ambassador whereas by the time of the third round the Ambassador may have been proved much more sanguine in tactfully expressing his doubts about the weaknesses of the government's negotiating position. Turkey may thus be more blunt in the way it negotiates; but it is also – understandably - also more effective.

Our fourth and concluding observations have in part appeared above but now need to be recapitulated in a slightly more detailed form. The hospitality offered to the immigrants free of any economic expectations from the EU since Greece is not a country which "puts a price on humanity" are, on closer examination, uncomfortably close to the nature of the Greek demands. For prominent among the economic *quid pro quo* demands put to Mr Shultz was a lowering of the VAT level charged on islands, a request already turned down by the EU and, most recently denied yet again by the visiting German Foreign Minister.

So what has already been turned down by our 'friends' is now – not so subtly put to them again in the somewhat crude form that "here are we doing our best to make these poor humans as comfortable as we can on our impoverished islands while you are asking us to keep the VAT levels at the exorbitant and unprecedented height of 23% thus adversely decreasing their living standards by affecting their hotel-restaurant tourist based industry".[6] This then is an example of a foreign policy dripping with sentiment even if its core is a cynically oriented attempt to rectify the mistakes of the economic package which the Prime Minister himself negotiated with Europe last June. As for its difference with the Turkish negotiating position, well it is obvious: the Turks demand in advance billions; we plead pathetically *ex post* for pennies.

Reading the way his press conference with the President of the European Parliament - Mr Shultz – was reported in the Greek Press[7] thus leaves little doubt that Greek foreign policy is not exercised through the medium of traditional diplomatic language but takes the form of an 'oriental bargain' with all the pejorative connotations which such a term implies. For in such situations both sides are trying to say one thing about the subject matter which may be about to change hands while hiding the compromise decision which they both know they

---

6. This sentence, though placed in inverted commas represents a paraphrase – albeit I believe an accurate one - of the argument employed by the Prime Minister.
7. For instance *Vima* of 5 November 2015 –

will probably reach in the end. The oriental merchant is thus as cunning as they make them while the European purchaser is learning that when in the orient you do as the Orientals do namely, you say one thing but mean another, plead poverty, crawl before the vendor but, when all is said and done, you know full well that you will end up paying more for the thing you trying to acquire than it really costs.

Mr. Tsipras' already alluded to open condemnation of the hypocrisy and disorganisation attributed to EU policy-making process when they meet behind closed doors was thus both revealing and perfectly timed.[8] In the last few months he has been exposed to such meetings more than his young years would normally warrant and traumatic they must have been. Having seen this behaviour at close quarters in all its full ugliness – and let us not play here with beautifying words for ugly it is - I hope he has at least now learnt that his allies in Europe are fair-weather friends and will thus continue – erroneously - to disabuse his innocent compatriots who place so much faith in their good feelings and the moth-eaten idea of European solidarity.

Yet, deprive the Europeans of years of a long standing media propaganda and one discovers that they are as tough as Mr Putin's boot nails and just as efficient on trampling on others if given half a chance. Mr Tsipras joint interview with Mr Shultz suggests that he, at least, is a fast learner even if as a citizen of the most Eastern part of the disunited Europe he still conducts his diplomacy with garments found in a Turkish or Arab bazar. The Greeks' ambivalence, mentioned in earlier chapters, as to whether they belong to the East or the West can thus be found even in the context of their contemporary diplomacy.

How Greece can survive, if at all, with such a mentality is not the topic of this book. This question, however, may soon become more urgent as well as more acute. For as European states are moving towards closing their borders to more immigrants Greece runs the very serious risk of being landed for a long time with 200 or 300,000 immigrants – possible even more - within its borders. This would be a total and unmanageable result; one which courts of law might one day have to review and decide whether those who took them may bear some form of legal as well political responsibility.

How Europe will fair is another matter. My readers will have, of course, noted my own (sad) conclusion is that Europe is slowly and unstoppably sinking though its band – as in the case of the Titanic – is still playing on its main deck happy tunes. For those who see the

---

8. This argument, as well, formed part of his speech in Parliament.

world as it is and not as they would wish it to be, one last corrective move thus needs to be made. This is a corrective action which must be taken by all the lesser players such as Greece, Portugal, Spain – all probably headed by Italy – as well as countries from the eastern periphery of Europe. For them the above state of affairs in Europe thus points in one direction only: NOT for Greeks to abandon their old friends; but to hurry to add new ones to their address books so that they, like all small or larger but wise states, have other possible supporters to turn to when the going in their own neighborhoods or back yards gets rough. In considering this proposition let us reflect also on whether Europe, herself, should be thinking along these lines.

First, has Europe gained – and of so what - by aligning herself with America's foreign policy *since the end of the Cold War?* It is difficult to give to this question a positive answer given that both entities treated in a radically different way the so-called end of the Cold War dividend.

Second, let us try – and a big effort will be needed here – to think laterally. Let us enquire weather Western Europe and Eastern Europe, including Russia, complement each other in their needs and their strengths or are they by fate doomed always to find themselves in opposite camps? For does not Russia need access to credits, advanced technology, a large market of over 500 million people? And do they not possess what we will need more and more which, inter alia, includes energy, a huge variety of minerals, especially if one includes under the term Russia is central Asian allies, and also an under-exploited market? I say nothing of the benefits which could flow of both sides by releasing the tension which American has generated by picking a fight in Russia's back yard. Finally, could not Russia assist in the immigration crisis – both its causes in Syria and its consequences if Europe was not fixated on keeping the Ukrainian crisis alive?

Third, who is to blame for the fact that the rapprochement attempted with China has not yet been also tried with Russia? Two important reasons jump to mind. The question is: are they still valid as once they were?

The first must be Britain's special relationship with the US has been one reason why this link with Russia has never been fully developed even though many a notable Englishman – including former Foreign Secretary Douglas Hurd - is on record in a speech delivered at the British Academy - stating that this relationship has worked more in favour of America than England.[9]

---

9. "The British Contribution to the Europe of the Twentieth-First Century", *The British*

The second fear must emanate from the Eastern Europeans who believe that Russia is becoming again militarily aggressive. These are obstacles no doubt; and the dangers arising from the second are perfectly legitimately raised. Yet given the growing strength of the immigration storm ahead, combined with the growing power of European movements now feeling unsatisfied with the way the Union is run, and everything is possible with people who have imagination. How else can one explain the fact that the Dalai Lama was so unceremoniously thrown overboard to make more room for his real lord and master, residing a few thousand miles to the east of his own decaying temples, to come on board? Is this nice? No. Is it kind? Again the answer is 'No'. Is what I am foreseeing a sign of realism? I believe absolutely so. So why should we react romantically on other issues?

How the convergence in sociological attitudes and behaviour could bring about more changes in the structures of the EU

So, let us continue developing the conclusion of my overall thesis contained in this book by returning our attention from divergences, which may be on the verge of being weakened or altered, to the more constructive phenomenon of convergence which has also been growing for years in Europe albeit occurring in different areas of human conduct – the kinds discussed in the earlier chapters of this book.

To be sure the convergences I have discussed in my early chapters are reflected in personal behaviour, tastes, attitudes, predilections, family patterns, apparel and, more generally, in inchoate but not inimical feelings towards a changing world. In theory one could argue they are encountered in relatively secondary matters though this does not mean that they cannot and do not generate heated debates. Certainly, these are not of the kind topics that easily catch the headlines in the way that military or financial confrontations do; nor do they touch upon matters of life and death. To give them and all-embracing – and in the eyes of many, degrading but not entirely accurate tone - we might describe then as sociological or anthropological in nature. Still, these growing similarities are affecting human beings; their overall thought patterns; the changing views as to how their lives should (or should not) be affected by government regulation. This means that the

---

Academy Centenary Lectures (ed. by Prof. Basil Markesinis, Hart Publishing (2002) at pp 215 ff, esp. 225 ff.

electorates can be influenced by such views and, in turn, exert their influence on society in favour of like-minded people. The press and social media can then enhance this influence and this affect can, its own turn, affect human behaviour.

The interesting thing about the above is that because these varied issues arise in all countries we are no longer talking of influencing the behavior of the citizens and the electorates of one country but of many if not all of them. For instance, Germans may still live under the Weimar nightmare and hate the idea of deficit spending; but that fear does not cross the mind of other European nations, at any rate with the intensity that it does with Germans. But the wider matters we discussed in the preceding chapters pertaining to sex, social comportment, dress, family, holidays, and the creation of 'images' we associate with the icons of our society arise in all countries. This means changing views in these matters can, eventually be reflected in the laws of all countries. Homosexual marriage is one; many aspects of political correctness could also, easily, be given a legal dress – e.g. discriminatory behavior or, even more dangerous, discriminatory speech – and thus once again influence international legislators – e.g. those sitting the European Parliament or in simply in the local Parliaments of individual countries.

My sociological 'changes' in the European character are also the result of enhanced travel, hugely extended communications through social media – face book and twitter for instance - and the increasing multi-ethnicity found in large cities which is making – slowly but as systematically as can be done - humans less frightened to cohabit with other 'strangers' provided the existing mixture of races and religions is not seriously – worse still suddenly - disturbed. The increase in mixed marriages among different races attests to this change having already occurred more during the last fifty years than the preceding one hundred years. Caution, however, reinforced by experience, demand us to admit that the present social equilibrium can be easily unbalanced. The kind of problems which massive immigration could raise are the kind to which I have alluded to already and which I fear may turn out to be one of the most unwanted future legacies of what is happening today.

The increase and spread of current Muslim fundamentalism is one of such potential destabilizing factors for it frightens and repels, not attracts the locals who feel 'invaded' – and that, indeed, is how often they feel. The current waves of massive immigration could easily be a gross impediment or, alternatively, a catalyst towards the ability of different religions and ethnicities to learn to live together. Of course, if the first occurs – and the size of displacement is likely to make the more likely reaction, then the destruction of what has been achieved since the end of the Second War could be a disaster of a different kind.

My starting point in trying to guess how this conundrum might end is that *cohabitation and co-existence with 'foreigners and people considered as different – ethnically and religiously - has its limits.* Two reasons argue in favour of this view, especially if these newcomers arrive with a mentality which demands their hosts to adapt to their – the invaders (for that is how they are seen) – mores, legal and religious rules and does not de facto force them to fit in the flexible parameters of most societies which they are asking to become their hosts.

Then we have to consider the economic consequences that massive displacements can have on their budgets e.g. housing, social security costs, education and possible payment of unemployment benefits. Germany knows better than most how costly it was to absorb in the existing structure of the Federal Government – once described as West Germany – the bankrupt part of its country, i.e. former Eastern Germany. Would absorbing two or three or even four million of 'genuine' foreigners' – many totally untrained and not even speaking a word of German – prove more costly and if so by how much? Would this cost come from increased taxation? Would it retard the growth of Germany's economy at a time when it is facing the first serious challenges for years? Would it not nourish the slowly growing opposition within Germany as well as the existing pan-European unhappiness – and I deliberately choose to phrase this growing tide in the mildest possible way – against the current assertiveness of that indisputably great country? Or, last but by no means least, might not all this lead many Europeans to think that Germany is, in principle, favouring this movement partly in order to whitewash its bleak past during the nazi years but also because it may now be to receive these newcomers as a kind of "cheap if not slave labour." Horrible thought this but I have heard it used 'approvingly' by some of my German friends; and have also become aware of it being practiced in my Texas days when the wealthy Texan farmers would facilitate illegal entry from Mexico in exchange for then using these poor creatures to work at the farms for pittance.

Intellectually, I owe much too much to German humanism and German law to criticise an entire nation. Goethe, one of my literary heroes, expressed a similar thought when, after the Prussian defeat at the battle of Iena, he was asked to comment on the French as a nation. He refused to utter a single bad word about a Nation to which he owed intellectually so much. I feel flattered to be able to re-use his phrase. This, however, does not mean that I am either blind or deaf to the many pan-European signs who have seen in Mrs. Merkel's promotion of the interests of her country an obvious danger of destabilisation of European institutions, especially in the face of the seriously weakened counterbalancing power which France once possessed.

The most troubling argument cuts across internal political divisions of Right or Left. Put simply it is this: would not such a *massive and sudden* invasion disturb the way of life, thought patterns, basic life styles, values, and even neighbourhood lives of the indigenous population? The *size* and the *suddenness* of such an influx would, I strongly believe, affect all of the above and – my main concern - destroy such progress as has been made thus far in the gradual familiarization of indigenous populations with foreign ones. I made this point already in earlier chapters; but it bears repeating for it is one thing to fear massive and uncontrolled immigration and quite another to object to the presence of individual foreigners in your country, especially if they come from cultures (such as Hindu's, Sikhs, or Buddhists) who have *a proven* record of easy and useful assimilation by the host country. Those whom I have met from these religious backgrounds have been most impressive on all fronts.

One could also argue that most of the wider topics discussed in the first part of the book may be of the kind that interest sociologists rather than politicians in the belief that such a twist in seeing them would belittle them in the eyes of most observers. Accepting this kind of argument would mean that the reader interested in the problem of immigration could ignore the earlier chapters of the book and focus on the last three (admittedly much longer) chapters which are totally devoted to the problematic aspects of mass immigration. It would be idle, however, to deny that what is occurring across so many different fields and shaping the attitudes of people on matters of sex, religion, morality, ideas and attitudes in general will not one day affect the changing psychology and values-system of the EU since it will reflect the changing psychology and attitudes of its members; and these changes run deeper than many realise. What I began by describing – tentatively - as a sociological set of attitudes and habits can thus easily acquire a political dimension which the massive immigration crisis could seriously affect.

The current massive immigrations, if they continue - and I think they will - can thus seriously affect the progress that has been made in inter-religion and inter-ethnicity relations in Europe since the Second World War. I repeat this point for now I wish to stress that this gradual improvement in the understanding of "the other" could be manifested in the geopolitical relations and allegiances of various countries.

This improvement in geopolitical relations as a result of enhanced understanding of each other was never full realized during this period. This is because the neo colonial policies of the West, especially when its arrogance increased after the end of the Cold War, impeded such a development which, I am among those who believe, would have been beneficial to all countries. The War against ISIS /terrorism – or whatever replaces it if or when it is eventually defeated *and something else will* – could still affect geopolitical alliances and even lead to diminution of influence of Middle Eastern states which, not that long ago and because of their wealth and geographical situation, wielded a disproportionate amount of power on the world scene. A state, more wobbly in my layman's view than most would admit, is Saud Arabia; and yet its alleged involvement with the funding of ISIS must fast be making it despised by countries with political links both with the East and the West.

In our potentially shifting world of state alliances the closer relations I always advocated should be with the Russian Federation. Indeed, depending upon who is elected to the Presidency of the USA, such an outcome might even end being acceptable to part at least of the American establishment. Moreover, the fact that former President Sarkozy has already spoken of the need for France to cooperate with Russia suggests that the days of quarreling over the delivery of the Mistral aircraft carriers may happily be something of the distant past. What I have been writing for over eight years now – a rapprochement with Russia may – just may – thus become possible and even desirable by changed circumstances. l thus maintain my view that a change in that direction would be a most welcome development for European trade, tourism, energy and technological cooperation. I do not of course delude myself into thinking that many if not most of my readers may find this idea distasteful if not dangerous; but those who have read some of my earlier books know full well that I do not flinch from my duty as an author to tell my readers exactly what I think. So, once again, I will again attempt to prophecy the future and predict that such a rapprochement with Russia would simply be beneficial to both sides – Western Europe and Russia – since they booth *compliment* each other on quite a range of issues.

Indeed, much of what I have described above is, I think, already showing signs of beginning to happen in the economic field and even in the emerging attitudes towards the Syrian and Iranian problems where, for instance, the older European animosity towards Russia seems to have been toned down given the Americano-European inability to cope with the problem. This attitude may even be approaching the point of assuming the form of commercial deals if this new climate of a more regularized relationship with Iran continues. If I am at all right in claiming the above I see advantages in the normalization of such relationships – especially between America and Iran - if this could lead to more talking and less threatening of each other. That all this was almost totally inconceivable some five years ago needs to be stressed for much of; what I will say in the next paragraphs may strike some of my readers as equally inconceivable. But great crises can either cause unfathomable harm to the societies they mainly affect or, alternatively, can prompt them into new initiatives which can mark a new era in their relationships with others, including old enemies. So I hope that few of my readers will take the *a priori* view that what follows is inconceivable.

To the above, we must also add the fact that electoral results may also be generating political changes in the Iberian Peninsula while Mrs. Lepen's remarkable show of force in the most recent regional elections in France may also be pointing to a change of feelings in France towards militant Islamism but also towards the need to tone down somewhat the criticism of the Russian Federation and even begin thinking of the need to modernize the structure of the European Union. If this, in turn, leads to a reduction in the barely concealed "suspicion" which undoubtedly has grown in recent years between northern and southern Europe that, too, would also be a net benefit for us all in the general political climate in Europe. That, in turn, could help many come around to the need of re-defining the competences of the Union in a way that would recognise a more active association of potentially autonomous provinces of existing member states. This would bring the Union closer to local democracy than any other single step I can think of.

If I am thinking of the unthinkable it is because I believe that in moments of transition or great tensions the unthinkable can become the obvious. Establishing special European links with important regions such as Scotland, Catalonia, or even Lombardy, would bring the Union closer to local democracy and enhance its positive image among citizens who see Europe as a distant organization. Indeed, why should we even omit from our list the possibility of using such closer links with different ethnic communities with one and the same member state to assist this state to function better. Could we thus not attempt to solve the perennial Belgian problem which results from its two admirable but in practice uncooperative ethnic communities – the Francophones and Flemish - to work better with each other if they what brought them together was their separate association with the European Union, an entity – an entity which has greatly helped their country and their capital to acquire their special prominence and could thus be trusted by both minorities.

Horror again some might say; and I can hear with dismay Belgian friends crying out thus since I have seen with my own eyes the incredibly nonsensical decision of separating the great Library and University of Leuven into the Flemish and Francophone side. If Belgium as a state could not prevent such a division, could Europe help patch it up without hurting the feelings of either community?

Such initiatives might just be possible if the two communities enjoyed an equal associate association with the wider Europe with all European ethnic communities being entitled to be heard and to have their legitimate interests examined and respected. Is it not what I propose better than seeing Belgium, after each general election, take up many months before even agreeing to form a coalition government? I think so; and, in any event, I am convinced that if every time someone proposes *bona fide* reforms for discussion is opposed by the argument "that is impossible" because "vested interests" are *automatically* likely to oppose new ideas one should keep reminding them "has the status quo they wish to preserve worked in practice?" Has Europe solved Greece's economic problems or has it helped them spread in other southern countries? Has Europe done anything to improve, let alone solve the Syrian crisis? The Palestinian issue? The unnecessary – in the first place - creation and the then subsequent enlargement and prolongation of the Crimean dispute? Over the last thirty years has Europe, as a whole, benefitted from the desire to play a subservient role to American geopolitical adventures in Iraq or Afghanistan or Libya? How have European citizens benefited from the EU's role in all this? For it the interests of the European citizens which the EU must have first and foremost at heart and not those of America or of long suffering immigrants – especially pure economic immigrants.

To be sure, all of the above remedies floated as possible remedies to the current European malaise contain a large element of speculation; many would even argue that the ideas presented in this book may belong more to the sphere of dreaming while awake than the real world. Yet foolish would be the commentator who would exclude a series of substantial European reforms being triggered off by what at present looks like a series of mismanaged crises linked to the absence of efficient structural ways of taken European decisions.

Giving *more* rights to regions while at the same time *reducing* the EU's ambition to operate a united foreign and defence policy, and focusing instead on an enhanced and more internally coordinated trade, might help bring the switch from internal divisions and apprehension to enhanced individual opportunities and hope. Add to this re-structuring closer business links with the Russian Federation and China and one might have the chance of putting an end to conflict between the two entities largely prompted by the American perennial desire to push their own sphere of influence further into the Eastern and South Eastern of Europe and the Caucuses even if this is not in the commercial interests of Europe.

Those who love and benefit from the status quo will, of course, brand this thinking in its totality as utopian and dangerous. I said this before and I repeat it now for I can already hear these words in my ears. Yet what these vested interests and their puppet politicians are currently operating is, quite simply, not working and, as a result, it is rapidly losing the confidence of the ordinary citizens of our Continent. Massive immigration could thus – if managed with imagination - unexpectedly cease being the huge danger it now is and become the chief stimulus for European review of the Continets aims, role and ways of achieving these things in a quick and efficient manner with the maximum possible way reducing its huge annual operating costs.

Incidentally, it is in this context that I see room for significant regional involvement who have substantial and potentially useful to the whole of Europe regional presence being given a special status within the Union and being allowed to play a role which would enhance the democratic legitimacy of the Union.

How could all these monumental changes come about? To give them a chance of being implemented one would have to start stressing the principles of gradualism and incrementalism. To put in simpler language: thinking and implementation of new ideas step by step is needed not rushed decisions, though decisions always agreed upon against a background of positive and democratically inspired philosophy.

On a European level these changes could thus first become apparent only after the next European elections took the composition of the European Parliament a step further away from its prevailing mental-

ity which is squarely based on preserving the privileges of its bureaucracy, the pre-eminence of one or two countries which no longer is acceptable to the remaining members, and the limitation of the Union's
powers in matters such as military and foreign policy, which cost a lot
and which cannot work given the differences of views between the
member state on such issues. Indeed, the Union has given adequate
proof how divided and ineffectual it is on these two topics.

All of the above could thus begin to happen if the number of parties
or elected EMP's that oppose the current status quo goes up. We saw
the beginning of this happening at the last European elections. The
Union's slow moving and, overall, mishandled Palestinian, Libyan,
Ukrainian, Syrian, Greek and wider immigration crises, offer reasons
to hope that the European electorate will seize the one and only way
it has for getting its ideas heard by the otherwise isolated from reality
internal but super-privileged European elites.

A change, which would better express the desire to make substantial alterations to the aims and structure of the EU world could come
if we further moved gradually away from MP's belonging to European parties which reflect the traditional but dated divisions which
were born within the member states. Talking of Conservatives, Socialists, Independents and the like is dated for these words do not
represent slogans which would reflect the kind of aims Europeans
would, I think, be willing to consider and even adopt. For everyone
in Europe is broadly agreed that they want a mixture of free trade,
and market ideas linked to key social notions expressing our tangible
sympathy and understanding for the least privileged of our societies.
Un-coordinated yet linked new alignments capable of operating outside the existing but dated structures do exist; the question is to find
ways to energise them and through such rejuvenate party structures
make the European Parliament both more modern, democratic, and
forward looking.

One must not at this early stage thus spend too much time talking about new structures and changing party labels lest one gives the
opponents of modernisation the chance to kill attempts to reform the
efficiency and costliness of the Brussels-based super-structure. But
this structural reform will have to be faced one day if Europe's competences and role be both cut down in amplitude yet at the same time
also expanded where no needs so demand.

The need for deep changes, I repeat, will be resisted; but it will also
be helped by the continuing political mess which remains centered
in the Ukraine, the growing destabilisation of the Middle East which

will reach danger levels as Saudi Arabia's position becomes more openly contestable as will that of the other Gulf States which, allegedly, are currently using their wealth to help international terrorism spread its destructive activities. Add to the above the obviously unhealthy economic growth rates of our once important Continent and you will see that arranged against some formidable European interests are the problems which their incompetence has helped augment. To put it differently, I do not think those with vested interests in the current state of affairs will not, one day, be persuaded to change their views about the need for reform (provided some reasonable solution is found – and such solutions can always be found) to preserves some, at least, of their own interests. So it will be up to thinkers and, above all, ordinary citizens to grasp the opportunities which the current multiplication of crises buffeting Europe are creating and use them to persuade those resisting change that this is as an opportunity which not be allowed to be missed.

In this intellectual battle with those who by temperament always fear change we can invoke further powerful arguments. For instance, what is nowadays appealing to increasing number of citizens of different countries is the fight against corruption and the corrupters and a foreign policy which is hypocritical in its application and should no longer be based on the animosities of the past but on the pursuit of common economic interests.

However much one wishes to demonise Messrs Putin or Xi Jaoping they, too, are more than willing to take huge strides towards capitalist or market ideas while also make some pragmatically inspired concessions towards the amorphous doctrine of the rule of law.[10] No one but 'inflexible' ideologues living in the clouds believe that we can rid humanity of military conflicts; but all of us are obliged to see the mismanagement of the world of yesterday comes to an end and use this growing lack of confidence in its surviving representatives and begin thinking, planning, and eventually building a new future based on the *hope* for a greater degree of peaceful co-existence. As far as immigration is concerned a compromise that could work – possibly the best one can invent at present – is the one which would allow foreign citizens to settle in the European space on the basis that (a) the pro-

---

10. I discussed these issue in a series of lectures delivered in Beijing and Shanghai and censored summary of my proposals has appeared in book form under the title *The Market Economy and the Rule of Law or How to Learn from Others*, printed privately by Bicester Print in 2015 (and available while the few copies last to anyone who write to the author.) The book has also appeared in Chinese, Italian and Greek.

vided the kind of services the potential host country needs e.g. doctors, nurses, engineers, teachers etc); (b) this means that the entrants were self-supporting or could be self-supportive by virtue of the need which the host country has of their services; and (c) spoke the language of the country they were planning to settle in. Obviously, the absence of a criminal record would be *a sine quae non*. Such person should, with the passage of time, be also eligible to obtaining the nationality of the country they chose to settle in.

One way the above aims – and especially the stemming of the current tides of immigrants - could be furthered would be to convince Europeans – and above all the Americans - to stay at home and let other nations sought out their problems on their own. We will not - should not - interfere in the Afghanistan of the world whether we wish to put an end to the poopy trade (which we patently failed to do) or to ensure that their young women were entitled to receive a full and proper education. This last right should, indeed, be valued, protected and promoted. But it is not for Eurpean countries to try and make it respected in other countries by means of using their troops. Whatever the views of ideologues, politics is the art of the possible and the cost of wars to enforce such rights is not one which realistically can be placed on the shoulders of any country or, even, a combination of countries.

Non-interference in the internal politics and laws of another country is based on a healthy respect of sovereignty, a legal principle which goes back to the days of Treaty of Westphalia of 1648. In return for the West staying out of the daily lives of other countries, their citizens should be made clearly and fully aware that their right to settle in European lands would be limited and, ideally, redrafted with the recent experience in mind. Where possible the help richer countries may offer to poor ones or less developed nations can take the form of foreign investment in them in areas where they decide the need support though, to combat local corruption, the administration of these funds necessary to carry out the desired investment could be retained in the hands of expert Westeners who, however, would be subject to careful and continuing judicial and legal scrutiny that they did not misuse funds advocated for the benefit of a different country. This last requirement should form part of whatever legal agreement was reached by a donor or investing country to the country needing this assistance; and let us be clear why we attach such importance we should never assume that the inhabitants of an undeveloped country are, by the nature of things, corrupt and dishonest whereas as the Westeners are living paradigms of virtue. Finally, *on the very rare occasion where other forms of European intervention are needed,* - e.g. pre-emptive military strikes clearly aimed to protect the country undertaking them – the permission of such an action should come from some kind of internal reputable body – e.g. the United Nations - following a unanimous recommendation of the Security Council. Additionally, if there was ever any doubt that military action was, in effect, undertaken to protect the economic interests of the intervening country this issue should be aired in an open session of the appropriate committee of the international body entrusted to giving the green light to such operations. I personally regard these kinds of safeguards as essential for we know from recent practice – Iraq, Afghanistan etc. – how the notions of pre-emptive self-defense or humanitarian cause – can be abused.

As for the subject occupying us in this book all I can add is that if the clash between 'humanity' and 'personal economic interests' should become more pronounced – as I think it will unless we stem these ever- growing displacements soon - the solutions the EU or individual countries take should be dictated by taking into account the interests of those countries which are forced to act as hosts and not by loose liberal thinking, however attractive it may be on paper. *To put it differently if controversially for the eyes of some. The primary duty incumbent upon state leaders is towards their own citizens and not those, however, meritorious, fleeing from unstable parts of the world, even less because they cannot earn a living in their own countries.* Our societies cannot and will not be those who will solve the essential problem that underlies today's crisis: human conflicts and poverty resulting from acts of nature and the indescribable misery they cause. The best one can do is to provide limited help to modernize primitive economies, or charity. Hard this may sound and it is; but life will not cease to be hard, unjust, and even brutal because of a few 'good doers' who believe they can change these characteristics of human existence.

Strange as it may seem I believe such a shift in thinking might strengthen not kill the European idea. I believe it could make it more willing to entertain more normal and mutually beneficial relations with its big Eastern neighbour with which culturally as well – and we must not forget this - it enjoyed for at least two to three centuries closer links than it has with the USA until it began enjoying the latter's food, and drink, and wearing its apparel.

With the passage of time Europe's funds could also help advance relations with the Arab world if they were spent as I suggested above *in situ* and not used to set up sorting camps in countries which really cannot cope with 'herds of immigrants' (to use the expression of the British Prime Minister uttered in Parliament during Prime Minister's question time on the 27ᵗʰ January 2016.

The lack of true leaders

Effective peace as much as war needs 'inspired and inspiring leaders' but Europe as an Economic Union and Europe as a Continent has not had in recent times many individuals who could be so described. For decades now no European country has produced a Churchill and Adenauer or a De Gaulle; and the EU has not had a true dreamer (and efficient administrator) since the days of Jacques Delors.

The point I am making is often missed by many and yet it is important. Presidents and Prime Ministers may serve in posts which nominally put them in charge of running institutions or countries. Of these, Europe was never short. But being Prime Minister is by no means the same as being a leader. This is because, especially in our times, our so called leaders are widely seen as individuals who wish to remain glued to their chairs or (political) thrones and get re-elected rather than lead which, nine times out of ten, means taking decisions in which one believes but also knows may prove unpopular and thus not beneficial to the incumbent's own ambitions. Their economic probity has, alas, not always been above suspicion. The topic I am addressing here is both important and to complex to discuss with even a semblance of completeness. One only has to look at the number of special laws passed in, say, one country – France – to see how endemic political corruption appears to be even in the most *civilised* countries of Europe. So, rather than be personal, let us just limit our observations to some essential points presented in the form of short paragraphs.

Leaders must not be beholden to supporters – especially business supporters – thereby limiting their freedom of future action. Most modern political leaders need considerable funds to run their campaigns. Few countries – and I am delighted to note that England is one of them – have strict rules as to who can give, how much he can give, and how or what he gives must be declared. A variety of rules can be found in other countries though the variations they present do not mean that the relevant laws have worked in practice. The question then is not the presence of laws but how are they enforced in practice? A summary reply will suffice for present purposes: unevenly! The country's temperament, tradition, and sense of propriety are usually determinant factors.

Leaders, including EU leading officials, depend for their election on the support of major countries. What subtle relationships of 'control' and 'indebtedness' does this 'relationship create? It is difficult to say much about this sensitive topic without generating defamatory innuendos. Suffice it once again to stress that this is a topic that now and again concerns average European voters and will need to attract the attention of would reformers. It is interesting to speculate, however, whether in a reformed Europe the huge patronage power given to one or two European states will be able to survive.

Large European countries cannot avoid responsibility in their role in choosing the holders of the key European posts by pleading that these persons come from small countries and are not favouring or indebted to the major economies who favour their appointment.

The relationship of indebtedness is not one of brief duration. Someone elected to an important – often very lucrative – post invariably wishes to be renewed in it. The person who once proved 'useful' in helping a particular individual to obtain this post invariably retains a certain hold over him or her for precisely the above-mentioned reason; for the elected person invariably wishes to be renewed in this post. Might it be a thought worthy of serious consideration if one argued in favour of rules stating that no one individual should be allowed to hold one of the top ranking EU posts for more than two consecutive sessions?

Leaders are often elected on the basis that they are 'compromise characters'. Humans, especially in a democracy, politicians even more so than average citizens, are scared of strong personalities. When elected President Rumpoy of Belgium was praised for his ability to negotiate constant compromises when forming or heading Belgian government. The weaker a leader – and this is no comment on President Rumpoy - the more his lieutenants will retain some measure of freedom and power for themselves and the governments or the Commission will tend to drift instead of moving forward towards a preset target. Alas, strong leaders rarely emerge from popular votes; it is grave circumstances that force their second rate colleagues to elect them to high office; and once such an 'emergence' becomes unavoidable all the weaker participants in the election process fall into line. Such leaders tend to survive while the crisis that helped catapult them to power lasts; once gone, supporters and electors forget quickly their services; and the once 'irreplaceable' leader will be ousted unless he or she had the foresight to leave voluntarily before his 'friends' remove him. How many of my readers have heard of Cincinnatus? Again, if politicians react in that way these days, should rules be passed making it obligatory that all key posts must be subject to renewal?

Being a leader is sought by many for economic or ego reasons; alternatively, because his 'shelf life' in his own country has expired. To many posts in the European Union have been filled in this way. Words to the effect that by electing such persons the European electors are putting themselves forward in order to serve are – on the whole – rarely (and rightly) not believed by the wider electorate which in these days of social media and the free circulation of gossip (rightly) displays a considerable degree of cynicism. Europe should make visible efforts to recruit the very best from the citizens of its member states, and not take 'used; politicians because their own country's bosses are anxious to get them out of their way back at home.

Whatever the reasons that propel an individual to the highest posts – especially *the* top post (whatever it may be called) – few of these holders realise before it is too late how lonely such posts will be. The loneliness has been described in modern biographies on, for instance, Presidents Nixon, Carter, and Bush (father) – to offer some examples – and how all three agonized deeply before forced to take grave decisions. The loneliness is even more dramatically described in works of literature. Yet this is the very moment when the metal the leader is made of is tested in practice. Mrs. Thatcher's handling the Falklands crisis was such a moment; and it reinforced the image the public had of her. Of course, powerful or not, determined or not is one set of possible reactions. Another would be to evaluate the decisions taken; and here we may note that a particular decision may be evaluated in one way at the time when it was taken and then, with the passage of time, it may be reappraised in a different way. Mr. Blair was, indisputably an able and exceptionally charismatic leader who brought his party out of the doldrums. Yet to this day many of his compatriots have refused to 'forgive' him for his stance over the war in Iraq. The continuing criticism he receives over this issue must be painful; many – including this author - are beginning to see it as excessive even though the present author was one of those who was strongly opposed to that piece of American bravado. The fact, however, remains that it did have one indisputable good effect on the attitude of subsequent Prime Ministers: for it has made them very careful to obtain the full support of Parliament before committing the country to armed conflict, especially if it is at the behest of others.

Leader = Imagination, experience, and courage

These words call for a separate treatment for they represent some key ingredients found only in successful leaders. All three are needed, though at times, one of these attributes may be more decisive than others. In the study of history once again we can probably discover useful precedents which may help us understand the huge importance of these attributes.

Scipio decision not to fight Hannibal on Italian soil but move the war to his homeland in Carthage is an excellent example of lateral thinking prompted by imagination and then courage to apply such an unexpected move. The first element is obvious, the second clear, too, from the fact that he had to convince his Senate that the risk was worth taking. A good example this which shows that often one imaginative and courageous man can be of greater use to his country than many old sages who, because they are old hands tend to do the same things over and over again.

We have in modern history and almost exact equivalent in General Sharon's decision to attack Egyptian armed forces from South of Cairo and move upwards until he forced Egypt – which up until that moment had the upper hand in the Yom Kippur war - to plead for peace. The general's imagination was here prompted by the Scipio precedent; in that sense, he was not that original. But the courage was a hallmark of his character; and in later times it made him the object of severe criticism and even took off much of the shine his image had acquired in his earlier years, perhaps because in his case it seemed to have been combined with arrogance.

In this case I just mentioned, however, experience also played a key part in the success of the operation; for the Israeli army has had – alas – for most of the life of its re-created country much experience in fighting in difficult circumstances. Well trained and experienced troops thus enabled this otherwise risky move to succeed and in the case saved Israel from the unthinkable possibility of a humiliating defeat.

These two illustrations given above present an interesting side issue worth considering. In modern times, but not in the ancient world, the question often is who decides on such daring initiatives since military and political power is divided between political (i.e. civilian) hands and military experts. How exactly differences of opinion were settled in such cases in days gone by can only be clarified by reading memoirs and other accounts of historical events dealing with such issues.

Greek, as well as European history shows how this division can lead to problems if not defeat. In Israel's case, however, the troubled modern history of that country has given to many a leading politician who was earlier in his life a successful General a way of minimizing this potential clash. This coexistence of roles in one person is not, however, likely to be a precedent in western democracies, though Hitler's own intermeddling with the advice of his well trained professional generals often proved disastrous to his country.

The most crucial area in which imagination counts is what these days is called geopolitics – a new discipline which demands the pooling of knowledge from different parts of human experience – history, diplomacy, geography, economics, religion, climatic conditions, means for moving forces from A to B, accurate intelligence and some understanding of even local customs – in an attempt to second-guess what will happen if the leader takes decision A rather than decision B. Imagination in this kind of situation again must be accompanied by courage; for beyond a certain point planning is not possible and the result may well go in favour of whoever is able to calculate risks better.

President Putin offers an example of a contemporary statesman who has proved to have a knack for 'unexpected' interventions. He showed this while attending the China Olympics when the Americans prompted the Georgians to secede from the Russian Federation. Most journalists and political commentators believed that Mr. Putin would wait and act after the World Olympics were over. He did not. Before anyone really had a chance to digest his rapid reaction, two strategic parts of Georgia - (with a pre-existing dominance of Russian inhabitants) were annexed officially to Russia. The then American educated President of Georgia is now acting in some advisory capacity in Odessa. His Harvard training no doubt was first class; but academe does not tend to equip humans for international politics. Such posts usually require talent, physical and mental endurance, obstinacy, self-confidence and ability to think laterally. As stated, like most of my ordinary fellow citizens, I look around me and simply do not see many who fulfill these criteria.

In more recent times Mr. Putin has twice moved swiftly in the highly complex zone – Syria - to protect his own interests in the ports of Lattakia and Tartus as well as prop up his political ally, President Assad. In both he, once again, surprised America and Turkey. In both he proved decisive while the Americans proved victims of their polyphony or, maybe indirectly, their economic exhaustion after their failed wars in Iraq and Afghanistan. The indications are that he may yet pull off this, his second, bet; and if he does, his prestige in this volatile region will inevitably rise. For Arab states are astute in observing which of the major powers is more adroit at moving its military pieces across the world chess board; and their own actions take very seriously into account how decisive the leaders of the great powers who play a role in their part of the world can be. At this stage, however, another digression is called for.

Political planning and military action go together. In principle the politicians decide and the military develop the plans and execute them. This combination did not give rise to problems in days gone by when the political leader was also, in effect, the supreme military commander – e.g. Alexander the Great; Napoleon – though, at times, political leaders who also fancied themselves as military Supremo's – Adolf Hitler for instance - caused much harm to the interests of their own countries. Nowadays that the two roles – political and military – have, in theory at least, been clearly delineated such clashes between strong personalities have been reduced. Otto von Bismarck and Count von Moltke are examples of men with big ego's and big brains as well who could clash in practice. Eberhard Kessel, one of many biographers of Bismarck, has, however, remarked that after the Franco-Prussian War of 1871 the Field Marshall worked hard to minimize the possibilities of diverging views with his Chancellor.[11]

To conclude this section an example from Greece reveals an instance of bad cooperation between Prime Minister and the Chiefs of the General Staff which occurred during the Imia crisis in 1997. Unusually, both the then Prime Minister and the Head of the Joint Chiefs of Staff wrote their accounts, while journalists also saw their chance to shine in areas where their knowledge was purely secondary to that of the main protagonists. Though war was avoided, the final result was most unfortunate for Greece while the role played at the time by the USA was never clarified entirely even though the Greek politicians in power, accustomed to servile action, rushed to thank the USA for their help.

The legal status of uninhabited islands was not, however, resolved in the way Greece would have wanted and was, in fact, widely understood to be, until the incident occurred. This result was finally confirmed at a Meeting in Madrid – apparently in a document which was never even officially published! Worse still, it became part of the Helsinki Accords of 2001. Both accords left a large and unclarified is-

---

11. *Moltke* (Stuttgart: K. F. Koeler Verlag, 1957)

sue between Greece and Turkey which to this day is giving the chance to the ever- simmering dispute between the two countries to flare up. The responsibility of the then Greek Prime Minister is now forgotten by those he governed. History, however, never forgets; and it certainly never forgives mistakes.

EPILOGUE

At the time of writing – winter 2015 - a day hardly goes by without a paper, journalist, or political commentator of some standing mentioning the worsening situation in the world. Crises of different kinds dominate the news from North Africa, the Middle East, the Gulf States, the Balkans, Eastern Europe, the Caucuses, Afghanistan (back in the news to spoil President Obama's retirement). In the Far East, the emphasis is shifting from North Korea's unpredictability (which remains a problem) to the West's constant attempt to understand China's true plans and evaluating whatever role Japan might be able to play in the event of matters heating up in the region. Talk of a new era of Cold War has become a self-fulfilling prophecy; some go further and drop hints of a Third World War (which can always begin by accident wherever one finds large concentrations of arms and soldiers). I suspect, the only section of any community which must feel content with such loose talk must be the American Far Right which has assiduously worked during the last two to three years to create an anti-Russian and anti-Chine paranoia.

Paradoxically, the full extent of the immigration problem has still not dawned in all its 'glory' for most people except those who are in the front line and are increasingly feeling its effects. The latest massacres which shook Paris and the world have added a new dimension to immigration, especially since it was revealed that one at least of the murders followed the well-trodden "refugee highway" through Greece, the Balkans, ending up in Brussels which, we already noted earlier on in the book, has become a hot-bed of militant neo-immigrants. *This does NOT mean that immigration equals terrorism; but it does mean that it will allow Islamic militants to exploit it to its advantage. The signs that it is happening are already there for most who work in the secret services to see and try to forestall future attacks.*

This linking of the two issues is vehemently denied by those of leftist inclinations who are letting their liberalism run wild. Against this background Europe's internal decay is becoming obvious even though it is constantly covered up by its diplomats and those who have an interest in preserving the *status quo*. At the same time the number of countries and organised political groups that are seeking some kind of serious re-thinking of its future role are undoubtedly growing though the progress made is disproportionately slow compared to the speed with which the crises are multiplying and growing in their destructiveness. In my humble view the longer it takes before the EU can be renovated the more likely it becomes that it might even shatter into pieces. This, is not just my view but also shared by others; and in this context I remind my readers of the headline spread across almost the entire front page[1] of the *International New York Times* which, on the 19th-20th of December 2015 asked "Has Europe reached the breaking point?"

In this fluid world I would keep a close eye on what was once Eastern Europe. For Soviet dominance has produced tougher characters in those lands than the ones we find in the more consumer –oriented Western Europe. I would thus put money on the former Eastern Blok increasingly asserting its views within the framework of the older Europe. Hungary gave us an example with its "no nonsense" stance in erecting its protective war. Slovenia followed; and Austria gingerly half imitated the decision; Poland made no bones about its decision to accept only Syrians; while the Danish Parliament recently voted to confiscate financial assets of refugees exceeding the first 1000 pounds (and strictly personal belonging). Far more dangerous, however, are the tentative moves taken by the former Yugoslav Republic of Macedonia to close it borders with Greece. The EU, in a state of barely concealed panic is leaning in a similar direction which, if accepted, would throw Greece into a tizzy by trapping within its borders hundreds of thousands of immigrants who were originally using the Greek soil as a highway towards the richer lands of central/ north Europe.

Personally I am not over-anxious to condemn such moves as to note what they indicate about the unity of the European Disunion. After all, it is not that long ago that the former Soviet satellites freed themselves from their own misery and poverty and they are therefore understandably anxious to preserve their national identities and safeguard their nascent economic recovery wherever this is occurring. I find this to be mature behaviour and I contrast it to the flippant hot air

---

1. The article, including its pictures, covered the entire end page as well.

rhetoric which dominates my country of birth; but then, I hope, we are *all* - not only some - entitled to our honestly held views.

The combined pressure which Poland, the Czech Republic, Slovenia Hungary, Sweden could thus, one day, place on the old European order such pressure which, few considered as possible when over a decade ago one after the other joined the EU and NATO with expectations which, I suspect, are now proving only half justified. These countries, taken together, represent a sizeable part of the EU population; a culturally rich past; and a restlessness which to me suggests that they will not tolerate for long being treated as 'second league' players in the European game.

Odd as it may seem, I suspect many of these state might also one day join cause with countries of the South leaving countries such as the Netherlands and Finland in Germany's gravitational pull but not half as many as have been up to now. In economic terms Italy and Spain (and what is left of Greece) could easily see eye to eye with all the above in their attempt to put an end to German-inspired austerity; and a sudden increase in immigration coming directly from Africa and crossing from Morocco into Spain and from Libya and Tunisia to Italy, could also place these countries in the group of pragmatists and not 'fluffy' ideologues. If what I predict as being only possible at present but maybe become probable in the near future, the Europe of the post-Second World War could change in a profound way, not least since most of its energy wealth is hidden in the Eastern Mediterranean waters. Personally, I would not object to a serious institutional rethink taking place with the EU which would – should? - include: reducing the powers of the Commission; increasing the powers of the European Parliament; removing its competence to become involved in 'oversees' wars or armed conflicts, especially in order to please the Americans; moving parts of the European administrative juggernaut closer to the locations from which, depending on the specification of their duties, their work could be conducted better thus achieving greater decentralisation from a hydrocephalus Brussels; stop the wasteful and time-consuming 'toing and froing' between Brussels and Strasbourg (where legal issues could be centralized to make up for the loss of other activities) and so on. But let us not jump the gun. For the moment it will suffice to state that matters for Europe cannot get much worse. Or can they?

Turning now to the relationship between the two classical rivals - the USA and the Russian Federation – we also note that they have seriously worsened (except for the strange yet optimistic in its own improbable way friendly exchanges between Mr. Putin and the Republican Presidential Candidate Donald Trump.) American propaganda is, as repeatedly stated in this book, in full swing in generating a deep dislike of Russia and its leaders are making a huge mistake in encouraging this. I believe that when the time comes for some kind of thaw to set in – and such a time *will come since these crises are cyclical in nature* - changing the public opinion from its current state of Putin-paranoia to tolerance towards Russia's legitimate demands will thus prove neither easy nor quick. The bombings in Paris could even act the catalyst which convinces the West that they cannot fight the Muslim threat while also quarreling with the Russians. In the meantime, embargoes or not, rhetorical threats notwithstanding, Mr. Putin is, once again, proving that he knows how to dominate the international chess board. One may hate him and I suspect many westerners do; but only those who judge through emotion rather than observation of facts could deny that he is a master operator and true leader. The Forbes Magazine of 4th November 2015 – an American publication especially read by high-powered businessmen - was thus correct to state that

"Russian President Vladimir Putin emerged as the world's most powerful person for the third year running. Putin continues to prove he's one of the few men in the world powerful enough to do what he wants – and get away with it."

Among his political achievements was

"making the U.S. and NATO look weak in the region, and helping rebuild Russian influence abroad."

If my own assessment differs in any way from the above it is because I keep stressing that this kind of image is not one which goes 'un-noticed' in the world, the Middle East in particular, where more and more countries are losing their faith in the USA to protect their interests, even their existence.

For me, however, even more notable and regrettable in the last thirty years or so is the fact that the USA has moved closer to the 'illegal', 'immoral', 'ruthless' attitudes – I have placed these words in inverted commas because these characterisations are attributed to the USA *not by me but by those who follow its deteriorating record in civil rights issues* - which were once associated with the USSR. A few examples may be worth giving as a starting point for further developing this thesis at some future date but, more importantly, making seriously-minded Americans reflect carefully whom they elect to succeed President Obama as their President. Having worked as a Visiting Professor in the United States for thirty four years my guess is that the need to make a clean break with the older generation of politicians who are still hanging around hoping to make it to that high post would be the best of all worlds. The same thoughts and warnings are also addressed to my predominantly European audience as part and parcel of my attempt to look at the immigration crisis from a global point of view.

My complaint that American standards have dropped dramatically in the domain of human rights' protection is supported by the Snowden saga which revealed the extent of America's electronic snooping. So, for instance, is not the State's growing neglect for the privacy rights of the leaders of its formal allies a backward step? And has not the same occurred with phone and computer hacking which in England even revealed a certain degree of complicity on behalf of a limited number of policemen? Does not Guantanamo and its continued existence despite Presidential promises to the contrary, prove that Gulags now exist even in the USA? Has not rendition showed that American torture was practiced outside the USA with the demeaning agreement of foreign governments – which exactly? - consented in the kidnapping of individuals whom the Americans wished to 'interrogate' outside their jurisdiction with all the extra freedoms this gave to their 'freedom-loving' interrogators? Laws allowing the American secret services to snoop on their own citizens even within the USA have multiplied; but even more developed are now the technical means available and in use by American agencies to listen into the private discussions of 'suspected' but, otherwise, very ordinary citizens.

America's hypocrisy reaches astonishing levels when they complain what the Chinese are doing to them and their corporations – various forms of cyber-space violations - but this is then replaced by silence when news leaks and appears to suggest that they, too, are perfecting this game themselves. In my youth – the fifties and sixties - these were, again, practices associated with the KGB. No one, but no one, would ever argue that they were known within the USA or, if known, practiced on Americans and their allies. Now they indisputably are; and the only way to defend their existence is by arguing that if such things happen in the USA (or are practiced by American agents abroad) they are much less frequently resorted to than they are in Russia.

This is an ingenuous argument which, in terms of morality, is utterly disingenuous; for in matters of morality 'quantity arguments' matter less than 'qualitative accusations'. For instance, the Ten Commandments order me not to commit murder or adultery; they do not say, "you can do these things once or twice but simply do not overdo them." Snowden's service to human rights consists of revealing the true attitude of the United States towards them and many around the world. For the Americans he may be a traitor; to those illegally followed and taped his work could be seen as an invaluable if *sui generis* service to the human rights movement.

Enhanced Western interference to the detriment of poorer countries has also increased manifold by the expansion of globalization. Here the exploitation takes different economic forms. Thus, the ways globalization has enhanced the possibility of internationally operating companies to exploit tax legislation is important and sad but not my concern in this book. The profit made at the expense of poor countries in various international agreements is another example of corporate exploitation and, more importantly, one with political consequences. Experts can, of course, shower us with figures of the amounts of aid given to these countries. The disproportionality of what the Westerners 'take out' from these countries compared to what they 'put in' is, however, less well projected simply because the poor and the victims do not have the access to the modern media which the international corporations and banks do.

This argument is not made because the writer of this book is an unreformed socialist let alone communist who believes that bashing the successful entrepreneurs will solve the problems of the world - *quite the contrary*.[2] It is, however, made in the belief that this continued exploitation of the weak by the powerful of the world – and here we may include Chinese and Russian interests among the exploiters – fuel local wars, increase hunger, deprivation, unrest and, ultimately, enhance the main problem explored in these last three chapters namely, unwanted and unwelcome immigration.

I thus referred to earlier on that issue in expressing my view that American neo-colonialism and the wars it has generated is a major factor of the current waves of immigration. These things will increase further if America and the West continue to assist (allegedly) corrupt countries such as Saudi Arabia and Qatar to finance and arm the modern Islamic fundamentalists to fight in the Middle East. What is more, as the pressures of uncontrolled immigration increase, the liberal

---

2. The emphasis is added and necessary if for no other reason than to demonstrate that those disillusioned with the USA include traditional supporters (such as the present author) and, of course, a sizeable section of the American electorate.

views of the West, developed when peace allowed the luxury of developing attractive ideals – may suddenly begin to give way to pragmatism. I foresee and will welcome such a change not least because it will have the salutary effect of revealing that much of the West's supposed liberalism and idealism existed when the West was not under siege and could afford the luxury of promoting its image in this way.

Much of the above are facts not opinions and are known to the press, the governments, and the powerful establishments the world over, but are not dealt with. The EU now even has a Commissioner for Immigration; and during his reign the problem far from being solved gives the impression of getting worse. For the highest ranking officials as much as all public officials the world over as well as the army of well-paid experts they have hired to assist them, can only come up with periodic payments of money (of which Europe is running out) but remain unable or unwilling to address openly the deep structural causes of the European weaknesses.

So how many naïve people honestly believe that the immigration problem will be eased, let alone solved, by forcing upon a Greece and other semi-bankrupts Balkan states to open immigration sorting out Centres? All these moves will achieve is temporary and very partial solutions until the next big waves start arriving in Europe, this time perhaps through the Turkish frontier in Thrace. The Europe I loved and served as best I could for all my life is thus in my view sleepwalking into an even greater disaster on this issue.

Of course, some might argue, what can our European officials do?

Well, apart from considering (if not implementing) some at least of the suggestions I mentioned above they could tell the Americans – secretly if they so prefer but firmly - to stop training Muslim terrorists in Syria; make it clear to them once and for all that they are hypocrites for not ticking-off Turkey when it is daily violates Greek air space but quick to reprimand Russia for violating Turkey's air space once or even twice over a week end; cease aiding Turkey at a time when this country's human rights record is so dubious. These matters have been frequently acknowledged even by the American press; but the cabals which make foreign policy remain untouchable and succeeded, at least in part, to derail even President Obama from his obvious dislike of military solutions.

To explain such omissions I am forced to return to my very last point in the preceding chapter in which I complained of lack of true leadership in the West; for the current presence of three persons with the title of President in the European Union does not mean that there is one *leader among them.* It simply means that three countries – Luxembourg, Poland and Germany - shared among themselves the three best paid jobs in Europe in the belief that the rest of the citizens of the Union will go on suffering such arrogance without a murmur.

Readers of this book will note that the tone of this last chapter is more strident than that used in earlier ones. This is because the book tried to explain why a more consensual, compromise, tolerant way of thinking was, in one sense, trying to emerge with the frontiers of Europe and, maybe, appear in other countries of the world and should be understood and encouraged. However, this ideal in the making will be destroyed if we continue to tolerate the practices and attitudes mentioned in this epilogue.

Like the vast majority of European citizens I do not wish to see any of the predictions mentioned at the beginning of this Epilogue become a reality. I only wish to see the thesis for reasoned tolerance and compromise and convergence in tastes and behavior described and advocated in the preceding pages, develop further. As writer I can do no more than argue in its favour and register my sadness at the levels of political hypocrisy of those who are at the very top and who try to sweep under the carpet official neglect over decades when electorates could still be hood-winked.

So my overall conclusion is that the average European resembles more and more the other inhabitants of his Continent when it comes to tastes, views, attitudes – much more at any rate rather than those that prevailed when the EU was launched under the name the "Common Market. Whether this growing convergence can gradually help produce common reactions of the kind I have advocated, un-stitching much of the needle work of recent EU administrations, I do not know; but I do hope it will prove a common first step. Beyond externalising some fears and some hopes and indicating in very general terms the directions they should take I can do no more. Time alone will show whether I am right in at least hoping that some new common base is emerging which might eventually blow some fresh air in musty corridors of power in Brussels.

Printed in Great Britain
by Amazon